# TOWARD A FREE ECONOMY

# HISTORIES OF ECONOMIC LIFE

*Jeremy Adelman, Sunil Amrith, Emma Rothschild,*
*and Francesca Trivellato, Series Editors*

# Toward a Free Economy

SWATANTRA AND OPPOSITION
POLITICS IN DEMOCRATIC INDIA

ADITYA BALASUBRAMANIAN

PRINCETON UNIVERSITY PRESS
PRINCETON & OXFORD

Published by Princeton University Press
41 William Street, Princeton, New Jersey 08540
99 Banbury Road, Oxford OX2 6JX

press.princeton.edu

All Rights Reserved

ISBN 9780691205243
ISBN (e-book) 9780691249292

British Library Cataloging-in-Publication Data is available

Editorial: Priya Nelson & Emma Wagh
Production Editorial: Jaden Young
Jacket/Cover Design: Karl Spurzem
Production: Danielle Amatucci
Publicity: Alyssa Sanford & Charlotte Coyne
Copyeditor: Leah Caldwell

This book has been composed in Arno Pro

Printed on acid-free paper. ∞

Printed in the United States of America

10 9 8 7 6 5 4 3 2 1

To Amma

# CONTENTS

# FREQUENTLY USED TERMS AND ACRONYMS

BJP Bharatiya Janata Party (1984–). A Hindu nationalist party tracing its origins in the Rashtriya Swayamsevak Sangh; the successor to the Bharatiya Jana Sangh Party (1951–77). Formed a coalition government at the Center between 1998–2004 and again from 2014, the second time with an absolute majority in the lower house in parliament.

CONGRESS Indian National Congress party (1885–). The umbrella organization that led the nationalist movement and dominated Indian electoral politics for most of the first three decades of Indian independence, suffering its first all-India defeat only in 1977.

DALIT Preferred modern term for formerly untouchable communities in India.

DHARMA Cosmic Hindu law underlying just behavior and order; can also mean duty.

JATI Birth group typically corresponding to region and associated with a particular *varna*.

KHADI Hand-spun cloth.

MOFUSSIL Relational term connoting spaces in between the hinterland and urban areas. Can also mean riverside and railway towns.

PANCHAYAT Village council.

RYOTWARI Colonial land tenure system under which revenue was collected straight from the landowning peasant cultivator.

RSS Rashtriya Swayamsevak Sangh, or Organization of National Volunteers (1925–). A cadre-based Hindu nationalist paramilitary group out of which the Bharatiya Jana Sangh and Bharatiya Janata Party came.

SATYAGRAHA Literally, "soul-force." Term used for a range of activities associated with Gandhian nonviolent protest.

SWARAJ Self-rule.

VARNA Fourfold ranked order of castes consisting of Brahmins (scholars and priests), Kshatriyas (rulers, warriors, and landed seigneurial groups), Vaishyas (traders), and Shudras (servile toilers). Dalits were considered to be "without caste."

ZAMINDARI Colonial land tenure system under which absentee *zamindars* held a title to land and collected revenue from the cultivator.

# NOTE ON NAMES AND SPELLINGS

THE PRESIDENCIES OF British India were officially disestablished upon independence and turned into provinces between 1947 and 1950 (i.e., Bombay Province). Upon the establishment of the Republic, the provinces became states (i.e., Bombay State) and remained as such, or they were renamed (as in the case of Madras State becoming Tamil Nadu in 1969) or divided into new states along linguistic lines.

For the purposes of this book, the important states are Andhra Pradesh (1953), Gujarat (1960), Mysore (1956), Maharashtra (1960), and Madras (1956). Previously, Bombay State consisted of Maharashtra and Gujarat, which had been part of the colonial-era Bombay Presidency. Madras State consisted of Andhra Pradesh and Madras, which had been part of the colonial-era Madras Presidency. Mysore consisted of both the former princely state of Mysore and the Kannada-speaking areas of princely Hyderabad, the Bombay Presidency, and the Madras Presidency. References to state names during periods in which they did not exist are as ethnolinguistic regions rather than entities in India's federal system. Because city names were not changed during this time (i.e., Bombay to Mumbai), their earlier versions have been used.

The text and footnotes refrain from using diacritical marks for proper nouns and words with common Anglicizations (i.e., *Swarajya, samachar, satyagraha*). Book titles and direct quotations in Gujarati, Hindi, and Tamil appear italicized and in diacritics. For words or phrases without common Anglicizations used multiple times, the diacritical spelling is provided in parentheses the first time but omitted subsequently. For Gujarati, I follow the usage in the *Oxford Universal English-Gujarati Dictionary*. For Hindi, I have broadly adhered to the *Oxford Hindi-English Dictionary*, deviating occasionally for the convenience of the reader. For Tamil, I have followed the University of Madras Lexicon Scheme.

# MAPS OF INDIA

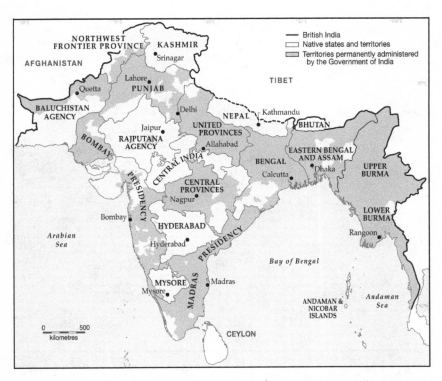

MAP I: India on the Eve of Independence, 1947 (Jenny Sheehan and CartoGIS, College of Asia and the Pacific, Australian National University, 2022).

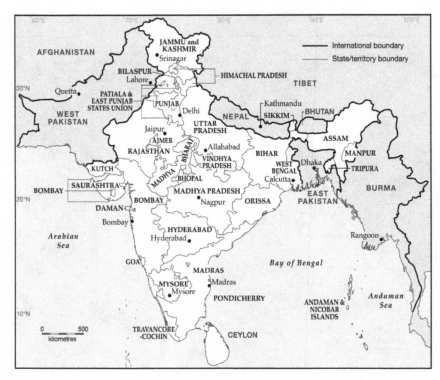

MAP II: India, 1947–53 (Jenny Sheehan and CartoGIS, College of Asia and the Pacific, Australian National University, 2022).

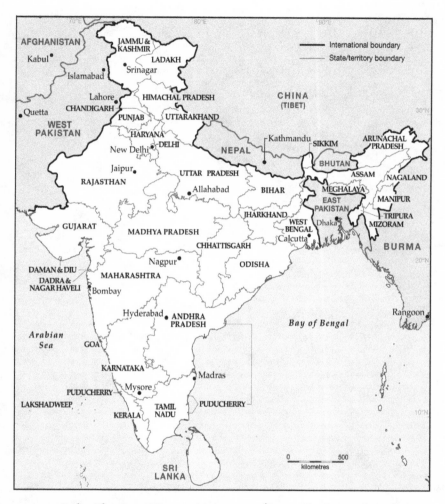

MAP III: India After States Reorganization, 1960 (Jenny Sheehan and CartoGIS, College of Asia and the Pacific, Australian National University, 2022).

# ACKNOWLEDGMENTS

MY BIGGEST DEBT is to Srinath Raghavan. He has been my university, my most dedicated friend, and my inspiration.

Tim Harper took me on as a PhD student, offered incisive feedback on my draft chapters, and lifted my spirits at critical times. His erudition and kindness are unique.

As he is for many other junior scholars, Rohit De has been a magnanimous friend and my guide to the opaque world of the academy. He has always been patient and indulgent with me, even when I have not deserved it.

Emma Rothschild introduced me to the study of the history of economic ideas and supervised the undergraduate thesis where this project started. She has commented on almost all my writing and offered advice on matters small and large at every step of the way. Those familiar with her work will detect its influence on this book. Working as Amartya Sen's research assistant was an education of its own; his interest in this project has been humbling.

A. R. Venkatachalapathy, whom I call Professor, taught me that everything has a history, from coffee drinking to slang. He has given unstintingly of his time, knowledge, and affection. Over the years, he has cheered me on as I learned to read and write in my mother tongue, encouraged me to incorporate new materials into my analysis, directed me to the spots where such materials could be found, and welcomed me to his home and his family.

Sunil Amrith examined the dissertation upon which this book is based with great sensitivity and care. His enthusiasm for it has more than a little to do with why it is appearing in the *Histories of Economic Life* series. Since I have known him, he has been a model of grace and generosity. The projects I hope to undertake in the future have been conceived of after reading and learning from his extraordinary work.

David Washbrook, my late MPhil supervisor and PhD adviser, has sadly passed away. I am sorry not to be able to share this book with him. But I take comfort in the fact that he knew what it was about all along. His big-picture questions have shaped and continue to shape my approach.

My colleagues at the Australian National University have done much to create an encouraging and friendly atmosphere for me, especially the three Heads of School: Frank Bongiorno, Nick Brown, and Carolyn Strange. I also want to thank Alex Cook, Barry Higman, Melanie Nolan, Carroll Pursell, Kim Sterelny, and Angela Woollacott for welcoming me with open arms. They have taken both personal and professional interest in their new colleague. I am grateful to Rabee Tourky of the Research School of Economics for his championing of history, and to Martine Mariotti and Tim Hatton for making me a part of the Center for Economic History.

Shameem Black, Assa Doron, and Andy Kennedy have gone above and beyond to bring me into the community at ANU. I thank them warmly. Robin Jeffrey has been a fount of wisdom and enthusiasm. He has kept South Asian studies alive in Australia for several decades now. Thejas Krishna, the only member of my family Down Under, continues to bring fun and joy to my life. Justin D'Ambrosio, fellow *estadounidense* in Canberra, sustained me throughout the pandemic.

Quinn Slobodian's scholarship has been crucial to me and others studying the history of economic thought. Over the years, he has championed my research. He generously shared the materials from German archives cited in this book. Contributing to *Market Civilizations,* a volume edited by him and Dieter Plehwe, was an honor and a privilege.

This book is a substantially revised version of my doctoral dissertation completed at the University of Cambridge. My friends and teachers from graduate school and the friends I made in the wider South Asianist community during those years taught me a great deal, among them Darinee Alagirisamy, Tom Arnold-Forster, Oliver Crawford, Anjali Bhardwaj Datta, Sarah Gandee, Rotem Geva, Devyani Gupta, Manav Kapur, Arun Kumar, Vatsal Naresh, Harshavardhan Raghunandhan, Pedro Ramos Pinto, Ornit Shani, Michael Sugarman, Tara Suri, Vineet Thakur, Nilesh Tripuraneni, Gilles Verners, and William Whitham. Ishan Mukherjee and Partha Pratim Shil are the closest friends I made in Cambridge. In our informal conversations they illuminated—and continue to illuminate—so much. Since those years, I have been in touch so often with Aditya Ramesh and Bérénice Guyot-Réchard that it feels like they are never far away. Inga Huld Markan was like my local guardian; she is the most cheerful and cheer-spreading person I know. It has been greatly enjoyable to get to know and work alongside Mary-Rose Cheadle and Amy Price. The Center of

South Asian Studies was my home while I completed my PhD; Dr Kevin Green-bank, Barbara Roe, and Rachel Rowe made it so.

Ira Guha, Dominic Leggett, Rohini Pande, and Jamie Scott cheerfully put up with me, put me up, and fed me well on the multiple occasions when I escaped the town for the city. My colleagues in the collective endeavor of trying to build an economic, social, and political history of postcolonial South Asia—Nikhil Menon, Eleanor Newbigin, Mircea Raianu, Matthew Shutzer, and Benjamin Siegel—have been gracious and friendly comrades.

Because this is my first book, I would like to thank some of my teachers from the period before I undertook doctoral study. My introduction to South Asian history came from Gitanjali Surendran in a panoramic course taught by Sugata Bose. There, I first met my friend Tariq Omar Ali. Benjamin Friedman, Eric Nelson, William Mills Todd, and Richard Tuck introduced me to the history of texts in context, sensitive to both genre and audience. And the late Lahore-born Roderick MacFarquhar, who retained a lifelong affection for the subcontinent, taught the most exciting lecture and seminar classes I have taken.

Sana Aiyar, Fahad Bishara, Shane Bobrycki, Rohit De, Diana Kim, Nikhil Menon, and Julia Stephens guided me through the postdoctoral fellowship and academic job market application process, sharing samples, reading drafts, offering words of encouragement. Mircea Raianu's comments on my book proposal were instructive. Kumar Anand, Milinda Banerjee, and Shuvatri Das-gupta helped me secure key publications of the Libertarian Social Institute. Mou Banerjee helped me secure a crucial pamphlet and offered helpful advice on conducting a book manuscript workshop via Zoom. Sarah Gandee took photographs of a few of the Gujarati texts cited here. Alden Young guided me through some of the new scholarship on the history of democracy in decolonizing societies.

As this book went to press, I learned that Amy Offner was one of the anony-mous peer reviewers. This was fortunate. Amy's book has changed our under-standing of twentieth-century political economy. I have kept it by my side and turned back to it time and time again while revising this work. It says some-thing about her generosity, and that of the other reviewer, that their feed-back together comprised sixteen single-spaced pages. I have thought long and hard about their comments and hope they detect their imprint on the final work.

Ritu Birla, David Engerman, Jonathan Levy, Karuna Mantena, and Sumathi Ramaswamy participated in a book manuscript workshop organized by the Center for History and Economics in November 2021. Each read with great care and offered constructive suggestions. I have drawn deeply from their comments. Special thanks to David for sharing his annotated version of the manuscript, which had useful thoughts on virtually every page.

I thank the interview committee of the Center for History and Economics for awarding me a yearlong postdoctoral fellowship. During that time, I revised the manuscript into its current form. I have greatly benefited from the tireless efforts of Emily Gauthier and Jennifer Nickerson and the camaraderie of Elsa Génard, Kalyani Ramnath, Michael O'Sullivan, Melissa Teixeira, and Lola Zappi. It was a joy to spend time once again with my college friend Ian Kumekawa. Now a prolific, sophisticated historian, he nevertheless retains his mischievous wit from those days. Arunabh Ghosh and Ping-hsiu Alice Lin have been wonderful friends and sharp interlocutors; as I completed my revisions, they became parents to a delightful daughter named Meena. Durba Mitra's pioneering scholarship and support of younger scholars are admirable. She came up with the title for this book and treated me and my friends to delicious meals.

Most of the research for this project was done at two storied institutions in New Delhi. At the National Archives of India, I am grateful to Balkishen Ji in the PA Section, and Sanjukta Didi and Rakesh Ji in the Research Room. Special thanks to the always energetic and helpful Anumita Banerjee, formerly archivist of the Research Room. At the Nehru Memorial Museum and Library, I thank Jyoti Luthra, the late Shakti Sinha, and Deepa Bhatnagar for always helping me. Mahesh Rangarajan was a legendary director of NMML. I am delighted to have been in touch with him ever since.

The best part of fieldwork was rediscovering Chennai, site of my annual childhood summer vacation, as a place of study. I am indebted to K. M. Ariff and his colleagues at *Dina Thanthi* for access to their digitized archive. It is an amazing collection of one of Asia's great periodicals. I thank my friend Pu Ko Saravanan of the Indian Revenue Services for making this possible. Saravanan was also a very helpful guide to the 1967 Madras elections. The staff of the Periyar Library in Chennai took a great interest in what I was doing and offered much help.

Ganesh Raghuveer took photos of the Lotvala Library while I was in Australia during the pandemic and unable to travel to India. One of these appears in the Introduction. Enid Zafran prepared the index, and Jenny Sheehan of ANU drew the maps. For financial support in revising and publishing this manuscript, I thank the Australian Academy of the Humanities and the ANU's Research School of Economics.

For summaries of Gujarati material, I thank Adhitya Dhanapal and Chitra Kudecha. Hiteshi Bhatt was a stellar and dedicated translator of Bhailalbhai Patel's memoirs. Ayesha Sheth translated a crucial letter from Ranchoddas Lotvala to Vallabhbhai Patel. For sharing their research with me and discussing various ideas, I thank Ole Birk Laursen, Aakriti Mandhwani, and Lisa Mitchell.

At Princeton University Press, I thank Eric Crahan and Priya Nelson, my editors, for giving me time, space, and freedom. They have always had the book's best interest in mind. Their colleagues Barbara Shi and Emma Wagh, and the production team of Susan Clark, Alena Chekanov, and Jaden Young worked with professionalism and alacrity.

My friend Keshava has been a pillar of support and a special companion ever since I met him in 2008. So, it is fitting that we celebrated the final submission of this manuscript together fourteen years later. Nandan's friendship I cherish, his appetite for knowledge I admire. I hope he returns to scholarly life soon, where he belongs. For infectious enthusiasm, support, and many generous introductions over the years, I thank Keshava's father, Ram Uncle. Rohit and Samir Mathew are my oldest friends. I have been so fortunate to have had them in my life, be it in Istanbul, Chennai, or New York.

Finally, I want to thank my family, extended and nuclear. Since my childhood, I have been spoiled by the love of Babu Chitappa, Balu Mama, Shwetha, my Periammas (Leela, Kamala, Vimala, Savitri, Chandra), and their respective families; there are simply too many of them to call out by name. Appa has been subjected to lots of drudgery over the years, helping me decipher many of the uncatalogued, barely legible handwritten letters to Rajagopalachari by people from all over Tamil Nadu and fielding several queries about Tamil paragraphs and sentences I did not quite understand. He has also taken the time to read and comment on everything I have written. I am grateful for his engagement and support. Anirudha has always been unconditionally proud of and attached to me, which is particularly special given his unsentimental disposition. Amma, who taught me how to read, is the best person I know. This book is for her.

# TOWARD A FREE ECONOMY

INTRODUCTION

# "You, Too Can Be an Economist"

ON THE THIRD FLOOR of a building nestled at the intersection of Vallabhbhai and Vithalbhai Patel roads, in the bustling Girgaum locality of Mumbai (formerly Bombay), the Ranchoddas Lotvala Library provides students with an inner-city space for quiet reading. Signs on the building's facade indicate that it is home to multiple small businesses. None of them carries any suggestion of the library's existence (see Figure I). It receives few visitors. Inside, a few dusty shelves hold dated books, their pages yellowing. Occasionally, students visit the reading room to study for exams. The librarian complains that funding has dried up.[1] Handsome profits from the flour mill on nearby Duncan Road, once the library's financial lifeline, no longer sustain it. For decades, nobody has opened the wooden bookshelf onto which the words "Libertarian Co-Op Bookstore" are painted. Dust and decay have set into a space once characterized by intellectual discovery and debate.

The library and its books are the barely visible remnants of a forgotten history of apostasy and evangelism. In a dramatic turn, Bombay's leading patron of socialism, Ranchoddas Lotvala, and his accomplished sportswoman and radio host daughter, Kusum Lotvala, abandoned their earlier activities. Instead, as the Cold War intensified during the 1950s, they dedicated themselves to convincing compatriots of the dangers of statism.[2] They sought to prepare Indians, newly freed from British rule, to live in "an economic age" by offering them the tools to do so. "You, Too Can Be an Economist" began one appeal to join their Libertarian Social Institute.[3] During the course of the 1950s, the

1. Telephone conversation with Mr. Govind Keluskar, February 15, 2021.
2. Prakash Karat, "A Publishing History of the *Communist Manifesto*," in *Essays on the Communist Manifesto*, ed. Prakash Karat (New Delhi: Leftword Press, 1999), 131–40, 131.
3. B.S. Sanyal, ed., *Supplement of the Research Department of the R. L. Foundation* (July 1, 1957).

1

FIGURE 1. An Unexceptional Façade (Ganesh Raghuveer).

Lotvalas' institute agitated for what its founders called "free economy," which at that point was more of an aspiration toward an economy free from domination by any one social group or the state rather than anything concrete. Their *Indian Libertarian* magazine occupied the central node in a connected cluster of broadly anticommunist English-language journals and associations across urban India, in which free economy developed and spread. Several of these were operated by fellow lapsed Marxists and publicists now working to shape public opinion in a gentler fashion.

As it spread, free economy took on multiple meanings. In a negative sense, it signified opposition to the incursions being made into economic life by the Indian state as the then-dominant Indian National Congress party launched a program of centrally directed economic planning aimed at creating a "socialistic pattern of society." But free economy also became associated with positive imaginaries and ideas in practice. It could mean a self-employed economy of peasants, a country of small-businesspeople embedded in a free trading international order, or a kinship-based cooperative enterprise and educational town. These ideas came primarily from South and West India. These regions had histories of long-distance waterborne trade and were designed to be spaces of landowning cultivation in the colonial era.[4]

Kinship groups from these regions often united by occupation—classified by the more specific *jati* rather than the fourfold ritual caste order of *varna*—began to move away from or had moved away from agriculture and trading toward capital accumulation of different forms.[5] The state stood in the way of their activities.[6] These groups did not seek to disrupt the social order to unleash the power of free markets.[7] Rather, they sought "ordered progress," which, in the economic arena, would be directed by themselves. They hoped for a state that would either facilitate or remain aloof from economic processes, not conduct or regulate them.

The promise of free economy brought diverse agrarian and commercial constituencies together under the banner of the Swatantra ("Freedom") Party, founded in 1959. Its key figures had walked alongside Mahatma Gandhi in the anticolonial nationalist movement. With freedom from the British Raj having been achieved in 1947, Swatantra's leaders directed their animus against what they dubbed the "permit-and-license *raj*." In their eyes, this was an oligarchic coalition of big businessmen, Congress politicians, and corrupt bureaucrats who wielded their power by forcing Indians to navigate a thicket of regulations in their economic lives. The Gandhian legacy exerted other pulls as well; it

4. David Washbrook, "Towards a History of the Present: Southern Perspectives on Nineteenth and Twentieth Centuries," in *From the Colonial to the Postcolonial: India and Pakistan in Transition*, eds. Dipesh Chakrabarty, Rochona Majumdar, and Andrew Sartori (New Delhi: Oxford University Press, 2007), 332–57.

5. The four *varnas* of the caste order are Brahmin, Kshatriya, Vaishya, and Shudra. Those outside the four varna order were historically considered "untouchable." These latter communities are known as Dalit. In this book, I use caste and community interchangeably to mean *jati*. See Susan Bayly, *Caste, Society and Politics in India from the Eighteenth Century to the Modern Age* (Cambridge: Cambridge University Press, 1999), 8–10.

6. Debate on to what extent landed communities transitioned to "agrarian capitalism" in the Marxist sense and whether this transition merely accelerated or changed qualitatively between the colonial and postcolonial period has been extensive. See Utsa Patnaik, ed., *Agrarian Relations and Accumulation: The "Mode of Production" Debate in India* (Bombay: Sameeksha Trust, 1990). Characterizing these changes is not so important to the concerns of this study. Rather, what is important is their connection to changing forms of political-economic ideation and mobilization.

7. In this way, they differ from the conservatives in Gary Gerstle, *The Rise and Fall of the Neoliberal Order: America and the World in the Free Market Era* (Oxford: Oxford University Press, 2022).

predisposed Swatantra's leaders against the religious sectarianism of some contemporaries and toward patriarchy.

The Swatantra Party offered a strategy to pursue influence outside the
one-party dominant system that characterized India's Westminster-style
parliamentary democracy. In this system, theorized by the erstwhile Lotvala
Library visitor and eminent political scientist Rajni Kothari, Congress was a
*party of consensus* within which intraparty groups across the ideological
spectrum vied for influence to make the party's agenda.[8] Outside, *parties of
pressure* sought to "pressurize, criticize, censure and influence it," both by
persuading the subgroups inside the *party of consensus* and by posing an
outside threat to displace it from power by coming together in the event of
inadequate performance.[9]

Unsatisfied with this system, Swatantra's founder, C. Rajagopalachari, contended that "government by the majority without an effective opposition is
like driving a donkey on whose back you put the load in one bundle."[10] An
effective opposition party could "steady movement by putting a fairly equal
load into each pannier" and "furnish the healthy opportunity for beneficent
osmosis."[11] Swatantra sought to bring balance to Indian democracy by offering
a counterweight to the Congress. The party sought to bring ideological conservatism into a political discourse dominated by various forms of progressive
thought. Simply accommodating diversity within the dominant party, by
contrast, was "meaningless dilution," according to Rajagopalachari. This book
explores Swatantra's project of opposition politics—or making effective
opposition a reality—a process that involved imagination, communication,
and mobilization of various kinds.

In the first instance, opposition politics meant presenting a conservative alternative to the Congress as salutary for the health of a postcolonial democracy

8. Rajni Kothari's studies of Indian democracy defined over a generation of scholarship in
the field. He is best known for the idea of the Congress Party as a system rather than a party
accommodating factionalism within its units. See Paval Tomar, "Rajni Kothari," *Social Scientist*
43, no. 3–4 (2015): 119–121. Kothari mentions first learning of "global movements, especially the
communist, anarchist and other such offshoots of Left leanings" in Lotvala's library. See Kothari,
*Memoirs: Uneasy Is the Life of the Mind* (New Delhi: Rupa, 2002), 23. I am indebted to Professor A. R. Venkatachalapathy for this reference.

9. The classic statement is in Rajni Kothari, "The Congress 'System' in India," *Asian Survey* 4,
no. 12 (1964): 1161–73.

10. C. Rajagopalachari, "Our Democracy," *Swarajya*, August 17, 1957.

11. C. Rajagopalachari, "Wanted: Real Two-Party System," *Swarajya*, December 31, 1960.

with progressive ideals. Swatantra's leadership cast their version of economic conservatism—free economy—as the economic equivalent of independence from British rule itself. "Swatantra" was the word used for political indepen-dence, with connotations of a more abstract freedom. Leaders emphasized the continuity between their project and the anticolonial nationalist movement for swatantra. At times they used the liberal idioms of early nationalist dis-course to signal their affinity to that movement.[12] They also brought decen-tralization and antistatism—albeit not anarchism—from Gandhian anti-imperial thought to the debate on economic development in postcolonial politics, even though the spirit of the times tended toward its opposite. They appropriated tenets of classical liberalism and constructed an appeal as an alternative to the dominant Congress. Like conservatives in the Western world, they caricatured their opponents as headed down the road to communist to-talitarianism with its statist policies.[13] Like American rural cooperativists with whom they exchanged ideas, they also mobilized the image of the smallhold-ing peasant proprietor to legitimate the existence of much larger rural land-holding practices.[14] They thus covertly rendered acceptable the profound hereditary exploitation of lower-caste labor embedded in traditional agrarian practices and turned a blind eye toward major inequalities. This constructed

12. This must be understood in the context of imperial liberalism's profound role in inform-ing colonial governance in India rather than as evidence of a liberal sensibility. See Karuna Mantena, *Alibis of Empire: Henry Maine and the Ends of Liberal Imperialism* (Princeton: Prince-ton University Press, 2010); Jennifer Pitts, *A Turn to Empire: The Rise of Imperial Liberalism in Britain and France* (Princeton: Princeton University Press, 2005); C. A. Bayly, *Recovering Liberties: Indian Thought in the Age of Liberalism and Empire* (Cambridge: Cambridge University Press, 2012).

13. Michael Freeden, *Ideologies and Political Theory* (Oxford: Oxford University Press, 1996), 335. The standard definition of classical liberalism draws from John Stuart Mill's formulation as an individualist philosophy that assigns paramount importance to liberty and rationality and is underpinned by the understanding that these two concepts are interlocked with a notion of progress. See Freeden, *Ideologies and Political Theory*, 147–67. On the appropriation of its tenets by conservatives in the twentieth century, see Roger Scruton, *Conservatism: An Invitation to the Great Tradition* (New York: All Points, 2018), 103–26.

14. Their interlocutors, rural cooperativists, drew on a long tradition of invoking the symbol of the fabled yeoman farmer. Consider, for example, its invocation by the slaveholder in Drew McCoy, *The Elusive Republic: Political Economy in Jeffersonian America* (Chapel Hill: University of North Carolina Press, 1980), and by populists in the nineteenth-century southern United States. See Steven Hahn, *The Roots of Southern Populism: Yeoman Farmers and the Transformation of the Georgia Upcountry, 1850–90* (New York: Oxford University Press, 1983).

self-image also allowed economic conservatives to join with feudal landholders to build a viable political coalition.

Next, opposition politics meant bringing economic affairs into the domain
of public consciousness and debate and mobilizing people around these issues
rather than concerns of caste or religion.[15] Consistent with the "pedagogical
politics" of both the Indian state and other parts of the decolonizing world,
Swatantra's leaders spoke and behaved like teachers to the masses.[16] They
presented themselves as peer educators and addressed audiences in a didactic fashion.[17] They sought to teach Indians how to participate meaningfully
in the new republic through such forms of address, not unlike their Congress counterparts.

Swatantra produced a wide range of printed and visual literature that sought
to teach Indians to contest the dominant economic imaginary and register
their democratic choice to vote for opposition. It imagined a "middle-class"
economic citizen as its ideal voter. The party pursued popular mobilization
activities like Anti-Inflation and Anti-Excess Taxation days and small-town
protest marches against legislation to amend the right to property. It managed
to court a select group of correspondents who wrote in with letters and petitions. These interlocutors hailed mainly from upper-caste professional backgrounds. They engaged with the Swatantra Party's materials and began to look
at it as a vehicle for making claims on the state.

Third, opposition politics meant using the institutions of India's tripartite
system of government to check the power of the ruling party. After Swatantra
members got elected to parliament, they brought their perspective to parliamentary debates. At times, they provided lengthy critiques of economic policy
that would be reproduced in newspapers the following day. Swatantra members introduced the first successful no-confidence motion to Indian parliament by collaborating with opposition parties. They chaired committees of

15. C. Rajagopalachari, letter draft, May 21, 1967, Installment VI–XI, C. Rajagopalachari Papers (CRP), Nehru Memorial Museum and Library, New Delhi, India (hereafter NMML).

16. Madhav Khosla, *India's Founding Moment: The Constitution of a Most Surprising Democracy* (Cambridge, MA: Harvard University Press, 2020), 25; Dipesh Chakrabarty, "The Legacies
of Bandung: Decolonisation and the Politics of Culture," in *Making a World after Empire: The
Bandung Moment and Its Political Afterlives,* ed. Christopher J. Lee (Athens, OH: Ohio University Press, 2010), 45–68.

17. Nikhil Menon, *Planning Democracy: Modern India's Quest for Development* (Cambridge:
Cambridge University Press, 2022); Srirupa Roy, *Beyond Belief: India and the Politics of Postcolonial Nationalism* (Chicago: University of Chicago Press, 2007).

inquiry into abuses of power by the Congress. Outside the legislature, Swatantra leaders lobbied the court system to defend the right to property, helping to win two major Supreme Court cases that defined the era. Most subversively, Swatantra entered cross-party coalitions against the Congress, helping to unseat incumbents from power in multiple states.

One-party dominance no longer seemed a foregone conclusion for a brief period after the 1967 general elections.[18] Congress lost power in seven out of sixteen states. Its majority decreased from 361 to 283 in the 523-seat Lok Sabha, the lower house of parliament. Swatantra became the largest opposition party, with forty-four seats. It won more than a tenth of the seats in the legislative assembly elections of three Indian states, clearing the threshold to be recognized as the official opposition party. As Kothari himself noted, while this was far from evidence of a new party system, it did signify the birth of "a new active phase" of Indian politics. Swatantra's rise was making politics "more ideologically oriented."[19]

Swatantra did not always win more seats than the other opposition parties. Nor did it bring about the end of one-party dominance. The party disintegrated in the early 1970s after the Congress split and its conservative faction captured much of Swatantra's support. Sharp and quick as the decline was, its founders themselves would not have been surprised. Responding to a devastating assessment of the party's prospects by the American political scientist Howard Erdman in 1964, Rajagopalachari had written to the party's general secretary, "Historical parties rest on the firm foundations of inherited mass support. A new party like ours must stand or fall on the strength of our principles and our promises, and the present appeal of such principles and pledges to the masses of the country who have to vote."[20]

Swatantra's significance lies in its aspiration to end the one-party dominant system by bringing balance and stability to the political system through opposition. Its leaders considered democracy to be an end in itself. By contrast, the Communist Party of India saw democracy as a step on the way to the dictatorship of the proletariat. And unlike the Hindu sectarian Bharatiya

18. On these aspirations and the more sobering realities, the best account is Francine Frankel, *India's Political Economy, 1947–2004* (New Delhi: Oxford University Press, 2005).

19. Rajni Kothari, "The Political Change of 1967," *Economic and Political Weekly* 6, no. 3/5 (1971): 231–50; Rajni Kothari, "Developing Political Pattern," *Seminar* (June 1962).

20. C. Rajagopalachari to Minoo Masani, February 27, 1964, Subject File 42, Installment VI–XI, CRP, NMML.

Jana Sangh party, forerunner of today's dominant Bharatiya Janata Party (BJP), Swatantra did not seek to disenfranchise or subordinate the minority Muslim population. The fact that its ranks swelled with right-wing ex-Congress members suggests a conscious choice of a new strategy for political influence. This study examines the various ways in which Swatantra strove to bring opposition consciousness to a young democratic society around issues of political economy. It is far less concerned with Swatantra's electoral performance.

———

The history of free economy and opposition politics is a history of India in the two decades after it won independence from British rule. It is part of the mid-twentieth century decolonization of Asia and Africa, which was the heyday of schemes of economic modernization and development.[21] A powerful Center, or central government, sought to assert itself over India's regions in the country's federal system during this period. It retained emergency powers from the colonial era and reworked wartime laws to handle the violence and migration accompanying the partition of British India into Hindu-majority India and Muslim-majority Pakistan, thwart regional insurgencies, and suppress dissent.[22]

After having stabilized the country by about 1950, the Indian state pursued two elitist antipolitical strategies to maintain the integrity of the nation and usher in a new era of modernity. The first was a cultural anti-politics of unity in diversity. Whereas in private, individual communities could pursue their

21. Ramachandra Guha, *India after Gandhi: The History of the World's Largest Democracy* (London: Picador, 2007); Els Bogaerts and Remco Raben, eds., *Beyond Empire and Nation: The Decolonization of African and Asian Societies, 1930s–1970s* (Leiden, Netherlands: Brill, 2012); Sara Lorenzini, *Global Development: A Cold War History* (Princeton: Princeton University Press, 2019); Corinna Unger, *International Development: A Postwar History* (London: Bloomsbury, 2018).

22. Sunil Purushotham, *From Raj to Republic: Sovereignty, Violence and Democracy in India* (Stanford, CA: Stanford University Press, 2021); Taylor Sherman, *State Violence and Punishment in India* (Abingdon, UK: Routledge, 2010); William Gould, Taylor Sherman, and Sarah Ansari, eds., *From Subjects to Citizens: Society and the Everyday State in India and Pakistan, 1947–70* (Cambridge: Cambridge University Press, 2012); Rohit De, "Between Midnight and Republic: Theory and practice of India's Dominion status," *International Journal of Constitutional Law* 17, no. 4 (2019): 1213–34; Vazira Zamindar, *The Long Partition and the Making of Modern South Asia* (New York: Columbia University Press, 2007); Rotem Geva, *Delhi Reborn: Partition and Nation Building in India's Capital* (Stanford, CA: Stanford University Press, 2022); Dipesh Chakrabarty, Rochona Majumdar, and Andrew Sartori, eds., *From the Colonial to the Postcolonial*.

own practices and exclude others, in the public realm the state sought to make diverse communities symbols of the nation that everyone could embrace. As Thomas Blom Hansen describes it, the state sought to "disentangle community practices from their localized or historical context and reinstate them as national monuments, tales and legends in children's books, historical narratives in schoolbooks—as a national-modern aesthetic."[23] The second anti-politics was an expert-directed, technocratic project to develop India along rational, ordered lines. Activities under this broad umbrella included the creation of new institutions to train scientists and bring India into the atomic age, the design of planned cities like Le Corbusier's Chandigarh, and the expansion of the remit of bureaucratic authority to control resource distribution.[24]

Perhaps the biggest of these activities was the project of economic development. Prime Minister Jawaharlal Nehru and his closest associates of the Congress sought to transform a chiefly agrarian economy and extractive state into a planned, developmental state. Armed with one of the world's foremost statistical data-gathering infrastructures, India pursued heavy industry-led import-substituting industrialization. This took place under a mixed economy framework of private and public sector industries and directed along technocratic lines.[25] As in the case of cultural anti-politics, the state undertook a huge effort to publicize and popularize planning and encourage Indians to buy into it as part of their citizenly duty.[26] The logic ran that by saving and participating in five-year-plan projects, Indians could shed their poverty and raise their country to the ranks of the world's economically powerful nations.

Both these projects of anti-politics broadly succeeded during the Nehruvian era. The developmental project has most influentially been interpreted by social scientists as part of the passive revolution of capital.[27] This interpretation

23. Thomas Blom Hansen, *The Saffron Wave: Democracy and Hindu Nationalism in Modern India* (Princeton: Princeton University Press, 1999), 53; Roy, *Beyond Belief.*

24. Sunil Khilnani, *The Idea of India* (New York: Farrar, Straus and Giroux, 1997); Vikramaditya Prakash, *Chandigarh's Le Corbusier: The Struggle for Modernity in Postcolonial India* (Seattle: University of Washington Press, 2002); Jahnavi Phalkey, *Atomic State: Big Science in Twentieth Century India* (Ranikhet: Permanent Black, 2013); Gyan Prakash, *Another Reason: Science and the Imagination of Modern India* (Princeton: Princeton University Press, 1999).

25. Sukhamoy Chakravarty, *Development Planning: The Indian Experience* (Oxford: Clarendon Press, 1987).

26. Menon, *Planning Democracy.*

27. Another hypothesis, advanced by sociologist Vivek Chibber, is that the bourgeoisie actively organized to thwart the progress of the developmental state and perpetuate their

suggests that the weakness of the Indian bourgeoisie led to a collaboration with rural landowners and the bureaucracy to bring about economic transformation without violent political revolution.[28] Class conflict could be contained while the state, imbued with progressive ideals, pursued rational economic management by central planning. However, the prerequisites for such management, like land reform, went unmet thanks to the exodus of left parties from this coalition. Subsequently, the progressive Congress top brass led by Nehru was forced to contend with a conservative agrarian support base that stopped the revolution dead in its tracks by the mid-1960s.[29]

Left opaque by this account—and until very recently by historical treatments as well—are the actual changes that took place during this period in the state, society, and economy, and their relationship to each other. This book illuminates aspects of these important but underappreciated dimensions of life in Nehruvian India, the period formally associated with his tenure as prime minister (1947–64) but more loosely spanning until the end of the 1960s. The

---

dominance along existing lines of economic activity. See Chibber, *Locked in Place: State-Building and Late Industrialization in India* (Princeton: Princeton University Press, 2003). Nasir Tyabji argues that India's big business firms clung to their activities as "merchant capitalists" or "usury capitalists" by privileging speculation over investment and resisted the state's project of social engineering to submit to the logic of industrial capitalism. See Tyabji, *Forging Capital in Nehru's India: Neocolonialism and the State, 1940–70* (New Delhi: Oxford University Press, 2015). Against this hypothesis, historians have argued that the state refused to provide the investment climate and resources required for business. See David Lockwood, *The Indian Bourgeoisie: A Political History of the Capitalist Class* (London: I. B. Tauris, 2013); Medha Kudaisya, "The Promise of Partnership: Indian Business, The State, and the Bombay Plan of 1944," *Business History Review* 88, no. 1 (2014): 97–131.

28. Frankel, *India's Political Economy*. Pranab Bardhan gave the most sophisticated articulation of the dominant class coalition framework in *The Political Economy of Development in India* (Oxford: Oxford University Press, 1984), while Partha Chatterjee first used "passive revolution" in the Indian context to describe the form in which nationalism became situated in state ideology in *Nationalist Thought and the Colonial World: A Derivative Discourse?* (London: Zed Books, 1986), 132.

29. Sudipta Kaviraj's classic essay, "Critique of the Passive Revolution," *Economic and Political Weekly* 23, no. 45/47 (1988): 2429–44, and Chatterjee, *The Nation and Its Fragments: Colonial and Postcolonial Histories* (Princeton: Princeton University Press, 1993) expanded on this notion. Susanne and Lloyd Rudolph wrote of the primacy of the state over labor and capital and the weakness of either left-wing or right-wing politics at the national level. See Rudolph and Rudolph, *In Pursuit of Lakshmi: The Political Economy of the Indian State* (Chicago: University of Chicago Press, 1987), 2.

Indian state remade its relationship to the economy during this period. It erected a highly regulated framework for economic activity managed by an expanding army of bureaucrats.[30] New businesses required permits to pursue their activities under this framework. The Government of India levied and collected new taxes, managed commodity prices, and tightly controlled the supply of import licenses and foreign exchange. The face of the new state was the increasingly numerous and powerful government employee.

These new faces of the state encountered new civilians in spaces growing with people. As India's population rose and the country made strides in public health, villages became towns. Towns became cities. Cities became metropolises. People moved increasingly between these spaces and felt the dislocations of leaving home. Millions of Indians became the first in their families to enjoy literacy, as the state took responsibility for increased educational investment. Others were the first college graduates in their household. These new professional classes concentrated in the cities and took advantage of opportunities in a growing economy. Meanwhile, in the towns and smaller cities, agrarian landowners adapted to the gradual industrialization of the country by embracing new activities like agroindustry and real estate.

Both the new urban professionals and commercial groups broadly began to feel the pinch of the state and the power of the bureaucrat. That might be through rising prices brought on by deficit financing of the five-year plans, as the professionals experienced. Or it might be through a rising tax burden, which the businessmen of Bombay never missed an opportunity to lament. Or it might be in having to contend with legislation seeking to impose ceilings on landholdings, as the Patidar community of Gujarat nearly experienced.

Frustration with these aspects of everyday life came to feature in daily conversations, debates in associations, and the pages of newspapers and magazines.

---

30. Rohit De, *A People's Constitution: The Everyday Life of Law in the Indian Republic* (Princeton: Princeton University Press, 2018), 226. Recent scholarship encourages interrogation of the diverse ways in which the state carries out "intervention," operating through both private and public intermediaries. See, for example, Amy Offner, *Sorting Out the Mixed Economy: The Rise and Fall of Welfare and Developmental States in the Americas* (Princeton: Princeton University Press, 2019); Nicholas Barreyre and Claire Lemercier, "The Unexceptional State: Rethinking the State in the Nineteenth Century (France, United States)," *American Historical Review* 126, no. 2 (2021): 481–503. Where appropriate, the book points to such entanglements between public and private. However, it is more concerned with the state's entry into domains previously left untouched and with my protagonists' rhetorical adoption of a binary between state and nonstate corresponding to public and private.

India's vibrant print culture, which had played a crucial role in the anticolonial nationalist movement, took on a range of new causes in the aftermath of the nationalist movement. Newspapers and magazines in both English and regional languages grew steadily. They provided a threshing ground for ideas about economy and society. Politicians and publicists who managed to intermediate between regional and national publics developed and disseminated their ideas in these spaces and strung together new and unlikely alliances.

This book also brings a situated or "emplaced" perspective, of "local social formations and patterns of accumulation" rather than "global flows of ideas and capital," to the study of neoliberalism.[31] It demonstrates how a set of actors located far away from the purported origins of neoliberal thought, operating in a specific sociocultural context, came to their own common-sense understandings about political economy to pursue their politics. In the process, they selectively encountered and interpreted transnational currents of neoliberal thought as appropriate for them. This situated approach also focuses on the creation of *economic consciousness* via informal cultures of economic argumentation in the public sphere rather than the formulation of *economic theory* and its (assumed) outward diffusion into policy and popular thinking.[32] Caste practices, everyday work, and regional political economy—that is, the experience of economic and social life—shaped the emergence of this consciousness.[33] Communication took place in voluntary associations, through exchanges fostered in longstanding social networks, and in a once substantial but now forgotten connected cluster of periodicals. It occurred in metropolitan cities and *mofussil* areas—spaces in between urban centers and rural areas, like riverside and railway towns—alike.[34]

31. James Vernon, "Heathrow and the Making of Neoliberal Britain," *Past and Present* 252, no. 1 (2021): 213–47.

32. I am borrowing from a parallel distinction drawn between political theory and the history of political consciousness made in Eric Nelson, "What Kind of a Book Is *The Ideological Origins of the American Revolution*?" *The New England Quarterly* 91, no. 1 (2018): 147–71. Ben Jackson points out the importance and possibilities of this distinct focus in relation to Offner's work in "Putting Neoliberalism in its Place," *Modern Intellectual History* 19, no. 3 (2022): 982–95.

33. My thinking here is guided by the way in which remembered pasts and a turn to industry shape the self-identification of the Tamil-speaking Gounder community in Sharad Chari, *Fraternal Capital: Peasant-Workers, Self-Made Men, and Globalization in Provincial India* (Stanford, CA: Stanford University Press, 2004).

34. In colonial parlance, mofussil meant "the provinces—the country stations and districts, as contra- distinguished from 'the Presidency;' or relatively rural localities of district as

Neoliberal discourse came to India as part of the Cold War battle of ideas between communism, socialism, and capitalism.[35] Its South Asian history complicates our picture of India in the nonaligned era, when the country deliberately abstained from aligning itself with the United States or the Soviet Bloc.[36] Despite India's own position of neutrality, the Cold War was also a battle of hearts and minds fought inside the nonaligned world by local actors. Indians used global events and idioms to frame domestic concerns in the rhetoric of the Cold War.[37] Free economy developed within anticommunist networks inside India and in connection with, although independently of, transnational anticommunist and free market groups abroad. This aligned print culture flourished underneath the surface of India's formal nonalignment and alongside more popular left-leaning literature. It stood one step removed from official superpower propaganda efforts.[38]

---

contra-distinguished from the sudder or chief station, which is the residence of the district authorities." See Henry Yule and A. C. Burnell, *Hobson-Jobson: A Glossary of Colloquial Anglo-Indian Words and Phrases and of Kindred Terms, Etymological, Historical, Geographical and Discursive* (London: J. Murray, 1903), 570. It is a relational term; mofussil connotes a space of a smaller agglomeration of people from the perspective of a larger one. In this case, following Tariq Omar Ali, I use it to connote the spaces between the hinterland and urban areas, which began to become politically active from the early decades of the twentieth century. See Tariq Omar Ali, *A Local History of Global Capital: Jute and Peasant Life in the Bengal Delta* (Princeton: Princeton University Press, 2018). Chapter 3 discusses mofussil economic life and ideas in greater detail.

35. It is revealing that in a recent handbook on the history of neoliberalism—see Simon Springer, Kean Birch, and Julie MacLeavy, eds., *The Handbook of Neoliberalism* (New York: Routledge, 2016)—not a single chapter covers the Cold War.

36. Recent work has shown how superpower competition played out in the politics of economic aid to India and compromised development aid imperatives. It has unearthed how powerful domestic bureaucrats developed ideological affinities for specific donor countries. See David Engerman, *The Price of Aid: The Economic Cold War in India* (Cambridge, MA: Harvard University Press, 2018).

37. Jürgen Dinkel, *The Non-Aligned Movement: Genesis, Organization and Politics* (Leiden, Netherlands: Brill, 2018); on the importance of nonalignment to studies of India in the Cold War, see David Malone, C. Raja Mohan, and Srinath Raghavan, "Introduction," in *The Oxford Handbook of Indian Foreign Policy*, eds. Malone, Mohan, and Raghavan (Oxford: Oxford University Press, 2015), 23–43. On the aim of nonalignment to keep India aloof of superpower conflict, see Andrew Kennedy, "Nehru's Foreign Policy," in ibid., 127–40, 133–35.

38. On formal propaganda efforts, see Paul McGarr, "'Quiet Americans in India': The CIA and the Politics of Intelligence in Cold War South Asia," *Diplomatic History* 38, no. 5 (November 2014), 1046–82.

This situated history raises questions about the relationship between neo-liberalism and democracy, and indeed about the nature of democratic projects themselves. The free economy political project of the Indian interlocutors of neoliberals actually went hand in hand with a particular historically contingent idea of democracy.[39] Recovering this history revises the scholarly understanding of neoliberalism as antidemocratic. Swatantra's leaders conceived of democracy as a stabilizing institution more than an egalitarian or emancipatory one. In that way, they paralleled anticommunist actors in other parts of the world. However, they operated far more independently of the United States than these counterparts.[40] They reckoned that a two-party system could prevent a democracy from veering toward authoritarianism by producing a moderation in political outcomes and keeping the electorate safe from false promises of socialism. Although it regarded the Communist Party with contempt, Swatantra's primary concern was with the far more influential Congress.[41] The key constituency of the Swatantra idea of democracy was a loosely defined "middle-class" economic citizen suffering from red tape, inflation, and taxes.[42] Such a citizen might be an urban professional, a peasant proprietor, or

39. Wendy Brown, *Undoing the Demos: Neoliberalism's Stealth Revolution* (Brooklyn: Zone Books, 2015); Brown, *In the Ruins of Neoliberalism: The Rise of Antidemocratic Politics in the West* (New York: Columbia University Press, 2019); Quinn Slobodian, *Globalists: The End of the Empire and the Birth of Neoliberalism* (Cambridge, MA: Harvard University Press, 2018); Aldo Madariaga, *Neoliberal Resilience: Lessons in Democracy and Development from Latin America and Eastern Europe* (Princeton: Princeton University Press, 2020). This book follows John Dunn's insight that democracy can take on a staggering variety of forms and "does not specify any clear and definite structure of rule" and Ricardo López-Pedreros' call to "historicize democracy not as a gift from the West to the rest of the world but as a worldwide question over which different historical actors engaged in hard-fought battles over its meanings, practices, subjectivities, and institutions." John Dunn, *Democracy: A History* (New York: Atlantic Monthly Press, 2005), 123. See Ricardo López-Pedreros, *Makers of Democracy: A Transnational History of the Middle Classes in Colombia* (Durham, NC: Duke University Press, 2019), 18.

40. Greg Grandin, *The Last Colonial Massacre: Latin America in the Cold War* (Chicago: University of Chicago Press, 2001); Jennifer Miller, *Cold War Democracy: The United States and Japan* (Cambridge, MA: Harvard University Press, 2019). However, this understanding of democracy came from Indians themselves rather than part of concerted U.S. foreign policy efforts.

41. The central government unseated the world's first democratically elected communist government of the state of Kerala in 1959 using its emergency powers. On this episode, see Guha, *India after Gandhi*, 281–300.

42. See López-Pedreros, *Makers of Democracy*, for discussion of a contemporaneous parallel phenomenon in Colombia, albeit one that achieved much more success.

a small business owner. This figure was threatened by the bureaucrat, the Congress politician, and the big businessman.

Although incompletely articulated, this middle-class citizen was always a man in Swatantra's propaganda literature. Swatantra had a gendered idea of democracy. While women appear in the pages that follow as important organizers and institution builders, this is always in a subservient capacity to men.[43] Their involvement in public life chiefly consists of service, and their prominence often owes to influential male spouses. To the extent Swatantra's politicians made appeals to the female electorate, it was in their capacity as householders and homemakers.[44] Swatantra's few female members analogized the polity to the family and the household in their rhetoric. Women were invited to participate in anti-inflation marches through appeals to their roles as food purchasers. The enfranchisement of women did not imply their political emancipation but rather the extension of their private subordination to their public political participation for Swatantra's leadership. The party was not among those with an outspoken feminist contingent, although this was not particularly unconventional for the time.[45]

Unequal gender relations underpin the institution of the family, which exists and continues across generations thanks to various kinds of unpaid labor. However, the family itself features explicitly in the discourse of this book's protagonists only on occasion.[46] Family reproduces social stratification through practices of caste endogamy. It forms the unit for certain kinds of political and economic activity, not least in the cases of the Lotvala's flour mill and their Libertarian Social Institute. And at times, it provides a powerful analogy for conveying ideas of duty. Politicians like Rajagopalachari opposed the changes proposed to Hindu personal law that sought to give women power to inherit

43. See especially chapters 2 and 5.

44. Margaret Power and Paola Bacchetta, eds., *Right-Wing Women: From Conservatives to Extremists around the World* (New York: Routledge, 2002), 5–7.

45. Anjali Bharadwaj-Datta, Uditi Sen, and Mytheli Sreenivas, "Introduction: A Country of Her Making," *South Asia: Journal of South Asian Studies* 44, no. 2 (2021): 218–27; Nirmala Banerjee, "Whatever Happened to the Dreams of Modernity? The Nehruvian Era and Woman's Position," in *Economic and Political Weekly* 33, no. 7 (1998): WS2–WS7.

46. By contrast, see the commercial protagonists of Ritu Birla, *Stages of Capital: Law, Culture, and Market Governance in Late Colonial India* (Durham, NC: Duke University Press, 2007), and Eleanor Newbigin, *The Hindu Family and the Emergence of Modern India: Law, Citizenship, and Community* (Cambridge: Cambridge University Press, 2013). The protagonists here are diverse enough that they include votaries of both the nuclear and the undivided joint family.

property, considering such reform an attack on the gender hierarchy of the family. Reading between the lines, it appears that the patriarchal family would provide the social stability for free economy as opposed to the welfarist or developmental state. Unlike in the history of American postwar conservatism and neoliberalism, the political coalition behind free economy did not generally include individualists standing alongside its "family men."[47]

The three parts of this book cover the origins of free economy and opposition politics, the regionally situated ideas and practices of Swatantra's key leaders, and the presentation and publicity of free economy as a political platform across diverse forums. They do not offer a party history of Swatantra, which multiple political scientists have successfully attempted.[48] Part I shows how the discourse of free economy emerged and developed in response to changes in the Indian economy and society, before the birth of the Swatantra Party. Chapter 1 provides an overview of the aims, achievements, and failures of economic policy during the first two decades of independence. It highlights the underlying dynamics that produced discontent with India's development model and offers glimpses of these discourses of discontent. Moving from an all-India perspective to the west-coast city of Bombay, India's commercial capital, chapter 2 shows how the millowner and political patron Lotvala and his family fashioned an Indian libertarianism professing free economy through their Libertarian Social Institute. Contact with neoliberal publicists and agrarian decentralists in the Western world played some role in the development of this set of ideas, but the key process of articulation and diffusion occurred in a connected cluster of periodicals and voluntary associations spread across urban India. It was in this intellectual environment that the seeds of the idea of an opposition party to the Congress first germinated during the mid-1950s.

Part II excavates constitutive visions and practices of economic conservatism from southern and western India through a study of four founding leaders of the Swatantra Party. Caste, locality, and region helped shape the economic common sense these politicians developed out of their life's activities. Chapter 3 peels back the diverse layers of influences that led to the emergence of the

---

47. Melinda Cooper, *Family Values: Between Neoliberalism and the New Social Conservatism* (Brooklyn: Zone Books, 2017); Gerstle, *The Rise and Fall of the Neoliberal Order*.

48. Interested readers may turn to Howard Erdman's classic book, *The Swatantra Party and Indian Conservatism* (Cambridge: Cambridge University Press, 1967), and Vasanti Pratapchandra Rasam's *The Swatantra Party: A Political Biography* (Nagpur: Dattsons, 1997), which brings the discussion up to the decline and death of Swatantra.

Tamil Brahmin politician C. Rajagopalachari as an economic commentator who went on to demand the creation of a Swatantra Party to free India from "permit-and-license raj." It probes the symbiotic relationship between regional and national print publics and the intersection between a localized economic sensibility and neoliberal language. Chapter 4 complements Rajagopalachari's essentially negative view of free economy with three alternative economies of varying levels of concreteness coming from the Kammas of Andhra Pradesh, the Patidars of Gujarat (see Map II), and the Parsis of Bombay. It identifies distinct conceptions of the relationship between the scales of community, nation, and world economy in the practices of these communities and the writings of its Swatantra leaders. This scalar analysis reveals that their antistatism concerned centralized government power and bureaucratic regulation of economic activity; it was not a wholesale rejection of the state as a force in economic life.

Part III shows how the Swatantra Party constructed an ideological platform from the ideas examined in part II as it rewrote free economy for popular consumption and attempted to provide useful opposition to the Congress in Indian democracy. Chapter 5 reconstructs Swatantra's attempt to communicate its project of antistatist political mobilization through the construction of a "middle-class" citizen, and it surveys some of the responses these efforts courted. Chapter 6 highlights how the Swatantra Party pursued its ideal of democratic balance in office: by organizing coalitions, using parliamentary procedure to improve legislative accountability, and lobbying the judiciary to check the power of the Congress. With this discussion in mind, it assesses the recent revival of interest in the Swatantra Party and offers conclusions to the study.

# PART I

# Situating Free Economy

# 1

# Making a New India

## DREAMS, ACCOMPLISHMENTS, DISAPPOINTMENTS, CIRCA 1940−70

THE FILMS DIVISION OF India released a short documentary called *Tomorrow Is Ours* in 1955, toward the end of the country's First Five-Year Plan.[1] These shorts conveyed dimensions of the country's nation-building project.[2] They were screened before feature films at commercial theaters. A *gram sevak (grām sevak)*, a government employee tasked with assisting villagers in community welfare and development schemes, serves as the narrator. The film opens with a group of villagers and reviews changes at both the local and national levels. Newly built canals, tube wells, and tanks have helped improve agricultural output and reduce dependency on the annual monsoon. The village has built an all-weather road, a railway station, a trading center, a school, and refuse pits. The country has built several large dams, roads, and railway lines. By listing these feats, the gram sevak suggests the unity of ambition between village and nation.

Still, he notes, India must do much more to "catch up with the rest of the world in the shortest possible time." As the film cuts to the spectacle of factories and large machines, the narrator continues, "The throb of the machines captures the new spirit of India" (see Figure 1.1).[3] The country stands on the threshold of a new dawn. *Tomorrow Is Ours* evoked the optimism of the planning exercise. Films like these sought to drum up nationalist fervor. They invited Indians to

1. T. A. Abraham, dir., *Tomorrow Is Ours* (New Delhi: Films Division, 1955), https://www .youtube.com/watch?v=6F0b7tv5IhU&feature=emb_logo.

2. Roy, *Beyond Belief*, 32–65.

3. See the brief discussion in Peter Sutoris, *Visions of Development: Films Division of India and the Imagination of Progress, 1948–75* (New York: Oxford University Press, 2016), 134.

FIGURE 1.1. A Scene from *Tomorrow Is Ours* (1955) (Films Division of India).

partake in an economic transformation requiring the imagination and effort of everyone from the ordinary villager to the government minister. This was one way that the country sought to implant ideals of citizenly duty and participation.[4] More broadly, the developmental project attempted to bring change to India in a "scientific," orderly, and rational manner.[5]

Some fourteen years after the appearance of this film, the Indian bureaucrat Shrilal Shukla's farcical 1968 novel, *Rāg Darbārī* (The Melody of the Court), lampooned state propaganda like *Tomorrow Is Ours* for its tone-deafness and paternalism. The book consists of a series of episodes increasing in absurdity about how the noble intentions of the Indian leadership in Delhi are disconnected from the on-the-ground realities of the village. It is set in the fictional village of Shivpalganj in India's largest state of Uttar Pradesh, where state resources are dissipated or usurped by traditional elites who use them to further entrench existing power structures.

In one chapter, the villagers are subjected to political speeches encouraging them to increase their agricultural output, part of the "Grow More Food" campaign. All the speeches offer some variation of the following: "India is a

4. Menon, *Planning Democracy*. On duty toward nation-building as a dimension of citizenship, see Niraja Gopal Jayal, *Citizenship and Its Discontents: An Indian History* (Cambridge, MA: Harvard University Press, 2013), 171–74.

5. Blom Hansen, *The Saffron Wave*, 59.

farming nation. You are farmers, you should farm well and produce more grain." Supplementing these are advertisements. The most well-known of them depicts a healthy farmer cutting wheat with a sickle and a laughing woman behind him. The government "hoped that as soon as they saw the man and the laughing woman, the farmers would turn away from the poster and start growing more grain like men possessed," the narrator sarcastically comments.[6] Instead, the poster provokes a discussion in Shivpalganj about which villager the man and woman pictured most closely resemble. Meanwhile, a debate rages on the issue of whether it is inadequate food production that forces the country to "display the scars of its poverty to bring in the wheat they ate from abroad" or if the problem is instead greedy traders hoarding the wheat produced.[7] The narrator thus casts doubt about whether the incompetent state is even clear about its own resource position.

Both the dreams of *Tomorrow Is Ours* and the disillusionment of *Rāg Darbārī* have loomed large in historical memory and even in scholarship on India's experiment with statist development.[8] On the other hand, the nature and experience of socioeconomic change during these times has received scant historical consideration.[9] At least some appreciation of the salient changes over this time is crucial to understand the backdrop against which economic conservatism emerged and became expressed in politics. It was a momentous era. India designed and executed a program of planned economic development tethered to an aspirational scientific rationality of the state.

6. "*Bhārat ek khetihar deś he, tum khetihar ho, tumko accī khetī karnī cāhiye, adhik anna upajanā cāhiye*"; "*Unse āśā kī jātī tī ki ādmī ke pīce hastī huī aurat kī tasvīr dekhte hī ve uskī or pīṭh perkar dīwānoṁ ki taraf adhik anna upajānā śurū kar deṅge.*" Shrilal Shukla, *Rāg Darbārī*, 2nd paperback edition (New Delhi: Rajkamal Prakashan, 2021), 59–60. The original version appeared in 1968.

7. Shukla, *Rāg Darbārī*, 236; "*Jo gehū unhoṃne khāyā hai vah apnī garībī kā khoṛ dikhākar bāhar se maṅgāyā gayā hai,*" 250. On this debate, see Benjamin Siegel, *Hungry Nation: Food, Famine, and the Making of Modern India* (Cambridge: Cambridge University Press, 2018), 119–51.

8. Classically, Khilnani, *The Idea of India*. See, also, Guha, *India after Gandhi*; Pratap Bhanu Mehta, *The Burden of Democracy* (New Delhi: Penguin, 2003); and, more recently, Menon, *Planning Democracy*. For a juxtaposition of audiovisuals of dream and disillusionment pointing to the way that these binaries still seize the scholarly imagination, see Vikrant Dadawala, "The Films Division of India and the Nehruvian Dream," *South Asia: Journal of South Asian Studies* 45, no. 2 (2022): 220–35.

9. Notable exceptions are Engerman, *The Price of Aid*, and De, *A People's Constitution*. However, the social scientific treatments of scholars like Francine Frankel and O. V. Malyarov have been more comprehensive. Nikhil Menon, "Developing Histories of Development," *History Compass* 19, no. 10 (2021); O. V. Malyarov, *The Role of the State in the Socioeconomic Structure of India* (New Delhi: Vikas, 1983).

Development helped India consolidate a heavy industrial base, increase its population, and escape the colonial growth trap. In the process, it adjusted the relationship between citizens and the state and gave rise to new classes of people. But it never quite met its ambitious aims, culminating in disillusionment about the inconveniences and shortcomings of the developmental model. Political consequences would follow.

## Planned Transformation: From Early Days to Holidays

After India became independent from colonial rule in 1947, its people finally got the chance to take concrete steps toward development, something that they had thought about and debated for over six decades.[10] The Directive Principles of State Policy of the republican constitution, adopted in 1950, asserted some of the objectives of this project.[11] The broadest of these was the state's commitment to "securing and protecting as effectively as it may a social order in which justice, social, economic and political, shall inform all the institutions of the national life."[12] Other principles under this umbrella elaborated on this broad objective. They included committing to reducing inequality, securing the right to work and education, aiding the unemployed and disabled, and guaranteeing a decent standard of life.[13] Planned economic policy promised to bring about such changes. In the constitution, it appeared

10. On development and early Indian nationalism, see Bipan Chandra, *The Rise of Economic Nationalism in India* (Bombay: People's Publishing House, 1966). On colonial laissez-faire and its eclipse, see John Gallagher and Ronald Robinson, "The Imperialism of Free Trade," *The Economic History Review* 6, no. 1 (1953): 1–15; and Sabyasachi Bhattacharya, "Laissez-Faire in India," *Indian Economic and Social History Review* 2, no. 1 (1965): 1–22. See also Manu Goswami, *Producing India: From Colonial Economy to National Space* (Chicago: University of Chicago Press, 2004), 31–72. On Listian political economy and Indian nationalist thought, see Goswami, *Producing India*, 209–41. On cooperatives, see Nikolay Kamenov, "The Place of the 'Cooperative' in the Agrarian History of India, c. 1900–1970," *Journal of Asian Studies* 79, no. 1 (2020): 103–28. The quotation comes from Benjamin Zachariah, *Developing India: An Intellectual and Social History, c. 1930–50* (New Delhi: Oxford University Press, 2005), 6.

11. An exciting vein of law and society research examines the republican constitution as a product of contestation between progressive impulses to transform India and attempts to arrest radical change. See Arvind Elangovan, *Norms and Politics: Sir Bengal Narsing Rau in the Making of the Indian Constitution* (Oxford: Oxford University Press, 2019); Khosla, *India's Founding Moment*; Newbigin, *The Hindu Family and the Emergence of Modern India*; Saumya Saxena, *Divorce and Democracy: A History of Personal Law in Post-Independence India* (Cambridge: Cambridge University Press, 2022).

12. Article 38, Part VI, *Constitution of India*.

13. Articles 39, 41, 43, 47, Part IV, *Constitution of India*.

in the concurrent list of powers shared between states and the Union. This feature would prove important to its execution.[14]

Planning began to take shape after the cabinet passed a resolution calling for the creation of a planning commission in 1950. According to the resolution, the commission's work would be defined by the following aims: the right to livelihood for everyone, a more equitable pattern of ownership and control of resources, and the prevention of undue concentrations of economic power.[15] However, creating an apex body responsible for delineating development's contours along these progressive lines was a controversial proposition. Deputy Prime Minister Sardar Patel opposed central planning and believed that government's role was to create a suitable environment for business investment.[16] Countering ideas for a planning commission, he instead suggested a body comprising businesspeople, economists, and heads of government departments who might coordinate existing activity. His opinion held sway over the propertied majority comprising the dominant Congress Party's ranks.[17] Only after Patel's death in December 1950 could Prime Minister Nehru establish himself as the party's unquestioned leader and redirect planning along progressive lines.

The Planning Commission became the "nerve center of national thinking— on matters of planning and development."[18] From 1951 to 1967, its staff grew from 157 to 961.[19] Nehru leveraged his seniority in the Congress after Patel's death to transform the commission into an extension of his personal authority.[20] He gave members responsibilities and prestige paralleling those of cabinet ministers. By controlling the membership of the commission himself, he

14. Granville Austin, *The Indian Constitution: Cornerstone of a Nation* (Oxford: Clarendon Press, 1966), 235.

15. Frankel, *India's Political Economy*, 84–85.

16. Frankel, *India's Political Economy*, 85.

17. During the transfer of power between 1946–47, Congress assumed the reins of the Government of India. On this, see Rakesh Ankit, *India in the Interregnum: Interim Government, September 1946–August 1947* (Oxford: Oxford University Press, 2019). After the first elections in 1951–52, Congress formed the government with 364 of the 489 seats in parliament. It also won every state election. Although the party began to lose individual states from 1957, when Kerala voted for the Communist Party of India, Congress remained in power at the Center until 1977. See Stanley Kochanek, *The Congress Party of India: The Dynamics of One-Party Democracy* (Princeton: Princeton University Press, 1968).

18. D. R. Gadgil, quoted in Malyarov, *The Role of the State in the Socioeconomic Structure of India*, 251.

19. Malyarov, *The Role of the State in the Socioeconomic Structure of India*, 256.

20. Frankel, *India's Political Economy*, 113–15.

brought together like-minded figures who sympathized with the aim of socialist transformation. Outnumbered by the more conservative elements in the Congress and in parliament at large, Nehru concentrated the power of the executive branch in his person to advance the most radical program of economic policy possible.[21]

A top-down development apparatus spread from the mandarin in Delhi to the *gram sevak* of the village to implement the First Five-Year Plan. The commission comprised five layers of officials, numbering 1,816 by 1968.[22] A senior civil servant, the Department of Economics and Statistics, and a development commissioner liaised with the commission at the state level. Underneath this layer, government workers across India oversaw the allocation of resources in India's villages as part of community development.[23]

From its inception, the Indian planning apparatus created anxieties among certain leaders due to its potential to bypass the structures of representative government. The original Planning Commission consisted of six members: the prime minister, two politicians, two civil servants, and a businessman.[24] The body defined India's resources position, formulated a plan to utilize these resources, and determined priorities and stages for five-year plan completion. It also identified pitfalls along the way, selected the appropriate machinery for the plans, apprised plan progress at regular intervals, and made interim recommendations for revisions in plan strategy to the cabinet as needed.[25] In most respects, the Planning Commission resembled a separate ministry of the central government. However, it had no formal constitutional sanction.[26] Worried that this body would "gradually reduce the Cabinet to practically a registering authority," Finance Minister John Matthai resigned from his post in 1950.[27] He

21. Sudipta Kaviraj, *The Enchantment of Democracy and India: Politics and Ideas* (Ranikhet: Permanent Black, 2011), 85–116, 88.

22. This paragraph and the statistics cited follow from A. H. Hanson, *The Process of Planning: A Study of India's Five-Year Plans, 1950–1964* (London: Oxford University Press, 1966), 50–88. These figures appear in *Administrative Reforms Commission: Report on Machinery for Planning* (New Delhi: Government of India, 1968), i.

23. Chapter 4 offers a more detailed treatment of community development.

24. Raghabendra Chattopadhyaya, "The Idea of Planning in India, 1930–51," (unpublished PhD diss., Australian National University, 1985), 321.

25. Hanson, *The Process of Planning*, 50.

26. Austin, *The Indian Constitution*, 235–36.

27. John Matthai to Jawaharlal Nehru, June 17, 1950, Roll 1 (microfilm), Serial No. 30, John Matthai Papers, NMML.

found the commission "totally unnecessary and in fact hardly qualified to do its work."[28]

The First Five-Year Plan (1951–55) served as a trial period of sorts.[29] The plan invested in irrigation and rural electrification to improve agricultural output. It also coordinated the distribution of fertilizers, agricultural implements, and building materials. The first plan rebuilt the transportation architecture of the country. This was particularly urgent after World War II. The migration of millions of people after the partition of British India into India and Pakistan had left the overstretched railways crumbling.[30] To increase the output of factories and enterprises, the plan promoted schemes for improved capacity utilization. At this stage, responsibility for industrial development lay in the hands of private enterprise. In the domain of cottage and small industries, the state provided subsidies and sought to coordinate cooperative marketing and distribution of outputs. By the end of the first plan, labor, goods, and services flowed around the country without the political interruptions of the previous decade. Solid harvests drove down the price of food.[31]

To pinpoint the particularities of India's social and economic profile for this planning exercise, India developed a world-leading statistical infrastructure and introduced standardized weights and measures.[32] The most important data collection method that emerged from this project was the National

28. "Grave Misgivings on Delhi Pact: Dr. Matthai's Reasons for Resignation—Government Spending Criticized," *Times of India (hereafter ToI)*, June 3, 1950.

29. This paragraph follows Chattopadhyaya, "The Idea of Planning in India, 1930–51," 320–39.

30. Srinath Raghavan, *India's War: The Making of Modern South Asia* (London: Allen Lane, 2016), 325–50; Yasmin Khan, *The Great Partition: The Making of India and Pakistan* (New Haven, CT: Yale University Press, 2007). On the challenges and violence of postwar and postpartition stabilization, see Sherman, Gould, and Ansari, "The 'Flux' of the Matter: Loyalty, Corruption, and the 'Everyday State' in the Post-Partition Government Services of India and Pakistan," *Past and Present* 219, no. 1 (2013): 237–79; Sherman, Gould, and Ansari, eds., *From Subjects to Citizens*; Purushotham, *From Raj to Republic*; Rotem Geva, *Delhi Reborn: Partition and Nation Building in India's Capital* (Stanford, CA: Stanford University Press, 2022). For an overview of the vast scholarship on Partition, see David Gilmartin, "The Historiography of India's Partition: Between Civilization and Modernity," *Journal of Asian Studies* 74, no. 1 (2015): 23–41.

31. P. D. Ojha, "Inflation Control and Price Regulation," in *India's Economic Development Strategies, 1951–2000 AD*, ed. J. N. Mongia (Dordrecht, Netherlands: Reidel, 1985), 239–90, 244–48.

32. J. K. Ghosh, P. Maiti, T. J. Rao, and B. K. Sinha, "Evolution of Statistics in India," *International Statistical Review* 67, no. 1 (1999), 13–34. On the standardization of weights and measures, see A. Velkar, "Rethinking Metrology, Nationalism and Development in India, 1833–1956," *Past and Present* 239, no. 1 (2018): 143–79.

Sample Survey. The survey organization sent a group of statisticians and workers across India's villages to ascertain information ranging from income levels to height. The survey's pioneer, polymath P. C. Mahalanobis (1893–1972), became the grey eminence of Indian planning during the 1950s.[33] His Indian Statistical Institute and the Central Statistical Organization assumed prominence during the planned era, housing the seers of India's economic transformation.[34] It attracted a slew of foreign visitors, including Chinese officials who came to study large-scale random sampling.[35]

Alongside statisticians, quantitatively minded economists provided expertise to the project of planning in India. Economics began to incorporate sophisticated techniques of mathematics and focus on questions of growth theory at this time.[36] Economists created new metrics for conceptualizing the economy and reimagined its possibilities, across the world.[37] "What is a young man's ambition today? They think of becoming economists, because an economist plays a big part in the modern world," Nehru had mused in 1948.[38] Economists could do a number of things for India. They might offer advice to the government, work in a growing number of universities and think tanks, or—from 1961—join the Indian Economic Service.[39] The most highly regarded feeder of economists to these institutions was the Delhi School of Economics. Aspiring to be "an institution with the characteristics of a public school, an Oxbridge college, and an Indian version of the Brookings Institution," the school came forth as the country's leading center for social science.[40]

33. Ashok Rudra, *Prasanta Chandra Mahalanobis: A Biography* (Delhi: Oxford University Press, 1996).

34. Nikhil Menon, "'Fancy Calculating Machine': Computers and planning in independent India," *Modern Asian Studies* 52, no. 2 (2018): 421–57, 424–26.

35. This fascinating episode of Indo-Chinese knowledge exchange ended with the Great Leap Forward (1958–61). See Arunabh Ghosh, *Making it Count: Statistics and Statecraft in the Early People's Republic of China* (Princeton: Princeton University Press, 2020), 213–248.

36. E. Roy Weintraub, ed., *MIT and the Transformation of American Economics* (Cambridge, MA: MIT Press, 2014).

37. Adam Tooze, *Statistics and the German State, 1900–1945: The Making of Modern Economic Knowledge* (Cambridge: Cambridge University Press, 2001); Timothy Mitchell, *Rule of Experts: Egypt, Techno-Politics, Modernity* (Berkeley: University of California Press, 2002).

38. Nehru, quoted in Khilnani, *The Idea of India*, 61.

39. S. Ambirajan, "The Professionalization of Economics in India," *History of Political Economy* 28 (1996) Supplement, 80–96, 82.

40. P. N. Dhar, "The Early Years," in *D-School: Reflections on the Delhi School of Economics*, eds. Dharma Kumar and Dilip Mookerjee (New Delhi: Oxford University Press, 1995), 7–23.

The Second Five-Year Plan (1956–61) sought to reorient India economic policy toward greater "self-sufficiency." The term had antecedents in Mahatma Gandhi's idea that India must reclaim an imagined precolonial restraint and eschew greed. "Self-sufficiency" now connoted India's desire to escape its colonial-era vulnerability to shocks in the global economy and the whims of policy defined by the India Office in London.[41] The country had to shed its identity as a raw materials exporter and finished goods importer by generating industrial capacity of its own. To do so, India pursued import substitution, introduced a series of tariffs on imports, and offered subsidies for Indian enterprises.[42] It also deliberately refrained from cultivating large export markets for fear of becoming too dependent on foreign economic interests. As a result, foreign exchange earnings were minimal.[43]

The second plan's theoretical underpinnings came from the so-called Mahalanobis model, which prioritized capital-goods-led industrialization.[44] The logic ran that investing in heavy industries that produced capital goods like steel would create the conditions for self-sustaining growth and generate demand for consumer goods, like cloth. Mahalanobis's model required that a country maintain a high enough savings rate and repress consumption to invest in such goods. This also meant investing fewer resources in consumer goods industries.[45]

India's planning model aimed at consolidating a "mixed economy" with private and public sectors.[46] But the aim was to move the country toward a "socialistic pattern of society," as articulated by the Congress in 1955. The socialist tenor of this policy lay in the fact that 80 percent of the second plan's resources were marked out for the public sector and that the nationalization of multiple industries was in the cards. The private sector received lower priority.

41. Tirthankar Roy, *The Economic History of India, 1857–1947* (New Delhi: Oxford University Press, 2000); Dietmar Rothermund, *India in the Great Depression, 1929–39* (New Delhi: Manohar, 1992). For more on Gandhi, see chapters 2 and 3.

42. Jagdish Bhagwati and Padma Desai, *India: Planning for Industrialization* (London: Oxford University Press, 1970).

43. Manmohan Singh, *India's Export Trends and the Prospects for Self-Sustained Growth* (Oxford: Clarendon, 1964).

44. This paragraph follows Chakravarty, *Development Planning*, 13–17.

45. Leslie Hempson, "The Social Life of Khadi: Gandhi's Experiments with the Indian Economy, c. 1915–65," (unpublished PhD diss., University of Michigan, 2018), 130–78.

46. "Mixed economy" was also used to describe policy regimes in other parts of the developing world. See, for example, Offner, *Sorting Out the Mixed Economy*.

Instead of "socialist," a better description would be an aspiring developmentalist state capitalism comprising state-owned firms and a regulated private sector. "Mixed economy" connoted the state ownership of priority sectors combined with private sector ownership of other sectors of the economy.[47] The planners considered this a "middle way" in development, avoiding the extremes of either laissez-faire or complete state ownership of the means of production.[48]

The strategy found acceptance and aid from both sides of the Iron Curtain.[49] Indeed, a great contradiction of India's capital-goods-led import-substituting industrialization was that self-sufficiency involved becoming dependent on generous resource contributions from foreign countries. The largest donors were the United States and the Soviet Union. Both saw India as a crucial site in the global Cold War and sought to tilt the nominally non-aligned country in their direction. The Americans, advised by modernization theorists, sought to help give India a "big push" and become a major market for U.S. exports. The United States offloaded its agricultural surpluses onto food-insecure India and sought to persuade the country to dedicate greater resources to private sector and small industrial development. The Soviets, wanting India to industrialize so that its proletariat could develop and seize the means of production, provided resources in support of heavy industry products.

State propaganda vividly conveyed the ambition of the globally supported second plan, the centerpiece of India's dominant economic imaginary. The Films Division released the Hindi-language *Working for the Plan* just before it commenced.[50] The film begins with a postman delivering an invitation to a theater performance titled, *Sāre Jahāṃ Se Accā, Hindustān Hamārā* (Better than the Rest of the World, Our India).[51] Named after a famous patriotic song, the play weaves planning into a history of India. This history commenced with ancient glory, followed by colonial decline. It ended in national regeneration built

47. Mahalanobis devised his model independently, though it paralleled the 1928 model developed by Soviet economist Feldman. Chakravarty, *Development Planning*, 14.

48. P. C. Mahalanobis, *Talks on Planning* (Calcutta: Indian Statistical Institute, 1961).

49. Engerman, *The Price of Aid*; Jag Parvesh Chander, *India's Socialistic Pattern of Society* (Delhi: Metropolitan Book Company, 1956).

50. Curiously, however, there does not seem to be a Hindi title for the film. Kumar Chandrasekhar, dir., *Working for the Plan* (New Delhi: Films Division, 1956), https://www.youtube.com/watch?v=I6BXQQ07N9k.

51. Sutoris, *Visions of Development*, 160.

FIGURE 1.2. A Diverse People Coming Together in *Working for the Plan* (Films Division of India).

on the backs of a diverse group of peoples working together for the greater good (see Figure 1.2). Near the end, the camera cuts from the ancient Ashokan wheel of the Indian flag to the turning gears of a machine, emphasizing the connection between the past and the aspired future.[52] The narrator boldly proclaims, "*Yah ek naye Bhārat banāne kā yojanā hai*" (This is a plan to make a new India).

The second plan's ambition and relative neglect of agricultural investment sowed the seeds of its demise. Shortages of foreign exchange and food put brakes on the process.[53] The Third Five-Year Plan (1961–66) shifted the resources away from the public sector and more toward agriculture (see Table 1.1), even as it retained a slight heavy industry focus.[54] A more decentralized process of resource allocation allowed state governments to pursue new policies to improve agricultural yields. Still, India persistently underproduced its targets. State-level resistance from landed interests on matters such as the reform of agrarian holding structures and production arrested further

<hr/>

52. Srirupa Roy, "'A Symbol of Freedom': The Indian Flag and the Transformations of Nationalism, 1906–2002," *Journal of Asian Studies* 65, no. 3 (2006): 495–527.

53. Engerman, *The Price of Aid*, 159–89.

54. Hanson, *The Process of Planning*, 188–89.

TABLE 1.1. Plan Outlays and Financing at a Glance

| Expenditure Heads | Plan Outlays (in crores,* current) | | | Shares of Total Allocation (%) | | |
|---|---|---|---|---|---|---|
| | First (1951–56) | Second (1956–61) | Third (1961–66) | First | Second | Third |
| Agriculture/Community Development | 361 | 568 | 1068 | 17 | 12 | 14 |
| Irrigation/Power | 561 | 913 | 1662 | 27 | 19 | 22 |
| Village Industry | 27 | 200 | 264 | 1 | 4 | 4 |
| Industry/Mining | 146 | 690 | 1520 | 7 | 14 | 20 |
| Transport/Communications | 497 | 1385 | 1486 | 24 | 29 | 20 |
| Social Services/Miscellaneous | 477 | 1044 | 1500 | 23 | 22 | 20 |
| Total | 2069 | 4800 | 7500 | 100 | 100 | 100 |

| Resources | First (1951–56) | Second (1956–61) | Third (1961–66) | First | Second | Third |
|---|---|---|---|---|---|---|
| Domestic Resources | 1258 | 2400 | 4750 | 61 | 50 | 63 |
| External Assistance | 521 | 800 | 2200 | 25 | 17 | 29 |
| Deficit | 290 | 1200 | 550 | 14 | 25 | 8 |
| Gap | | 400 | | | 8 | |

*Source:* Reproduced from David Engerman, *The Price of Aid: The Economic Cold War in India* (Cambridge, MA: Harvard University Press, 2018), 12l, and (built from *Government of India,* various).

*crore = 10 million

progress. While India's new, world-class capital-goods-producing firms met their plan targets, older uncompetitive businesses churned out subpar consumer goods well into the 1960s.[55]

Financial constraints now overwhelmed the heady dreams and enthusiasm characteristic of the earlier years of planning. India's wars with China (1962) and Pakistan (1965) drove up military expenditures. A poor harvest in 1966 produced further economic pressures.[56] By that year, India had steadily run out of foreign exchange and could no longer pay for imports. It was forced to devalue the rupee and liberalize import policy by the World Bank and International Monetary Fund to secure the requisite foreign exchange.[57] The inflation rate was about 14 percent that year, ten times greater than the 1.5 percent annual average for the first half of the 1950s.

Such events undermined the original development strategy. Indian development planners lost autonomy to foreign interests, dropping several industrial controls and trade licensing policies.[58] Over the entire third plan period, India's economy grew at an annual average of just 0.3 percent.[59]

The country subsequently went on a Plan Holiday from 1966 to 1969. In the face of sustained foreign pressure, Indian policymakers made virtue of necessity and articulated a new policy for agriculture. Lal Bahadur Shastri, Nehru's successor, did not share his predecessors' views on development. He showed more sympathy to private sector efforts and interests in the agrarian economy relative to heavy industry.[60] From 1966–67, Indian policymakers embarked on what would come to be known as the Green Revolution. India introduced high-yielding varieties of seeds from Mexico and chemical fertilizers by providing price incentives to private farmers who would adopt them,

55. Frankel, *India's Political Economy*, 180–90.

56. Chirashree Das Gupta, *State and Capital in Independent India: Institutions and Accumulation* (Cambridge: Cambridge University Press, 2016), 100. This also complicated India's relationship with foreign donors as it required the purchase of foreign weaponry and technology. See Engerman, *The Price of Aid*, 191–223.

57. Rahul Mukherji, "India's Aborted Liberalization–1966," *Pacific Affairs* 73, no. 3 (2000), 375–92; Frankel, *India's Political Economy*, 315–16.

58. Mukherji, "India's Aborted Liberalization."

59. Engerman, *The Price of Aid*, 304.

60. Medha Kudaisya, "'Reforms by Stealth': Indian Economic Policy, Big Business and the Promise of the Shastri Years, 1964–1966," *South Asia: Journal of South Asian Studies* 25, no. 2 (2002): 205–29.

aided by the Rockefeller Foundation.[61] Farmers received direct payments for investment in improved agricultural technology under this scheme.[62] By pursuing this strategy, India became self-sufficient in food production, ending a period of its economic history of persistently inadequate domestic food supply. However, the policies tended to concentrate power in the hands of rich farmers and clients of landowners and made increasing numbers of agricultural laborers redundant.[63]

During the second half of the 1960s, the Center conceded greater resources to the states and left more activity to the private sector. The liberalization of certain forms of licensing and removal of controls from strategic industries compromised the "planned" character of the economy. Once seen as the formidable agent of industrial transformation, the public sector lost its widespread regard. Even the Soviets, who welcomed India's aim of public-sector-led development, grew frustrated with the inefficiency of the country's public enterprises.[64] The introduction of greater price incentives for farmers and the slow retreat of the state from primary markets in agriculture signaled the end of an era.[65] Turning things over to the states and private markets was a fresh approach.

Planning ended two hundred years of per capita income stagnation for good.[66] The Indian economy slowly but surely moved away from agriculture and toward heavy industrial production. India's industrial sector grew at 7 percent annually. The composition of this growth moved away from consumer goods and into capital goods production.[67] Planning also shifted the balance between private and public sectors. The public sector's share of

---

61. Scientific exchange during this time between India and Mexico is now emerging as an important part of the history of South-South exchange. It challenges the picture of the Green Revolution as a simple story of the Indian uptake of American advice and resources. See Gabriela Soto Laveaga et al., "Roundtable: New Narratives of the Green Revolution," *Agricultural History* 91, no. 3 (2017): 397–422. On the ideological origins of the Green Revolution, see Siegel, *Hungry Nation*, 183–219.

62. Frankel, *India's Political Economy*, 274–76.

63. B. H. Farmer, "The 'Green Revolution' in South Asia," *Geography* 66, no. 3 (July 1981): 202–7.

64. Engerman, *The Price of Aid*, 285–96.

65. This follows from Frankel, *India's Political Economy*, 246–92.

66. Bishnupriya Gupta, "Falling Behind and Catching Up: India's Transition from a Colonial Economy," *Economic History Review* 72, no. 3 (2019): 803–27.

67. Prabhat Patnaik, "Industrial Development in India Since Independence," *Social Scientist* 7, no. 11 (1979): 3–19, 7; Das Gupta, *State and Capital in Independent India*, 154; Jagdish Bhagwati and T. N. Srinivasan, *Foreign Trade Regimes and Economic Development: India* (New York:

national output rose from 7.4 percent to 13.3 percent between 1950 and 1965.[68] At the same time, the independent Indian state failed to achieve its aims. The capital-intensive techniques of planning generated inadequate employment for India's population, which grew 70 percent between 1941 and 1971 thanks to declining death rates.[69] And growth exacerbated vectors of both economic and social inequality such as income, gender, and caste.[70]

## Seeing and Feeling the State: Bureaucracy, Controls, Extraction

The state went beyond producing long outlines and propaganda films to make its plans work. It expanded its personnel and either intensified or introduced new mechanisms of economic extraction and control. These trends traced antecedents in World War II, when the British used India as a supply base for the war in Asia. Wartime measures introduced a raft of emergency economic laws and prompted a lopsided process of industrialization.[71] They created a template that would characterize the management of economic life for decades to follow.[72] These wartime measures became codified in economic laws following the cessation of hostilities, reflective of an understanding of underdevelopment as a permanent emergency.[73]

---

National Bureau of Economic Research, 1975), 17; Ayesha Jalal, *Democracy and Authoritarianism in South Asia* (Cambridge: Cambridge University Press, 1995), 123–36.

68. Malyarov, *The Role of the State in the Socioeconomic Structure of India*, Appendix 8.

69. P. N. Chopra, ed., *The Gazetteer of India: Indian Union Vol. 3–Economic Structure and Activities* (New Delhi: Government of India, 1975), 128 (hereafter, *Gazetteer*, vol. 3); Nirmala Banerjee, "Women Workers and Development," *Social Scientist* 6, no. 8 (March 1978): 3–15.

70. This is an important topic for which there is inadequate space to discuss here. A good volume evaluating planning is Terence Byres, ed., *The State, Development Planning, and Liberalization in India* (New Delhi: Oxford University Press, 1997); see also the essays in Sugata Bose and Ayesha Jalal, eds., *Nationalism, Democracy and Development* (Oxford: Oxford University Press, 1998), and Bardhan, *The Political Economy of Development in India*. I discuss some of these issues in the following chapters.

71. Raghavan, *India's War*, 320–55.

72. Rohit De, "'Commodities Must Be Controlled': Economic Crimes and Market Discipline in India (1939–55)," *International Journal of Law in Context* 10, no. 3 (2014): 277–94; Aditya Balasubramanian, "Anticorruption, Development, and the Indian State: A History of (Incomplete) Decolonization," (working paper); Indivar Kamtekar, "The Foundations of State Expansion: War and Government in India, 1939–50," paper delivered at "The Indian Predicament: South Asia in World War II," Hebrew University of Jerusalem, June 5–6, 2016.

73. De, *A People's Constitution*, 77–122.

From the outbreak of World War II onward, the Government of India had created new departments, hired more personnel, and granted them more power over resource allocation.[74] In part, this bureaucratization owed to the state's expanded duties. Whereas in the colonial era, the smallest unit of administration had been concerned almost exclusively to collect revenue, the postcolonial state sought to direct and expand production and provide a modicum of welfare as well. Table 1.2 shows how, during the 1940s alone, the central secretariat's personnel ballooned at every level, from stenographers to influential department secretaries. The trend continued in subsequent decades. The number of central government departments soared from eighteen to forty-two. Employment rose from six thousand to fifteen thousand in the first twenty years of independence.[75] Overall, between 1939 and 1971, the number of central government employees nearly quadrupled, from 809,000 to three million.[76]

The central government bureaucracy was organized in a pyramid-style hierarchy. A small minority of Class I officers wielded power over larger numbers of subordinates in Classes II to IV. Class I bureaucrats assumed key responsibilities and enjoyed a range of perquisites—housing, expense accounts, and vehicular transportation among them.[77] Those appointed Custodians of Evacuee Property in states like Punjab and cities like Delhi had the power to redistribute these assets.[78]

Even within this elite group of Class I officers, members of the Indian Administrative Service (IAS) enjoyed the greatest prestige. They were descendants of the Indian Civil Service, the steel frame of the British Government of India. These mandarins passed selective entrance examinations to join a gentlemanly, middle-class, and conservative subculture. Advocates of the IAS considered these officers to share a set of service-minded norms and values.

74. Rohit De, "A Republic of Petty Bureaucrats: Upendra Baxi and the Pathologies of Civil Service Jurisprudence," *Jindal Global Law Review* 9, no. 2 (2018): 335–50.

75. Malyarov, *The Role of the State in the Socioeconomic Structure of India*, 291.

76. P. N. Chopra, ed., *Gazetteer of India: Indian Union Vol. 4–Administration and Public Welfare* (New Delhi: Government of India, 1978), 105 (hereafter *Gazetteer*, vol. 4), 105.

77. M. N. Srinivas, *Social Change in Modern India* (Berkeley: University of California Press, 1966), 94; André Béteille, *Castes: Old and New: Essays in Social Structure and Social Stratification* (Bombay: Asia Publishing House, 1969), 234–35.

78. Rohit De, "Evacuee Property and the Management of Postcolonial Economic Life in India," in *The Postcolonial Movement in South and Southeast Asia*, eds. Gyan Prakash, Michael Laffan, and Nikhil Menon (London: Bloomsbury, 2019); Rotem Geva, "The Scramble for Houses: Violence, a Factionalized State, and Informal Economy in Post-Partition Delhi," *Modern Asian Studies* 51, no. 3 (2017), 769–824.

TABLE 1.2. Growth of Staff of the Central Secretariat during the 1940s

| Posts | 1939 | 1948 | Increase in Staff |
|---|---|---|---|
| Secretaries | 9 | 19 | 111% |
| Additional Secretaries | 0 | 5 | — |
| Joint Secretaries | 8 | 35 | 338% |
| Deputy Secretaries | 12 | 84 | 600% |
| Under/Assistant Secretaries | 16 | 191 | 1094% |
| Superintendents | 68 | 293 | 331% |
| Assistants | 501 | 2406 | 380% |
| Clerks | 641 | 2569 | 301% |
| Stenographers | 90 | 515 | 472% |

Source: P. N. Chopra, ed., *The Gazetteer of India: Indian Union Vol. 3–Economic Structure and Activities* (New Delhi: Government of India, 1975), 58.

Critics regarded them as unabashed elitists and even neocolonialists.[79] The IAS officers rose to fame when Deputy Prime Minister Sardar Patel used them to unify the Indian nation in the aftermath of Partition. Subsequently, Nehru relied on them to implement the machinery of the development state.[80] Their ranks swelled from 803 to 2,754 between 1948 and 1966.[81]

The IAS officers were generalists without expertise. They looked after a range of economic activities. They might collect revenue from a district of rural India, run a large public-sector industry, or manage food-grains distribution. As the investment in the public sector of the economy expanded by over 300 percent during the first three plans, these administrators began to control an increased proportion of India's economic resources (see Table 1.3). Some 320 designated district officers supervised the development schemes and allocation of economic resources in rural India through a nationwide system of subordinates spread over India's 560,000 villages.[82]

Numbers and responsibilities for government officials increased at the division, district, regional, and state levels as well.[83] All in all, between 1947 and 1968, employment rose from 3 million to 9.9 million across layers of

79. David Potter, *India's Political Administrators: From ICS to IAS, 1919–1983* (New Delhi: Oxford University Press, 1996), 80–120; 246–50.

80. Sudipta Kaviraj, *The Trajectories of the Indian State: Politics and Ideas* (Ranikhet: Permanent Black, 2010), 144–71, 155.

81. Malyarov, *The Role of the State in the Socioeconomic Structure of India*, 291.

82. Angus Maddison, *Class Structure and Economic Growth: India and Pakistan Since the Moghuls* (New York: Norton, 1971), 117, 94–95.

83. On bureaucratic discretion and commodity controls, see De, *A People's Constitution*, 87.

TABLE 1.3. Public Sector Plan Outlay (in Rs. crores)

| Sector | First Five-Year Plan | Second Five-Year Plan | Third Five-Year Plan | Increase between First and Third Plans |
|---|---|---|---|---|
| Agriculture | 290 | 530 | 1090 | 276% |
| Irrigation | 310 | 420 | 650 | 110% |
| Power | 260 | 440 | 1190 | 358% |
| Industry | 120 | 1080 | 1890 | 1475% |
| Transport | 520 | 1300 | 1940 | 273% |
| Social Service | 460 | 830 | 1440 | 213% |
| Total | 1960 | 4600 | 8200 | 318% |

Source: Chopra, ed., Gazetteer, vol 3., 58–59.

government.[84] These employees supervised activities ranging from tax collection to electrification. The number of new jobs created in individual departments could be enormous; one state secretariat increased its staff from 320 to 2,226 people between 1947 and 1965. And in the 1960s alone, the number of government officials in India's states rose 40 percent.[85] Sarkārī (government) employees became the human face of the expanding Indian state. They enjoyed stable jobs and oversaw the dissemination of resources and practice of policy in an economically insecure country.

Bureaucrats administered a regime of rations, price controls, and industrial licenses.[86] Essential commodities that came under the purview of control legislation included various foodstuffs, cloth, and steel. Control also meant that a private corporation needed government consent to issue shares and debt securities. Only those firms whose expansion advanced plan objectives would be able to do so. Private citizens needed to apply for foreign exchange from the Reserve Bank. Importers applied for goods under a quota system. Taken together, these controls profoundly touched Indian economic life.

The apparatus of procurement and distribution and set of laws devised by the Ministry of Food for the management of the most important controlled commodity is a case study in the statist contours of the postcolonial

84. Maddison, Class Structure and Economic Growth, 93.
85. Administrative Reforms Commission Report on State Administration (New Delhi: Government of India, 1969), 73.
86. Malyarov, The Role of the State in the Socioeconomic Structure of India, 194, 222–27.

economy.[87] The ministry divided the country into zones of food surplus and deficit and redistributed from the former to the latter. Private actors could not move food across zones. To guarantee livelihoods, the government paid minimum support prices to farmers. It also paid procurement prices to acquire grains from sellers for redistribution to deficit states. When necessary, the Government of India augmented the total food supply with imports.

By the late 1950s, the government supplemented these forms of intervention by building up its own buffer stock of food to stabilize the price system. It absorbed excess food-grains in years of good harvests and released extra grains into circulation in years of shortage. For the poorest sections of the populace, the ministry oversaw the rationing of approximately a tenth of the country's food resources. Licensed dealers across the country sold fixed quantities of food at fair price shops to citizens presenting ration cards. This process of procurement and distribution ran alongside parallel processes conducted by state-level civil-supplies departments. This system connected local, state, and central levels of government with the everyday economic lives of Indians.

The state's functionaries also oversaw the management of industrial policy. The Government of India's Industries Development and Regulation Act (1951) and Industrial Policy Resolution (1956) reserved seventeen industries for exclusive public-sector enterprise participation, twelve for both private and public enterprises, and the remainder exclusively for the private sector, subject to licensing and regulation by the government.[88] This legislation required private businesses to secure government permits to operate and obtain licenses for scarce resources like foreign exchange.[89] The state reserved the right to prescribe prices, determine the methods and volume of production, and control channels of distribution of output in all industries under the terms of this policy.[90] Further, it could nationalize businesses and determine adequate compensation. It went on to do so in the fields of aviation and life insurance.

87. This paragraph follows R. N. Chopra, *Evolution of Food Policy in India* (New Delhi: Macmillan, 1981), 1–17.

88. Ruddar Datt and K. P. Sundharam, *Indian Economy*, 5th edition, (New Delhi: Niraj Prakashan, 1969), 181–83. The features of the resolution, sometimes called the "economic constitution of India," were passed as amendments to the 1951 Act.

89. Uma Kapila, "Industrial Development and Policies since Independence," *Indian Economy since Independence*, 23rd edition, ed. Kapila (New Delhi: Academic Foundation, 2012), 389–456, 389–91.

90. Datt and Sundharam, *Indian Economy*, 185–86.

Between 1950 and 1971, the state's share in the national capital stock—reproducible tangible wealth—rose from 15 percent to 35 percent.[91]

Taxes provided a source of financing for planning. Because only a small proportion of Indian citizens earned enough to pay income tax, the Government of India increased the burden on the wealthy by introducing direct taxes: a wealth tax (1957), a gift tax (1958), and, subsequently, an estate duty (1963).[92] Nevertheless, direct taxation accounted for the minority of tax receipts. The infamous income tax collector only really affected a small sliver of the population.[93] More than double that amount came from regressive indirect taxes on transactions typically paid by the urban population. These included sales taxes, excise duties, and the entertainment tax. The share of indirect taxes in government revenue increased over time, driven by raising duties and increasing the number of commodities subjected to excise taxation.[94] These included everything from sugar to pressure cookers. Between 1950 and 1971, rising receipts from indirect tax collection doubled tax receipts as a percentage of national output from 4 percent to 8 percent.[95]

Debasing the currency furnished another source of development funding. The plan's ambitious expenditure requirements for producing capital equipment required India to run an unfunded budget deficit. To meet it, India printed more currency. This contributed to prices rising during the period of the Second Five-Year Plan (see Graph 1.1). The country's export earnings paled in comparison to the foreign exchange costs of imports. As a result, foreign exchange reserves steadily diminished. An anxious Nehru wrote to his cabinet in June 1957 of "great stress on the foreign exchange which is causing us so much trouble."[96] In the event of their exhaustion, India faced painful devaluation and

91. Malyarov, *The Role of the State in the Socioeconomic Structure of India*, 89.

92. Frankel, *India's Political Economy*, 218–19; Nanasaheb Rajendra Lavand, "A Study of Income Tax Revenue and Buoyancy in India since 1991," (unpublished PhD diss., Dr. Babasaheb Ambedkar Marathwada University, 2016), 1–72.

93. *Report of the Committee on Taxation of Agricultural Wealth and Income* (New Delhi: Ministry of Finance, 1972), 3–5.

94. This paragraph follows M.M. Sury, "Tax Structure Developments in India: 1950–90," *Journal of Indian School of Political Economy* 3, no. 1 (1991), 1–37, 6–9.

95. M. M. Sury and Vibha Mathur, *India: Sixty Years of Planned Economic Development* (New Delhi: New Century Publications, 2010), 341.

96. Jawaharlal Nehru, untitled memorandum, June 8, 1957, Correspondences with Jawaharlal Nehru, NMML. In the event, the commission was bypassing the Commerce Ministry and requesting statistical information directly from businesses.

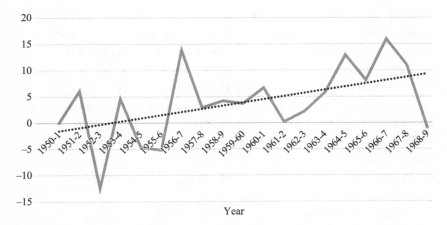

**GRAPH 1.1.** Wholesale Price Inflation (Year on Year, Percent).
*Source:* H. L. Chandhok, *Wholesale Price Statistics in India, 1947–78* (New Delhi: Economic and Scientific Research Foundation, 1978), 147.

accepting higher rupee costs of imports. That could in turn further exacerbate inflation.[97] Poorer harvests during this period further drove up the cost of food.

A key aspiration of the central government in bringing the planned economy into being was to redistribute unequally held land to organize it in a more equitable and economically productive fashion. The record of measures toward this end highlights some of the challenges of Indian federalism.[98] Under the constitution, the states held the exclusive power to pass land reform legislation. The right to property (article 19), enumerated as one of the seven guaranteed fundamental rights, and the right to just compensation for property acquired by the government for public purpose (article 31), constrained the process of transformation. The issue of what constituted just compensation became a sticking point in the courts.[99] Between 1951 and 1970, judicial enforcement of the property clause provoked four amendments to the constitution.[100]

97. Engerman, *The Price of Aid*, 159–70.

98. For a useful overview, see Louise Tillin, *Indian Federalism* (New Delhi: Oxford University Press, 2019).

99. Granville Austin, *Working a Democratic Constitution: A History of the Indian Experience* (New Delhi: Oxford University Press, 1999), 69–122.

100. Namita Wahi, "Property," in *The Oxford Handbook of the Indian Constitution*, eds. Sujit Choudhry, Madhav Khosla, and Pratap Bhanu Mehta (New Delhi: Oxford University Press, 2016), 944–64.

Land reform measures sought to end the greatly unequal ownership patterns and exploitative relationships characterizing agrarian life. Broadly, they encompassed laws to regulate rents, to prevent tenants from being thrown off land by owners, and to redistribute land ownership.[101] Over the 1950s and 1960s, the Government of India sought to introduce reforms to areas governed by each of the three major colonial-era land tenure systems—*zamindari, mahalwari*, and *ryotwari*.[102] Of these, conditions in the former zamindari regions of the Bengal Presidency and other parts of northern India were the worst. This system resembled a kind of absentee landlordism. Property and revenue rights were vested with the zamindar, who collected rent from the peasant and passed on 10/11 of the sum to the British.

Under the mahalwari system prevalent in much of northern and central India, *mahals* (estates of one village or more) supervised revenue collection from peasants who owned their own land. By contrast, under the ryotwari system prevalent in the Bombay and Madras presidencies of southern and western India (see Map I), the British collected 50 percent of the revenue of dry lands and 60 percent of the revenue of irrigated areas directly from the *ryot*, who had effective property rights.[103] Although notionally a form of peasant proprietorship, large ryots could sublet their land or charge high rents to tenants and operate like zamindars.[104] Manifold local variations, special forms of these tenures, and exceptions further complicated matters.[105] Still, India managed to abolish the zamindari system in these years.[106]

The everyday lives of India's people became increasingly entangled with the personnel and processes of the state as planning took shape. Bureaucrats controlled prices, distributed resources, issued licenses, and collected taxes. This could be a less pleasant phenomenon for the citizen than pictured in films like *Working for the Plan*. It might mean experiencing lengthy delays in

---

101. Datt and Sundharam, *Indian Economy*, 350–58; Ronald Herring, *Land to the Tiller: The Political Economy of Agrarian Reform in South Asia* (New Haven: Yale University Press, 1983).

102. Land reforms receive greater attention in chapters 3, 4, and 6.

103. This paragraph follows B. H. Baden-Powell, *A Short Account of the Land Revenue and its Administration in British India: With a Sketch of the Land Tenures* (Oxford: Clarendon, 1907).

104. Datt and Sundharam, *Indian Economy*, 347.

105. To take one example, there were five different kinds of tenure in the northern city of Allahabad alone. See C. A. Bayly, "Rural Conflict and the Roots of Indian Nationalism: Allahabad District Since 1800," 1–23, appendix to *The Local Roots of Indian Politics: Allahabad, 1880–1920* in *The C. A. Bayly Omnibus* (New Delhi: Oxford University Press, 2009).

106. Frank J. Moore, "Land Reform and Social Justice in India," *Far Eastern Survey* 24, no. 8 (1955): 124–28.

receiving permits, paying more and more for food, or being subjected to everyday bureaucratic hurdles. In this environment, civil servants and the state came under both deserved and unmerited suspicion.

## New Concerns, New Classes

A current of cynicism about independent India's developmental dreams appeared in literary culture from the time the second plan began to lose steam. The Hindi novelist and short story writer Krishan Chander's *Ek Gadhe kī Ātmakatā* (The Autobiography of an Ass) offers a compelling example.[107] Published as a pocketbook, the novella was part of a growing genre of middlebrow reading material of the literate urban classes.[108] It satirizes the political economy of development through the tale of a witty talking donkey's misadventures journeying from an Uttar Pradesh village to the capital city of New Delhi. On a quest to claim *harjānā* (government compensation) for the family of his recently deceased washerman owner, the donkey goes from government department to government department. At every step, his interlocutors offer new excuses about how they cannot help him. One tells him that the matter is not in the department's jurisdiction. Another points out that the washerman does not fall under the definition of a government worker to qualify for compensation. A third lambasts the donkey for not having the adequate paperwork.

Undeterred, the donkey perseveres by approaching increasingly important officials until he reaches Nehru. The prime minister offers help and asks to take a ride on the donkey. By making Nehru ride a donkey rather than the more honorable horse, the author suggests that he is a fool. The meeting with Nehru attracts the attention of a *sēṭh* (small businessman or merchant, possibly from a hereditary merchant caste) who hopes to procure a lucrative contract to supply goods to the government. He courts the animal, offering the donkey shelter in his home and the hand of his daughter in marriage. Chander's tale points to the inadequate welfare provision of these times and the bureaucratic indifference and petty corruption associated with the statist development model.

107. Krishan Chander, *Ek Gadhe kī Ātmakatā* (New Delhi: Hind Pocket Books, n.d.). The English translation appeared in 1968, suggesting an earlier publication date for the original Hindi version. See Krishan Chander *Mr. Ass Comes to Town*, trans. Helen Bouman (New Delhi: Hind Pocket Books, 1968).

108. Aakriti Mandhwani, "Everyday Reading: Commercial Magazines and Book Publishing in Post-Independence India," (unpublished PhD diss., School of Oriental and African Studies, 2018), 102–5. The discussion in this paragraph draws from Mandhwani's excellent analysis of the book, supplemented by my own reading.

Indians living in the country's growing urban spaces might have found their experiences resonating with those of the donkey. Not for nothing did the song about the perils of the city, "*Bombay Merī Jaāṃ*" (Bombay, My Heart), become wildly popular. Its refrain—"*zarā haṭke, zarā backe, ye hai Bombay merī jaāṃ*" (Move aside, watch out, this is Bombay my love)—conveys the need to be careful and watch one's back.[109] Between 1941 and 1971, India's urban population grew from 44 million to 109 million, rising from 14 percent to 20 percent of the total population.[110] Both the mofussil areas and the major cities of Bombay, Calcutta, Madras, and Delhi expanded in size. Although India remained predominantly rural, it was in the urban areas where the majority of a million new members of the professional classes lived.[111] This included 265,000 new engineers, 41,000 new doctors, 100,000 teachers in higher education, 62,000 scientists, 3,000 journalists, and 50,000 lawyers.[112] With ties to agrarian India through family or trade, these professionals had a unique perspective of industrialization, urbanization, and the advent of a state with welfarist aspirations. Although they progressed economically during this period, they could also witness and comment on the shortcomings of India's attempted political and economic transformation. They had the capacity to witness how income inequality rose in areas with greater population density. The poorest Indians in the cities often clustered in slums of migrants.[113]

The proliferation of small business enterprises of fifty employees or less was a no less profound but much less understood, dispersed phenomenon of these times. Unlike cottage industrial enterprises, these businesses utilized

109. Sudipta Kaviraj, "Reading a Song of the City: Images of the City in Literature and Films," in *The Invention of Private Life: Literature and Ideas* (New York: Columbia University Press, 2015), 253–73.

110. Statistics from Census of India, tabulated in Chinmay Tumbe, "Urbanization, Demographic Transition, and the Growth of Cities in India, 1870–2020," *International Growth Centre Working Paper* #C-35205-INC-1, 2016, 20.

111. Chopra, ed., *Gazetteer*, vol. 3, 129. Absent detailed time series, it is difficult to ascertain the number of new school graduates and university degree holders who settled in urban areas. However, what we do know about the clustering of hospitals and universities in urban areas, figures on the expansion of higher education, the spatial concentration of growth, and urbanization more generally makes this plausible.

112. Maddison, *Class Structure and Economic Growth*, 88.

113. *Report on the Committee on Distribution of Income and Levels of Living, Part I* (New Delhi: Planning Commission, 1964). On the worsening conditions of the urban poor, see V. M. Dandekar and N. Rath, "Poverty in India-I: Dimensions and Trends," *Economic and Political Weekly 6*, no. 1 (1971): 25, 27, 29–48.

electricity and machinery. They produced products such as metal utensils, bicycle parts, and sewing machines.[114] The government helped with financing and allocating industrial permits to deserving units. High taxation rates incentivized them to reinvest profits in allied ventures and diversify.[115] Smaller units fit into the planned economy as providers of consumer goods that would help India attain the ideal of self-sufficiency.[116] Although not a strategic focus of policy until after 1960, the private sector accounted for between a third and a half of increased manufacturing capacity during the first three plans.

The small-scale sector grew about 7 percent to 8 percent annually during the first three plans. It came to account for about a third of industrial output by 1971.[117] Policies that helped catalyze the emergence of these smaller modern commercial entities chiefly took the form of concessionary terms of credit and tax incentives.[118] Bodies such as the State Finance Corporation, the State Bank of India, and National Small Industries Corporation provided loans at the national level. The state-level Aid to Industry Acts, which passed in the 1950s, offered decentralized forms of financial support.[119] The Reserve Bank took a role in stimulating private investment, offering credit guarantees to banks loaning to small businesses.[120] By the end of the 1960s, small-scale manufacturers accounted for 40 percent of their sector's output and employed 75 percent of its labor force.[121] The government estimated that there were

114. P. N. Dhar and H. F. Lydall, *The Role of Small Enterprises in Indian Economic Development* (Bombay: Asia Publishing House, 1961), 4.

115. By 1966, the Government of India's industrial development institutions financed a quarter of all private sector investment. See Adnan Naseemullah, *Development after Statism: Industrial Firms and the Political Economy of South Asia* (Cambridge: Cambridge University Press, 2017), 80–81.

116. Quoted in Dhar and Lydall, *The Role of Small Enterprises in Indian Economic Development*, 10.

117. *Report of the Working Group on Industries* (New Delhi: Government of India Committee on Unemployment, 1972), 11.

118. The Industrial Policy Resolution of 1956, for example, stipulated that the government extend more loans to encourage small and medium enterprises through state-level development corporations. See Sumit Majumdar, "Fall and Rise of Productivity in Indian Industry: Has Economic Liberalization Had an Impact?" *Economic and Political Weekly* 31, no. 48 (1996): M46–M53; Das Gupta, *State and Capital in Independent India*, 150.

119. Dhar and Lydall, *The Role of Small Enterprises in Indian Economic Development*, 69–74.

120. Balachandran, *The Reserve Bank of India, 1951–67* (Bombay: Reserve Bank of India, 1998), 553–92.

121. Maddison, *Class Structure and Economic Growth*, 126.

approximately 120,000 registered and 250,000 unregistered units of such enterprises by 1968. Most were less than fifteen years old.[122]

Regional dynamics drove this national trend. In particular, small industrial concentration in the former Bombay and Madras presidencies increased.[123] In these historically ryotwari regions, colonial irrigation schemes and state-sponsored cooperative credit programs had helped dominant castes generate agricultural surpluses. These might then be invested in productivity improvements and new economic activities.[124] During World War II, provincial capital filled the void left by big business, which vacated smaller regional concerns to consolidate their national enterprises.[125] Subsequently, provincial capital leveraged political representation in state assemblies to secure favorable policies. As mofussil and rural elites could most easily secure supplies of food and labor for entering these businesses, the plurality of these new small- and medium-sized firms specialized in food processing and textiles. They also began to urbanize their rural bases of power by setting up private educational institutions for their youths.[126] Small industrialists from the village to the metropolis used both traditional and modern methods of production. They leveraged joint family provisions in Hindu personal law to bring down tax burdens and maintain

122. *Small-Scale Industries in India* (New Delhi: Ministry of Industrial Development and Company Affairs, 1968), iii.

123. Chopra, ed., *Gazetteer*, vol. 3, 631; R. K. Hazari, *Industrial Planning and Licensing Policy: Final Report* (New Delhi: Planning Commission, 1967), 4–5; Das Gupta, *State and Capital in Independent India*, 164.

124. Balachandran, 229–64. On the colonial legacy of cooperative development in these regions, see Bruce Robert, "Agricultural Credit Cooperatives in Madras, 1893–1937: Rural Development and Agrarian Politics in Pre-Independence India," *Indian Economic and Social History Review* 16, no. 2 (1979): 163–84; I. J. Catanach, *Rural Credit in Western India, 1875–1930: Rural Credit and the Co-operative Movement in the Bombay Presidency* (Berkeley: University of California Press, 1970); D. Parthasarathy, "The Poverty of (Marxist) Theory: Peasant Classes, Provincial Capital, and the Critique of Globalization in India," *Journal of Social History* 48, no. 4 (2015): 816–41. Less sensitive to questions of caste and more concerned with whether the phenomena observed corresponded to a rigid Marxist definition of capitalism, the older debate on the mode of production unfolded in the 1980s. See Utsa Patnaik, ed., *Agrarian Relations and Accumulation: The "Mode of Production" Debate in India* (Bombay: Oxford University Press, 1990).

125. Sanjaya Baru, *The Political Economy of Indian Sugar: State Intervention and Structural Change* (New Delhi: Oxford University Press, 1990), 70–71; Damodaran, *India's New Capitalists: Caste, Business and Industry in a Modern Nation* (London: Macmillan, 2008).

126. D. Parthasarathy, "The Poverty of (Marxist) Theory: Peasant Classes, Provincial Capital, and the Critique of Globalization in India," *Journal of Social History* 48, no. 4 (2015): 816–41, 836–37.

continuity of enterprise and assets across generations.[127] This could apply even when joint families split into nuclear families and when younger members moved to the city.[128]

Expressions of discontent captured the tension that developed between new interests like the urban professionals and regional capitalists, and the state and its bureaucracy. A sarcastic Air India poster from the year 1968 read: "Income tax, super-tax, surcharge, wealth tax, gift tax, estate duty, corporation tax . . . A Happy New Year."[129] Frustration with bureaucratic red tape and perceived abuse of office was reflected in a rising number of complaints lodged against government employees (see Table 1.4). Responding to popular pressures like these, the Government of India convened a Committee on the Prevention of Corruption in 1962.[130]

Official government investigations corroborated some of these allegations. One found that industrial licenses accrued disproportionately to large industrial houses. Bureaucrats delayed the process unduly for smaller industrial concerns and did not follow up on incidents of failed implementation. Lax administration and susceptibility to influence by vested interests bore at least part of the responsibility for these shortcomings.[131] By the end of the 1960s, a series of reports by the Administrative Reforms Commission suggested decentralizing administration further to the states and simplifying and dismantling parts of the central government's administrative structure.[132] "Expected to supervise all aspects of activity, from managing the army and running the administration to running the railways and postal system and providing schools and hospitals," the Indian state "became ubiquitous, but also universally unreliable."[133]

---

127. This practice rolled over from the colonial era. Of that period, Ritu Birla has argued influentially that the British established exceptions to universal market norms by coding kinship-based firm activity as 'cultural' rather than economic. In so doing, they brought business practices under the purview of 'private' Hindu personal law. See Birla, *Stages of Capital*. We expand on this in subsequent chapters.

128. Das Gupta, *State and Capital in Independent India*, 123–29.

129. Cited in M. R. Masani, "How Are We Doing?" Undated [1968], speech notes, Serial No. 43, File Six, M. R. Masani Papers, National Archives of India, New Delhi (hereafter NAI).

130. Balasubramanian, "Anticorruption, Development, and the Indian State."

131. These findings all come from *Report of the Industrial Licensing Policy Inquiry Committee* (New Delhi: Planning Commission, 1969), 51, 53–74, 100, 183. See also the discussion in Jalal, *Democracy and Authoritarianism in South Asia*, 38–40.

132. Shriram Maheshwari, *The Administrative Reforms Commission* (Agra: Lakshmi Narain Agarwal, 1972); Frankel, *India's Political Economy*, 311.

133. Sudipta Kaviraj, *The Imaginary Institution of India* (New York: Columbia University Press, 2010), 210–33, 222–24.

TABLE 1.4. Complaints Lodged against
Government of India

| Year | Cases for Disposal |
|---|---|
| 1956–57 | 4,676 |
| 1957–58 | 8,540 |
| April–Dec. 1958 | 8,313 |
| 1959 | 10,649 |
| 1960 | 10,721 |
| 1961 | 10,481 |
| 1962 | 20,461 |

Source: Report of the Committee on the Prevention of Corruption
(New Delhi: Ministry of Home Affairs, 1964), 14.

The state's attempts to project national culture and discipline via modernization and the drama of development in the 1950s gave way to disillusionment
and a feeling of malaise in the decade that followed.[134] Bengali playwright Badal
Sircar's 1962 Evam Indrajit explored feelings of being trapped and the aimless-
ness of life. The protagonist Indrajit's contemporaries move on with their lives
without much reflection. They harbor bourgeois aspirations, pay bribes, and file
papers for a living. By contrast, Indrajit wants something more. He rejects the
conventional employment of stamping files in an office. But Indrajit is unable
to grasp precisely what he is after. Asked about how he has been getting on in
life, he responds that he "walks between the rails of the railway line . . . What is
behind is ahead. There is no distance between the past and the future. What's there
in the past is in the future as well."[135] The railway line, a symbol of movement,
should take Indrajit forward. Instead, he stands trapped in between its rails.
Around the same time, Evam Indrajit's English translator, the Kannada playwright
Girish Karnad, wrote the play Tughlaq. It is a historical drama about the fourteenth-
century Delhi Sultan Muhammad Bin Tughlaq's failed aspirations despite his
great capability. Karnad would later recall how discovering this historical figure's
reign reminded him of India in the 1960s and of Tughlaq's similarity to Nehru.[136]

---

134. Dilip Menon, "Lost Visions: Imagining a National Culture in the 1950s," in Land, Labor
and Rights: The Daniel Thorner Lectures, ed. Alice Thorner (New Delhi: Tulika, 2001), 250–68, 252.

135. Badal Sircar, Evam Indrajit, reproduced in Three Modern Indian Plays, trans. Girish Karnad (New Delhi: Oxford University Press, 1989), 55.

136. Girish Karnad, quoted in U. R. Ananthamurthy, "Introduction to Tughlaq," in Three
Modern Indian Plays.

In July 1959, the retired civil servant V. P. Menon wrote a journalist friend in London about the birth of the Swatantra Party. Menon enclosed the copy of a lengthy article that would appear on Independence Day, August 15. "Freedom is primarily a negative concept . . . But the Sanskrit word 'Swatantra' combines a positive inner discipline with a negative external freedom," he wrote. "From this principle stems the entire attitude of the Party towards the State and the individual and to all forms of activity like industry, agriculture, trade, public and private charity, and legislative and administrative functions." [137] Menon had served as reforms commissioner to the British viceroy. He had a worm's eye view of the transfer of power to Indians.[138] He had recently finished writing a book on the integration of India's princely states into the Union, a process in which he had been an active participant. His article associated inflation and black-market activity with the expansion of the state's role in "practically every kind and aspect of industry and trade" tracing back to World War II. According to Menon, all of this had intensified after independence in 1947, to the detriment of the Indian public. Swatantra hoped to arrest these trends and restore "freedom."

Halfway across the world, the eminent development economist Peter Bauer made a parallel observation. He alleged an atmosphere of "widespread disillusionment with the Congress Party." This assessment appeared in a pamphlet for the free-market American Enterprise Institute, written to persuade the U.S. Congress against ramping up aid to India. Something was brewing among the "small landowners, small industrialists, traders and artisans, who used to be the bulwark of the Congress Party . . . now acutely apprehensive of current Indian economic policy, of which a Socialist regime is the avowed objective, and a Sovietized economy a possible eventual outcome." These people expressed their "growing apprehension . . . in letters and articles in the press, in pamphlets written by members of this class or addressed to them." In a footnote, Bauer mentioned the recent creation of a party under the leadership of the veteran politician C. Rajagopalachari to "combat some of the principal trends of current Indian economic planning."[139] To continue

137. Menon to Geoffrey Tyson, July 26, 1959, and enclosure, "Swatantra Party," Papers of the India, Pakistan and Burma Association, MSS Eur 158/356, European Manuscripts, Asian and African Studies Collection (hereafter AASC), British Library, London (hereafter BL).

138. On Menon, see Narayani Basu, *V. P. Menon: The Unsung Architect of Modern India* (New Delhi: Simon and Schuster, 2020).

139. Peter Bauer, *United States Aid and Indian Economic Development* (Washington D.C.: American Enterprise Institute, 1959), 2–3, 113. Peter Bauer, a British development economist of Hungarian descent, taught for many years at the University of Cambridge (1948–60) and the London School of Economics (1960–82). Following his academic career, he was elected to the

foreign aid would be to underwrite the regime led by the Indian National Congress and forestall these new developments.

The Government of India took on new roles in the postcolonial period as part of the Congress vision to make a new India. It dammed rivers, built new railroad tracks, and lit up rural homes with electricity. State-owned power plants and factories, which Nehru christened the temples of modern India, sprung up across the country. The Ministry of Food sought to control the prices of consumer commodities and ration food to the poorest. These activities helped put the country on a path to growth and leave colonial economic stagnation behind. They also reordered certain kinds of social relations. A growing number of people became officials of the state. Those officials became increasingly powerful. Laws were implemented to manage and distribute scarce resources carefully for the sake of industrial progress. Indians migrated into growing cities and embraced new professions. Villages became towns and began to see new forms of enterprise take off as prominent agrarian communities diversified their economic activities.

Planning required the incursion of the postcolonial state into economic life in ways that rendered it far more visible than before to Indians. In the name of development, the state fixed prices, taxed, and made decisions about who did and who did not get to pursue commerce. This could be frustrating to navigate. It pinched the pocket any time goods and services were transacted. Powerful currents of dissent became visible in Indian society as the momentum of the early years of planning slowed down. They were expressed by professional classes and small capitalists directing their animus against the state and its functionaries. Social and economic change brewing in India's regions culminated in the political expression of alternative ideas of political economy outside the corridors of power in New Delhi. Some of the Congress' old guard— among them defenders of property rights at the Constituent Assembly, anticommunists, and quintessentially agrarian thinkers—no longer found the party an appropriate vehicle for themselves. Breaking away, they caught on to waves of dissent from their communities and regions of origin. They organized and leveraged this dissent in a way only possible in the context of an open electoral democracy: through the creation of an opposition party.

---

House of Lords. A synthetic collection of his essays appeared as Bauer, *From Subsistence to Exchange and Other Essays* (Princeton: Princeton University Press, 2000).

# 2

# Indian Libertarians and the Birth of Free Economy

THE ORIGINS OF "FREE ECONOMY" were at once unlikely and unsurprising. They were unlikely because the person responsible for this formulation and the spread of its associated ideas had retreated into obscurity. They were unlikely, too, because at a time when men dominated the public sphere, it was a woman named Kusum Lotvala who made free economy viable. They were unsurprising because free economy emerged in Bombay. In this port city of ideological churn, traders of various sects of Islam from all over the Indian Ocean came to exchange their wares, communism spread across the working classes, and big business wrote its plan for postcolonial economic development.[1] India's commercial hub was a city of real and reel life, intrigue, underground activity, and the media.[2] Bombay teemed with life and bubbled with a spirit of its own.

After being overshadowed by mass movements, the elite associational culture in which Indian nationalism originated in the late nineteenth and early twentieth centuries came back to life in independent India. Actors who had

1. Nile Green, *Bombay Islam: The Religious Economy of the West Indian Ocean* (Cambridge: Cambridge University Press, 2011); Raj Chandavarkar, *The Origins of Industrial Capitalism in India: Business Strategies and the Working Classes in Bombay, 1900–1940* (Cambridge: Cambridge University Press, 1994), 21–71; Raj Chandavarkar, "Bombay's Perennial Modernities" in Chandavarkar, *History, Culture and the Indian City* (Cambridge: Cambridge University Press, 2009), 12–30; Sumit Sarkar, *Modern India: 1885–1947* (Basingstoke: Macmillan, 1983), 246–60.

2. Gyan Prakash, *Mumbai Fables* (New Delhi: Harper Collins, 2010); Debashree Mukherjee, *Bombay Hustle: Making Movies in a Colonial City* (New York: Columbia University Press, 2020).

partaken of mass politics went back to the associational mold under the constraints of parliamentary democracy. Others never deviated from their associationalist practices and experienced a second wave of energy in the postcolonial context. They directed their energies against the state once again, now for different reasons. For both sets of actors, being against a centralizing statism, or antistatist, was just as important as being anticolonial. Their lives, causes, and connections to each other disrupt our picture of the hegemonic nationalism of these times. They offer a perspective from outside the state and its institutions.[3]

These figures drew upon networks and experiences of the anti-imperial struggle to come together again in 1950s India. Old friends reunited. Foes of yore became friends of the present. Down the street from Ranchoddas Lotvala's Libertarian Social Institute were the Bharatiya Vidya Bhavan and Forum of Free Enterprise. The heads of both organizations had participated with him in the Gurjar Sabha of the 1920s. This was an association of Gujarati-language speakers in Bombay who promoted their native language and supported progressive political movements. Now, two decades later, a couple of key differences became salient. India's urban centers were much larger. And the idiom of politics was, increasingly, one of political economy.

Associations of various stripes and commitments took an interest in economic issues, even if it was not their primary concern. Yesteryear's anticolonial activists and personages of public affairs became today's anticommunists. They built a vibrant, widely circulated, and largely forgotten print culture from English-language periodicals run out of their associations. Their periodicals originated in large cities but reached deep into the mofussil. In their pages, readers might encounter warnings of how the country was headed toward totalitarian excess, the case against nonaligned foreign policy, and even literary criticism from the Anglo-American world. Although the founders' lives remain largely mysterious, the traces these magazines left offer a picture of this hidden world, the world in which "free economy" and opposition politics was born.

Who were the Lotvalas? Why did they have a Libertarian Social Institute? What were the origins of free economy? How did it spread?

3. Partha Chatterjee, *The Nation and Its Fragments: Colonial and Postcolonial Histories* (Princeton: Princeton University Press, 1993).

## Profit, Press, and Politics in Interwar India

The world wars, organized anticolonial nationalism, regional linguistic move-ments, and the advent of industrial capitalism all left their indelible imprint on Ranchoddas Lotvala's home city of Bombay during his lifetime.[4] He was no passive observer of these developments. Based in the thriving middle-class locality of Girgaum in South Bombay (see Figure 2.1 and Map 2.1), he estab-lished himself as a leading patron of a range of educational initiatives, political causes, and personalities.[5] The money for them came from the profits of his successful Duncan Road flour mill. Ranchoddas' early involvement in three organizations formed the foundations of a lifetime of engagement with in-terconnected movements of social and political reform. They demonstrated his conviction toward religious revivalism, regional linguistic identity, and the organized politics of self-rule. Lotvala's life before Indian independence in 1947 intersected with some of the major currents of the country's political history. The activities of the final decades of his life would draw upon these foundations.

The Lotvalas came from the Halai Lohana *jati* community, traditionally of the Kshatriya (warrior) *varna*. They hailed from the region of Sindh in the northern part of the Bombay Presidency. A group of Lohanas settled in Gujarat and originally served as administrators for local rulers.[6] They came to take part in Gujarat's vibrant commerce in the early modern period in the Indian Ocean region. Some Lohanas moved there as the British con-verted Bombay into a more viable hub for commerce. They were one of several Gujarati-speaking communities that would come to dominate Bom-bay's commercial scene.[7]

---

4. Prakash, *Mumbai Fables*; Chandavarkar, *History, Culture and the Indian City*. On the forces of capital and the remaking of urban space, see Sheetal Chhabria, *Making the Modern Slum: The Power of Capital in Colonial Bombay* (Seattle: University of Washington Press, 2019). See D. M. Kulkarni, "Selections from Indian Libertarian—Part II," in *Selections from the Indian Lib-ertarian*, ed. Kulkarni (Bombay: Libertarian Publishers, 1984).

5. Chandavarkar, *The Origins of Industrial Capitalism in India*, 41; Chandavarkar, *History, Culture and the Indian City*, 166.

6. Pierre Lachaier, *Firmes et entreprises en Inde: La firme lignagère dans ses réseaux* (Pondi-cherry: Karthala, 1999), 65–92.

7. Although the Lohanas were secondary in importance to the Zoroastrians (Parsis) and the Ismaili Muslim Khojas and Boras. Chandavarkar, *The Origins*, 55–56.

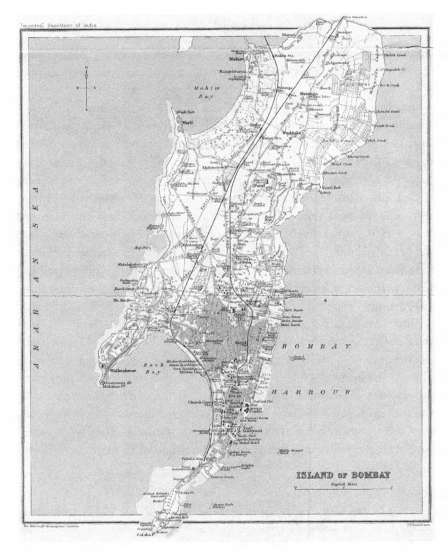

FIGURE 2.1. Bombay, 1909 (J. G. Bartholomew, *Imperial Gazetteer of India*, downloaded from Digital Library of South Asia).

Ranchoddas' own prosperity came from mechanizing the flour milling and trading business (*lot* is the Gujarati word for flour) of his family, who migrated to Bombay in the seventeenth century. After his father passed away, Ranchoddas borrowed from business associates to buy out his father's partners' shares of the enterprise and establish himself as the sole proprietor. During

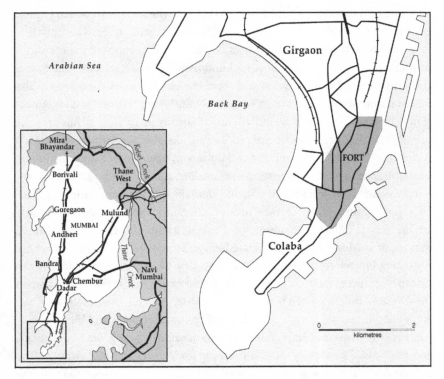

MAP 2.1. Girgaum and the Inner City (Jenny Sheehan and CartoGIS, College of Asia and the Pacific, Australian National University, 2022).

World War I, he leveraged wartime increases in food prices and strategically hoarded supplies to reap handsome profits.[8] Lotvala's was a modern small enterprise, linked to some extent to wider processes of industrialization but independent of wage labor.[9]

8. Dick Kooiman, "Bombay Communists and the 1924 Textile Strike," *Economic and Political Weekly* 15, no. 29 (July 1980): 1223–25, 1227–36.

9. Given the limitations in available evidence, it is hard to classify this firm as straightforwardly merchant or industrial capitalist. It has been impossible to decipher the role of external finance, the connection of the firm to larger processes of industrialization, and the importance of wage labor. But what seems clearer is that the firm exhibited more capitalist characteristics than the family concern operated by Lotvala's ancestors. And in converting raw grain to flour, it partook of more than just the circulation of commodities corresponding to a straightforwardly merchant capitalist firm. On this debate, see Jairus Banaji, *A Brief History of Commercial Capitalism* (Chicago: Haymarket, 2020), chapter 1.

Some of Ranchoddas' profits went to support the local Arya Samaj ("Society of the Aryan Race"), a prominent Hindu revivalist reform association. Responding to the threat from missionary activity that exposed the iniquities of social life under traditional caste Hinduism, organizations like the Samaj sought to bring back converts and stem the exodus from their ranks. The Samaj committed to a return to scriptural Hinduism. It promoted an educational agenda to cultivate an individual's relationship to God rather than via priestly intermediaries. And it embraced a so-called meritocratic caste system.[10] Activities included reconversion to Hinduism, cow-protection movements based on an exaggerated perception that Muslims and Dalits who ate beef threatened the survival of these animals, and *shuddhi* (purification) rituals.[11] Ranchoddas first attended the lectures of one of the Samaj's holy men during his early adulthood. He found great appeal in the Samaj's assault on orthodoxy and ritual in favor of an idealized, scripture-based Aryan Hinduism devoid of hierarchies. Throwing himself into its activities with zeal, he became vice president of the Bombay chapter (1904–24). He ran the Samaj newspaper for years and named the Girgaum building from which he would direct several subsequent activities Arya Bhavan.[12] Lotvala even called his mill's produce "Cow Brand Flour."

Then, there was the Gurjar Sabha. This association of young "writers, scholars, and reformists" met every Sunday morning for lectures and discussion.[13] The Sabha's name came name from the region of western India associated with the language of Gujarati.[14] Under Mughal and colonial rule, this region was

10. Indulal Yagnik, *Life of Ranchoddas Bhavan Lotvala* (Bombay: Libertarian Social Institute, 1952), 20–21; J.T.F. Jordens, *Dayanand Sarasvati: His Life and Ideas* (New Delhi: Oxford University Press, 1978); Rosalind O'Hanlon, *Caste, Conflict and Ideology: Mahatma Jotirao Phule and Low Caste Protest in Nineteenth-Century Western India* (Cambridge: Cambridge University Press, 1985), 50–102.

11. On cow protection, see Gyanendra Pandey, "Rallying around the Cow: Sectarian Strife in the Bhojpuri Region, c. 1888–1917," in *Subaltern Studies 2: Writings on South Asian History and Society*, ed. Ranajit Guha (New Delhi: Oxford University Press, 1983), 60–129. On Shuddhi, see R. K. Ghai, *Shuddhi Movement in India: A Study of its Socio-Political Dimensions* (New Delhi: Commonwealth Publishers, 1990).

12. Yagnik, *Life*; Kulkarni, ed., *Selections from the Indian Libertarian*, 8.

13. John R. Wood, "Indulal Yagnik: Patriot, Polemicist, Politician," in *The Autobiography of Indulal Yagnik*, trans. Devavrat N. Pathak, Howard Spodek, and John R. Wood, vol. 1 (New Delhi: Manohar, 2011), 38, 177 (hereafter *Autobiography*); Yagnik, *Life*, 26–27.

14. The region was first unified by the Chalukyas in the twelfth century and became linguistically homogeneous in the fifteenth century. This Gurjara-bhumi or Gurjaratta included areas that are part of today's Gujarat and Rajasthan. See Samira Sheikh. *Forging a Region: Sultans, Traders, and Pilgrims in Gujarat, 1200–1500* (New Delhi: Oxford University Press, 2009), 25–27.

subdivided into differential geographic units of administration. Bombay became the center for the revival and modernization of the Gujarati language against the backdrop of the migration and success of various Gujarati-speaking communities now based in the city.[15] The Sabha was the most significant political association of Bombay's Gujaratis. Through it, Lotvala established lifelong relationships and encountered local figures from the Indian National Congress.

The Congress had a long association to Bombay, where in 1885 it formally convened for the first time. Originally an elite organization of professionals who pressed "gentlemanly resolutions at staid annual sessions which still eagerly asserted their basic loyalism," it morphed into an umbrella organization for Indian nationalism comprising varying stripes of political actors.[16] The Swadeshi (Own Country) movement of 1905–8, launched to protest the partitioning of the province of Bengal into Muslim and Hindu majority areas, was a watershed in this regard. During the movement, Swadeshi nationalists promoted national industries and schools, participated in village reform, and boycotted British goods and industries. A small section of them also pursued terrorist activities.[17] Newly created labor unions and volunteer movements mobilized unprecedented numbers of people toward these causes. While the movement faltered within a few years of its initiation, the next viceroy reversed this partition in 1911.

A basic split in philosophy within Congress ranks crystallized by this time. On one side, the "moderates" led by Gopal Krishna Gokhale advocated for generally peaceful means of self-development. They did not forsake earlier forms of polite protest, but by this time they began to ignore the British. On the other side, the "extremist" faction led by Bal Gangadhar Tilak endorsed mass protest to attain *swaraj* (self-rule), although this remained a nebulous aim. Both men hailed from the Bombay Presidency.[18]

Lotvala supported both factions. He sympathized with Gokhale's interest in peer education and social service and donated to Gokhale's Servants of India Society.[19] However, he also appreciated Tilak for using the press to

15. Francoise Mallison, "Bombay as the Intellectual Capital of the Gujaratis," and Sonal Shukla, "Gujarati Cultural Revivalism," in Sujata Patel and Alice Thorner eds. *Bombay: Mosaic of Modern Culture*, (Bombay: Oxford University Press, 1996), 76–87, 88–98.

16. Sarkar, *Modern India*, 2.

17. Sumit Sarkar, *The Swadeshi Movement in Bengal, 1903–1908* (Bombay: People's Publishing House, 1973).

18. Sarkar, *Modern India*, 135–37.c

19. "Social Service League: Progress of Traveling Libraries," February 4, 1914; "Social Service League: Fourth Annual Report," January 31, 1916; "Gokhale Education Society," December 8,

FIGURE 2.2. Lotvala in his Youth (n.d.)
(Yagnik, *Life of Ranchoddas Bhavan
Lotvala*).

disseminate political ideas and opinions, and for endorsing labor protest.[20]
Lotvala's Arya Samaj colleague and Congress "extremist," Lajpat Rai, presided
over the first meeting of the All-India Indian Trade Union Congress (AITUC).

Over and above being a financial turning point for Lotvala, World War I
transformed Bombay. Gandhi returned to India from South Africa, arriving
first in Bombay in 1915 and bringing with him a new ideology for the Congress
that would help bring mass nationalism to India. With the reemergence of
international travel after the war, the communist ideology lying at the heart
of the 1917 Bolshevik Revolution made its way to Bombay alongside new visitors to the city. Politicians mobilized sections of the city's dwellers and awakened their political conscience. Migration by the aspiring literati and artists
from other parts of the country elevated Bombay's status as a hub of intellectual

1919; "Indian Education Society's Meet," December 8, 1919; "Educational Work: The Gokhale
Society," September 25, 1920 (all *ToI*).

20. Both Tilak and Lotvala were directors of the "National Democratic Publishing Co.,"
created in 1920 to sponsor an English-language evening newspaper "to put before the public the
Indian point of view on all matters concerning the welfare of the people. "The National Democratic Publishing Co.," *BC*, January 17, 1920.

ferment and experimentation.[21] Making use of the wartime spike in profits, Lotvala patronized various social and political causes and bought multiple newspapers to disseminate radical ideas.[22]

Economically, Bombay kept up its wartime profitability during the interwar period by developing a larger domestic market.[23] Merchant communities, many of them Gujarati, emerged as patrons for new ideas and anti-imperial politics. Possessed of a strong sense of regional pride, they resented attempts to tax their increasing prosperity and demanded political change. They rose to positions of prominence in political organizations. Girgaum was a particularly important area in which the new Gujarati nationalists sought to cultivate supporters through pamphleteering, organizing lectures, and hosting discussion groups.[24]

Lotvala made a series of annual travel tours overseas.[25] He cultivated Indians abroad through his political networks and maintained a student hostel in London.[26] Several of his peripatetic contacts used European capitals as bases in their transnational Asian project to bring about the end of empire by any means necessary at the time.[27] Lotvala generally refrained from joining these activities. He typically provided the revolutionaries with venues to meet. His own interest lay in consuming the latest radical political writings and news from the Soviet Union. Lotvala brought back texts to India to publish or summarize in his newspapers because much of this literature was proscribed in India.[28] So

---

21. Prakash, *Mumbai Fables,* 119.

22. S. Natarajan, *A History of the Press in India* (Bombay: Asia Publishing House, 1962), 182. In fact, Lotvala is referred to in this book as "the prominent figure in the Gujarati press" in his capacity as owner of *Hindustan, Prajamitra,* and *Parsi.*

23. Sujatha Patel, "Bombay and Mumbai: Identities, Politics and Populism," in Sujata Patel and Jim Masselos eds. *Bombay and Mumbai: The City in Transition,* (New Delhi: Oxford University Press, 2003), 1–22, 7–8.

24. Jim Masselos, "Some Aspects of Bombay City Politics in 1919," in Masselos ed. *The City in Action: Bombay Struggles for Power,* (New Delhi: Oxford University Press, 2007), 153–95.

25. Yagnik, *Life,* 64.

26. "Indian Students' Central Association Abroad," *BC,* May 25, 1931.

27. These included Har Dayal, Lajpat Rai, M. N. Roy, and V. D. Savarkar, among others. See Tim Harper, *Underground Asia: Global Revolutionaries and the Assault on Empire* (Cambridge, MA: Harvard University Press, 2021). These were not always left-wing revolutionaries, and some had no qualms taking support from racist, authoritarian regimes. On Nazi patronage of some of these figures, see David Motadel, "The Global Authoritarian Moment and the Revolt Against Empire," *American Historical Review* 124, no. 3 (2019): 843–77.

28. Prabhas Kumar Sinha trans. Muzaffar Ahmed, *Myself and the Communist Party of India, 1920–1929,* (Calcutta: National Book Agency, 1970); Yagnik, *Life,* 49.

as not to attract undue suspicion, he and his son Narottam traveled under pseudonyms.[29]

Despite his commitment to obstructing imperial rule by multiple methods, Lotvala grew increasingly impatient with Gandhian politics. He objected especially to Gandhi's ambiguous attitude toward modernity, his mixing of religion with politics, and his adherence to nonviolent methods of political practice. When Gandhians boycotted elections to provincial legislative assemblies for the sake of the "constructive program" of hand-spinning *khadi*, promoting Dalit uplift, and living in the village, Lotvala aligned himself with politicians who instead preferred active obstruction of the British from within the legislature.[30]

Lotvala also patronized a young leftist named S. A. Dange, who went on to become a storied figure in India's communist movement. A one-time devotee of Tilak, Dange authored a pamphlet called *Gandhi vs Lenin* (1921) at the age of 22. In it, he criticized Gandhi for his idealism and lauded Lenin's aims despite the latter's violent and dictatorial tendencies. An impressed Lotvala offered the young man the opportunity to undertake a self-study of communism and disseminate Marxist ideas in print. Dange and Lotvala published both the country's first avowedly socialist weekly, *The Socialist*, and the first Indian edition of the *Communist Manifesto*.[31] While Lotvala sourced materials from London and continued his travels in Europe, Dange conducted propaganda activity and cultivated a network of communist contacts nationwide.[32]

Censorship, religion, and caste defined the context in which Indian communism was incubated in Bombay. It meant different things to different people. Notably, Indians had limited access to the full canon of communist texts available to their comrades in other parts of the world. As a result, a figure like Dange had not even read the *Communist Manifesto* before writing *Gandhi vs Lenin*. Indians also interpreted the available literature in their own localized context and with their own blind spots. So, the Brahmin Dange's brand of communism equated the colonial state with capitalism. He understood

---

29. "Ranchoddas Bhavan (Lotwalla) and son Narotam," IOR/L/P&J/12/167, India Office Records, AASC, BL: "Passport holder charged: alleged false personation," *ToI*, April 14, 1931.

30. Shekhar Bandyopadhyay, *From Plassey to Partition: A History of Modern India* (New Delhi: Orient Longman, 2004), 336; Sarkar, *Modern India*, 227.

31. Karat, "A Publishing History of the *Communist Manifesto*," 131; Juned Shaikh, *Outcaste Bombay: City-Making and the Politics of the Poor* (Seattle: University of Washington Press, 2021), 47–53.

32. Harper, *Underground Asia*, 475–77, 580. Although he avoided the limelight, Lotvala was not totally aloof from political activities. See "Girni Kamgar Mahamandal," *ToI*, November 27, 1926.

communism to be compatible with the caste system, which he described in its idealized form as a division of labor in the prerevolutionary commune. By contrast, Dalit communists understood communism and caste abolition to be coterminous.[33] Examined alongside Lotvala's other pet causes, his patronage of Dange shows that even if he was comfortable with caste reform, Lotvala was never fully comfortable with the abolition of caste.

Tilak had once assigned the young Dange the task of organizing labor, toward which the latter worked assiduously. During the 1920s, workers came together to protest threats of rationalization and extended working hours. This was the byproduct of stringent labor conditions and low capital investment in Bombay's textile industry. A 1924 textile strike helped develop the labor movement, and the communists, Dange among them, built up the Girni Kamgar Union in its aftermath. The union played a crucial role in the unprecedented 1928–29 general strike, which lasted over a year. At its peak, the general strike counted over 150,000 workers.[34]

Employers used Muslims as strikebreakers and turned the general strike into a violent Hindu-Muslim riot.[35] Most labor leaders were upper-caste Hindus and downplayed religious tensions to present class rather than faith as the grounds for disputes.[36] However, the reality of the 1920s was of increasing Hindu-Muslim strife, duly exploited by the millowners. The colonial state did little to smooth out differences. The animosity fit in with their tactics of divide and rule. One can only imagine that Lotvala's later prejudices against Muslims in India would be shaped by the events of these years, although he no longer participated in the Samaj and does not appear to have sponsored any anti-Muslim literature at this time.

Various factors account for the deterioration of Hindu-Muslim relations. But one overarching explanation is that Gandhi's pivot to mass nationalism relied on co-opting religious leaders of multiple faiths.[37] This provided a way for

33. See the discussion in Shaikh, *Outcaste Bombay*, 46–83, 58.

34. Chandavarkar, *Imperial Power and Popular Politics: Class, Resistance and the State in India, c. 1850–1950* (Cambridge: Cambridge University Press, 1998). It was also this class focus that relegated the caste question to the margins during this period. See Shaikh, *Outcaste Bombay*, 14.

35. Sabyasachi Bhattacharya, "Capital and Labor in Bombay City, 1928–29," *Economic and Political Weekly* 16, no. 42–3 (1981): PE36–44; Raj Chandavarkar, "Questions of Class: The General Strikes in Bombay, 1928–29," *Contributions to Indian Sociology* 33, no. 1–2 (1999); *Report of the Bombay Strike Enquiry Committee, 1928–29* (Bombay: Government of Bombay, 1929).

36. See Patrick Hesse, "Communism and Communalism in the 1920s: Notes on a Neglected Nexus," *South Asia Chronicle* 5 (2015): 259–87.

37. Bandyopadhyay, *From Plassey to Partition*, 335.

religious zealots to create sectarian groups. Both the extremist Muslim ulema and fundamentalist Hindus perceiving an existential threat from the Muslim Other set Indians against each other to advance their political aims. Organized Hindu nationalism traces its origins to this period. In 1925, K. B. Hedgewar, from the Bombay Presidency, founded the Rashtriya Swayamsevak Sangh (National Organization of Volunteers, or RSS). This was a cadre-based paramilitary organization, built of volunteer *pracāraks* (preachers), seeking to strengthen Hindu society through physical fitness, marches, and political education for the cause of Hindutva (Hinduness).[38] The dimensions of Hindutva were a shared geography of the subcontinent, a common Vedic blood, and Hindu culture.[39]

The British cracked down hard on the strikers. They arrested Dange alongside thirty other communists and tried them for conspiring against the Raj in the city of Meerut.[40] Conducted on an epic scale, the trial drove a wedge between internationalism and nationalism. It stimulated the formation of a Congress Socialist Party and amplified anticommunist sentiments in the public.[41] Police searches of Lotvala's home and office shook him to his core. The millowner began to fear for the safety of his family.[42] Meanwhile, in the USSR, Stalin asserted the primacy of "socialism in one country" and temporarily sidelined the international movement.[43] By 1929, India's key internationalist in Moscow, M. N. Roy, fell afoul of Stalin and was expelled from the Comintern as a "renegade."[44] From jail, Dange was expelled from the Communist Party, as tensions with a breakaway faction from his Girni Kamgar Union

---

38. Christophe Jaffrelot, *The Hindu Nationalist Movement in India* (New York: Columbia University Press, 1998), 33

39. Janaki Bakhle, "Country First? Vinayak Damodar Savarkar (1883–1966), and the Writing of *Essentials of Hindutva*," *Public Culture* 22, no. 1 (2015): 149–86.

40. Sarkar, *Modern India*, 272.

41. This sophisticated, revisionist reading of the legacies of Meerut comes from Ali Raza, *Revolutionary Pasts: Communist Internationalism in Colonial India* (Cambridge: Cambridge University Press, 2020), 201–6.

42. "Is It War against Labor?" *BC*, March 21, 1929.

43. Harper, *Underground Asia*, 558. Stalin further tarred his internationalist opponent Trotsky as an elitist ignorant of the realities of workers and peasants and had him expelled from the party in 1927 and the Soviet Union in 1929. For his part, Trotsky published a stern denunciation of Stalin and labeled him totalitarian. See Vladimir Borovkin, *Russia After Lenin: Politics, Culture and Society* (London: Routledge, 1998); Dmitri Volkogonov, *Stalin: Triumph and Tragedy* (Grove Weidenfeld, 1991), 133–44.

44. Harper, *Underground Asia*, 470, 629–30. For more on this, see Sobhanlal Datta Gupta, *Comintern and the Destiny of Communism in India: 1919–43* (Kolkata: Seribaan, 2006).

led party leaders to believe he was encouraging factionalism.[45] A shattered Lotvala kept abreast of these developments.[46] He ended various friendships with erstwhile fellow travelers.[47] From then on, Lotvala's publishing practices started to diverge from those of active Communist Party members.[48]

Lotvala foreswore communism and retreated to the associational politics of an earlier era during the 1930s. He now chiefly supported research activities and more intellectual pursuits.[49] Religious tensions between Hindus and Muslims in Bombay intensified during this period. Extremism and divisions about whether Indian self-government would involve separate electorates and safeguards for the Muslim minority who made up about 13 percent of the 1931 population drove this intensifying animosity.[50] Lotvala threw his financial and intellectual support behind an Indian Rationalist Association that listed its primary objective as "to combat all religious and social beliefs and customs that cannot stand the test of Reason and to endeavor to create a Scientific and Tolerant Mentality among the masses of this country." And yet there was a majoritarianism to this "reasoning." The association's *Reason* magazine alleged Muslims' inferior reasoning ability and Catholics' fanaticism.[51]

The more progressive thrust of Lotvala's "reasoning" concerned reforming Hindu society around "rational" lines. At the time, upper-caste Hindu revivalist organizations like the Samaj and the Hindu Mahasabha sought to consolidate Hindus as a community against those of other religions. Ranchoddas opened an Institute of Sociology in Bombay that sponsored essay competitions and published journals and books. Topics ranged from birth control, eugenics, and political economy to social reform.[52]

Hindu personal law reform became one of the institute's pet causes. During the interwar period, nuclear families began to cleave off from joint families.

45. This was the Girni Kamgar Mahamandal. See "Mill Workers' Reign of Terror in Bombay," *ToI*, January 4, 1929; Sheikh, *Outcaste Bombay*, 58.

46. Ahmed, *Myself and the Communist Party of India*, 115.

47. Yagnik, *Autobiography*, vol. 2., 418.

48. Charles Wesley Ervin, *Tomorrow Is Ours: The Trotskyist Movement in India and Ceylon, 1935–48* (Colombo: Social Scientists' Association, 2006), 84.

49. He allegedly lost his faith in communism in 1932. See C. G. Shah, *Marxism, Gandhism, Stalinism* (Bombay: Popular Prakashan, 1963), ix.

50. *Census of India*, 1931. See Ravinder Kumar, "From *Swaraj* to *Purna Swaraj:* Nationalist Politics in the City of Bombay, 1920–32," in *The Congress and the Raj*, ed. D. A. Low (New Delhi: Oxford University Press, 2004), 77–108.

51. *Reason: The Journal of the Rationalist Association of India* 1, no. 1 (1931): 13–14, 40.

52. Yagnik, *Life*, 73–74.

Accounting for this trend was migration, changing patterns of employment and the enduring influence of later Victorian discourses of conjugality.[53] Hindu upper-caste male elites sought changes in succession and inheritance law with respect to joint family property with the objectives of reducing taxable income and reconstituting patriarchy around the individual rather than the family estate. These elites argued in the press and legislative assemblies that a clearly delineated share of the family assets for nuclear families would allow them to better provide for their wives and daughters and cleave off from joint families if necessary. Consistent with a reconstituted idea of patriarchy and the idea of "respectable" womanhood, they also sought greater inheritance rights for widows from their deceased spouses' shares of the joint family estate (limited estate).

As of 1938, legislation passed demarcating individually owned salary income from jointly owned family property and asserting a widow's right to maintenance payments.[54] However, provisions for extending the right of unmarried daughters to inherit from the family estate after the death of the head of the family had been eliminated from the final legislation. In its aftermath, a government-appointed Hindu law committee submitted its recommendations to codify Hindu personal law.[55]

The Institute of Sociology ran an essay competition on the reform of Hindu personal law in 1939 and published a pamphlet in 1942 on the need for improving the Indian woman's treatment in Hindu personal law. Both the winning essay and the pamphlet applauded bills circulating to strengthen the rights to divorce and separate. They also argued for fortifying the status of the widow's estate and granting daughters inheritance rights. These writings further encouraged Indians to author wills when they wanted other close female relatives to inherit property. When convenient, they made recourse to ancient Hindu law treatises to justify these reforms.[56]

Although it would be inaccurate to label him an advocate of gender equality, Ranchoddas evinced an interest in the improvement of women's status within a

---

53. Newbigin, *The Hindu Family and the Emergence of Modern India*, 94.

54. Newbigin, *The Hindu Family and the Emergence of Modern India*, 93–127. This would come in 1956, as discussed in the next chapter.

55. Newbigin, *The Hindu Family and the Emergence of Modern India*, 128–61.

56. K. B. Gajendragadkar, *Prize Essay on Why the Present Hindu Law of Survivorship Applicable to Joint Family Property Should Be Abolished* (Bombay: Indian Institute of Sociology, 1939); Gajendragadkar, *Legal Rights of Hindu Women: Discussion of Some Necessary and Urgent Reforms* (Bombay: Indian Institute of Sociology, 1942). Gajendragadkar's younger brother would go on to become chief justice of India from 1964 to 1966.

patriarchal system. This position possibly owed to the peculiar features of his own nuclear family. His wife had died early, leaving him responsible for the upbringing of his children. No dogma governed the occupational choices they made. Remarkably, the women of the family made their own, prominent careers. Daughters Bachuben and Kusum fit the profile of the "public woman" who had emerged in 1930s Bombay society.[57] Bachuben, a social worker, became a leading figure in the Bhagini Samaj, a female wing of Gokhale's Servants of India Society. She was also among the first women elected to the Bombay Municipal Council in 1922 and served for a decade.[58] Six years after her first council election, Bachuben became the first Indian woman to run a daily newspaper.[59] A keen participant in Gandhian civil disobedience during the 1920s, she helped her father set up scholarships for women undergraduates and students at vocational institutes in the 1930s.[60] Younger daughter Kusum made a career as a radio journalist and sportswoman.[61] Neither daughter married. Lotvala's daughter-in-law was the all-India badminton champion Mumtaz Chinoy. A Muslim woman, she looked after her family radio business before becoming manager of a travel agency.[62] Marriage did not require her to give up her career.

Ranchoddas was a well-connected man of public and commercial affairs with a demonstrated nationalist politics. He was one of many small but prosperous businessmen who typically remain nameless in the historical record but provided key patronage for political causes. During his lifetime, the encounter with Hindu revivalism, the left, and the Congress had been transformational. However, Lotvala parted company with the mainstream of all three causes, never willing to go beyond moderate patronage. While undoubtedly

57. Mukherjee, Bombay Hustle, 26.

58. Gail Olivia Pearson, "Women in Public Life in Bombay City with Special References to the Civil Disobedience Movement," (unpublished PhD diss., Jawaharlal Nehru University, 1979), 232; "Social Service League: Annual Meeting of Women's Branch," ToI, April 14, 1925; "Mutual Helping Society," ToI, August 5, 1926; "Bombay Municipal Elections," ToI, February 9, 1932.

59. "Indian Womanhood," The Modern Review, 45, no. 1 (January 1929): 86.

60. Pearson, "Women in Public Life in Bombay City," 232; "Scholarships for Women," ToI, June 15, 1936.

61. D. M. Kulkarni, "Shri R. B. Lotvala: The Prophet of Human Freedom—A Life Sketch," Indian Libertarian (hereafter IL) April 1, 1971. On Kusum's sporting activities, see "Hindu Gymkhana 'B' Lose on Sunday," ToI, June 14, 1937; "Preparing for Pentangular," ToI, August 22, 1942; "Grand Display by Mugwe: C.C.I. Open Badminton," ToI, August 24, 1942; "Indu Desai Eliminated from the Singles," ToI, October 25, 1949. At one point, Kusum did a radio show reviewing sporting events of the fortnight. See "Broadcasting Programmes," ToI, May 15, 1952.

62. "Partners On and Off the Court," ToI, November 15, 1970.

idiosyncratic, his associations with various political causes shared some loose objectives of progress and popular sovereignty. Lotvala spoke and patronized those who spoke the language of revolution but refrained from such activity and tended not to associate with the most radical of causes. Caught on the cusp of a transition in the mode of anti-imperial politics, he primarily associated with city notables and aligned with upper-caste Hindu movements. Lotvala went on to make his most idiosyncratic pivot yet in the twilight of his life. Daughter Kusum oversaw the associated activities.

## (Lotvalan) Liberty, Equality, Fraternity

Ranchoddas Lotvala renamed his Indian Institute of Sociology the Libertarian Socialist Institute on August 7, 1947, eight days before India became an independent nation.[63] He believed that the advent of political independence required a radical overhauling of India's socioeconomic structure. The institute would be "the testament I bequeath to my friends at home and abroad, to my country," he wrote, because old age and frail health prevented him from starting a small utopian community.[64] This was not an incidental choice. According to Lotvala, "Libertarian socialism" aimed at "a classless society" without a state. Production of output would take place in cooperatives wherein all shared ownership equally and "each individual could develop his own talents and personality." Such a world would be "economically equalitarian, politically libertarian, and socially and in community fraternal."[65]

Omissions in Ranchoddas' biography, gaps in the memoirs of his interlocutors, and his own minimal corpus of published or collected output make it a serious challenge to fully account for his intellectual transformation from the 1930s without jumps. Even still, the surviving record allows some terms in his unique amalgam of political-economic thought to be decontested.[66] This

63. Yagnik, *Life*, 83.

64. Anthony Elenjimittam, *Cosmic Ecumenism via Hindu-Buddhist Catholicism: An Autobiography of an Indian Dominican Monk* (Bombay: Aquinas Publications, 1983), 306. Elenjimittam served as the director of the Ranchoddas Lotvala Trust's short-lived Research Institute for Eastern Philosophy between 1951–53 and participated actively in the institute for a time. See *The Libertarian* 1, no. 1 (April–June 1951): xv.

65. *The Libertarian Socialist*, April–June 1950.

66. By decontestation, I follow Michael Freeden's usage, as some precise delineation from the various alternatives that political concepts linked to an ideology can conjure. See Freeden, *Ideologies and Political Theory*.

partial history offers a window into how ideas develop in the minds of publicists. They are shaped by the selective availability of canonical texts, debates in obscure forums, and local political and economic contexts.[67]

Freedom of occupation and the diffusion of political power as much as possible became the foundation of what Lotvala called "free economy." What did this connote? Lotvala left the matter vague. He provided glimpses of what he meant in the institute's magazine by reproducing correspondences with others in print. In one such exchange, he defined it as follows: "It is an economy which is free from monopoly, privilege, and control of State in various forms, as for instance, monopoly of exchange, credit, quotas, licenses, etc. in land, money and trade. All of these should be free." Understanding what kind of a currency standard and mode of credit extension should be practiced was something he wanted his institute to research. Clear in his mind by this time, however, was that this was a capitalist system: "As to economics, only one that is practicable in these days of mass production and division of labor and specialization, none can work satisfactorily except that is capitalist i.e. dependent on making money the means of exchange, to be settled in the market."[68] Despite its merits, Lotvala found communism to be utopian and infeasible. Bombay's erstwhile patron and propagandist of communism had by now decisively shed his old attachments.

Lotvala's transition must be considered in the wider global context of the rightward shift of the Trotskyites, the internationalist wing of the communist movement opposed to Stalin and sympathetic to Leon Trotsky.[69] They became uncomfortable with communism after Trotsky's 1929 expulsion from the Soviet Union and further drifted away from their erstwhile comrades after the news of Stalin's pogroms came out. A parallel to the experiences of Lotvala and several of his associates is the particularly well-documented history of the Trotskyists who came to be known as the New York Intellectuals. They pursued an anti-Stalinist leftism committed to communism and democracy in

67. Robert Darnton, *The Literary Underground of the Old Regime* (Cambridge, MA: Harvard University Press, 1982); Darnton, "Two Paths Through the Social History of Ideas," in *The Darnton Debate: Books and Revolution in the Eighteenth Century*, ed. Haydn T. Mason (Oxford: Voltaire Foundation, 1998), 262–301.

68. "What is Individualist Philosophy and Free Economy?" *Free Economic Review* (hereafter *FER*), June 1954.

69. John Patrick Diggins, *Up from Communism: Conservative Odysseys in American Intellectual History* (New York: Harper and Row, 1975). Classically, R.H.S. Crossman, *The God that Failed: A Confession* (New York: Harper, 1949).

the 1930s.[70] However, the rise of fascism and the promise of job opportunities in the literary establishment dimmed their revolutionary zeal. Their "anti-Stalinism" soon morphed into an anticommunist slogan to bring together varying stripes of people against radical change as they became influential writers and editors of the establishment. Among their journalistic ventures was the anticommunist *Encounter* magazine, later revealed to be funded by the CIA.[71] And at least a few of their members became part of the neoconservative movement that gained steam in the 1970s. The observation made by the standard history of this group about "the suddenness of their shifts, the extremes to which they went" and the assumption of positions "sometimes blithely contradicting what they had earlier professed" applies equally to the Indian story.[72]

Free economy differed from free market. Lotvala understood free market to be indistinct from laissez-faire, which "weighed heavily on the side of the persons in control of money through Banks and private ownership of land" and would result in "accumulation of wealth on the one side and poverty and destitution on the other." This implied—again, without elaboration—that free economy connoted some form of intervention in land and credit by the state to prevent such an accumulation.[73]

Lotvala had taken quite the intellectual journey to get to this point. He had read widely and deeply, and changed course when appropriate.[74] Inspired by Peter Kropotkin's communist anarchism, Lotvala originally favored common ownership of the means of production with a provision for individual rights to personal property. Centralized production and distribution took place via the principle of "from each according to ability" and "to each according to need." In the last twenty years of his life, Lotvala most faithfully embraced ideas of American individualist anarchists. They were part of a current of American rural decentralism in the post–World War II era.[75] Individualist anarchists' concern with personal liberty extended beyond property rights and

70. There is a vast literature on the New York intellectuals, of which the most well-regarded account is Alan M. Wald, *The New York Intellectuals: The Rise and Decline of the Anti-Stalinist Left from the 1930s to the 1980s* (Chapel Hill: University of North Carolina Press, 1987).

71. Hugh Wilford, *The New York Intellectuals: From Vanguard to Institution* (Manchester: Manchester University Press, 1995).

72. Wald, *The New York Intellectuals*, 4.

73. "Politics versus Economics," *FER*, February 1955.

74. Ahmed, *Myself and the Communist Party of India*, 113.

75. See Allan Carlson, *The New Agrarian Mind: The Movement Toward Decentralist Thought in Twentieth Century America* (New Brunswick, NJ: Transaction Publishers, 2000).

freedom from the state. They rejected the concentration of production in large units altogether, irrespective of ownership. Lotvala came particularly under the influence of a man named Ralph Borsodi, who conducted a social experiment in New York called the School of Living. It was from here that the kernel of Lotvala's free economy originated.

Born in Manhattan in 1886, Ralph Borsodi became an active campaigner by the 1920s for decentralism and a return to rural ways of living from urban industrial life. He moved to rural New York and ran a successful homestead farm. The experience provoked him to consider social reorganization around decentralized units of production. Borsodi believed that advertising and distribution introduced complications and distortions in economic life that could be cut out in self-sufficient economies.[76] Assaulting industrial life from a philosophical perspective, Borsodi wrote three bestselling books between the late 1920s and the outbreak of World War II. They advocated a return to family-based units of production.[77] It was a nuanced and modernist critique. Borsodi was not an enemy of the machine but rather of the large factory, mass production, and the legal institution of the American corporation. He believed that machines associated with the industrial revolution implied superior forms of organization in the factory but that more recent technology such as the small electric engine reoriented production advantages toward the small unit. Production in the United States concentrated in corporations because of the legal benefits granted to such organizations, benefits that families did not share. Borsodi wanted to return the world to the agrarian life of the preindustrial era, incorporating modern technology to remove its hardships.[78]

Consciously or not, Borsodi was updating the figure of the rural smallholder so central to American thought and politics. This idealized construct was part of the United States' origin story as a nation of yeoman farmers who moved westward to fulfill their manifest destiny. This figure was sometimes invoked to downplay inequalities of race, as in the case of slaveholders in the antebellum period.[79] Or, in the case of the late-nineteenth-century south, it

76. William H. Issel, "Ralph Borsodi and the Agrarian Response to Modern America," *Agricultural History* 41, no. 2 (1967): 155–66.

77. The titles are: *This Ugly Civilization* (1928), *Flight from the City* (1933), and *Prosperity and Security: A Study in Realistic Economics* (1938).

78. Carlson, *The New Agrarian Mind*, 55–66.

79. Drew McCoy, *The Elusive Republic: Political Economy in Jeffersonian America* (Chapel Hill: University of North Carolina Press, 1980).

could be used to paper over class differences to build rural coalitions against urban industrial corporate power.[80] Borsodi's constructed ideal would find appreciation from those asserting the virtues of the Indian peasant proprietor in the former ryotwari areas. They also downplayed other kinds of inequalities and simplified landholding patterns in the process.[81]

Pursuing this agenda required implementing decentralism in practice and actively re-educating civilization about its benefits. To experiment with these ideas, Borsodi created a School of Living in upstate New York. Each of its divisions—homemaking, agriculture, crafts, buildings, applied exchange— produced research and conducted practical experiments. The school consisted of multiple homesteads. Residents formed a mini economy. A small "state," accepted as a necessary evil, administered a tax on land. A currency was denominated in units of labor. Those who more actively farmed received more rights to pieces of land.[82]

Based on his experiences running the school, Borsodi wrote *Education and Living* (1948), his magnum opus. Lotvala loved it. The school incorporated the ideas of two thinkers Lotvala particularly admired: Pierre-Joseph Proudhon and Henry George.[83] Lotvala saw traces of Proudhon's mutual credit bank that charged only the cost of administration in Borsodi's currency system. The currency was denominated in units of labor. It could never be subjected to inflation, such as the kind that had gripped India during World War II and persisted until the end of the 1940s. The taxation scheme put in place by Borsodi drew on American progressive Henry George's idea of a single tax based on the output potential of land, which would smooth out inequalities that

80. Steven Hahn, *The Roots of Southern Populism: Yeoman Farmers and the Transformation of the Georgia Upcountry, 1850–90* (New York: Oxford University Press, 1983); Charles Postel, *The Populist Vision* (Oxford: Oxford University Press, 2007).

81. See chapters 3 and 4.

82. Carlson, *The New Agrarian Mind*, 66–67.

83. Pierre-Joseph Proudhon, a key anarchist thinker of the nineteenth century, was particularly known for his theory of mutualism. In a mutualist system, the residents of a society operated a mutual credit bank and organized in voluntary cooperatives. See George Woodcock, *Pierre-Joseph Proudhon: A Biography* (New York: Macmillan, 1956). Henry George was a journalist and public intellectual of the American Progressive era. His *Progress and Poverty* (1879) was the bestselling American book of its age. George became well known for his critique of industrialism and identification of rising inequality in the United States, and his work paved the way for the school of thought known as Georgeanism. His most famous idea was the land tax. See Edward T. O'Donnell, *Henry George and the Crisis of Inequality: Progress and Poverty in the Gilded Age* (New York: Columbia University Press, 2015).

arose due to differences in land value. This system sought to prevent financiers from profiting through exchange and tied value as closely as possible to labor and land.[84]

While Borsodi gave Lotvala ideas about economic organization, debating two former Marxist internationalists helped him reach a position that the nation was the ideal unit of political organization. The first, in Bombay, was M.P.T. Acharya. At the time, Acharya was living out his final years practicing Gandhian nonviolence and social service for the poor. Once a revolutionary anarchist who participated in everything from armed rebellions to assassination attempts spanning North America and Europe, he abandoned the Bolsheviks because of their authoritarian tendencies. He subsequently observed anarchist cooperatives in Germany and Sweden in the interwar period before returning to India. It was Acharya who introduced Lotvala to the term "libertarian socialism" as a free and decentralized social order in which the individual could live with complete autonomy to flourish.[85] The second interlocutor, in Calcutta, was M. N. Roy. Roy and his wife, Ellen, had settled down to a career of "Radical Humanism" by the 1940s. This philosophy stressed democracy, individualism, and the importance of decentralized production on cooperative lines.[86] Like Acharya, Roy and the Radical Humanists maintained their internationalism. They, too, pitted the blame for most of the violence and oppression of the contemporary world on nation states.[87] Lotvala, on the other hand, had been more profoundly shaped by the communalization of politics along Hindu and Muslim lines. The riots in Bombay of the 1930s and 1940s and the influx of refugees into his city after the events of Partition loomed large in the millowner's mind.[88]

---

84. Yagnik, *Life*, 81–84.

85. Maia Ramnath, *Decolonizing Anarchism: An Antiauthoritarian History of India's Liberation Struggle* (Oakland: AK Press, 2011), 125–34; C. S. Subrahmanyam, *M.P.T. Acharya: His Life and Times* (Madras: Institute of South Indian Studies, 1995). The definitive treatment of Acharya is Ole Birk Laursen, *Anarchy or Chaos: M.P.T. Acharya and the Indian Struggle for Freedom* (London: Hurst, 2023).

86. Harper, *Underground Asia*, 568–600, 643–62.

87. M.P.T. Acharya, "Libertarianism versus Dictatorship," *The Libertarian* 1, no. 2 (July–September 1951). Sibnarayan Ray, *In Freedom's Quest: A Study of the Life and Works of M. N. Roy*, vol. 4, pt. 2 (1946–54), (Kolkata: Renaissance Publishers, 2007), 298–304.

88. Meena Menon, "Chronicle of Communal Riots in Bombay Presidency, (1893–1945)" *Economic and Political Weekly* 45, no. 47 (2010): 63–72. In total, the majority of approximately 150,000 people migrating to Bombay State during this time settled in the city. The government constructed thirty-two refugee camps to house them. *Rehabilitation of Displaced Persons in*

As he saw it, the nation state was not only more practical but also more appropriate for a polity united by a superior, Hindu culture.[89]

Complementing a decentralist political economy and a world order of nation states was Lotvala's idea that India should be religiously "fraternal." However, Lotvala's concept of fraternity was tinged with a prejudice informed by the momentous events of Partition and the majoritarianism of his Samaj past. Lotvala rejected Gandhi's belief in interreligious harmony. He also criticized the Constituent Assembly's adoption of nonintervention in religious affairs, equality of religions before the law, and retention of distinct personal laws for religious minorities.[90] Instead, he believed that the creation of Pakistan and India as separate states with Muslim and Hindu majorities obviated the possibility of India's secularism.[91]

Alongside the Nehruvian state's pursuit of expert-directed technocratic planning and presentation of this exercise as rational and scientific, the state sought to construct secularism as a composite culture embracing religious diversity and pluralism.[92] These forms of anti-politics sought to limit the domain of the political and unify a greatly heterogeneous society marked by class, caste, and religious tensions. Together with the efforts to project and

---

*Bombay State: A Decennial Retrospect* (Bombay: Directorate of Publicity, 1958); Yasmin Khan, *The Great Partition*, 163.

89. "Creed of New Humanism," *FER* 2, no. 11 (May 1953).

90. On Gandhi's notion of interreligious unity and Nehru's idea of secularism as the isolation of religion from politics, see Khilnani, *The Idea of India*, 164, 177–78. On the Constituent Assembly and secularism, see Shabnum Tejani, *Indian Secularism: A Social and Intellectual History, 1890–1950* (Ranikhet: Permanent Black, 2007), 234–65. The assembly stopped short of adopting a uniform civil code, which has both secular and majoritarian proponents and remains debated to this day.

91. Two-nation theory, the idea that the people of South Asia belong to two nations corresponding to Islam, had its origins in the late nineteenth century. Although it formally entered the discourse of the Muslim League during the 1930s, Ayesha Jalal argued influentially that this did not constitute a serious demand for separate nation states and was a bargaining chip used by the Muslim League leader Mohammad Ali Jinnah against the Congress. See Ayesha Jalal, *The Sole Spokesman: Jinnah, The Muslim League, and the Demand for Pakistan* (Cambridge: Cambridge University Press, 1985), 57. More recently, Venkat Dhulipala contested this hypothesis by referring to a long-running corpus of writing by the influential Deobandi ulema (Muslim religious leadership) of Uttar Pradesh. See Venkat Dhulipala, *Creating a New Medina: State Power, Islam, and the Quest for Pakistan in Late Colonial North India* (Cambridge: Cambridge University Press, 2014).

92. This paragraph follows Blom Hansen, *The Saffron Wave*, 50–59.

consolidate a dominant economic imaginary, the state untethered diverse religious practices from their local contexts and repackaged them as part of a composite Indian culture visible in various public fora. The contradiction was that equal treatment of religions at times tilted toward favorable treatment of the Hindu majority. And in private, communities could go on practicing their own activities to the exclusion of others.

Lotvala contested both technocratic and cultural antipolitical projects. In possibly the first usage of a term that has since gone on to become mainstream in Hindu nationalist discourse, he labeled the Indian state "pseudo secular."[93] Official secularism was "anti-Hindu attitude by multi-religious ruling clique [sic]" which "under the guise of protecting minorities is putting a premium in allowing anti-national activities by a large section of exotic religious minority which owes allegiances not to the land of their birth but to Mecca, Rome or foreign governments."[94] Hindu revivalist organizations like the Arya Samaj had by now been portraying their religion as under threat by Muslims and Christians for decades.[95] Such rhetoric provided a fillip for organizational recruitment and assisted in the creation of groups like the RSS.[96] Carrying on along on these lines, Lotvala transposed this threat onto the independent nation state and raised the question of the loyalty of the minorities.[97]

Truly "fraternal" relations, then, required redressing this imagined anti-Hindu bias. Lotvala believed that Hindus were subordinate citizens in Pakistan

93. Emma Goldman, "The Individual, Society and the State," *Libertarian Socialist*, April–June 1950, 6–22, 10. This was possibly the first usage of "pseudo-secular," a term that has come to dominate Indian right-wing political discourse after a BJP-led group of fanatics demolished the Babri Masjid (Mosque) in 1992, claiming it was the birthplace of the Hindu god Ram. See Ramesh Thakur, "Ayodhya and the Politics of India's Secularism: A Double-Standards Discourse," *Asian Survey* 33, no. 7 (1993): 645–64. Scholars have previously dated the original usage of "pseudo-secularism" to K. R. Malkani, *Principles for a New Political Party* (New Delhi: Vijay Pustak Bhandar, 1951), 60, and Anthony Elenjimittam, *Philosophy and Action of the R.S.S. for the Hind Swaraj* (Bombay: Laxmi Publications, 1951). Both books were reviewed in the institute magazine, and Elenjimittam worked for Lotvala at the time.

94. Lotvala, "Review of *Principles for a New Political Party*," *TL*, July–September 1951, 48–52.

95. Ganga Prasad Upadhyaya, *The Origin, Scope and Mission of the Arya Samaj* (Allahabad: Arya Samaj, 1940).

96. Jaffrelot, *The Hindu Nationalist Movement in India*, 19–45.

97. Following Partition, various Congress politicians, the most prominent of them Sardar Patel, also questioned Muslims' loyalty to India. See Gyanendra Pandey, "Can a Muslim Be an Indian?" *Comparative Studies of Society and History* 41, no. 4 (1999): 608–29.

and Muslims therefore did not deserve equal treatment as Hindus in India. Identifying himself as someone who took pride in Hindu culture, he addressed a concerned 1950 letter on a related issue to Deputy Prime Minister Sardar Patel counseling him to treat Muslims in India as aliens.[98] At this time, Nehru and Pakistani Prime Minister Liaquat Ali Khan were on the verge of negotiating a pact declaring that both countries would safeguard the interests of their minorities.[99]

However, in the same letter, Lotvala demarcated where he parted company with the Hindu nationalists. He condemned the RSS as reactionary because of their desire to restore the disputed region of Kashmir to a fabricated ancient Hindu past dominated by Brahmins.[100] The following year, he attacked the Hindu nationalists' conception of the ancient past as a golden age of Hindu rule and their defense of "everything Hindu . . . [as] children's love of dolls, no logic of a critic or historian." By contrast, Lotvala believed in constantly reforming Hinduism along progressive lines to preserve its "wheat" and throw out the "chaff" like idol worship and priestly hegemony.[101] Notably, Lotvala never joined or supported the RSS-affiliated Bharatiya Jana Sangh party.[102]

Lotvala's synthesis of free economy, nationalism, and Hindu majoritarianism—though not Hindu nationalism per se—was an idiosyncratic form of "libertarian socialism." It was fashioned out of curiosity, the excitement of attaining independence, and prejudice. The process of creating this libertarian socialism involved engaging with lapsed communist internationalists, Hindu nationalists, and American decentralists. There was a tension between Lotvala's ideal of decentralized cooperatives trading freely all over the world and religio-culturally chauvinistic nation states coexisting in a postwar global order. Here, the informality of his thought process must be emphasized. As his institute concretized its activities, it would disavow socialism altogether. It dedicated itself to spreading economic ideas, pushing the majoritarian agenda aside.

98. Lotvala had been a patron of Patel's elder brother Vithalbhai. See Yagnik, *Life.*

99. Pallavi Raghavan, *Animosity at Bay: An Alternative History of the India-Pakistan Relationship, 1947–72* (London: Hurst, 2020), 47–72.

100. Lotvala to Sardar Patel, February 3, 1950, Microfilm Accession 54, Sardar Patel Papers, NAI. I am grateful to Ayesha Sheth for the translation from Gujarati.

101. Lotvala, "Review of *Cultural State in Bharatvarsha*," *TL*, 1, no. 1 (1951): 38–42.

102. Bruce Graham, *Hindu Nationalism and Indian Politics: The Origins and Development of the Bharatiya Jana Sangh* (Cambridge: Cambridge University Press, 1990), 17.

## Indian Libertarians

Lotvala's institute in Girgaum morphed into a site for the development and dissemination of what it called "Indian Libertarianism" during the 1950s. Its name changed from Libertarian Socialist Institute to Libertarian Social Institute. "Socialism is a thin end of transforming it into Communism," one institute magazine op-ed declared.[103] As in other parts of the world, this slippery slope argument would be made by a diverse range of anticommunists in India time and again.[104] It would go on to assume a position of prominence in the rhetoric of the Swatantra Party.

With the advent of the second plan and a program for the linguistic reorganization of Indian states (1956), the institute came around to an agenda of libertarianism for India. It displayed the slogan "Make English the lingua franca of India" on its magazine cover. The institute committed itself to "propaganda and education" now "necessary for the intelligent section of the Indian public" that would show them libertarian philosophy as the way out from the "socialist [sic] pattern of society."[105] Indications of the defining features of this libertarianism came in bits and pieces in the institute magazine. Drawing its foundations from anarchism and utopian projects and developed through the activities and debates of the institute, Indian libertarianism was a loosely defined set of positions articulated in opposition to the conventional wisdom of the times.

The institute aimed to help get people ready for an "economic age" of "economic freedom."[106] "You, Too [sic] can be an economist" because "you are capable of understanding and forming intelligent opinions on the so-called economic events that control your present and future," read one flyer advertising

---

103. "What is Individualist Philosophy and Free Economy?" *FER*, June 1954.

104. In the American context, for example, see Robbie Maxwell, "'A Shooting Star of Conservatism': George S. Benson, the National Education Program and the 'Radical Right,'" *Journal of American Studies* 53, no. 2 (2019): 372–400, 379. The economist F. A. von Hayek most famously advanced this line of argument in his 1947 *The Road to Serfdom*. See Neil McInnes, "The Road Not Taken: Hayek's Slippery Slope to Serfdom," *The National Interest* 51 (1998): 56–66. However, libertarian commentators have argued that it is a more nuanced work. See Peter Boettke and Rosolino Candela, "The Intellectual Context of F. A. Hayek's *Road to Serfdom*," *The Journal of Private Enterprise* 32, no. 1 (2017), 29–44.

105. Kusum Lotvala, "What we stand for," *IL*, January 1, 1958.

106. "LIBERTARIAN SOCIAL INSTITUTE: WHAT IT STANDS FOR," *IL*, January 15, 1958.

its mission.[107] It was an economic age, as discussed in the previous chapter, because the Indian state had hitched its legitimacy to the promise of economic development. It was an economic age, too, because economics had ascended to a privileged place in public policy. Consistent with Lotvala's embrace of individualism, the institute saw itself as a place of learning that would help people help themselves. It sought to persuade people of the merits of libertarianism and anarchist thought through deliberation and study, not overnight conversion.[108] Like the Indian Rationalist Association that Ranchoddas had been a part of in the 1930s, the institute considered itself a place for reasoners rather than believers.

Even if it was not overtly exclusionary, this mission of economic enlightenment for everyone through reading, debate, and discussion was not in fact open to all. The language for conducting affairs was always English, spoken by less than 5 percent of the population.[109] Lotvala considered the English language to be standardized across communities and free of the caste vocabulary of Indian languages. Not a single Muslim was ever a party to the activities of Lotvala and his followers as far as one can tell from the records. The occasional Christian might appear at an institute talk or contribute something to the magazine. Nothing indicates that the institute barred Muslims from participating, but articles and books published or reprinted by the institute committed to discussing the history of Islam exclusively as one of violent territorial conquest. One of the articles in the institute magazine asserted the author's prejudices directly: "From the point of view of Freethought and of Rationalism, represented by the present writer, Islam, the religion of the Koran, represents one of the most formidable obstacles to both intellectual and political progress."[110] These currents of majoritarian sentiment owed specifically to the creation of Pakistan and annoyance at the state's attempts to improve the second-class status of Muslims in India. However, this sentiment was never tied to any organized political agenda.

107. "You, Too Can Be an Economist," in *Supplement of the Research Department of the R. L. Foundation*, ed. B. S. Sanyal, July 1, 1957.

108. Its statement of aims and objectives read: "WE DO NOT ASK YOU TO FOLLOW US . . . We ask you to stop depending on others for leadership and to think and act for yourself." *The Libertarian Socialist*, April–June 1950, not paginated.

109. Barbara Metcalf and Thomas Metcalf, *A Concise History of Modern India*, 2nd edition (Cambridge: Cambridge University Press, 2006), 248.

110. F. A. Ridley, "Pan Islamism," *FER*, July 1955. Apart from a few similar articles by Ridley, the institute also published its own edition of his book *The Assassins*, advertised as "A Must Book For Those Interested in Detailed information of Islam and Historical Record of Fanaticism and Heresies," in *FER* July 1955.

Kusum sacrificed a career as a sports journalist to run the day-to-day operations of the institute during the 1950s. Her dedication and everyday labor made Indian libertarianism viable.[111] By this time, her septuagenarian father had retired to a life of reading and writing in the nearby town of Deolali.[112] Nevertheless, consistent with the patriarchy of the times, the historical record offers far more information about Ranchoddas than Kusum. Ranchoddas' obituary merely described Kusum as "the devoted co-worker and collaborator in Mr. Lotvala's journalistic and ideological work."[113] Perhaps she subtly asserted her independence from the strictures of matrimony by signing off documents as "Miss Kusum Lotvala." And yet, even this choice took place in the context of performing clerical activities on Ranchoddas' behalf.

The institute bustled with activity. It housed university students who participated in its lecture and discussion series. It published a biweekly magazine, maintained a press and bookshop, and ran a library. Some forty-five-odd students residing in the hostel, typically degree candidates at Bombay University, pursued independent study of topics in economics and sociology after consultation with Kusum or her father. Research outputs appeared as stand-alone pamphlets and contributions to the journal. Weekly discussion groups involved intense debates, some of which went on for hours.

One such initiative, the short-lived Youth Forum, encouraged students to partake in serious debates about their research and involved several female students. Individualist and anarchist thinkers visited from abroad. College lecturers streamed in from all over the city. Participants could be of various ideological persuasions. Discussion topics ranged from the imbrication between ethics and economic systems, to foreign policy, to the history of Islam and territorial conquest. Other than students, visitors normally came from academia or journalism. Most did not share the views of the institute's directors. A firsthand account of a hostel discussion about libertarianism that followed a lecture by Ranchoddas regretted the "pro-Marxist" and "dogmatic attitude of most of the participants."[114]

---

111. D. M. Kulkarni, "Shri R. B. Lotvala: The Prophet of Human Freedom—A Life Sketch," *IL*, April 1, 1971; Yagnik, *Life*, 10.

112. Lotvala to Yagnik, May 13, 1951, Indulal Yagnik Papers, NMML.

113. Kulkarni, "Shri R. B. Lotvala." My attempts to learn more about the Lotvala family through contacting the trustees of the Lotvala Library unfortunately yielded no more information.

114. Kishore Valicha, "Mr. R.B. Lotvala Addresses Hostel Students: Advocacy of Libertarianism," *IL*, September 15, 1957.

The institute published a biweekly magazine from 1952 and sold pocket-sized books at the reasonable price of 2 rupees each (see Table 2.1 for a sampling of the titles).[115] Commentary on current affairs and syndicated material from foreign periodicals appeared regularly. Editors reproduced epistolary correspondences of Ranchoddas' on a range of philosophical issues for readers' edification. Some correspondents were local college lecturers. Others came from far away, as in the case of an Australian anarchist poet. These correspondents hailed increasingly from the United States by the second half of the 1950s.[116] Most of the pocket-sized books focused on issues of political economy and philosophy. The occasional book struck a belligerent tone on India-Pakistan tensions. These had nothing particularly libertarian about them. Rather, they came out of the institute's nationalist position that India was a territorial entity constantly under threat by a perpetually hostile, Muslim-majority neighbor and enemy called Pakistan.[117]

The institute library held approximately six thousand books in its collection.[118] Primarily in English, they covered economics, philosophy, and sociology. Between three hundred and four hundred people visited the library daily by the year 1957, according to records reproduced in the institute

115. Paralleling the institute's own evolution, its offerings changed over the course of the decade and its name changed five times: *Cooperative Democracy* (1947–50), *Libertarian Socialist* (1950–51), *The Libertarian* (1951–52), *Free Economic Review* (1952–56), and *Indian Libertarian* (1957 onward). The original search for a utopian political-economic system that safeguarded human freedom (1947–52) gave way to a second, worldly phase (1952–56) of trying to interpret this philosophy as a set of positions on the political and economic affairs of the moment.

116. Examples include the Australian poet Harry Hooton and monetary economics writer Lucas George DeGaris. Both were figures associated with the Personal Rights Association of Britain. Another correspondent was the French anarchist individualist Emile Armand. Letters of these correspondents show up in the pages of *Libertarian Socialist* or *The Libertarian*. Anarchist individualists like Frank Chodorov, Hugo Fack, and Henry Hazlitt wrote in the *Freeman* magazine of New York's Foundation for Economic Education. *FER* and *IL* reprinted selected columns with permission.

117. For example, future Indian Supreme Court Justice Mehr Chand Mahajan's *Background of the Kashmir Problem* (Bombay: Libertarian Social Institute, 1959), detailed Pakistan's violent invasion of the state of Jammu and Kashmir in 1947, involving Pathan tribesmen supported by the Pakistani army. That year, as prime minister of the state, Mahajan navigated these tensions and helped secure the Kashmir maharaja's accession to the Indian Union. On this and Mahajan's role in negotiations between the Indian Union and the Kashmiri maharaja, see Srinath Raghavan, *War and Peace in Modern India* (Basingstoke: Macmillan, 2010), 101–48. Like Lotvala, Mahajan had been associated with the Arya Samaj in his youth.

118. *FER*, April–May 1954; *FER*, January 1955.

**TABLE 2.1.** Sample List of Titles Published by Libertarian Book Shop

| Title | Author |
| --- | --- |
| *The Analysis of Usury* | Jeffrey Mark |
| *Anarchism in Socialistic Evolution* | Pierre Kropotkin |
| *Anarchism and Other Essays* | Emma Goldman |
| *Anarcho-Syndicalism* | Rudolf Rocker |
| *Annihilate Orthodoxy* | Dr. K. N. Kini |
| *The Assassins* | F. A. Ridley |
| *Background of the Kashmir Problem* | Justice Meher Chand Mahajan |
| *Bakunin's Writings* | Guy A. Aldred |
| *Charwak—An Ancient Rationalist* | P. J. Sabnis |
| *Cause of Business Depressions* | Hugo Bilgram |
| *Compulsory Military Training* | Dr. K. N. Kini |
| *Diamat* | Philip Spratt |
| *Does God Exist* | Sabastein Faure |
| *Economic Planning* | Ludwig von Mises and Rufus Tucker |
| *Economics of Liberty* | John Beverly Robinson |
| *Evolution & Revolution* | Elsce Reclus |
| *Footprints of Treachery* | Baburao Patel |
| *God and the State* | Michael Bakunin |
| *India's Foreign Policy* | Om Prakash Kahol |
| *Life of Ranchoddas Bhavan Lotvala* | Indulal Yagnik |
| *Libertarian Anthology* | |
| *Libertarian Manifesto* | Ralph Borsodi |
| *Meet Kropotkin, the Master* | Herbert Reed |
| *Men over Industry* | Paul Derrick |
| *Modern Idolatry* | Jeffrey Mark |
| *Mutual Banking* | William B. Greene |
| *Nationalism & Its Relation to Culture* | Rudolf Rocker |
| *New World Through Co-operative Democracy* | James Peter Warbasse |
| *Political Justice* | Selections from Godwin |
| *Principles of Land Value Taxation & Free Trade* | E. C. Craigie |
| *Psychology of Political Violence* | Emma Goldman |
| *Rebuilding the World* | John Beverly Robinson |
| *Root Is Man* | D. Macdonald |
| *RSS from the Inside* | K. Nagaraj |
| *Saving and Spending* | Jeffrey Mark |
| *Science of Society* | Stephen Pearl Andrews |
| *Social Relations and Freedom* | A. Symposium |
| *Socialism & State* | Rudolf Rocker |
| *A Study of Money Question* | Hugo Bilgram |
| *What Is Cooperation* | James Peter Warbasse |
| *What Is Mutualism?* | Clarence Lee Swartz |
| *What Is Pluralism* | The Pluralist Society |

*Source*: Back Cover of A. Ranganathan, *English or Linguistic Chaos?* (Bombay: Libertarian Social Institute, 1959).

magazine. Roughly a hundred people enjoyed borrowing rights to the collection, which increased in size by about a hundred new titles each month.[119] The library subscribed to about thirty foreign and thirty Indian periodicals in multiple languages. A substantial proportion of the texts published and collected by the institute traced a foreign provenance. Several of these could not be easily sourced in India.

The institute secured these materials by collaborating with and embedding itself in networks of parallel organizations run by anarchists, cooperativists, and free enterprise conservatives from other parts of the world. Kusum made do with limited amounts of foreign exchange tightly controlled by the government and appealed to a mission of "propagating radical ideas in India" to secure discounts from sympathetic publishers.[120] Where possible, the institute even borrowed and returned books to suppliers.[121] Contacts included the consumer advocacy-focused Cooperative League of the USA, the New York-based Foundation for Economic Education, the anarchist Joseph Ishill's Oriole Press of New Jersey, the Libertarian Group of Los Angeles, and the Personal Rights Association of Britain.[122] The institute magazine reproduced articles from *Freedom* and *The Free Trader* in the UK and from such U.S.-based publications as *Analysis, The Henry George News, The Individualist, Ideas on Liberty,* and *Freedom and Plenty.* Diverse as they were, these organizations and periodicals shared a common conviction for the freedom of the individual and an associated weariness of the coercive powers of the state.

Measured by the titles published by their bookshop and the articles printed in the pages of its magazine, the institute's most important contacts were a group

119. *IL*, August 15, 1957; See the list of 101 accessions for the month of April 1955 in *FER*, May 1955.

120. R. B. Lotvala (transcribed by Kusum Lotvala) to Joseph Ishill, July 23, 1948, Folder 17, Box 1C, Joseph Ishill Papers, Special and Area Studies Collection, George A. Smathers Libraries, University of Florida, Gainesville, Florida. Ishill (1888–1966) was a Romanian American anarchist and owner of the Oriole Press in New Jersey.

121. Lotvala to Ishill, June 30, 1953, Ishill Additional Papers, MS AM 1614.1, Series II, Folder 23, Houghton Library, Harvard University, Cambridge, MA, USA.

122. A number of these groups, such as the Oriole Press, no longer exist. See Marion Brown, *Joseph Ishill and the Oriole Press* (New Jersey: Oriole Press, 1960). However, the Cooperative League of the USA, which brought together small businesses to negotiate attractive input prices, survived and grew. Now, it is called the National Cooperative Business Association. See Clarke A. Chambers, "The Cooperative League of the United States of America, 1916–61: A Study of Social Theory and Social Action," *Agricultural History* 36, no. 2 (1962): 59–81.

in the United States that has been called free enterprisers. These figures argued that the free enterprise system was seminal to national identity and was under attack in the aftermath of the New Deal, a series of interventionist policies undertaken in the United States that increased public spending to combat the Great Depression.[123] Notably, these figures never quite defined the "free enterprise" system they supported. Instead, they persistently characterized it in opposition to the status quo and produced simple stories in defense of its virtues. Originally, this coalition consisted of small businesses, larger firms, "moderate Republicans, conservative Democrats, reactionary newspaper publishers, libertarians, and many others." [124] A free enterprise orientation became a defining feature of postwar American conservatism. The Republican Party incorporated it into the party platform by the 1970s. Out of the constituencies of the free enterprise coalition, it was with the libertarians that the Bombay-based institute engaged most closely.

It is highly possible that Kusum modeled certain activities on the libertarian Foundation for Economic Education (FEE) in New York. The FEE (1946–) produced everything from "one-page leaflets" to "moderate length pamphlets and short books" to long empirical studies and philosophical meditations.[125] It sponsored debate and essay competitions. Such activities were intended to provide mass education and to link "far-flung adherents" to its cause. Like Ranchoddas Lotvala himself, its founder, Leonard Read, evinced a key interest in disseminating ideas as widely as possible and never secured copyright for FEE publications. Between 1946 and 1950, it mailed out four million bits of literature that would be featured in over four hundred American newspapers. It was greatly skilled at publicity and outreach. The FEE took over a fortnightly publication called the *Freeman* in 1956 and raised its circulation from four thousand to forty thousand in two years.[126] Contributions from the *Freeman*'s pages included short parables and metaphors in defense of free markets. In faraway Bombay, the institute reprinted them in service of its parallel, smaller-scale evangelical mission.

123. The New Deal has been the subject of a vast scholarship, too long to discuss here. One recent contribution placing it in the context of the crisis of global capitalism in the 1930s and interpreting its policies as part of the consolidation of post–World War II American hegemony is Kiran Klaus Patel's *The New Deal: A Global History* (Princeton: Princeton University Press, 2016).

124. Lawrence Glickman, *Free Enterprise: An American History* (New Haven: Yale University Press, 2019), 81, 141–66.

125. Henry Hazlitt, "The Early History of the FEE," *Freeman*, March 1984, 38–40.

126. Brian Doherty, *Radicals for Capitalism: A Freewheeling History of the American Libertarian Movement* (New York: Public Affairs, 2007), 165, 173.

The cooperative form discussed in the institute's correspondence with the Cooperative League of the USA differed from those in domestic Indian parlance. During the colonial era, cooperative credit societies had mainly extended loans from the Government of India to provide working capital for farmers. And the collective farms of the Soviet Union or the cooperative farms of China that the Government of India would investigate when studying land reform were owned by the state. By contrast, the American form was consistent with private owner- ship; it mainly involved joint marketing and sales initiatives or joint purchasing schemes for consumer groups. The animosity that Indian economic conserva- tives would direct against cooperative farming in the later 1950s was thus not against cooperatives per se. Rather, it was embedded in the exaggerated fear that such farms were a step toward cooperatives of the communist variety.[127]

Whereas American libertarians and cooperativists had turned their animus against the New Deal, labor unions, and the left, Indian libertarians attacked statist policy and what Sudipta Kaviraj calls the "hegemony of the left-wing construction" of political discourse around "socialism."[128] They raised suspi- cion that the Congress' rhetoric of social transformation was a worrying sign of things to come, even though rhetoric often went much beyond the reality.[129] The libertarians did not normally target the Communist Party, which was the largest opposition party. Rather, the point of their anticommunist rhetoric was to suggest that the dominant Congress was heading down the path to com- munism and ultimately totalitarianism.[130]

Editorials in the institute magazine attacked the centralizing and statist ten- dencies of policy in polemical fashion. An unsigned editorial warned that the Registration and Licensing of Industrial Undertakings Rules of 1952 "'spell[ed]

127. For more on this, see chapters 3, 4, and 6.

128. Kimberly Phillips-Fein, *Invisible Hands: The Making of the Conservative Movement from the New Deal to Reagan* (New York: Norton, 2009), 27–33, 53–55; Sudipta Kaviraj, "Democracy and Development in India," in *The Enchantment of Democracy and India*, 116–60, 130.

129. This rhetoric also comprised a more heterogeneous set of influences than they alleged. See C. A. Bayly, "The Ends of Liberalism and the Political Thought of Nehru's India," *Modern Intellectual History* 12, no. 3 (2015): 605–26.

130. In the 1952 elections, the Congress won 364 seats in the Lok Sabha, the lower house of parliament. The communists won sixteen seats. Its results were stronger in some individual states, but it did not win any of these elections either. The 1957 elections were similarly lop- sided, with Congress winning 371 seats to the communists' 27. See *Statistical Report on Lok Sabha Elections, 1951–52* (New Delhi: Election Commission of India, 1953); *Statistical Report on General Election, 1957* (New Delhi: Election Commission of India, 1958).

the end of freedom in industrial enterprise and development" and would privilege more well-connected large firms over smaller ones.[131] The rules in question required new businesses to register and secure licenses from the government before engaging in commercial activity.

The editorial page turned its animus against the Essential Commodities Act three years later. The act in question placed temporary price controls on a permanent footing in the interests of economic development and extended them to new domains.[132] Through this legislation, the government introduced a scheme of licensing that gave petty bureaucrats power to regulate the manufacture, production, price, storage, transport, supply, and distribution of commodities. Controllers for each commodity could inspect the records of traders and search their premises without a warrant.[133] One article argued that the legislation was odious because it originated "in the recommendations of the Planning Commission," which envisaged "such economic dictatorialism [sic] . . . tolerated only during an emergency such as war or the threat of an external aggression."[134] Hyperbole notwithstanding, it was true that these laws codified underdevelopment as a permanent emergency.

That same year, the fourth amendment to the constitution went into effect. It gave the government the right to assume control over corporate entities and property without having the amount or principles of compensation awarded subjected to judicial scrutiny.[135] Pointing to this legislation alongside the nationalization of the airlines (1953), bus routes (1953), life insurance (1956), and the institution of the State Trading Corporation (1956), the editorial page warned of the possibility of more to come. It also took the view that these enterprises under state ownership could not be profitable and therefore nationalization made no sense.[136]

Another point of attack was the financing provisions of the ambitious Second Five-Year Plan and its attendant consequences for economic life. Both increased taxation and deficit financing would be required to meet greater capital expenditures from the previous plan period. "It is clear that we are in

131. "How 'Mixed' is 'Mixed Economy'?" *FER*, September 1952.

132. De, *A People's Constitution*, 77–122, 88.

133. De, "'Commodities Must Be Controlled,'" 284.

134. "Pursuing a Mirage," *FER*, October 1954.

135. Austin, *Working a Democratic Constitution*, 101–10.

136. J. K., "Planning or Muddling," *FER*, September 1955; A. C. Ramalingam, "State Entry into Industrial Fields and its Adverse Effects," *FER*, January 1956.

for a period of inflation and hardship for all, particularly the middle classes," warned an institute op-ed.[137] Unlike private-debt-fueled inflation, which culminated in a credit bust and recession as part of the business cycle, another article noted, "political inflation" could "feed on itself. Create more debt to pay the present debt and interest thereon and thus leave the debt figure, [sic] to grow in an arithmetic progression."[138] The institute had long argued that money value should not be disconnected from labor value, following Ralph Borsodi.[139]

The libertarian critique of policy represented the class interests it sought to safeguard, which in turn led to an alternative understanding of how development should work. According to this critique, the socialistic pattern of society as envisioned ignored "needs of the small producer and trader."[140] Worse, the large-scale heavy-industry-led pattern of development could wipe these actors out. In this period, the trader and small businessperson could come under suspicion easily and go to jail for their offenses. To add to the atmosphere of suspicion, the government produced films vilifying shopkeepers and merchants, suggesting that citizens keep a watchful eye over them and report illicit behavior.[141] Over the course of the decade, these commercial actors also began to bear the burden of increased indirect taxes. The unprecedented nature of policy changes, combined with the uncertainty around the degree to which the government would go to make India socialist, provoked fear of a pathway "for the State to absorb economic sovereignty into political sovereignty."[142]

It appears from hints dropped throughout magazine articles that the libertarians began to gravitate toward an idea propagated by economist Joseph Schumpeter that entrepreneurs provided the innovation necessary for the development of an economy.[143] They acknowledged that "in the absence of

137. Sumant S. Bankeshwar, "Shaking the Foundation," *FER*, May 1955.

138. R. J., "The Potential Danger," *FER*, April 1953.

139. Although raising the bogey of the inflationary spiral was to some degree alarmist, the experiences of rampant inflation in India during World War II had not yet receded from popular memory. On wartime inflation and its socioeconomic effects, see Indivar Kamtekar, "A Different War Dance: State and Class in India, 1939–45," *Past and Present* 176, no. 1 (2002): 187–221.

140. Bankeshwar, "Private vs. Public Sector," *FER*, April 1955.

141. De, *A People's Constitution*, 96–106.

142. "Eye on Events: The Budget," *FER*, March 1956; J. K. Dhairyawan, "On the High Road to Totalitarianism," *FER*, January 1956.

143. Joseph Schumpeter, *The Theory of Economic Development* (Cambridge, MA: Harvard University Press, 1934). The first edition was published in 1912.

the genuine innovator the Government in a backward economy can act as an economic process which can be planned below if there is sufficient agreement among the people as regards to the objectives of the plan." The government might legitimately play a "positively useful role of innovator *initiating* the cumulative process of economic development in a democratic society" (emphasis mine) by creating a capital base of savings to be invested to bring about self-sustaining growth.[144] From then on, entrepreneurs would make long-term investments in the economy and raise productivity.[145] They would adopt modern means of production and trade freely with each other and the rest of the world.[146] Crucially, in the Indian libertarian conception, these firms would be small, competitive firms, never monopolies. The qualified endorsement of early government intervention came with a warning that it "need not be exaggerated." After providing this spark of sorts, the government could stand back. What was happening now was that the government was going too far.

The institute stated its cause and objectives in the October 1957 issue of the *Indian Libertarian*. "This Libertarian branch of social thought has a great function to fulfil, in offsetting the present centralizing totalitarian economies and politics, that are exercising an unhealthy fascination on our leaders owing to the example of Soviet countries," it declared. A prerequisite of the "free society" that the libertarians dreamed of was a "free economy," an economy "as free as possible from coercion." In such an economy, personal initiative and free choice would "have adequate scope, as unfettered as possible by the coercive apparatus of the State." The statement pointed out that this philosophy was distinct from "laissez-faire, and the sovereignty of capital and the business class." Rather "free economy . . . means an economic order which allows no monopoly of economic power to any class."[147]

Free economy became a keyword that bound people together and indicated certain kinds of thought.[148] It connoted a loose common belief in less state regulation of and participation in the economy than was currently being practiced. It was therefore malleable enough to fit multiple ideas and practices of

144. "The Need for Planning," *FER*, March 1953.

145. "Economic Program of the Jan Sangh: A Critical Review," *FER*, February 1953.

146. "Dark Days for Japan," *FER*, September 1952; "World Standards of Life," *FER*, August 1952.

147. "What the Libertarians Stand For," *IL*, October 15, 1957.

148. Raymond Williams, *Keywords: A Vocabulary of Culture and Society*, 3rd edition (New York: Oxford University Press, 2015), xxvii.

political economy. Yet precise details about the domains of state intervention and nonintervention, public-private partnerships, or the kinds of government activity in economic affairs that might be acceptable never appeared. Nor did any consideration of how to prevent the concentration of economic power in private hands. This vagueness allowed the term to spread more quickly.

Tempting as it may be to dismiss this as empty sloganeering, it is also worth noting the ways in which the Lotvalas sought to establish the intellectual legitimacy of free economy and elevate political discourse. They produced an unusually wide-ranging suggested reading list for those seeking a "quick and correct grasp of the libertarian philosophy." Readers were encouraged to study the "three naturalistic systems" and "three humanistic systems." They were pointed toward the works of a range of Western authors, including Epicurus, Herbert Spencer, William James, Jeremy Bentham, John Stuart Mill, Henry Sidgwick, and Immanuel Kant.[149]

The Indian libertarians demonstrated awareness of the evils of the private concentration of economic power, especially usury. But their urbanite aloofness from rural India's concerns prevented them from appreciating the major problems of that geography. They encouraged readers to consult the work of the Austrian-born American economist Ludwig von Mises, described by one American historian as the "fountainhead of modern libertarianism."[150] His work offered "a defense of the unhampered market as necessary and sufficient for social welfare."[151] The economist's name appeared in eleven separate *Indian Libertarian* articles between March 1957 and 1958, and twice as the author of syndicated *Freeman* articles.[152] One *Indian Libertarian* editorial conceded that although Von Mises' writings were inattentive to inequalities of land and credit, "we largely agree with von Mises."[153] Of particular appeal was his insight that "the market economy operates according to certain laws of nature, human and non-human, and . . . there is nothing wrong with these laws."[154] Von

149. "The Course in Social Sciences," *IL*, August 15, 1957.

150. Doherty, *Radicals for Capitalism*, 9.

151. Like their American contemporaries, the Indian libertarians interpreted the progressive George to mean that taxing land went along with leaving every other domain of economic activity free from the state. See Charles H. Hamilton, ed., *Fugitive Essays: Selected Writings of Frank Chodorov* (Indianapolis: Liberty Fund, 1980), 11–32.

152. Ludwig von Mises, "Full Employment and Monetary Policy," reprinted in *IL*, September 15, 1957.

153. B. S. Sanyal, "The Welfare Sentiments," *IL*, July 1, 1957.

154. "Editorial Note: Where Libertarians Differ from von Mises," *IL*, September 15, 1957.

Mises most likely came to India through Read's FEE, which reproduced and disseminated a number of the economist's writings and extended him regular invites to their lectures and seminars.[155]

Von Mises was associated with what would become known as the Austrian school of political economy. The school was distinguished by its adherence to methodological individualism and the notion that universal rules about economics could be derived from logic, aloof from empirical concerns.[156] He sought to identify the conditions for what he called "perfect capitalism"— open markets, low taxes, low wages, state protection for investments, and laws to promote competition.[157] An interest in extending the principle of the division of labor to its logical conclusion led him to reject the nation state and endorse British imperial policies of free trade and mobility of peoples.[158] Fleeing the Nazis, the Jewish Von Mises relocated to Geneva and then the United States. He became more skeptical of mass reasoning, particularly of those of peoples of color, and began to countenance selective immigration controls.[159] From 1945, Von Mises took up a long-term visiting professorship at New York University financed by business groups for whom he delivered lectures and seminars.[160] His magnum opus, *Human Action* (1949), made the case for a relatively unrestrained capitalism.

Von Mises himself had little faith in the capacity of Indians to grasp economic reasoning. "How can we expect that Hindus, the worshippers of the cow, should grasp the theories of Ricardo and of Bentham?" he asked in 1944.[161] Substantially engaging with Von Mises' ideas may have turned Lotvala away from the economist. The same can be said about the selection of texts by Mill and Spencer for the self-study course in libertarianism; there does not

155. Jörg Guido Hülsmann, *Mises: The Last Knight of Liberalism* (Auburn, Alabama: Ludwig von Mises Institute, 2007), 837–83.

156. On this latter point, they squared off against those of the empiricist German Historicist School in what came to be known as the *methodenstreit* (methods debate). See Janek Wasserman, *Marginal Revolutionaries: How Austrian Economists Fought the War of Ideas* (New Haven: Yale University Press, 2019); Erwin Dekker, *The Viennese Students of Civilization: The Meaning and Context of Austrian Economics Reconsidered* (Cambridge: Cambridge University Press, 2016).

157. Slobodian, *Globalists*, 30–45.

158. Slobodian, "Perfect Capitalism, Imperfect Humans: Race, Migration, and the Limits of Ludwig von Mises' Globalism," *Contemporary European History* 28, no. 2 (2019): 143–55.

159. Slobodian, "Perfect Capitalism."

160. Hülsmann, *Mises: The Last Knight of Liberalism*, 837–83.

161. Von Mises, quoted in Slobodian, "Perfect Capitalism."

seem to have been any attention paid to the racialized civilizational discourses present in the works of these writers. This paralleled the Indian communists' selective access to texts published overseas in the 1920s. For example, the first wave of literature that came into India did not include a single text by Marx himself. Multiple factors mediated the spread of texts and evolution of ideas as they moved, leading to rather surprising appropriations.[162] With respect to Von Mises, it is likely that foreign exchange scarcity limited the Indian libertarians' exposure to Mises to writings reprinted and circulated by the FEE. The editorial choices of organizations like these could shape the reception of thinkers in unanticipated, even undesired, ways.[163]

Editorial selections and omissions by intermediaries like the FEE may also account for the Indian libertarians' partial understanding and lack of much interest in a new set of ideas called neoliberalism. Coined for the first time in 1938 at a Paris conference attended by economists and journalists, "neoliberalism" sought to reinvent a liberalism in crisis. Crucially, neoliberals at this time rejected both laissez-faire and economic planning. Progenitors sought to protect the world economy from organized capital and organized labor, which they believed fomented totalitarianism. From 1947, the neoliberals gathered as part of the Mont Pelerin Society (MPS) and dedicated themselves to a project that would push the state to create conditions for markets to work more freely. In their early stages, they once even referred to their mission as one of securing a "free economy."[164] By no means a homogeneous group, MPS members nevertheless agreed on the need for the state to create laws and safeguards for market exchange to be free. In fact, Von Mises, who attended their first meeting, found them too interventionist and stormed out. However, when the institute reproduced a 1952 *Freeman* article by MPS president and future Nobel Prize winner F. A. von Hayek about "neoliberalism" emerging in the Atlantic world, the accompanying editorial note dismissed

---

162. Shaikh, *Outcaste Bombay*, 51–52.

163. In one prominent example, FEE editors sought to tone down the moderating language in American economists George Stigler and Milton Friedman's popular tract, *Roofs or Ceilings?*, which argued that rent controls produced housing shortages. The FEE also cut out the authors' affirmation of their commitment to decreasing inequality, prompting them to protest and reach a compromise in which the editors put in a clarifying footnote. See Angus Burgin, *The Great Persuasion* (Cambridge, MA: Harvard University Press, 2015), 165–68.

164. Ben Jackson, "At the Origins of Neo-liberalism: The Free Economy and the Strong State, 1930–47," *The Historical Journal* 53, no. 1 (2010), 129–51. On the Mont Pelerin Society, see Burgin, *The Great Persuasion*.

it as "fresh advocacy of 'Laissez-Faire' economics."[165] The appearance of Von Mises' and Hayek's writings suggest that the Indian libertarian project established points of connection to early neoliberalism in the United States. At this stage, Indians encountered aspects of neoliberal ideas in the process of defining their own. However, they considered the Indian project to be more interventionist.[166]

Complementing their economic program, the Indian libertarians adopted a clear position on the use of English in Indian society. They defended the language's salutary consequences during a period of political turmoil. Their use of English was originally a byproduct of the elite character of their activity in a polyglot city. By the late 1950s, this was deliberate. Across the country, regional agitations led to an investigation of the possible reorganization of states along linguistic lines by the Government of India in 1953. The report of the States Reorganization Commission recommended keeping Bombay as the capital of a bilingual, Gujarati- and Marathi-speaking state. Riots ensued. Maratha Kunbis led a Samyukta Maharashtra Samiti (United Maharashtra Association) for a Marathi-speaking state that retained Bombay as its capital.[167] Lotvala's biographer, Indulal Yagnik, led a Mahagujarat movement for a separate Gujarati state from the Gujarati-speaking city of Ahmedabad. Bombay State split into the linguistic states of Maharashtra and Gujarat in 1960. Bombay became Maharashtra's capital.[168] By upholding the use of English, the libertarians played neutral on this question.

The institute's pro-English position also signaled its opposition to giving Hindi status as the country's official language. Gandhi had promoted the adoption of the northern Indian dialect of Hindustani, an amalgam of Urdu (which drew from Persian and Arabic) and Hindi (which drew heavily from

165. Hayek, "A Rebirth of Liberalism," *Freeman*, July 28, 1952, 729–31, reprinted in *FER*, October 1952.

166. The spread of neoliberal ideas to Indian economic policy is a later phenomenon. See Aditya Balasubramanian, "(Is) India in the History of Neoliberalism?" in *Market Civilizations: Neoliberals East and South*, eds. Quinn Slobodian and Dieter Plehwe (Brooklyn: Zone Books, 2022), 53–79.

167. On the history of this movement, including the forerunner Samyukta Maharashtra Parishad, see Oliver Godsmark, *Citizenship, Community and Democracy in India: From Bombay to Maharashtra, c. 1930–1960* (London: Routledge, 2018), especially 54–82.

168. Jayant Lele, "Saffronization of Shiv Sena: The Political Economy of City, State and Nation," in *Bombay: Metaphor for Modern India*, eds. Sujata Patel and Alice Thorner (Bombay: Oxford University Press, 1995), 185–212, 187–88.

Sanskrit), across the country to bring people together in speaking an Indian tongue and unite Hindus and Muslims. At the Constituent Assembly, delegates struck a compromise that English would continue as the language of affairs for Union and interstate communication for fifteen years. In a break from Gandhi's Hindustani agenda, the Hindu majority in the assembly agreed that Hindi, which they perceived to be more authentic for Hindus, would become the official language. This decision would be subject to further review after five years.[169] That 1955 review recommended the adoption of Hindi the following year. Protests broke out in non-Hindi-speaking areas like Bombay until the government dropped the idea for the time being.[170] From then on, the slogan of the institute magazine became "KEEP ENGLISH THE LINGUA FRANCA OF INDIA."

The institute made plans for a special issue "justifying our slogan" and showing that "English has been the Binding Cement between States in the country."[171] Offering an economic reason for the "economic age," editorials in the magazine argued that English could make interstate activity more efficient and give the country global advantages. To counter arguments adduced by leaders in the Hindi-speaking northern states that English was the foreign language of the imperial masters, the institute published a book that traced a lineage of Indian demands for English education back to the nineteenth century. The book offered several examples of how nationalist leaders had used English effectively for Indian ends.[172] Consistent with the organization's elite commitments and its nationalist zeal, the libertarians sought to demonstrate that the argument from patriotism against English had no merit.

Their advocacy of English further differentiated the Indian libertarians from Hindu nationalists. The latter considered English to be a foreign imposition and associated with Western values. Hindu nationalists believed that Hindi could purify, unite, and thereby strengthen the nation. Since its inception the Bharatiya Jana Sangh pursued Hindi promotion as a key activity.[173]

169. Guha, *India after Gandhi*, 117–20.

170. D. D. Laitin, "Language Policy and Political Strategy in India," *Policy Sciences* 22, no. 3/4 (1989): 415–36. The institute's own response to the Kher Commission appeared in J. K. Dhairyawan, "Review of *Future of English in India*," *FER*, November 1955.

171. "To Our Readers," *IL*, October 15, 1957.

172. Airavatham Ranganathan, *English or Linguistic Chaos* (Bombay: Libertarian Social Institute, 1959).

173. Although at times they would have to downplay their advocacy of Hindi as the national language of India to court a broader base of support, this has been a core political

The Lotvala family sought to spread a right-wing, agrarian libertarianism in postcolonial India much as they had supported communism in the 1920s. Kusum drove this agenda forward. Free economy and the establishment of English as "the lingua franca of India" became the unique features of Indian libertarianism at a time when commercial regulation and regional ethno-linguistic assertion began to define economic and social life in Bombay and across India. These trends helped separate the libertarians from their earlier affinity for Hindu majoritarian politics and socialist forms of political econ-omy. Like the free enterprisers in the United States, the Indian libertarians practiced rhetorical strategies to ingrain libertarianism. They repeated terms like "free economy," offered cautionary tales about the slippery slope to com-munism, and used hyperbolic language. Still, key differences separated them. It was one thing for figures like the FEE's Leonard Read to advance the agenda of free enterprise in a literate, prosperous society and take forward an agenda defined in the 1930s. Compared to the *Freeman's* circulation of forty thousand copies, the *Indian Libertarian* circulated just a thousand copies in a largely poor country. How would the newly fashioned free economy spread?

## Spreading the Word:
## Midnight's Other Cold Warriors

"It may appear to the superficially-minded person that we are championing a lost cause," Kusum Lotvala conceded in a 1958 *Indian Libertarian* piece. And yet, the less superficial would know that recent global events painted an en-tirely different picture. The collapse of the socialist party in Britain, Moscow's program of de-Stalinization, the Gomulka program in Poland, and the Hun-garian Revolution, Kusum declared, "show that we, the Indian Libertarians, ARE CHAMPIONING A LIVE CAUSE."[174] As the Cold War intensified, free economy incubated in a web of interconnected organizations—periodical presses, book publishers, and associations—based in urban India. In several cases, energies unleashed at independence had transformed colonial-era organizations to attend to new purposes. All linked in some way or other to the Indian libertarians, these organizations published affordable short books, pamphlets, and periodicals. They conducted debates, conferences, lectures,

---

commitment of the Jana Sangh and its successor BJP. See Graham, *Hindu Nationalism and Indian Politics*, 6, 30.

174. "What We Stand For," *IL*, January 1, 1958.

and educational programs. The institute managed to open branches in seven other cities by 1960 thanks to such collaborations.[175]

Morphologically, the voluntary association is the classic unit of conservative political organization.[176] Such an association provided the necessary buffer between the individual and the state, according to the writings of its classic theorist Edmund Burke. Its emergence was a testament to the freedom of association and common interest of individual wills. This was a version of what he called the "little platoon," of which the family was the traditional example.[177] There was also a conservative intellectual disposition uniting these groups against state expansion and centralization.

These magazines in this web offer a rich picture of the views of middling figures interpreting India's experiment with democracy and development in a Cold War age. They provide a record of vibrant debate that unfolded outside of the corridors of Indian parliament, public universities, and research outfits where the Congress or left parties enjoyed overwhelming support. These periodicals enjoyed appreciable readership. Studying them together illuminates the networks forged by editors and contributors and makes apparent the strategies they adopted to amplify their reach.[178] Reading them exposes the ideological heterogeneity of this period and suggests that India's eventual abandonment of socialist rhetoric and planned economic policy had constituencies of support as early as the mid-twentieth century.

175. These were Bangalore, Baroda, Calcutta, Delhi, Madras, Nagpur, and Patna.

176. Robert Nisbet, *Conservatism: Dream and Reality* (Minneapolis: University of Minnesota Press, 1986), 38; Karl Mannheim, *Conservatism: A Contribution to the Sociology of Knowledge*, eds. David Kettler, Volker Meja, and Nico Stehr eds. and Kettler and Meja trans (London: Routledge, 1986), 99.

177. Robert Nisbet, *Conservatism: Dream and Reality* (Minneapolis: University of Minnesota Press, 1986), 38.

178. The neglect of this history until recently owes to the reliance of scholarship on postcolonial economic policy and the Cold War on official documentation available in state archives. See Bérénice Guyot-Réchard, "South Asia in the World," in *The Cambridge History of the Modern Indian Subcontinent*, David Gilmartin, Prasannan Parthasarathi, and Mrinalini Sinha eds. (Cambridge: Cambridge University Press, forthcoming); Menon, "Developing Histories of Development." In fact, it has been scholars of comparative literature who have recently started to use these sources seriously. See Francesca Orsini, "The Post-Colonial Magazine Archive," *South Asia: Journal of South Asian Studies* 45, no. 2 (2022): 250–267. A recent special issue of *South Asia* on postcolonial archives points to ways in which scholars must think more creatively about the use of sources for this period because of the relative paucity of easily accessible and extensive records compared to those from the colonial period. See Anjali Narlekar and Francesca Orsini, "Introduction: Postcolonial Archives," *South Asia* 45, no. 2 (2022): 211–19.

Prime Minister Nehru devised a novel and courageous policy of nonalignment with the superpowers to establish Indian autonomy in the international arena and avoid putting "all our eggs in one basket."[179] Influential as it was, the intellectual culture of this period of Indian history amounted to much more than just the nonaligned vision and practices of foreign policy.[180] Both superpowers waged a pitched war of texts in India. They sought to tap into the expanding reading culture of the period to penetrate hearts and minds. The United States opened libraries of the Information Agency in the country's largest cities of Bombay, Calcutta, Delhi, and Madras. Each of them received a few thousand books and presented visitors with open access to the holdings. The libraries offered "the best show-windows" of life in the United States and showcased various accomplishments in foreign policy, science, and technology.[181] Both the Americans and the Soviets disseminated tens of thousands of copies of official publications like *American Reporter* and *Soviet Land* and reprinted them in various Indian languages (see Table 2.2). The U.S. Information Agency also sponsored Indian reprints of American books by minor local publishers.

These organizations and their publications that made up the web or cluster in which free economy diffused stood one step away from official superpower propaganda efforts. They emerged as a category of extra-state actors in the nonaligned world offering consciously *aligned* positions to public discourse.[182] Their erstwhile anti-imperialist founders had retooled earlier versions of these associations to weigh in on Cold War predicaments.

179. Khilnani, *The Idea of India*, 31; Raghavan, *War and Peace in Modern India*, 20–21. Nehru enunciated these principles at the Afro-Asian Conference of 1955 at Bandung in Indonesia, which gave them purchase among decolonizing nations. Building from this idea, in 1961, Jozip Broz Tito of the former Yugoslavia founded a Nonaligned Movement. See Vijay Prashad, *The Darker Nations: A People's History of the Third World* (New York: New Press, 2007).

180. One example is the cultural Cold War's influence on the development of Indian literary modernism, see Laetitia Zecchini, "What Filters through the Curtain: Reconsidering Indian Modernisms, Travelling Literatures, and Little Magazines in a Cold War Context," *Interventions: International Journal of Postcolonial Studies* 22, no. 2 (2020): 172–94.

181. Madhukar Bhimrao Konnur, "Transnational Library Relations in the Indo-American Experience," (unpublished PhD diss., Savitribai Phule Pune University, 1986), 274–79.

182. The official vernacularization of Soviet texts in the Indian literary sphere by the USSR's Foreign Languages Publishing House/Progress Publishers is the subject of forthcoming work by Jessica Bachman and Lisa Mitchell. See Bachman, "Reader Influence on Soviet Urdu-Language Book Publishing during the Cold War," and Mitchell, "Translating the Political: Telugu Writers and Soviet Publishers, 1950s–1980s," *Progressive Reading Cultures and Communist Political Thought: between South Asia and USSR, 1930–80*, Association of Asian Studies Conference, March 22, 2021 (viewed online).

TABLE 2.2. Titles and Circulation of Official Propaganda Publications of the USA and the USSR

| Name | Language | Periodicity | Year Established | Circulation (1961) |
|---|---|---|---|---|
| American Embassy Newsletter | English | Weekly | 1960 | 23,720 |
| American Labour Review | English | Monthly | 1957 | 10,987 |
| American Review | English | Quarterly | 1956 | 7,800 |
| American Reporter | English | Fortnightly | 1951 | 69,097* |
| American Reporter | Hindi | Fortnightly | 1951 | 77,096* |
| American Reporter | Telugu | Fortnightly | 1956 | 17,944 |
| American Reporter | Bengali | Fortnightly | 1951 | 46,337 |
| American Reporter | Malayalam | Fortnightly | 1958 | 17,647 |
| American Reporter | Tamil | Fortnightly | 1951 | 49,352 |
| American Sandesh | Gujarati | Fortnightly | 1960 | 16,505 |
| American Vartahar | Maharashtra | Fortnightly | 1958 | 23,520 |
| News and Views from the Soviet Union | English | Triweekly | 1959 | 8,404 |
| Soviet Bhumi | Hindi | Fortnightly | 1950 | 43,833 |
| Soviet Bhumi | Telugu | Fortnightly | 1950 | 14,341 |
| Soviet Des | Punjabi | Fortnightly | 1956 | 8,541 |
| Soviet Desh | Assamese | Fortnightly | 1961 | 6,000* |
| Soviet Desh | Marathi | Fortnightly | 1957 | 13,458 |
| Soviet Desh | Urdu | Fortnightly | 1954 | 17,167 |
| Soviet Desh | Gujarati | Fortnightly | 1957 | 30,483 |
| Soviet Desha | Kannada | Fortnightly | 1957 | 10,175 |
| Soviet Desha | Kannada | Fortnightly | 1957 | 10,175 |
| Soviet Land | English | Fortnightly | 1948 | 40,000 |
| Soviet Nad | Malayalam | Fortnightly | 1956 | 12,624 |
| Soviet Nadu | Tamil | Fortnightly | 1954 | 19,666 |
| Soviet Okkutada Samachar Vichara | Kannada | Biweekly | 1961 | |
| Soviet Sang Ke Vichar Aur Samachar | Hindi | Triweekly | 1947 | 1,009 |
| Soviet Union Ceytikaḷum Karuttukaḷum | Tamil | Biweekly | 1956 | 425 |
| Soviet Union De Samachar Te Vichar | Punjabi | Biweekly | 1952 | 276 |
| Soviet Union Na Samachar Ane Vichar | Gujarati | Daily | 1957 | |
| Soviet Union Samarcharni Vichar | Marathi | Daily | 1957 | 490* |
| Soviet Union Ki Khabren Aur Raen | Urdu | Triweekly | 1947 | 663 |
| Soviet Union Varthakalum Abhi Prayan Galum | Malayalam | Triweekly | 1954 | 272 |

TABLE 2.2. (*continued*)

| Name | Language | Periodicity | Year Established | Circulation (1961) |
|---|---|---|---|---|
| Soviet Union Varthalu Vyakhyalu | Telugu | Triweekly | 1949 | 562 |
| Soviet Yuktaraster Sangabad-O-Abhimat | Bengali | Triweekly | 1957 | 700 |
| Soviet Unioner Sambad-O-Abhimat | Oriya | Triweekly | 1957 | 490* |

Source: *Press in India* (New Delhi: Ministry of Information and Broadcasting), various.
*1962 figures provided where 1961 figures are unavailable.

These founders were often "knit together by common prejudices and animosities rather than common convictions and principles," not unlike exiled interwar Indian revolutionaries with whom Lotvala had come in contact during the 1920s.[183] They had been bureaucrats, former revolutionaries, and journalists. Some were lapsed communists of the Trotskyist variety, whose anticommunist zeal heightened after the Government of India's temporary ban of the Communist Party of India in 1948.[184] Most had been involved in some way or other in the freedom movement. All had been profoundly touched by it. Some continued to speak of utopias. Others preferred to weigh in on worldly topics.

Anticommunism and the use of the English language were the lowest common denominator of these organizations. Their closeness to superpower propaganda efforts varied. The Indian branch of the International Congress for Cultural Freedom (ICCF) received CIA funding, news of which became public in the 1960s. It published propaganda through a Democratic Research Service, a current affairs magazine called *Freedom First*, and a literary magazine called *Quest*.[185] Foreign editorial oversight appears unlikely, although there may have been constraints on the kind of news and texts they received.[186] Of the others in the web, *Thought* (which lost ICCF funding by the mid-1950s), *Swarajya*, *Current*, and *MysIndia* magazines discussed current affairs (see Figure 2.3).

183. Evelyn Roy, quoted in Harper, *Underground Asia*, 408.
184. On the Trotskyists in Asia, see Charles Wesley Ervin, *Tomorrow Is Ours: The Trotskyist Movement in India and Ceylon, 1935–48* (Colombo, Sri Lanka: Social Scientists' Association, 2006).
185. The discussion of Minoo Masani in chapter 4 elaborates on this.
186. Margery Sabin, *Dissenters and Mavericks: Writings about India in English, 1765–2000* (New York: Oxford University Press, 2002), 141–56. In the Latin American context, see *Neither Peace Nor Freedom: The Cultural Cold War in Latin America* (Cambridge, MA: Harvard University Press, 2015).

FIGURE 2.3. MysIndia Cover (*MysIndia*, August 3, 1958).

The Bharatiya Vidya Bhavan, the Forum of Free Enterprise, the Radical Humanist Association, the Indian Rationalist Association, the Hindu nationalist Society for the Defense of Freedom in Asia, and the *Organiser* newspaper each supported specific causes or ideologies, sometimes of their own creation. The texts published by these organizations could move far from their origins in India's major cities, reaching readers deep in the mofussil and even overseas.

TABLE 2.3. Circulation Figures of Selected Magazines by 1960

| Periodical | Frequency | City of Origin | Free Copies | Sold Copies | Total Circulation |
|---|---|---|---|---|---|
| *Blitz** | Weekly | Bombay | 4,518 | 82,668 | 87,186 |
| *Current* | Weekly | Bombay | 1,158 | 9,510 | 10,668 |
| *Indian Libertarian* | Biweekly | Bombay | 513 | 150 | 663 |
| *MysIndia* | Weekly | Bangalore | 436 | 13,048 | 13,484 |
| *Organiser* | Weekly | Delhi | 915 | 6,733 | 7,648 |
| *Radical Humanist* | Weekly | Calcutta | 200 | 2,441 | 2,641 |
| *Seminar** | Monthly | New Delhi | 800 | 725 | 1,525 |
| *Swarajya* | Weekly | Madras | 737 | 15,719 | 16,456 |
| *Thought* | Weekly | Delhi | 497 | 9,397 | 9,894 |

Source: *Press in India 1960, Part Two*
*denotes inclusion for comparison.

The circulation figures of the periodicals in this web indicate an appreciable audience. As one might expect, they sold fewer copies than comparable magazines associated with the left, like *Seminar* and *Blitz*. The figures (reproduced in Table 2.3) suggest two distinct tiers of magazines. The *Indian Libertarian* and *Radical Humanist* fall into a more esoteric and lower-circulating category. *MysIndia*, *Swarajya*, and *Current* fall into a more popularly minded and higher circulating category. Articles on free economy appearing across these journals would reach tens of thousands of readers. The readership could include prominent men of affairs who might contribute similar material to mainstream newspapers and further spread and develop these ideas.[187]

Mutual reinforcement and support between the organizations constituting this web, or connected cluster, helped them keep each other alive. This collective action of those generally at the ideological margins of economic and political discourse became apparent around 1956, the year the Second Five-Year Plan commenced. Leaders opened branches for each other in different cities. They invited each other to deliver public lectures. Where possible, they tried to have kindred spirits open branches in other cities. Several struggled for funds. They knew that they were not popular. Bombay's Forum of Free Enterprise, for example, sent most of its pamphlets free of charge to libraries and universities. It did not expect to win its targeted audience over.[188] Readers had the option of purchasing bundled subscriptions to various magazines

187. See the next chapter.
188. Stanley Kochanek, *Business and Politics in India* (Berkeley: University of California Press, 1974), 204–6.

and buying the books of one organization under the auspices of another. And finally, exchanges between the proprietors of magazines could help them sharpen and define their views. The renaming of the institute journal in 1956 as the *Indian Libertarian* instead of the earlier the *Libertarian* (1951–52) came after vigorously debating Roy's Radical Humanists about the merits of the nation state.[189] Together, these organizations amounted to more than the sum of their parts.

Compared with the others in the web, the institute's magazine operated in the most self-consciously pedagogical fashion. The magazine interspersed aphorisms and short passages of philosophy and social theory alongside current affairs commentary and engendered a habit of "slow reading." Readers might store the magazine and turn back to it later for these pearls of wisdom.[190] A subscriber from a far-away town or regional university might use it as a form of distance education and seek clarification through a letter to the editor. There is evidence that the *Indian Libertarian* was read as far away as the village of Trikkur in the southern state of Kerala.[191] It was also the only magazine run by a woman other than the *Radical Humanist*, which Ellen Roy took over after her husband's death.[192]

The target audience for this literature would have been sections of Indian society growing increasingly literate and educated during this period, especially in larger cities. Enrollment in educational institutions across India rose more than fivefold during the first two decades after independence. The number of school graduates roughly replaced the number of literate people. The tertiary sector registered the largest enrollment gain. The number of Indian universities grew from twenty-five to eighty-nine. Enrollment increased by a factor of five.[193] Between 1955–60, when publications like the *Indian Libertarian* came into being, periodical circulation rose from eleven million to nineteen million.[194] The increase was concentrated in the four largest cities of Bombay, Calcutta, Delhi, and Madras.[195]

189. "Where We Differ from the *Radical Humanist*," *FER*, August 1, 1954.

190. I borrow this term from Isabel Hofmeyr's wonderful discussion of Mahatma Gandhi's *Indian Opinion*. See Isabel Hofmeyr, *Gandhi's Printing Press: Experiments in Slow Reading* (Cambridge, MA: Harvard University Press, 2013).

191. D. V. Nathan, "English—the National Language of India," *IL*, February 1, 1959.

192. The *Radical Humanist* continues in print to this day. See Sibnarayan Ray, *In Freedom's Quest: A Study of the Life and Works of M. N. Roy*, vol. 4, pt. 2 (1946–54) (Kolkata: Renaissance Publishers, 2007), especially 298–304.

193. Chopra, ed., *Gazetteer*, vol. 3, 143–49.

194. *Press in India* (New Delhi: Ministry of Information and Broadcasting, various).

195. *Press in India*, various.

Free economy's fuzziness aided its movement beyond the pages of the *Indian Libertarian*. As it spread across the web, it could become different things to different people. But all of them were convinced that the Indian state had appropriated too much control over the economy and was on its way to totalitarianism. Three old acquaintances of Lotvala's made unusually common cause with the Indian libertarians: K. M. Munshi, S. Ramanathan, and Philip Spratt. Munshi, who would go on to become vice president of the Swatantra Party, wrote for Lotvala's early newspapers and frequented the Gurjar Sabha in in the late 1910s and 1920s.[196] Ramanathan and Lotvala met in 1932 in London, where they discussed rationalism and caste reform.[197] Spratt came to India as an emissary of the Communist Party of Great Britain at a time when Lotvala had been a leading patron of the left.[198] Their distinct paths intersected once again with Lotvala's as they advanced alternative political programs and critiqued the trajectories of the Congress-led state.

K. M. Munshi oversaw the activities of the Bombay-based Bharatiya Vidya Bhavan (Institute of Indian Culture, 1938–) following a long and distinguished career as a lawyer and politician, and man of letters.[199] His association with Lotvala dated back to the Gurjar Sabha. Devoted to reinjecting Hindu cultural values into Indian life, the Bhavan took part in a range of educational activities. It created and managed schools across the country. The organization's biweekly *Bhavan's Journal* boasted an appreciable circulation of 26,839 copies by 1960.[200] The Bhavan became most famous for its accessibly priced books, especially translations of the Hindu epics.[201] Sometimes, it published affordable Indian versions of anticommunist works like *The God That Failed*.[202] Although the

196. Yagnik, *Life*, 27, 30.

197. A. R. Venkatachalapathy, "From Erode to Volga: Periyar EVR's Soviet and European Tour, 1932," in *India and the World in the First Half of the Twentieth Century*, ed. Madhavan Palat (New York: Routledge, 2018), 102–33.

198. Spratt, *Blowing up India: Reminiscences and Reflections of a Former Comintern* (Calcutta: Prachi Prakashan, 1955).

199. V. B. Kulkarni, *K. M. Munshi* (New Delhi: Ministry of Information and Broadcasting, 1983), 6.

200. *Press in India 1960–Part Two*, 85.

201. We discuss these and the Bhavan's role in a kind of commodification of religious texts in the next chapter. The price of the volume is taken from Munshi, "General Editor's Preface," in Rajagopalachari, *Mahabharata* (Bombay: Bharatiya Vidya Bhavan, 1958), v.

202. Another such title was philosopher John Dewey's *Freedom and Culture*. "Munshi's Correspondences reg. Bharatiya Vidya Bhavan, Bombay, 1954," File 173, Microfilm Accession 2277, K. M. Munshi Papers (hereafter KMM), NAI, 234–35.

organization typically steered clear of political conflict, it once published an
Indian edition of an American book with inaccurate, offensive depictions of
the Prophet Muhammad. Book sections reproduced in a newspaper set off
Hindu-Muslim riots in three states.[203] The event caused embarrassment to
Munshi and threw a shadow of doubt over the Bhavan's activities.

Munshi's political positions illustrate a kinship between Hindu revivalism
and anticommunism, both of which went against the Nehruvian program.[204]
He had been a major figure at the Constituent Assembly. Munshi sat in ten of
its thirteen subcommittees and authored the version used as the template for
the fundamental rights section of the constitution. Notably, his version, unlike
others, included no political safeguards for minorities or provisions to remedy
the country's social and economic inequalities. Instead, he prioritized unity.[205]
A similar attitude underpinned his opposition to separate electorates for
Dalits; he took the revivalist line that they could be integrated into Indian
society as equals without trouble.[206]

Munshi used the Bhavan as an anticommunist platform on occasion, connecting socialism to communism and the latter to the death of religion. At a
1957 "grand symposium on the Welfare State" held at Bhavan's College, he argued that a planned welfare state could not come into being without adopting
totalitarian methods. He bemoaned the rhetoric of socialism and the welfare
state for focusing purely on material ends and not ethical, religiously grounded

203. Munshi's defense was that the publication of the book was an editorial oversight and
that the newspaper had incited violence. See Devika Sethi, *War over Words: Censorship in India,
1930–1960* (New Delhi: Cambridge University Press, 2019), 233–45.

204. Munshi believed India to be a Hindu nation with a glorious past. "Fanatical" Muslims
created interreligious violence. Because he thought they had Hindu blood from generations
ago, Munshi did not consider them real minorities. In the 1940s, Munshi set up the Akhand
Hindusthan (Undivided India) Front to prevent Partition and assert the unity of the country.
Furthermore, as the agent-general to the Muslim-majority princely state of Hyderabad, he was
involved in the violent process of securing its accession to India. The author of a book called *Jai
Somnath* (1940), he also spearheaded the movement for the reconstruction of the Somnath
Temple in 1951, on the site of a standing mosque. See S. R. Sharma, *Munshi,* 19; V. P. Menon, *The
Story of the Integration of the Indian States,* 337–68; Raghavan, *War and Peace in Modern India,*
76; Bhagavan, "The Hindutva Underground."

205. Erdman, *The Swatantra Party and Indian Conservatism,* 101; Munshi, *Pilgrimage to Freedom,* 116; Shefali Jha, "Secularism in the Constituent Assembly Debates, 1946–1950," *Economic
and Political Weekly* 37, no. 30 (2002): 3175–80; Elangovan, *Norms and Politics,* 211–17.

206. Kulkarni, *Munshi,* 175.

ways of living.[207] On another occasion, addressing a Bhavan audience on "Despotisms Old and New," Munshi warned that "many and various are the slogans like nationalization and planned economy, which are intended completely to annihilate private property. In the name of secularism, it tries to kill religion." Munshi reckoned that parliamentary democracies around the world could easily swing in a totalitarian direction and that the United States and the United Kingdom were the two countries most able to avoid going down this path.[208]

Available evidence suggests that Munshi preferred individual effort and faith in God to active effort by the state to secure social and economic objectives.[209] On the matter of just compensation for the acquisition of private property by the state, he insisted on the right of judicial review.[210] He also sought unsuccessfully to include the right to free trade as a fundamental right in the constitution.[211] Later on, as republican India's first food minister (1950–52), Munshi encouraged citizens to forgo meals to conserve food resources.[212] He considered accepting foreign aid only as a last resort.

Neither the Congress nor the constitution defined Philip Spratt's life. Instead, the editor of *MysIndia* and the founder of the Bangalore branch of the Libertarian Social Institute spent his life reckoning with communism, first as its emissary and then as its bitter opponent. Sent by the Communist Party of Great Britain to help spread communism in India, Spratt went to prison in

207. B. S. Sanyal, "Mr. Nehru and his Critics," *IL*, October 1, 1957. The text was later reprinted as Munshi, "Welfare Implies Freedom," *IL*, October 15, 1957.

208. Munshi, "Despotism: Old and New," January 29, 1959, File 225, Microfilm Accession 2283, KMM, NAI, 49–56.

209. In one example, after good rains came to Madras in 1952, he complimented the state's erstwhile chief minister, C. Rajagopalachari: "I am sure you are going to go down to posterity as the miracle-worker, for you prayed to God for rain, as the great Bhakta, Narsi Mehta did, and lo and behold! The rains came." Munshi to Rajagopalachari, June 9, 1952 Correspondences with Munshi, Installment V, CRP, NMML.

210. Munshi, *Constituent Assembly Debates*, September 12, 1949; Munshi, *Pilgrimage to Freedom*, 302–5.

211. Elangovan, *Norms and Politics*, 220.

212. Siegel, *Hungry Nation*; Sherman, "From 'Grow More Food' to "Miss a Meal': Hunger, Development and the Limits of Post-Colonial Nationalism in India, 1947–57," *South Asia: Journal of South Asian Studies* 36, no. 4 (2013): 571–88. Considering spiritual and economic issues as entangled rather than separate, Munshi kept metaphysical diaries asking God to help resolve the problem. See "Diary Note," File 260A, Microfilm Accession 2288, KMM, NAI.

connection with the Meerut Conspiracy. He read widely and reflected critically upon his political commitments during the time in jail. For the first time, he read about Indian history and Gandhi's ideas. What struck him about Gandhi was that he had an ethics to his political practice, something Spratt found absent from Marxism. India's distinctive history made him skeptical of the notion that "all civilizations form the same course of evolution" that his admittedly "inattentive" reading of Marx gave him. Gandhi appealed to the puritan in Spratt. He embraced nonviolence after this carceral spell.

Spratt broke decisively with communism when the Soviet Union invaded Finland in 1939.[213] He developed pro-American and pro-private enterprise attitudes and served as Secretary for the Congress for Cultural Freedom as the Cold War unfolded.[214] His book, *Diamat as Philosophy of Nature* (1958), was published by the Libertarian Social Institute. It sought to strike at the analytical foundations of Marxist thought in dialectical materialism and thereby discredit communism.[215] Poking holes in this interpretation was an overtly partisan activity of the Cold War.[216] The Hindu nationalist Sita Ram Goel, who published anticommunist literature from his Calcutta-based Society for the Defense of Freedom in Asia, perceived the need for such a text in India. Like

213. Spratt, *Blowing Up India*, 55–65.

214. Ramachandra Guha, *Rebels against the Raj: Western Fighters for India's Freedom* (New York: Penguin, 2022), 322–24.

215. "Diamat" originated in Marx and Engels' desire to place the idealist philosopher G.W.F. Hegel's schema for explaining the unity of thought and being on a materialist foundation. Engels understood Hegelian logic to rest on three laws—the unity and conflict of opposites, the law of the passage of quantitative into qualitative changes, and the law of the negation of the negation. Marx and Engels "turned this on its head" by using this interpretive framework to explain material changes in the mode of production and social relations across epochs. However, the term "dialectical materialism" as such owes credit to their successors. See Z. A. Jordan, *The Evolution of Dialectical Materialism* (London: Macmillan, 1967). During the 1930s, Stalin produced a somewhat dogmatic interpretation of dialectical materialism meant to furnish a "science of the history of society" to guide all policy; he had it adopted formally by the USSR. Spratt played upon the inconsistencies in its articulation and said that it was no different from Hegelianism. By choosing the scientific, Stalinist reading of dialectical materialism and pointing to the normative quality of its Hegelian antecedent, Spratt believed he was discrediting dialectical materialism altogether. See Philip Spratt, *Diamat as Philosophy of Nature* (Bombay: Libertarian Social Institute, 1958).

216. On this, see *Collected Works of Lenin*, 2nd edition, vol. 38, (Moscow: Progress Publishers, 1965), 220–22, https://www.marxists.org/archive/lenin/works/1914/cons-logic/summary.htm; Stefan Kipfer, "Preface" in *Henri Lefebvre, Dialectical Materialism*, trans. John Sturrock, 2nd edition (Minneapolis: University of Minnesota Press, 2009), xiii–xxxii.

Spratt, Goel was also a lapsed communist. He encouraged Spratt to take on the task. Like Spratt, his organization had some connection to the institute: subscribers to the *Indian Libertarian* could apply to receive Goel's newsletter free of charge.[217]

The encounter with communism featured in a distinct but significant fashion in the life of S. Ramanathan. The Madras-based Tamil social reformer and thinker founded and edited the *Indian Rationalist* journal. His life paralleled Lotvala's most closely in its emphasis on social reform.[218] By 1925, he had started the Self-Respect Movement with the Tamil social reformer Periyar (Great One) E. V. Ramaswami. The atheistic movement contested Brahmin power in Tamil society and politics and advocated for social reform via "rationalism." However, following a dispute with Periyar over whether senior figures of the movement should contest elections under a communist banner, he left the movement in 1932. Ramanathan believed that partaking of electoral politics would dilute their mission of social reform. He reckoned that communism would not work in the Indian social system.[219]

By 1958, Ramanathan believed that rationalists in India should adopt a political ideology that espoused an economic system of "democratically controlled capitalism" in which "the government plays the part of the Umpire in industrial conflicts." Ramanathan called it "Libertarianism." It was to be distinct from both "Laissez-faire Capitalism and Socialism." Such a system promised to avoid monopolies on the one hand and a large "unscrupulous bureaucracy" on the other.[220] Ramanathan considered libertarianism to be both a decentralist political economy that avoided concentrations of power in either the state

217. Sita Ram Goel, *How I Became a Hindu* (New Delhi: Voice of India, 1982). In the 1980s, Goel went on to run a publishing house called Voice of India focused on the construction of the Hindu self and non-Hindu other through English-language writings on Hinduism. See M. Riza Pirbhai, "Demons in Hindutva: Writing a Theology for Hindu Nationalism," *Modern Intellectual History* 5, no. 1 (2008): 27–53.

218. In his youth, Ramanathan experienced caste prejudice from Brahmins while studying in school and college. Exclusion by Brahmins from a college picnic was a notable event in Ramanathan's life that informed his subsequent political career. See E. S. Visswanathan, *The Political Career of E. V. Ramaswami Naicker: A Study in the Politics of South India, 1920–1949* (Madras: Ravi and Vasanth, 1983), 18, 35–39, 71–72.

219. Visswanathan, *The Political Career*, 138–48, 174–75, 194. On the non-Brahmin movement, see M.S.S. Pandian, *Brahmin and Non-Brahmin: Genealogies of the Tamil Political Present* (Ranikhet: Permanent Black, 2003).

220. Ramanathan, "A Political Ideology for India," reprinted in *The Indian Rationalist*, November–December 1958, 8–11.

or private enterprise, and a rationalist school of thinking with antecedents in ancient Indian knowledge systems. In the pages of the institute magazine, he attempted to reconstruct an Indian lineage for rationalism by locating its origins in the materialist philosophy of *Lokāyatā*.[221]

A shared animosity toward communism knitted together the Hindu revivalist lawyer Munshi, the lapsed revolutionary and magazine editor Spratt, and the rationalist social reformer Ramanathan. They interpreted Indian libertarianism in their own ways. This reflected their understanding of its kinship to their political projects. It was also strategic; turning to economic issues allowed them to amplify their own projects in an "economic age."

The history of the connected cluster of associations and periodicals in India—run by figures like Lotvala, Munshi, Spratt, and Ramanathan—is part of a wider global history of anticommunism. It meant more than just ideological opposition to the idea that communism was the endpoint of history or opposition to communist parties. Rather, anticommunism could be a set of dispositions against collectivist organization or any form of statism. Inverting the communist conviction that the endpoint of historical development was communism, anticommunists often warned that any form of collectivism or state intervention could lead to a totalitarian state of the Stalinist variety. However, anticommunism did not amount to a well-theorized ideology. It was a "symbolic glue" that brought together figures with diverse and, at times, "divergent priorities, concerns, and interests."[222]

## Toward Electoral Politics

Having used this web to spread free economy, the institute's leadership next sought to use it to spread the idea of a new opposition party to the Congress in electoral politics. Although not the first to make this call, the institute's

---

221. He wrote a six-part series of articles in *IL* between September 1960 and February 1961 under the title "Lokāyatā: Indian Materialism." Followers of Lokāyatā consider perception the sole means to knowledge, consciousness a product of matter, and pleasure the only goal in life. See Pradeep Gokhale, *Lokāyata/Cārvakā: A Philosophical Inquiry* (New Delhi: Oxford University Press, 2015).

222. Lisa McGirr, *Suburban Warriors: The Origins of the American Right* (Princeton: Princeton University Press, 2001), 36. Indeed, this history dates back even before the Cold War in some cases. Consider, for example, the Vatican's transnational project in the interwar period to forge a Catholic anticommunist internationalism, which involved collaboration with Nazis and Italian Fascists. See Giuliana Chamedes, *A Twentieth-Century Crusade: The Vatican's Battle to Remake Christian Europe* (Cambridge, MA: Harvard University Press, 2019).

erstwhile research director B. S. Sanyal was perhaps the first person to outline a strategy for such a party's formation and a possible platform.[223] Sanyal was an anticommunist philosopher who dreamed of future order and of the peaceful coexistence of states and cultural systems under a "world liberal culture," wherein freedom would allow culture to flourish.[224]

Sanyal chafed against "welfare sentiments." The people to combat these were "eminent persons, from different ranks of public life, representing different interests and movements: the Libertarians, the Radical Humanists, the Forum of Free Enterprise, the Democratic Research Service, the Jan Sangh, some independent journals, economic and cultural, etc." This "group of economic thinkers" was "trying to make us aware of the growing dangers of state interventionism and propaganda by the believers in [sic] 'welfare' principle and socialist pattern." He suggested that "liberal" or "enlightened" Hindus—possibly thinking of Munshi's Bharatiya Vidya Bhavan—and "free enterprisers" could coalesce and make libertarianism the bedrock of a new political ideology. A philosophical affinity between the "neo-Hegelian" writings of Ludwig von Mises in defense of free market economy, and an "individualist theory of state," which he believed had Hindu philosophical origins, offered grounds for unity.[225] Given the tenor of the magazine by this time, "liberal Hindus" most likely excluded the Hindu nationalists of the RSS and the Jana Sangh. However, it may very well still have been compatible with majoritarian sentiments.

Next, two anonymous editorials in the *Indian Libertarian* laid out a doctrine and strategy for a new political party. These responded explicitly to calls by ex-Congress leaders for a new opposition.[226] A doctrine for "a Rightist Conservative Party," the first editorial observed, would be one that safeguarded property. It would have to undertake the difficult task of maintaining religious

223. Limited biographical details are available about Sanyal. He published a book called *Culture: An Introduction* (Bombay: Asia Publishing House, 1962), most of which he wrote under the auspices of the institute. Sanyal later took up a position in philosophy at the Indian Institute of Technology (IIT) at Bombay, publishing *Ethics and Meta-Ethics* (Delhi: Vikas, 1970) and *Introduction to Logic* (Ajmer: Sachin Publications, 1979) during this tenure there. He retired from IIT in 1980. See "Retired Faculty," *Humanities and Social Sciences Department,* accessed at Indian Institute of Technology Bombay, http://www.hss.iitb.ac.in/en/people/retired-faculty.

224. Sanyal, *Culture: An Introduction* (Bombay: Asia Publishing House, 1962), 33.

225. The 1957 *IL* pieces in which Sanyal made these points ran under the titles: "The Welfare Sentiments" (July 1), "Welfarism and Poverty" (July 15), "Bread and Circuses" (August 1, A–B), "Welfarism and Inequality" (August 15, C), "Thus Spake Nehru at Jammu" (October 1, 10, 14), and "Mr. Nehru and his Critics," (October 1, 13–14).

226. On this, see the next two chapters.

institutions and the social order from a "rational point of view," one that would observe traditions of tolerance and learning. This new conservative doctrine would provide a counterpoint to collectivism and assert consumer sovereignty. It would support a heavy land tax to redress income inequality. A thin state would ensure the abolition of unnecessary intermediaries between community and individual users in production relations. Government would exist to preserve the law and run public utilities. Private companies and voluntary agencies would provide insurance for the public. Pension schemes and minimum wage legislation could continue until self-help associations could replace them. Educational institutions were to be accessible to all and purely run by teachers, independent of any attempts to set their agenda by the state.[227] Fealty to this outline of the state would vary in free economy discourse and politics, especially the points about land taxation and wages. But it concretely broke from the dominant economic imaginary.

Mobilizing "tens of thousands of workers" behind these "new ideas" required creating a broad-based appeal. The editorial put down tactics for mobilization that self-consciously evoked forms of organization Indians had been using from at least the nineteenth century to wage "epistemic insurgency" as they formulated Indian political thought.[228] Here, proponents of a new party stood to gain from what the editorial described as the Congress' amorphousness as an umbrella party of consensus accommodating various constituencies. To woo its supporters away, the editorial suggested placing nation before religion, stressing democracy for all, and adopting a harsher tone against Pakistan. For the Congress was now devoid of a clear vision and suffered from a cadre of social climbers and careerists, the author alleged. There was an opportunity to develop "a sphere of alternative ideas, covering every field of current problems—economic, social, political and constitutional." The "libertarian ideology" could be spread through "Libertarian societies, Adam Smith Clubs, Liberal Clubs, Current Affairs Clubs etc." Debate, discussion and journals like "*Indian Libertarian* and *MysIndia*, *Thought* and *Organiser*, *Swarajya* and *Current*" could help generate "exchange of thought and mutual enlightenment." Over time, this might create a new, distinct political consciousness, "an all-India association for political action."[229]

227. Chanakya, "The Basis for a New Political Party," *IL*, October 1, 1957.
228. Bayly, *Recovering Liberties*, 105.
229. Chanakya, "The Sanction for a New Political Party," *IL*, October 15, 1957.

The institute increasingly devoted its energies toward promoting the Swatantra Party. Lotvala wrote to Munshi and another ex-Gurjar Sabha colleague M. A. Master, head of the Forum of Free Enterprise, to do the same. "The Congress government has created vested interests everywhere and it is no easy task to dislodge the Congress from power," he urged Munshi.[230] He lambasted Master for rejecting his earlier suggestion that the Forum of Free Enterprise "organize itself politically to fight the Congress government," because it was a "non-political organization" and "purely educational body."[231] In these two desperate pleas were faint echoes of the long dormant young radical who had not spared any risk or expense to propagate new political ideas earlier in his life.

———

Free economy came to life as a unifying rhetoric for various forms of discontent expressed against the developmentalism to which the Nehruvian state hitched its legitimacy.[232] It acquired purchase in an environment of new controls on business administered by the state, of rising inflation, and increasing taxes. As free economy matured, its originators jettisoned their Hindu bigotry and discomfort with Indian secularism. Instead, they embraced a more explicitly economic platform against the developmental anti-politics of the time. The early history of free economy in India parallels the American history of free enterprise in some respects. The Nehruvian state, like the New Deal state, was the defined enemy. The partisans of free economy and those of free enterprise shared contact with the early progenitors of neoliberalism. More generally, the rightward drift in the politics of those once associated with Indian communism and socialism has parallels across the postwar world.

In other ways, the Indian example is unique. Unlike the free enterprisers, who were later co-opted into the agenda of the Republican Party in the United States, the Indian libertarians pre-dated the creation of the Swatantra Party. It was these libertarians who called for opposition to the Congress. The Indian

230. Lotvala to K. M. Munshi, January 27, 1960, Microfilm Accession 2290, File 290, KMM, NAI, 291.

231. Lotvala to M. A. Master, January 28, 1960, File 290, Microfilm Accession 2290, File 290, KMM, NAI, 292.

232. Benjamin Zachariah, *Playing the Nation-Game: The Ambiguities of Nationalism in India* (New Delhi: Yoda Press, 2011), 252–53.

libertarians were also far removed from the Indian academy, whereas American free enterprisers had strong ties to university academics. Indian libertarians may have been elites, but they were not experts. More than other kinds of American libertarianism and free enterprise thought, Indian libertarianism's agrarian focus made it resemble rural decentralism.

Free economy's flexibility meant that it could bring together Indian anti-communists of various kinds and be reconciled with multiple visions of an alternative economic model. Those visions, and how constituencies became attached to the politicians advancing them, are explored in the chapters that follow. The Lotvalas paved the way for them.

# PART II
# People, Ideas, Practices

# 3

# Conservative Opposition to the "Permit-and-License *Raj*"

THE APRIL 15, 1960, issue of the *Indian Libertarian* featured an article with the Manichean title "Prosperity or Bankruptcy?" Its author, C. Rajagopala-chari, argued that prosperity required "private initiative, management with personal interest, and honest competition." India could draw lessons from the "three miracles" of West Germany, France, and Japan. Rajagopalachari, affectionately known as Rajaji, asserted that the country ought to steer clear of Congress' "wild-cat schemes" and "the hollowness of socialist promises." Plans merely increased the size of the bureaucracy and came with the heavy price of large, inflation-generating budget deficits. Rajagopalachari particularly warned of the consequences of an expanding bureaucracy in an environment where the boundary between party and government was porous: "It is here that a party which cannot command the government exchequer and the power that a regimented economy gives to the official party finds the greatest obstacle," he reckoned.[1] Citizens would not be able to resist the temptation to bribe wayward officials. The following year, Rajagopalachari quoted from the *Indian Libertarian*'s pages multiple times in his own writing. He sent a message of felicitation for its Diwali (Festival of Lights) issue, praising the "inspiring leadership of Shri R. B. Lotvala" as "most timely in this age of tyrannical demagogy."[2]

---

1. C. Rajagopalachari, "Prosperity or Bankruptcy?" *IL*, February 15, 1960.

2. "Rajaji's Message: 'The Work of the *Indian Libertarian* Timely and Important in this Age of Demagogy,'" *IL*, November 15, 1961. Examples of Rajagopalachari quoting the magazine include "Socialism in Deep Eclipse," *Swarajya*, March 12, 1960, and "Dear Reader," *Swarajya*, July 28, 1962.

The *Swarajya* (Freedom) magazine in which Rajagopalachari wrote almost weekly formed part of the same connected cluster of periodicals as the *Indian Libertarian*. It drew financial support from Tamil communities engaged in small enterprise and styled itself as a form of elite consumption for the thinking man. In *Swarajya*'s pages, Rajagopalachari interpreted the observations of neoliberal economists in light of the Indian present and struck an anticommunist tone.

Rajagopalachari worried that one-party dominance would breed authoritarianism and, later, military rule, as it had in other postcolonial societies. His lasting formulation, "permit-and-license raj," called into question the fruits of independence by suggesting that India now lived under the rule of permits and licenses controlled by bureaucrats. There was only one solution: "A real two-party system would alone furnish the healthy opportunity for beneficent osmosis. There would be no osmosis but meaningless dilution if we cut out this dividing membrane."[3] He cofounded the *Swatantra*, or Freedom Party, to help create this membrane in 1959. That year, he turned 80.

Rajagopalachari and his interlocutors came from an entirely different context than the lapsed leftists of the previous chapter. Well-versed in the intricacies of colonial law and administration, they sought to defend an agrarian order undergoing change on its own, against the designs of an expanding state.[4] They possessed a common-sense understanding of political economy, improvised from experience and observation of rural and mofussil life in the Madras Presidency and later Province. This contrasted the admittedly idiosyncratic, text-based understanding of Bombay's more cosmopolitan Indian libertarians.

For men like Rajagopalachari, free economy became a part of their political vocabulary for the defense of agrarian life and decentralized government. They did not frequently express opinions on the issue of gender and political economy; yet the occasional statements they made are revealing in this regard. These individuals had not engaged with ideas of political economy in the way that Lotvala had or spent their lives in commercial centers. They styled themselves as thinking men of affairs with cultivated tastes in history and literature,

3. Rajagopalachari, "Wanted: Real Two-Party System."

4. On the disconnect between language and consciousness, see Gareth Stedman Jones' classic extended essay "Rethinking Chartism" in his *Languages of Class: Studies in English Working-Class History, 1832–1982*, (Cambridge: Cambridge University Press, 1983), 90–178.

knowledge of Hindu scripture and observation of its Sanskritic rituals, and an appreciation of the regional Carnatic music. Their economic conservatism went along with a valorization of the institution of the joint family, appeals to continue with time-honored traditions, and celebration of culture.[5]

Rajagopalachari's understanding of economic issues was deeply imbricated in questions of morality. This may be traced to an earlier political career as a Gandhian, one so prominent that during the 1930s he was the leading candidate to be the Mahatma's political successor.[6] He repurposed the decentralization and antistatism of Gandhian thought and practice to a conservative political cause focused on issues of economy.

Long after the likes of Lotvala had abandoned their Gujarati-language publishing, Rajagopalachari and his associates maintained their position in the Tamil literary sphere. They used the widely circulated cultural magazine *Kalki* to bring discourses of economy into idioms intelligible to a much larger audience than the English-speaking elite. Reaching deep into Tamil society, *Kalki* conveyed Rajagopalachari's views in simple language. But, as he waded more deeply into policy debates in English during the second half of the 1950s, Rajagopalachari's writing increasingly referenced neoliberals and took on Cold War hues. His rhetorical register could become increasingly policy-oriented and disembedded from local context.

Although the Lotvalas had introduced free economy discourse, it was thanks to Rajagopalachari that an Indian economic conservatism blending anticommunism, neoliberal rhetoric, and the defense of property came together and was imagined as a platform for a democratic party. What were the intellectual origins of permit-and-license raj and the concerns about corruption and inflation that Rajagopalachari wrote about in the *Indian Libertarian*? How did English and Tamil print worlds become both threshing ground and conduit for his ideas and political project? And how does this revise our picture of the history of how economic ideas develop and spread?

5. On a parallel affinity between neoliberalism and social conservatism in the post–1970s United States, which helped drive a political movement to restore social welfare provision to the family, see Cooper, *Family Values*.

6. The key scholarly works on Rajagopalachari and his ideas are Anthony Copley, *The Political Career of C. Rajagopalachari: A Moralist in Politics* (New Delhi: Macmillan, 1978); Joanne Punzo Waghorne, *Images of Dharma: The Epic World of C. Rajagopalachari* (Delhi: Chanakya, 1985); and Vasanthi Srinivasan, *Gandhi's Conscience Keeper: C. Rajagopalachari and Indian Politics* (Ranikhet: Permanent Black, 2010).

## Rajagopalachari and (Embedded) Economic Common Sense: A Prehistory

Most Indians today would not know who Rajagopalachari was, despite his importance to the history of Indian nationalism and role in spearheading the formation of the Swatantra Party. A lawyer with a thriving practice in the large town of Salem in the region known before 1935 as Madras Presidency (see Map 3.1), C. Rajagopalachari was elected chairman of the Salem Municipal Corporation (1917–19) and cultivated a reputation as a social reformer. His central contribution to the nationalist movement was bringing South India behind the Congress through Gandhian politics.[7] For most of the 1920s and 1930s, he took with zeal to Gandhi's constructive program of social and economic practices outside of traditional forms of protest to widen the nationalist program to encompass everyday practices. Rajagopalachari especially embraced program objectives of simple living, anti-untouchability, prohibition, and hand-spinning of *khadi*.[8]

Rajagopalachari opposed the progressive turn in the Congress engineered by Nehru.[9] He made common cause with Patel and Rajendra Prasad (India's first president), and the three became known as the Congress Right. Although once touted as Gandhi's successor, Rajagopalachari lost favor with the Mahatma and the Congress by adopting the attitude that India should support the British effort in World War II and earn its freedom. This led Rajagopalachari to oppose the Quit India Movement (1942) and leave the party. He re-joined the Congress after a period away and came up with a "C. R. Formula" (1944) that allowed for the emergence of a separate Pakistan via plebiscite in Muslim-majority areas. The plan indicated a sincere understanding of minority rights and concerns but did not come to fruition. By this time, Rajagopalachari was sidelined in the Congress in favor of Jawaharlal Nehru and Vallabhbhai Patel. He served in the interim cabinet as minister of industry and supply, education, and finance and occupied the symbolic roles of governor of West Bengal, and governor general of India after independence.[10]

---

7. Christopher Baker, *The Politics of South India: 1920–37* (Cambridge: Cambridge University Press, 1976).

8. A. R. Copley, *Gandhi's Southern Commander* (Madras: Indo-British Historical Society, 1986).

9. Sarkar, *Modern India*, 412. A recent work on this group, which attempts to strip the term from all the negative connotations associated with use in the Western context, is Neerja Singh's *Patel, Prasad and Rajaji: Myth of the Indian Right* (New Delhi: Sage, 2015).

10. For a helpful review of the events of this period, see Bandyopadhyay, *From Plassey to Partition*, 405–72.

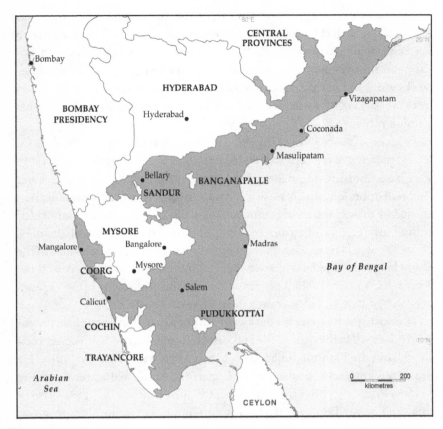

MAP 3.1. Madras Presidency (Jenny Sheehan and CartoGIS, College of Asia and the Pacific, Australian National University, 2022).

Following Patel's demise in 1950, Rajagopalachari spent a short period as home minister before retiring. He only managed to stay out of politics for two years. In the 1952 Madras State elections, the Communist Party performed much better than expected. Lukewarm results forced the Congress into a coalition partnership. Rajagopalachari emerged as a consensus figure to assume leadership of the state. Following a short term in office (1952–4), Rajagopalachari retired once again, continuing to read and write extensively. Sales of his abridged English translations of the *Mahabharata* (1951) and *Ramayana* (1957), published by K. M. Munshi's Bharatiya Vidya Bhavan, reached 100,000 copies by the end of the decade.[11]

11. Rajmohan Gandhi *Rajaji: A Life* (New Delhi: Penguin Books, 1997), 429–31. The size of the press runs appear in the frontmatter of Rajagopalachari, *Mahabharata* (Bombay: Bharatiya

These epics and his regular commentary in the mainstream press combined
to give Rajagopalachari the status of a wise man offering religious advice to
reflect on contemporary concerns.[12] In the Tamil public sphere, where Rajagopalachari already enjoyed a reputation as a major figure, reprints of his earlier
works appeared in magazines and new editions. Newspapers loyal to him
from the nationalist movement continued to cover his activities and carry his
opinion pieces.

Currents of progressive change brewing in Madras presented difficulties for
Rajagopalachari's regional career. He did not share the brewing interest in
state-based measures to ameliorate rural poverty through welfare schemes and
land redistribution, which arose as a response of sorts to social stratification
created by the expansion of commercial agriculture.[13] His rise also coincided
with a powerful Dravidian movement that asserted the historical distinctness
of the Tamil land from other parts of India and promoted a renaissance of the
Tamil language. The Dravidian movement attacked the hegemony of Rajagopalachari's native Brahmin community over the professions of the expanding colonial state and condemned them as Aryan invaders.[14]

Dravidian leaders rejected the Congress' brand of unitary nationalism consolidating itself in the region. The anti-caste reformer Periyar E. V. Ramaswami
singled out the Brahmin Rajagopalachari as a symbol of caste prejudice. He
organized protests against Rajagopalachari's attempts while premier of the
Madras Presidency to introduce Hindi teaching in schools.[15] Discourse of
this time painted Rajagopalachari as anti-Tamil and inimical to progress,

Vidya Bhavan, 1958), and Rajagopalachari, *Ramayana* (Bombay: Bharatiya Vidya Bhavan, 1968).
On the Bhavan, see the discussion in the section "Spreading the Word" in the previous chapter.

12. Ramachandra Guha, "The Wisest Man in India: Aspects of C. Rajagopalachari," in Guha,
*The Last Liberal and Other Essays* (Ranikhet: Permanent Black, 2003), 34–53.

13. David Washbrook, "Country Politics: Madras 1880 to 1930," *Modern Asian Studies* 7, no. 3
(1973): 475–531.

14. The South Indian varna order had no designations of Kshatriya (warrior) and Vaishya
(trader); there were only Brahmins, Sudras, and Dalits. The distinction between Brahmin and
non-Brahmin status was therefore even more stark than in other parts of the country. See Mar-
guerite Ross Barnett, *The Politics of Cultural Nationalism in South India* (Princeton: Princeton
University Press, 1976), 16–18.

15. See the discussion of Hindi language politics in the previous chapter. On the reaction to
Rajagopalachari's policies and leadership, see Sumathi Ramaswamy, *Passions of the Tongue: Language Devotion in Tamil India, 1891–1970* (Berkeley: University of California Press, 1997), 101–2,
169–72; M.S.S. Pandian, *Brahmin, Non-Brahmin: Genealogies of the Tamil Political Present* (Ranikhet:
Permanent Black, 2007) 188–92.

rejecting the Gandhian line that adopting a single Indian language would unify the country.

The progressive currents of Tamil politics stood in Rajagopalachari's way again when he served as chief minister of Madras (1952–54).[16] By this time, Congress had lost its electoral majority in the state elections, with communists making important headway. The regional leadership offered Rajagopalachari office to steady the boat. Rajagopalachari's undoing as chief minister the second time related to the authoritarian streak in his governing style and his inability to empathize with the social realities of caste. Claiming to widen the breadth of school education in a deficit state without increasing indebtedness, he introduced a scheme that reduced the length of daily classroom instruction and placed children in hereditary occupation training under their parents for the rest of the day. The measure promised to stretch teaching resources over a greater number of pupils and increase enrollment numbers.

Rajagopalachari rolled out the scheme without consulting anybody in his ministry. It provoked instant criticism from the leaders of the non-Brahmin Dravidian movement, especially Ramanathan's erstwhile comrade, Periyar E. V. Ramaswami. Rajagopalachari's rivals in Congress similarly rose in protest. Their argument ran that the hereditary occupation training would reify caste differences and entrench upper-caste privilege.[17] A stubborn Rajagopalachari doubled down and invested resources in publicizing and promoting the measure. Subsequently, leaders of the regional Congress apparatus successfully pressed for his resignation.[18] The era that followed saw the de-Brahminization of the Congress apparatus and an increase in the caste diversity of the personnel of the civil service.[19]

By the time he helped found the Swatantra Party, Rajagopalachari was a seasoned veteran of regional and national politics. His assumption of the mantle of political critic and opposition leader was the final act of the life of a man who rose to the forefront of Indian politics only to be relegated to its margins, come back, and then retreat once again into obscurity. Rajagopalachari was an

16. Gandhi, *The Rajaji Story: 1937–72* (Bombay: Bharatiya Vidya Bhavan, 1984), 224–56.

17. Pandian, *Brahmin, Non-Brahmin*, 200–10.

18. Copley, *The Political Career*, 310–20; Y. Vincent Kumaradoss, "Kamaraj Remembered," *Economic and Political Weekly* 39, no. 17 (2004): 1655–57.

19. D. Veeraraghavan's posthumously published book, *Half a Day for Caste? Education and Politics in Tamil Nadu, 1952–55*, ed. A. R. Venkatachalapathy (New Delhi: Leftword Books, 2019), gives a sophisticated social and political history of this episode.

independent-minded autodidact interested in an unusual range of subjects. He translated or adapted books on everything from plant biology to Marcus Aurelius' *Meditations*.[20] Despite being a moralist who projected himself as a wise man as the years went on, he never ignored the temptations or degradations of politics. Some principles he held on to dearly; others he did not hesitate to discard.

Rajagopalachari spent the majority of his first forty years of life in rural, and later mofussil, Madras Presidency. The contrast to the Lotvalas and most of their interlocutors could not have been greater. While he adhered to Gandhian politics like Nehru and Patel, unlike them he never studied in England or even traveled overseas until the 1960s. These mofussil origins shaped various aspects of his writing.

The increasing centralization of power by the provincial secretariat in Madras was the major political trend of the first half century of Rajagopalachari's life. Its insertion into the affairs of the mofussil provoked these areas to seek representation in politics.[21] Rajagopalachari's political importance to the nationalist movement lay in his ability to bring the mofussil behind Congress and wrest control over presidency politics from the Madras-based elites.[22] Throughout his life, the mofussil continued to help him maintain an enduring influence in politics. He used the Tamil press to reach beyond the urban centers.[23]

Rajagopalachari produced a prolific corpus of writing between the 1920s and 1940s. These included popular-education readers, short stories, articles, biographies of religious leaders, Tamil translations of scientific textbooks, and abridged editions of religious texts like the *Bhagavad Gita*. These appeared either serialized in periodicals, printed as standalone pamphlets, or collected as

20. Masti Venkatesa Iyengar, *Rajaji (A Study of His Personality)* vol. 2 (Bangalore: Jeevana Karyalaya, 1975), 99.

21. David Washbrook, *The Emergence of Provincial Politics: The Madras Presidency, 1870–1920* (Cambridge: Cambridge University Press, 1976).

22. Baker, *The Politics of South India, 1920–37* (Cambridge: Cambridge University Press, 1976), 247.

23. Washbrook, *The Emergence of Provincial Politics*, 226. The question of how the mofussil context related to a different envisioning and articulation of political ideas is discussed in Ali, *A Local History of Global Capital*, 108–36 and Mou Banerjee, "The Tale of the Tailor: Munshi Mohammad Meherullah and Muslim-Christian Apologetics in Bengal, 1885–1907," *South Asian Studies* 33, no. 2 (2017): 122–36.

low-cost paperbacks. During this period, economic issues appear embedded within other concerns but are rarely absent.

One can discern how Rajagopalachari's economic consciousness emerged by reading these texts in the context of his salient practices in office at the helm of Madras Presidency (1937–39) and later Madras State (1952–54). He came to espouse a broadly agrarian economic policy of restrained state intervention that accepted poverty as a feature of life. In this corpus, officers of the state are a distinct branch of government, powerful and prone to corruption. And economic change is always intertwined with ethical and social considerations. In Rajagopalachari's ideal conception, benevolent trustees would manage society's prosperity through a system of collective property. Citizenship meant an attachment to social duty so intense that it bordered on faith and entailed nearly constant activity.

Almost every one of Rajagopalachari's thirty-odd *cirukkathaikal* (*ciṛukkataikaḷ*, short stories) is intended to either publicize the evils of untouchability or encourage support for prohibition.[24] They date to the period when he ran a Gandhi ashram in Tiruchengode (1925–30) near Salem. The ashram was a key site of experimentation of the anti-untouchability and prohibition objectives of the Gandhian constructive program, pointing to the unity of thought and practice in these years.[25] The stories portray the consequences of economic change on social stratification and geography. Rajagopalachari wrote them against the backdrop of two longer processes and one shorter-term but more destabilizing phenomenon: the commercialization of agriculture, the urbanization of the Madras Presidency, and the Great Depression.[26]

24. One valuable attempt at bringing fiction into the history of economic thought is Craufurd Goodwin's "Observation through Fiction: Frank Norris and E.M. Forster," *History of Political Economy* 44 (annual supplement, 2012): 206–25.

25. Rajagopalachari used short stories to express concern about the evils of drink destroying the lives of the poor. They helped him win support for the temperance movement he led. As premier of Madras Presidency (1937–39), he instituted a policy of prohibition. See Darinee Alagirisamy, "The Politics of Alcohol in Colonial Tamil Nadu, 1886–1947," (unpublished PhD diss., University of Cambridge, 2016), 33–47.

26. Christopher Baker, *An Indian Rural Economy 1880–1955: The Tamil Nad Countryside* (Oxford: Clarendon, 1985). Rajagopalachari's short stories appeared mainly in the periodical press between the 1920s and 1930s before being collected and republished many times. I have consulted the sixteen Tamil stories in *Rājāji Kataikaḷ*, 10th edition (Chennai: Vanthi Pathipakkam: 2010). Those not available in Tamil appear in *Stories for the Innocent* (Bombay: Bharatiya Vidya Bhavan, 1964).

Rajagopalachari's cirukkathaikal offer a rich picture of how economic change can create social conflict, dislocate people, and erode morality. Reordering class relations can create caste-based resentment. Multiple stories show members of the mercantile Chettiar caste prospering.[27] Brahmins are in decline. Their poverty leads them to migrate to urban areas and enter the professions. Rajagopalachari stereotypes the Chettiar as greedy and incapable of understanding charitable behavior.[28] During the period that he wrote, rural indebtedness intensified and smaller cultivators suffered immiseration at the hands of bigger landowners.[29] His stories juxtapose the poverty of the village against the economic opportunities presented by the city. Avarice and pettiness could characterize new urban capitalist endeavors.[30] Movement from the village to the city is associated with selfishness and the disintegration of the family.[31]

Rajagopalachari's picture of upward economic mobility suggests that prosperity can come at the price of a narrowed humanity. In the story "Aṇṇaiyum Pitāvum" (Mother and Father), a Dalit man who has escaped the poverty of the village for employment in a mill in Bangalore and offered his Brahmin supervisor's sister in marriage lies that he is a Mudaliar (a vegetarian, non-Brahmin upper caste). Ashamed of his parents and brother, the protagonist prevents them from coming from the village to meet his wife. He turns down her requests to meet them by fabricating a cholera epidemic in the village and stops sending his parents remittances. They all end up dying of disease and poverty, leaving the protagonist struck by shame and guilt. When he finally reveals his caste identity to his wife, it does not bother her. His lies now pain him even more.[32] In other stories, protagonists of lower-caste origins leave India to make money from plantation labor in Ceylon or Southeast Asia. This is a process of dislocation and isolation. Even when they return and invest the money they made in agriculture, ending their poverty, their newfound prosperity meets with resentment.[33]

---

27. Baker, *An Indian Rural Economy*, 298–300.

28. *Stories for the Innocent*, 160–62, 196, 208.

29. *Rājāji Kataikaḷ*, 22–47.

30. *Stories for the Innocent*, 170–73; *Rājāji Kataikaḷ*, 208–17.

31. "The Conversion of Minister Sitaramaiyyar," in *Stories for the Innocent*, 200–4, 204.

32. *Rājāji Kataikaḷ*, 104–20.

33. On Tamil migration across the Bay of Bengal, which began to reverse in this period, see Sunil Amrith, *Crossing the Bay of Bengal: The Furies of Nature and the Fortunes of Migrants* (Cambridge, MA: Harvard University Press, 2013); *Rājāji Kataikaḷ*, 1–35, esp. 13–20.

Although typically considered a didactic moralist, Rajagopalachari the cirukkathai writer appreciates how material conditions can affect the relative morality of an action. Stealing under conditions of poverty deserves sympathy and forgiveness, for example.[34] His short stories provide a subtle understanding of the ethical and spiritual consequences of economic change and the tensions produced by the resulting ordering of social relations. They underscore how prejudice and poverty take on new forms in the context of urbanization and occupational change. However, they stop short of valorizing the past. The stories unequivocally portray poverty as degrading; they merely raise caution about the perils of prosperity.

Rajagopalachari shared Gandhi's skepticism of the modern state form. For Rajagopalachari, though, it was not so much the state's violence that he regarded as problematic as the proneness of those operating in its name— elected or appointed—to corruption.[35] Indeed, the corruption of officeholders had been a central preoccupation of the British in colonial South India. This was no doubt a regular theme of the court cases in which Rajagopalachari the lawyer was involved.[36] In his 1920 jail diary, he resigned himself to the fact that corruption would pervade public life "even under Swaraj."[37] Witnessing the petty corruption and abuse of office by Indian wardens in prison may have compounded Rajagopalachari's strong attitudes on this issue.[38] In "Oru Election Katai" (An Election Story), an unscrupulous Chettiar attempts to buy votes for the local government board elections. These efforts prompt a rival from the Mudaliar community to do the same. Both sides pay off the voters,

34. *Rājāji Kataikaḷ*, 1–35, 20–23, 94–104; *Stories for the Innocent*, 227–29.

35. Gandhi drew on an older genealogy of anti-statism in anticolonial thought and from thinkers like Henry Maine to posit a reconstituted village as the site for a postimperial polity. Rajagopalachari never went this far, but it is quite possible that his own thoughts were informed by earlier anticolonial nationalists like Naoroji and colonial administrators of the late nineteenth century like Maine. See Karuna Mantena, "On Gandhi's Critique of the State: Sources, Contexts, Conjunctures," *Modern Intellectual History* 9, no. 3 (2012): 535–63.

36. Bhavani Raman, *Document Raj: Writing and Scribes in Early Colonial South India* (Chicago: University of Chicago Press, 2012); Robert Frykenberg, *Guntur District: A History of Local Influence and Central Authority* (Oxford: Clarendon Press, 1965).

37. Mahesh Rangarajan, Deepa Bhatnagar, and N. Balakrishnan, eds., *Selected Works of C. Rajagopalachari*, vol. 2 (New Delhi: Nehru Memorial Library and Orient Blackswan, 2013/2014), 38.

38. David Arnold, "The Colonial Prison: Power, Knowledge and Penology in Nineteenth-Century India," in *Subaltern Studies VIII: Essays in Honor of Ranajit Guha*, eds. Arnold and Hardiman (New Delhi: Oxford University Press, 1994), 148–87.

who end up casting ballots based on their conscience.[39] Rajagopalachari's short stories portray a world of precarity and temptation, requiring constant vigilance. They do not portray income-generating work as a form of fulfillment. Rather, such work is necessary for survival. Politics can be inherently unethical and allegiances for sale. The less one seeks money and power, the better.

Politics therefore required principled action and constituted a form of *satyagraha* (a struggle for truth) according to Rajagopalachari. His first two published works were abridged Tamil translations of Plato's *The Trial and Death of Socrates* (1922) and Marcus Aurelius' *Meditations* (1928).[40] Socrates' commitment to the pursuit of knowledge and respect for the verdict of the courts are part of an active struggle for *satyam* (truth).[41] *Meditations* reminded Rajagopalachari of the Bhagavad Gita. He likened the Roman statesman's stoic idea of duty to Krishna's presentation of *niskama karma* (*niśkāma karm*, disinterested action).[42]

A more in-depth outline of civic duty, participation, and the ideal state form appeared during his time as premier of Madras Presidency (1937–39). With his journalist protégé K. Santhanam (see the next section), who went on to a distinguished career in national politics, Rajagopalachari authored the didactic popular reader *Ūrukku Nallatu* (Good for the Polity) in 1939.[43] Part of a literacy campaign, the text considered the role of the reading public as peer educators: "All the front verandas of homes should become like small schools. He who can read should not sit still. He should teach the others."[44] Newspapers required

39. *Rājāji Kataikaḷ*, 218–32.

40. Rajagopalachari *Cokraṭār*, and Rajagopalachari, *Ātma Cintaṇai (Meditations)* (Madras: Lodhra Press, 1935), v–vii.

41. Rajagopalachari, *Cokraṭār*, 15–16.

42. Rajagopalachari, *Ātma Cintaṇai*, v–vii. On how *niskama karma* became central to the nationalist imagination, see Sibaji Bandyopadhyay, "Translating Gita 2.47 or Inventing the National Motto," reproduced in his *Three Essays on the Mahabharata: Exercises in Literary Hermeneutics* (New Delhi: Orient Blackswan, 2015).

43. He went on to serve as union minister of state for the railways, member of the Rajya Sabha (upper house of parliament), and chairman of the Second Finance Commission. See Santhanam, *Looking Back: Memoirs of K. Santhanam (1895–1980)* (Bombay: Bharatiya Vidya Bhavan, 2001).

44. *Tiṇṇaikaḷellām ciṇṇa paḷḷikūṭaṅkaḷ āka vēṇṭum. Paṭikka terinta evaṇum cum'mā irukka kūṭātu. Marravārkaḷukku sollī tara vēṇṭum.* Rajagopalachari and Santhanam, *Ūrukku Nallatu* (Good for the Polity) (Madras: Rochouse and Sons, 1939), reprinted in *Rājāji Kaṭṭuraikaḷ* (Madras: Pudumai Pathippakam, 1944) 151–74, 151.

careful reading and engagement. Readers needed to distinguish between truth and falsehood, and between advertisement and news. They should study advertisements as well. From them, the citizen could discover where to purchase decent wares. Equally important were elections. The citizen was not to vote in exchange for money or favors, or to cast votes passively. Rather, she was to support honest candidates after having discussed them in groups and thought through the issues. If not, the polity would become sinful.[45]

Rajagopalachari and Santhanam presented the *uttiyōkastarkaḷ* (civil service) as the fourth branch of the *kuṭi aracu* (republic). The *kāval* (police) was one of this branch's constituent elements. This understanding had to with the fact that in largely rural Tamil society, police had played a key role in consolidating the colonial state and most often represented the state in the everyday life of ordinary people. Police both punished crime and enforced property rights as agrarian cultivation was extended.[46] Judicial procedure sheltered their violent activity from penalty.[47] It was therefore of paramount importance that these officers worked honestly.[48] The importance of administration and the risk of the abuse of administrative power lay at the heart of Rajagopalachari's political thought.

Civic duty was a commitment to one's *currantazhaal* (*currantaḷāḷ*), or the care of "those who surround," as Rajagopalachari pointed out in his 1937 translation and commentary on the ancient Tamil couplets of the second book of the *Kural*. *Curram* did not necessarily mean relatives, although this was often the case. It connoted sharing one's lawful possessions with an organic close community. This was distinct from nepotism, which defrauded the state and "prevails in countries prematurely forced from the currantazhaal culture into the individualist civilization by adventitious circumstances," he asserted.[49] "The crow does not hide it when it finds something to pick and eat, but cries out to its fellows and then starts eating. Prosperity comes only to men who develop this disposition," Rajagopalachari continued. As had come out in his earlier writings and practices, Rajagopalachari regarded family as the basic unit

45. Rajagopalachari and Santhanam, *Ūrukku Nallatu*, 168–69.

46. Baker, *The Politics of South India*, 85.

47. On this, see Radha Kumar, *Police Matters: The Everyday State and Caste Politics in South India, 1900–11975* (Ithaca, NY: Cornell University Press, 2021).

48. Rajagopalachari and Santhanam, *Ūrukku Nallatu*, 170–73.

49. *The Second Book of the Kural: A Selection from the Old Tamil Code for Princes, Statesmen, and Men of Affairs* (Madras: Rochouse and Sons, 1937), 20–22.

of social organization, rather than the individual, caste, or class.[50] Unusually for a village émigré—he left to pursue higher studies—Rajagopalachari never broke ties with his immediate family. He remained surrounded by family members until the end of his life.[51] A man who acknowledged his debts to Edmund Burke, Rajagopalachari valued the organic community over the individual.[52]

This family orientation translated into Rajagopalachari's understanding of individual ownership as collective in spirit. Addressing fellow prisoners in jail in 1930, Rajagopalachari likened Bolshevism to the joint family and presented an idea of ownership as trusteeship.[53] Collective property rights managed through the figure of the trustee had antecedents in the colonial Tamil region.[54] Custodianship of religious charitable endowments were vested with a trustee acting on behalf of the deity of the temple, which stood at the center of rural life.[55] Rajagopalachari also knew about Gandhi's notion of trusteeship as responsibility to the community by the holder of wealth or property.[56] His trustee appears to be a legal entity operating on behalf of the currantazhaal, with whom ownership rested. Rajagopalachari's position was conservative in

50. Biographer and grandson Rajmohan Gandhi described the Tiruchengode Ashram, for example, as a "family." See Gandhi, *The Rajaji Story I: A Warrior from the South* (Madras: Bharathan Publications, 1978), 156.

51. Joanne Punzo Waghorne, "Rajaji the Brahmin: A Style of Power," in *Religion and the Legitimation of Power in South Asia*, ed. Bardwell Smith (Leiden: Brill, 1978), 53–72, 55.

52. Copley, *Gandhi's Southern Commander*, 61.

53. A fellow inmate recorded this and other talks and published them as C. Rajagopalachari, *Chats Behind Bars* (Madras: S. Ganesan, 1931). See the chapter titled "Bolshevism," 16–41, 26–27.

54. David Washbrook, "Sovereignty, Property, Land and Labor in Colonial South India," in *Constituting Modernity: Private Property in the East and West*, ed. Huri Islamoğlu (London: I.B. Tauris, 2004), 69–99; Washbrook, "Law, the State, and Agrarian Society in Colonial India," *Modern Asian Studies* 15, no. 3 (1981): 649–721, 656; Mitra Sharafi, *Law and Identity in Colonial South Asia: Parsi Legal Culture, 1772–1947* (Cambridge: Cambridge University Press, 2014), 239–73.

55. Arjun Appadurai, *Worship and Conflict under Colonial Rule: A South Indian Case* (Cambridge: Cambridge University Press, 1981). From the late nineteenth century, the legal category of charitable endowments was codified and widened to encompass indigenous endowments of family and community groups, which aided in accumulation. Kinship-based firms could be registered as trusts if they showed public purpose and receive favorable tax treatment. See Birla, *Stages of Capital*, 67–139. However, it is unlikely that Rajagopalachari devoted much thought to the trustee of the mercantile firm.

56. Bidyut Chakrabarty, "Universal Benefit: Gandhi's Doctrine of Trusteeship," *Modern Asian Studies* 49, no. 2 (2015): 572–608. For a more cynical view, see Zachariah, *Developing India*, 157.

the context of the zamindari abolition and land redistribution debates taking place within the Congress during the 1930s.[57] In reality, trustees of temples and endowments could often use their powers in less than altruistic ways.[58]

The subtitle he appended to his translation of the second book of the *Kural—A Selection from the Old Tamil Code for Princes, Statesmen, and Men of Affairs*—strongly suggests that Rajagopalachari regarded the text as a how-to guide of sorts. He reorganized the *Kural*'s couplets into headings like "The Prosperous State," "Industriousness," "On Agriculture," "On Poverty," and "Labor" to derive practical guidance in these matters.[59] Labor on the soil was the engine that drove prosperity. Industriousness guaranteed greater agricultural yield. And honestly accumulated wealth could lead to *dharma* (the cosmic law underlying just behavior and order). Poverty was a fact of life, and donation motivated by compassion the best way to dispose of wealth. Leaving wealth idle was a sin and learning to live within the means of one's accumulated wealth a virtue. The state should tax lightly to allow people to keep a large chunk of their agricultural produce. This was not a redistributive state.[60]

Ideas first went into action during Rajagopalachari's tenure as premier of Madras (1937–39). During this period, Congress consolidated its power in the region on the back of tremendous support from rural smallholders. It made "adept use" of the powers given under the Government of India Act of 1935.[61] Rajagopalachari the premier had the power to borrow and tax, to hire and fire. He conducted his ministry with such ruthless efficiency that some perceived him as a one-man show. An obsessive administrator, his signature or scribblings appear on most office paperwork.[62] Drawing one-seventh of the authorized salary for himself, Rajagopalachari ran a frugal administration and implemented various cost-cutting and efficiency-enhancing measures.[63]

57. On the regional debates, see Baker, *The Politics of South India*, 207–10. On the debate at the national level, see Sarkar, *Modern India*, 354–64.

58. Appadurai, for example, shows how elected trustees could abuse their power to privilege certain devotees of temples over others on community lines.

59. Rajmohan Gandhi, *The Rajaji Story I*, 258.

60. Rajagopalachari, *The Second Book of the Kural*, 2, 37, 66–72, 124–29.

61. Christopher Baker, "The Congress at the 1937 Elections in Madras," *Modern Asian Studies* 10, no. 4 (1976): 557–89.

62. This is evident in the papers of the Madras government available at the Tamil Nadu Archives from the period.

63. Gandhi, *The Rajaji Story, 1937–72*, 2; S. Ramanathan, *Two Years of Congress Rule* (Madras: Madras Legislature Congress Party, 1939), 49–56.

Rajagopalachari's signature legislation during his two years in office indicates that he was most concerned with agrarian problems. He introduced prohibition, agrarian debt relief, and the sales tax. This was an adjustment to the changing nature of the Madras Presidency economy as it shifted toward commerce. To improve the fortunes of the agrarian economy within this changing environment, he widened the ambit of cooperative societies. These had previously been merely state-sponsored banks for subsidized credit.[64] Rajagopalachari tried to use them to promote consolidation of landholdings via joint cultivation, savings associations, and collective marketing and distribution of produce.[65] He capped the interest rate for all loans to cultivators disbursed since 1932 at 5 percent through the Madras Agricultural Relief Act.[66]

Rajagopalachari promoted moderate reforms for redressing inequality but resisted more radical approaches. He withstood pressures from colleagues to work toward abolishing the most unequal forms of land tenure prevalent in some parts of the presidency despite unequivocally condemning them.[67] Early signs of his future attitudes were on display when he arrested a Congress socialist on charges of sedition and attempted to scotch the subsequent bail application.[68] In Rajagopalachari's view, the left unnecessarily disrupted political order and fragmented society.

Rajagopalachari displayed some of these tendencies once again as chief minister of Madras fifteen years later (1952–54).[69] By this time, the Congress had lost its electoral majority in the state, with the communists making important headway. The regional leadership offered Rajagopalachari office to steady the boat. He emerged from retirement to inherit a deficit state reeling from five straight years of drought. During the first meeting of the legislative

---

64. Maanik Nath, "The State and Rural Credit Markets in South India, 1930–60," (unpublished PhD diss., London School of Economics, 2020). I am grateful to Dr. Nath for sharing his work with me.

65. "Establishment—Formation and Encouragement of Co-operative Societies for Consolidation of Holdings—Employment of Special Staff-Orders Passed," Government Order (hereafter G.O.) 1339 (P), May 23, 1939, Development Branch, Government of Madras, TNSA; "Rural Reconstruction—District Periodical Conferences—Proceedings for the Quarter Ending 30-6-1939—Papers Recorded," G.O. 2892, November 28, 1939, TNSA, 46–50; "Multipurpose Societies—Formation on a Large Scale," G.O. 79 (MS), January 10, 1939, TNSA.

66. Nath, "The State and Rural Credit Markets in South India," 125–26.

67. Copley, *The Political Career*, 39–171; See also Ramanathan, *Two Years of Congress Rule*.

68. Copley, *The Political Career*, 44–51.

69. Gandhi, *The Rajaji Story: 1937–72*, 224–56.

assembly, he told the communists that he was their "Enemy Number One."[70] Along with food and finance minister C. Subramaniam, a protégé from the Gounder community, Rajagopalachari dismantled the deeply unpopular food price controls. The measure reduced the possibility of abuse by food department officials and won approval. Other states adopted the policy shortly thereafter.[71]

Once again, Rajagopalachari pursued a light and financially sound administration. To balance the budget, he postponed rural electrification schemes and introduced regressive taxes.[72] Still, like before, he evinced moderate concern for the worst forms of poverty. He introduced legislation providing security for tenants in the dry region of Tanjore and guaranteeing tenurial rights for five years.[73]

Economic concerns were embedded in broader preoccupations of political and ethical life for the intellectually versatile and prolific C. Rajagopalachari. Despite his wide reading, there is no evidence of him ever having read a single economic text before the 1950s. And although the papers of his early life do not exist, it is far more likely that experiences, observations, and conversations informed his apprehension of economic issues. It was an economic common sense of sorts.

Gandhi played a role in helping him come to his convictions, but Rajagopalachari deviated from the Mahatma on multiple points. Crucially, Rajagopalachari did not reject material accumulation as sinful or unethical per se. Rather, it was excess caused by greed that he deplored. Foreshadowing his later positions, he was sensitive to the dislocations produced by economic change and the risk of moral degradation it might cause. Most notably, he derived a strong connection between economy and the administrative functions of the corruption-prone state. Theoretically, Rajagopalachari's ideal of active citizens serving their *currantazhaal* was distinct from individualism and paralleled the idea of family. As noted in his address to the second convention of the Indian Congress for

70. "Madras Budget and Sales Tax," *Economic Weekly*, January 2, 1954.

71. Rajagopalachari had been deeply troubled by wartime controls during the brief time he served as member for industry and supplies in the interim cabinet for several months in 1947. See Rajmohan Gandhi, *The Rajaji Story, 1937–72*, 136. However, he recognized them as a necessary evil. He did not yield to Sardar Patel's injunction on behalf of textile magnates to decontrol cotton prices at that time. See the letters from Sardar Patel dated 22.5.1947 and 24.5.1947, Subject File 43, Installment V, CRP, 53–55, 85. See also Ankit, *India in the Interregnum*, 51, 82–83, 108.

72. "Rajaji's Second Ministry in Madras," Microfilm Accession 10968, File 95, CRP, 41–63.

73. Copley, *The Political Career*, 288–306.

Cultural Freedom, Rajagopalachari understood the positive content of freedom to be self-control that could benefit society.[74] Although the economic became partially disembedded from these other concerns during the 1950s, they remained underneath the surface as he critiqued Nehruvian economic policy.

## Safeguarding Swarajya through Swatantra

Rajagopalachari recast himself as a teacher steeped in ancient wisdom that he could use to interpret the Indian experiment with democracy after becoming the ceremonial last governor general of India in 1947 (the position was subsequently abolished). He embraced the role of guide to the young republic. He valued mass enfranchisement but believed it would come to nothing without proper acceptance of civic and spiritual duty. Both of these he referred to as *dharma*.[75] The first issue of *Swarajya*, dated July 14, 1956, returned to the subject of his first book: "The need is great for a gadfly-Weekly-paper . . . of the Socrates pattern." *Swarajya* would offer "frank criticism" of Indian democracy, like Socrates, the gadfly of Athenian democracy in *The Apology*.[76] Personal and emotional motivations complemented this noble objective of providing an alternative perspective on political and economic affairs. By this time, Rajagopalachari was lonely, disappointed, and physically frail. His self-reinvention as a critic of Congress policy and leader of the Swatantra Party allowed him to both restore dignity to himself and vent feelings of betrayal against a party that ultimately sidelined him.

Rajagopalachari wrote extensively in *Swarajya*, a Madras-based weekly. The name was deliberately chosen. *Swaraj* was the term Indians used for the end-goal of anticolonial nationalism and self-rule. This was, therefore, the magazine interested in the salient points of life under Swaraj. Founding editor Khasa Subba Rau was reputed for his honesty. Rau had served three jail terms in the freedom movement and believed that the press was society's conscience.[77] In *Swarajya*'s pages, Rajagopalachari developed and expressed his opinions on contemporary topics. He attempted to problematize how governance became more challenging in the context of a democratic polity.

74. Rajagopalachari, "True Freedom," *Freedom First*, October 1953, 1.
75. Waghorne, "Rajaji the Brahmin."
76. Rajagopalachari, "Value of Frank Criticism," *Swarajya*, July 14, 1956.
77. Rajagopalachari to Subba Rau, April 7, 1947, Subject File 42, V Installment, CRP.

Rajagopalachari feared that the dual dangers of nuclear holocaust and greed confronted the Cold War world.[78] If one threatened physical destruction, the other risked the degradation of mankind's soul. He campaigned actively for world peace and nuclear disarmament and urged the embrace of religion to combat these dangers.[79] A pious Hindu, Rajagopalachari was nevertheless tolerant of whatever religion someone might want to assume. He stressed that the state should offer "impartial encouragement of religions."[80] This would help citizens cultivate the moral standards required to safeguard democracy.

Through weekly contributions to *Swarajya* and the occasional op-ed in national dailies, Rajagopalachari described administrative corruption as the major threat to democracy and proposed measures to limit the influence of money and vested interests on politics. In India and decolonizing Asia at large, he wrote, recent emancipation from monarchy and colonialism had not yet brought good government. Instead, government mainly served vested interests. Especially in societies without good traditions of popular government, he worried that an army leader could easily fill the leadership vacuum. Like the world at large, political order in a democracy was intrinsically fragile and required constant vigilance.[81] One reform he proposed was isolating administrative appointments and promotions from the influence of elections. This meant these appointments and promotions would be the sole responsibility of the administrative branch, like in the case of the judiciary.[82] Second, he suggested attacking the role of money in politics by conducting elections like the census. The government would send non-party-affiliated mobile units to

78. Rajagopalachari, "Almost Personal," *Swarajya*, February 28, 1959.

79. Rajagopalachari, "Positive Co-Existence," *New Reasoner*, iv (1958), 25–26. At the age of eighty-three, he left India for the first time to urge President Kennedy to stop nuclear testing as part of the Gandhi Peace Foundation. See "Chakravarti Rajagopalachari, Noted Indian Statesman, Dies," *New York Times*, December 26, 1972, https://www.nytimes.com/1972/12/26 /archives/new-jersey-pages-chakravarti-rajagopalachari-noted-indian-statesman.html.

80. Rajagopalachari, "Future of Democracy in Asia," *Hyphen*, September 1961, reprinted in C. Rajagopalachari, *Satyameva Jayate: A Collection of Articles Contributed to Swarajya and Other Journals* (Chennai, 2005), vol. 1, 219–22.

81. The discussion is around an article written by C. Rajagopalachari, called "Recipe for Good Government," *Illustrated Weekly of India*, August 15, 1957, as cited in Monica Felton, *I Meet Rajaji* (London: Macmillan, 1962), 68.

82. Rajagopalachari, "Expensiveness of Elections," *Swarajya*, January 26, 1957.

collect ballots at each house. Through such a reform, "the task of bringing voters to the booth—which in one way or another is the cause of all the expenditure now incurred by parties and individual candidates—would become a natural function."[83] Supplementing this idea, he proposed ceilings on corporate contributions and party spending in elections.

Centralization led to the neglect of "good government" independent of party influence, according to Rajagopalachari. Self-government had not yet led to good government. While the status of the civil service endured, their standards of efficiency and integrity had collapsed. This was a function of his belief that central government control of policy implementation in a country as diverse as India was nearly impossible. The bureaucrat had great incentive to please the elected official rather than do work for the society at large under the current model, he reckoned. Yielding to the elected official's desires might compromise the job of providing sound administration. To prevent this problem, he suggested taking administrative appointments and promotions squarely out of the electoral process. Instead, he proposed that a community like the judiciary, motivated by ethical conduct rather than the considerations of electioneering, make these appointments. "When a client goes to a lawyer, it is not the client's job to see the lawyer acts honestly. That is the business of the Law Society. It is a body of the same kind that is wanted," he wrote. To overcome the problem of money in politics, he suggested nationalizing elections.[84]

Rajagopalachari contended that socialism's broad popularity owed to a sycophancy toward the ruling elite. Opposition offered a way to create genuine political pluralism. He likened the enthusiasm for socialism to the enthusiasm for freedom from British rule. According to Rajagopalachari, the altered circumstances of independence required new emphases in political debate. Politics could no longer operate on the terms of the "revolution" that threw off the Raj. It needed to reorient itself away from sloganeering and "mutual encouragement" that lead to "parrot culture." Politics instead needed to focus on the practicalities of everyday administration.[85]

His next step was to equate socialism with communism, and communism with totalitarianism. In making these leaps, Rajagopalachari turned agonist.

83. Rajagopalachari, "Donations to Congress Party Chest," *Swarajya*, August 13, 1960; C. Rajagopalachari, "Company Donations to Party Funds," *Swarajya*, August 27, 1960.

84. Rajagopalachari, "Recipe for Good Government," *Illustrated Weekly of India*, August 15, 1957.

85. "Wanted: Independent Thinking," *Swarajya*, May 10, 1958.

He raised alarm that the Congress' proposals to introduce land ceiling legislation and encourage cooperative farming indicated the ruling party was headed the way of communist countries.[86] Instead, he argued for a return to contract and praised custom.[87] He oversimplified the complexity of debates about Indian socialism and framed political consensus around central planning as ideological stasis. Thus, opposition from "a Right party" was the need of the hour.[88]

In its earliest form, this demand for opposition was for a set of distinct state-level parties contesting the Congress.[89] This state-level opposition would play a balancing role and reorient the political Center. According to Rajagopalachari, centralization had compromised the constitution's federal character. The Planning Commission's allocation of fiscal resources during the Second Plan period furnished the clearest example. The way he envisioned it, every state election would be a battle of Center against regional opposition. States would work together to check the power of the Center and decentralize government. This was not an argument for the disintegration of the Congress, but for giving it competition.

Later, however, Rajagopalachari discarded the state-level opposition idea in favor of a national alternative. Calling India's democracy "one-footed," he reckoned that opposition could provide "true democratic balance" and counteract the "sadist passion" for socialism.[90] Rajagopalachari would thus by 1959 call for a "conservative party to stem the tide of statism in this country."[91] In a *Swarajya* article, he cited Soviet writer Boris Pasternak's *Doctor Zhivago* on the emptiness of idealist rhetoric—a calculated knock against the Congress' rhetoric of socialism. He affirmed that "to conserve is to look after what is good and not to let the thoughtless ruin what is essential and good, in a hunt after will-o'-the wisps."[92] Rajagopalachari would later compromise with General

86. These were much tamer than he suggested. For a basic narrative of these events, see B.R. Tomlinson, *The Economy of Modern India: From 1860 to the Twenty-First Century* (Cambridge: Cambridge University Press, 2013), 158–61.

87. "Compulsion in Agriculture," *Swarajya*, November 8, 1958.

88. Rajmohan Gandhi, *The Rajaji Story: 1937–72*, 282.

89. Rajagopalachari, "Autonomy of States," *Swarajya*, November 2, 1957.

90. Rajagopalachari, "One-Footed Democracy," *The Hindu*, January 6, 1959, reprinted in Rajagopalachari, *Satyameva Jayate*, vol. 1, 258–61.

91. Rajagopalachari, "Wanted: A Conservative Party," *Swarajya*, April 18, 1959.

92. *Doctor Zhivago* is a classic novel that unfolds between the Russian Revolution and the outbreak of World War II. The book captures the individual costs of progress for a society. Readers in the West understood it to be a major anticommunist work. Boris Pasternak, *Doctor*

Secretary Minoo Masani, who preferred "a Centre Party, a Liberal Party, or a Democratic Party" to "Right Party" or "Conservative Party." Nevertheless, the final choice of *Swatantra* should not obscure the clarity of Rajagopalachari's original theoretical impulse.[93]

What did Swatantra mean? Translated directly from Sanskrit, the adjective *swatantra* means "independent" or "autonomous." Splitting it into the word root *swa-* ("self") and *tantra* ("woven together") clarifies its meaning as a disposition whereby "the decision comes not by coercion from outside but from within."[94] Swatantra also calls to mind the freedom movement; Indian Independence Day is called *Swatantrata Diwas*, Swatantrata being the nominalization of swatantra. Rajagopalachari analogized the importance of his new party to that of Swaraj itself.

Rajagopalachari could not regard the modern state without suspicion. And he made the case for two-party politics in India as a shrewdly calculated attack on the Congress from which he had fallen out of the leadership. But despite his antiquarian proclivities and personal vendettas, he put his finger on the central problem of overreach in a one-party dominant political system. Rajagopalachari also delineated the challenge of abuse of office in the context of an expanding government machinery in a deeply unequal society. And as in his writings from previous decades, he raised caution about the consequences of economic change. Through *Swarajya*, Rajagopalachari found a new voice and a new cause—Swatantra.

## A New Conservatism Across Linguistic Publics

Rajagopalachari turned into an economic policy commentator as he reinvented himself as the most prominent agitator for a conservative opposition party to the Congress. This transformation took place in conversation with various interlocutors in *Swarajya* who reflected on changes in society and economy in its pages. The content of these discussions spread to the Tamil-speaking public thanks to *Kalki*, known primarily as a culture magazine. *Swarajya*'s close connection with *Kalki* was a function of their editors' strong relationship to Rajagopalachari. That connection strengthened further when

*Zhivago* (New York: Pantheon Books, 1958); C. Rajagopalachari, "Lost Its Anchor," *Swarajya*, April 11, 1959.

93. M. R. Masani to C. Rajagopalachari, January 14, 1959, Installment IV, CRP.

94. Masani, *Against the Tide*, 141, 159.

*Kalki* took over the finances and distribution of *Swarajya* in 1959.[95] Both magazines catered to consuming classes and featured eminent authors. They were also both run by Brahmins. The defense of large landholding and patrilineal inheritance that took place in their pages points to how a new economic conservatism emerged from a socially and culturally conservative milieu.[96]

Enmeshed in the connected cluster of English-language periodicals and associations in which free economy developed and diffused, *Swarajya* boasted an appreciable circulation of 16,456 by 1960.[97] Like others in this cluster, its editor and major contributors first came to know each other during the freedom movement. *Swarajya* commented mainly on economic and political affairs and aimed at a national audience. Its pages featured quotations in small boxes from the likes of Edmund Burke, Macaulay, John Stuart Mill, and Thomas Jefferson nested in the margins of article columns. Indicative of its Anglophile tenor, *Swarajya* once published the historian Percival Spear's article on "Life at Cambridge Today."[98] Articles focused on foreign policy, law and the courts, and economic affairs. Culture complemented current affairs. The magazine also featured articles on Hinduism, reviews of books and Carnatic music concerts, and the occasional short story.

Founded by R. "Kalki" Krishnamurthi, the former editor of Rajagopalachari's ashram temperance magazine *Vimōcaṇam*, *Kalki* fed into the linguistic and cultural renaissance being experienced in the Tamil-speaking region. It primarily featured illustrated short stories, segments of serialized novels, and short essays. Temporally, many of its fictional offerings were set in the ancient past.[99] Covers usually featured a scene from these stories, giving *Kalki* a classic, timeless appearance. The magazine also shared the name of the prophesied tenth incarnation of the god Vishnu, who first appeared in the *Mahabharata*.[100]

The politics section of *Kalki* that ran from 1954 typically covered economic affairs in at least one of its subsections—the unsigned main editorial, shorter

95. T. Sadasivam to Homi Mody, June 30, 1959, File 1, Box 6, SP.

96. Raymond Williams, *Marxism and Literature* (Oxford: Oxford University Press, 1977).

97. This was the first year the Government of India published the circulation figures of individual periodicals. See *Press in India—Part Two* (New Delhi: Ministry of Information and Broadcasting, 1960). On this cluster, see chapter 2.

98. Percival Spear, "Life at Cambridge Today," *Swarajya*, January 16, 1957.

99. M.R.M. Sundaram, *Eminent Tamil Writer Kalki: A Life Sketch* (Chennai: Vanthi Pathippakam, 1993), 123, 41, 85–104

100. Alt Hiltebeitel, *Reading the Fifth Veda: Studies on the Mahabharata: Essays, Vol. 1* (Leiden: Brill, 2011), 531.

subeditorials, or cartoons. *Kalki's* basic orientation strongly resembled the line taken in *Swarajya*. Its special symposia published over multiple weeks allowed eminent men of affairs to explain economic and political affairs in a more didactic vein. Pieces were around five hundred words in length.[101] Between 1957 and 1958, *Kalki* carried the twenty-part *Poruḷātāramum Potumakkaḷum* (The Economy and the Public); the eleven-part *Celvamum Svatantramum* (Wealth and Freedom); an eighteen-part *Ārāyacci Araṅkam* (Research Forum) on *Bhāratin Iṉraiya Poruḷ Nilai* (The Economic Condition of India Today); and a seventeen-part *Ceṅkōlum Jaṉaṉāyakamum* (Justice and Democracy).[102] The publication and content of these symposia reflected Rajagopalachari and his associates' commitment to peer education and the cultivation of public consciousness.

*Kalki* helped cement Rajagopalachari's enduring political force as both a symbol and purveyor of ideas. It published his renditions of the *Mahabharata* (1944–46) and the *Ramayana* (1954–55), and his annotated commentaries on the first book of the *Kural* (1957–59). Every year on his birthday, the magazine also carried Rajagopalachari's likeness on its cover and filled the issue with photographs and short hagiographical essays about him. One such article dubbed him "iraṇṭāvatu Cokraṭār" (second Socrates).[103] *Kalki's* offerings could be read easily, as they were written in a style resembling spoken Tamil.[104] By 1960, it became the second most widely sold Tamil weekly, with a circulation exceeding 100,000.[105]

*Kalki* and *Swarajya* occupied distinct but connected roles in India's "structurally bilingual public sphere" of regional Indian-language local publics and an elite English national public.[106] Intermediators like Rajagopalachari wielded important power because of their prominence to both kinds of publics. They fleshed out their economic ideas in dedicated associations across urban centers

101. Sadasivam was also the husband of the Carnatic musician M. S. Subbulakshmi and as her manager helped to make her a major national sensation. See Keshav Desiraju, *Of Gifted Voice: The Life and Art of M. S. Subbulakshmi* (New Delhi: Harper Collins, 2020), 110–14.

102. These ran from December 8, 1957, to April 6, 1958; April 13 to June 22, 1958; July 13 to August 17, 1958; and August 24 to November 2, 1958, respectively.

103. *Kalki*, December 30, 1956.

104. Sundaram, *Eminent Tamil Writer Kalki*, 124.

105. Despite fluctuations on an annual basis, these numbers were broadly consistent throughout the 1960s. *Press in India*, various.

106. Veena Naregal, "Colonial Bilingualism, Translation, and the Indian Social Sciences," Azim Premji Special Lecture, July 31, 2015, Azim Premji University, Bangalore, https://www .youtube.com/watch?v=NTNn0Oj9ktM. This ongoing work brings forward many of the issues identified in Naregal, *Language Politics, Elites and the Public Sphere: Western India Under Colonialism* (Ranikhet: Permanent Black, 2001).

or periodicals where the medium of communication was English.[107] These intermediators would then selectively communicate these ideas in Indian languages in the print cultures of their regions. They took on a more prescriptive tone as "peer educators" or pedagogues in their Indian-language writings.[108] When they addressed political rallies, it was more as proselytizers rather than debaters. *Swarajya* and *Kalki* overlapped to the greatest extent in the amount of coverage they gave to Rajagopalachari's writings and movements.

*Swarajya* and *Kalki* appeared during a period when the state was becoming increasingly assertive over regional economic life and the agrarian economy grew more industrialized.[109] As agricultural output declined in the early twentieth century, the state had taken on a more active role in the management of food-grains procurement and distribution. To the chagrin of mercantile interests, it instituted a bureaucracy for this purpose. New industries came into being and towns grew. Textile businesses that profited handsomely during World War II but saw demand collapse shortly thereafter diversified into new businesses: trucking fleets, cinema halls, printing presses, urban property, and consumer goods. Complementing this trend was the steady expansion of non-factory businesses specializing in tanning, carpet-making, *beedi*-rolling, and metalwork.[110] These businesses benefited from urban migration related to agrarian distress. Finally, the personnel of the state increased in size and asserted greater control over economic resources. They clustered in the capital of Madras or in large towns. The pages of both magazines carried advertisements for these new consumer products. They catered especially to urban readers.

Magazine contributions responded to national economic policy and ideology during the Second Five-Year Plan (1956–61). Over these years, states began to introduce tenancy reforms. Their intention was to either regulate rent, provide security of tenure so that tenants could not be thrown off the land, or bestow ownership rights in the non-Zamindari areas. The latter measure went hand in hand with land ceilings legislation, whereby land held over a certain

---

107. Metcalf and Metcalf, *A Concise History of Modern India*, 248.

108. On "peer education" as a context for the development of ideas in Indian intellectual history, see Bayly *Recovering Liberties*, 132–34; for a useful discussion on Indian-language versus English-language publics in the colonial era, see Neeladri Bhattacharya, "Notes Towards a Conception of the Colonial Public," in *Civil Society, Public Sphere and Citizenship: Dialogues and Perceptions*, eds. Rajeev Bhargava and Helmut Reifeld (New Delhi: Sage, 2005), 130–56.

109. This paragraph follows Baker, *An Indian Rural Economy*, 368–425.

110. *Beedi* is like a cigarette. It is a portion of tobacco flake wrapped in a tendu leaf.

ceiling limit would be acquired by the state and possibly turned over to tenants.[111] The government also evolved a more complex system of control-related laws; during the second parliament (1957–62) alone, the legislature passed over a hundred laws just to regulate finance.[112] Of the various personal law reforms during this period, the Hindu Succession Act of 1956 most directly affected landownership. For the first time, the act gave daughters claims to their ancestral property, though at half the amount of land that her brothers would inherit.[113]

Policymaker energy on the production side focused on the question of how to improve the productivity of small and fragmented land holdings. A seven-member study team newly returned from visiting agrarian co-operatives in China published a comprehensive Government of India Report in 1957 suggesting that the state encourage landowners to cultivate only as much land as they could by themselves. The report suggested that they rent out the rest to tenant farmers, who might then be granted state subsidies.[114] Congress subsequently introduced a resolution on cooperative farming at Nagpur in 1959. The measure sought to reap the benefits of economies of scale and raise agricultural production by encouraging landowners to cultivate joint plots of land. However, consultation with the Chinese and the context of land ceiling legislation aroused suspicion.[115] Unlike credit cooperatives or cooperative marketing organizations established from the early twentieth century in India onward, cooperative farming involved the production process itself.[116]

*Kalki* and *Swarajya* regularly registered their opposition to these changes and their implications. A special issue of *Kalki* that came out the week after Congress declared a "socialistic pattern of society" warned of the dangers of seemingly benign leadership morphing into authoritarianism.[117] *Swarajya*'s second ever issue bore the headline "Overdose of Socialism" and lamented the plight of the "small businessman," as the "raw deal he was getting under our Socialistic pattern" was unsatisfactory.[118] Another piece complained that the

---

111. Datt and Sundharam, *Indian Economy*, 350–58. See chapters 4 and 6.

112. Hanson, *The Process of Planning*, 94.

113. See chapter 1.

114. *Report of the Indian Delegation to China on Agrarian Co-operatives* (New Delhi: Planning Commission, 1957), 150–52.

115. Siegel, *Hungry Nation*, 174–77.

116. Kamenov, "The Place of the 'Cooperative' in the Agrarian History of India;" Nath, "The State and Rural Credit Markets in South India, 1930–1960."

117. Santhanam, *Araciyalum Poruḷātāramum* (Economics and Politics), *Kalki*, January 23, 1955.

118. "Sidelights," *Swarajya*, July 21, 1956.

increases in production of agricultural and consumer goods sectors aimed at by the second plan could not be met under the stringent licensing policies adopted for businesses.[119] Both magazines complained about the pinch of increased direct and indirect taxation.[120] "Wherever you look, taxes are rising," noted one editorial in *Kalki*, suggesting that this was the natural result of the government taking on an increasing number of responsibilities.[121]

These magazines sided with the landlord rather than the tiller when it came to questions of land reform. *Kalki* ran an editorial titled "Payir Toḷilē Keṭukka Vēṇṭām" (No Need to Ruin Agriculture) that commented on a law recently passed by the Madras legislature protecting agricultural tenants from eviction and imposing a ceiling on the rents that owners could collect.[122] The editorial argued that such measures ignored the way agriculture had been conducted since time immemorial. It cited a couplet from the *Kural* pointing to the necessity of both the cultivating tenant and an overseeing figure. The editorial argued that the legislation impaired landowners' incentives to invest in improvements to cultivation by weakening property rights. Tenants, without capital, would not be able to step into the vacuum. Agricultural output would therefore be in jeopardy. The editorial declared: "A society needs *mirasdars*. It also needs farm laborers. It needs cows. It needs manure. It needs seeds. And above all, it needs money."[123] The mirasdar, a category of landowner particularly prominent in parts of the former Madras Presidency, enjoyed rights analogous to the zamindar and in certain districts had estates of thousands of acres.[124] Unlike zamindari, mirasdari continued in practice.[125]

119. Saranga, "Discrepancies in the Second Plan," *Swarajya*, July 21, 1956; *Industrial Policy Resolution* 1956, 1–8.

120. "Austerity," *Swarajya*, June 15, 1957; Viji, *T.T.K. Taiyāritta Budget* (The Budget Prepared by T.T. Krishnamachari), *Kalki*, May 26, 1957.

121. *Eṅkē pārtālum varippaḷḷu atikamāki koṇṭu varukiṟatu. Enna Ceyti? Vari Paḷḷu* (What's News? Tax Burden), *Kalki*, March 6, 1955.

122. *Kalki*, October 14, 1956. The legislation immediately concerned was the Madras Cultivating Tenants (Payment of Fair Rent) Act. See G. Parthasarathy, "The Madras Land Reform Bill: A Critical Study," *Economic Weekly*, May 21, 1960, 771–76.

123. *Camūtāyattil mirācidārkaḷum irukka vēṇṭiyatu avaciyam. Paṇṇaikku vēṇṭiya thoḷilāḷikaḷum irukka vēṇṭiyatu avaciyam. Mātum veṇṭum. Eruvum veṇum. Vitaiyum vēṇṭum. Ellā veṟṟikum mēlāka paṇamum vēṇṭum.*

124. Baker, *An Indian Rural Economy*, 64–66; Washbrook, "Political Change in a Stable Society: Tanjore District 1880 to 1920," in *South India: Political Institutions and Political Change*, eds. Baker and Washbrook (Delhi: Macmillan, 1975), 20–68, 22–25. Washbrook, *The Emergence of Provincial Politics*, 86–89.

125. Austin, *Working a Democratic Constitution*, 78–92.

*Swarajya*'s and *Kalki*'s pages represented a distinct attitude toward the country's ideal strategy of development. "We must depend on local capital and local enterprise and the urge of honorable self-interest for this change of the face of India," Rajagopalachari would write. He believed that full employment could only be brought about "by smaller industries springing into existence in small towns and what may be called the rural areas round about the farm villages." Bringing small landowners together to engage in such enterprises sounded compelling but would not work in practice. Instead, he suggested that "richer landlords" might find rural industrialization "a good investment, supplementing their own interests." They were "the natural entrepreneurs of the smaller, decentralized rural industrialization that should come into existence." In other words, government should contribute to this mode of landlord-led industrialization via the investment of agricultural surplus. Other attempts risked empowering the state unnecessarily and normally produced inadequate outcomes.[126]

A conservative subtext underlay both the appeal to the peasant proprietor and a decentralized model of industry. Those who defended the constructed ideal of the small peasant proprietor could turn a blind eye to the massive inequalities produced by the diverse land tenure arrangements in these areas.[127] How small was "small"? This vagueness allowed a broader canvas of people to embrace such rhetoric. "Peasant proprietor" would come to function as a keyword to assert regional difference from the zamindari states. Decentralization was consistent with an anticommunist logic; it prevented labor from emerging as a class and unionizing.[128]

The two journals criticized measures aimed at giving women more economic independence in postcolonial society, consistent with this opposition to land reform. Rajagopalachari envisioned little else than a domestic life for women.[129] Both *Swarajya* and *Kalki* opposed Hindu personal law reform. Despite the fact that changes to personal law had been debated for over a decade after consultation with a range of experts across the political spectrum, a *Swarajya* editorial lamented that "these changes have not been properly examined in the background of Hindu social philosophy" and they "disrupt our

126. Rajagopalachari, "Why I Show the Red Flag," *The Hindustan Times*, February 16, 1959, reproduced in *Satyameva Jayate*, vol. 1, 283–87.

127. On the failure of ryotwari to generate a widespread and equitable pattern of smallholding, see Chari, *Fraternal Capital*, 147.

128. On how decentralization broke union power, see Chari, *Fraternal Capital*, 240–73.

129. Srinivasan, *Gandhi's Conscience Keeper*, 190–202; Guha, "The Wisest Man in India," 38.

homes and confuse the millions who are in no way parties to the changes."[130] One columnist blamed the actions of a "denationalized handful who have captured the machinery of power and are seeking to impose on Hindu society their outlandish notions" for destroying the joint family.[131]

*Swarajya* argued that the Hindu Succession Act would fragment holdings and create tensions between brothers and sisters. From a political economy angle, the smaller and smaller plots of land created would become uneconomic for cultivation.[132] Rajagopalachari warned that "it takes but a few years for a family of five becoming a fighting group of twenty."[133] *Kalki* ran a cartoon to this effect titled "*Urimai Pōr!*" (War of Rights!) when the bill was being debated. It depicts a father being pulled in opposite directions by his son and daughter. Meanwhile, the daughter herself is being pulled by her husband.[134] Rajagopalachari decried "personal laws affecting Hindus, laws relating to succession, marriage, adoption" and "changes in inheritance laws leading to over-fragmentation of land" in one of his 1957 speeches.[135] *Swarajya* reprinted a resignation letter from Congress of two Punjab parliamentarians that clubbed the Nagpur resolution alongside the Hindu Succession Act as "ruinous to the agriculturists." They warned that it would "lead to litigation of the worst kind and bad blood between brothers and sisters."[136]

Contributors to *Swarajya* converged in their attitudes to economic and political affairs. All objected to the increased incursion of the state into the economy during the second plan period. Each considered himself—most contributions came from men—to be qualified to provide commentary on current events because of age, experience, and learning. These men expressed a common feeling that Congress threatened to disturb the institutions guaranteeing social order and challenging the sanctity of the constitution. This related to their concern that the expanding size of government administration would compromise the government's integrity and lead to corruption. All shared an interest in fiscal rectitude, seen as the hallmark of good administration from the colonial era. Therefore, unbalanced budgets, as implied by deficit financing of five-year

130. Newbigin, *The Hindu Family and the Emergence of Modern India*, 128–61; "A Party for Welfare and Justice," *Swarajya*, November 3, 1956.

131. "Sotto Voce," *Swarajya*, December 22, 1956.

132. "Central Planning," *Swarajya*, October 24, 1959.

133. Rajagopalachari, "What We Are in For," December 27, 1958.

134. *Urimai Pōr!* (War of Rights!), *Kalki*, January 2, 1955.

135. "Rajaji on Need for Strong Opposition," *Swarajya*, March 9, 1957.

136. "'Nagpur Resolution Ruinous': Two Punjab MPs Resign from Congress," *Swarajya*, October 3, 1959.

FIGURE 3.1. *Geṭṭikkāra Kāvalkārar* (Outstanding
Guardian): Protecting the Plan from the Deficit (*Kalki,*
January 23, 1955).

plans, offended their sensibilities as wasteful expenditure. All regarded the rhetoric of socialism to be disingenuous and empty of practical content.

*Kalki'*s politics section provided greater coverage of regional affairs than
*Swarajya.* This section addressed itself more in the imagery and language of
the mainly agrarian Tamil-speaking world.[137] For example, *Kalki* made the
case for methods to redress the plight of handloom weavers and to reduce
taxes on cycles.[138] Sarcastic cartoons assaulted the Congress regime's economic
policy in an increasingly unsparing manner as the decade went on. The cartoon reproduced as Figure 3.1 portrays the finance minister as a farmer on his
knees, chasing away a goat called "deficit" eyeing an edible sapling called "Second
Five Year Plan." The caption reads: "Finance Minister Deshmukh believes that the
deficit will not interrupt the Second Five Year Plan," although the sketch suggests
this is hard work. The cartoon's title, "Outstanding Guardian," conveys a feeling
of improbability.[139] The cartoon is a perfect blend of the agrarian imagery and
sarcasm that pervade *Kalki'*s economic affairs commentary.

Contributors came from a stratum of professionals with some connection
to public life, as far as one can gather. They wrote occasional pieces in the

137. Scholars of colonial South Asia have examined vernacularization in terms of the ways
in which concepts are received and reworked in the subcontinent by Indian-language actors.
See, for example, Goswami, *Producing India;* Birla, *Stages of Capital;* and Sartori, *Liberalism in
Empire: An Alternative History* (Berkeley, CA: University of California Press, 2014). Here, I build
on this work to consider print culture and the process of translation.

138. See, for example, *Viḷā Muṭintatu; Āṇālum* (The Festival is Over; And Still) *Kalki,* April 3,
1955; *Enna Ceyti? Enna Seyti? Vāḻka Nakar Capai!* (Long Live the State Assembly), *Kalki,*
March 25, 1956; *Muṭṭakaṭṭai Vēṇṭām!* (No Need for a Stumbling Block!), *Kalki,* April 24, 1956.

139. *Nitipparrākuraiyāl irantāvatu aintu varuśa thiṭṭam thaṭaipaṭātu eṉra nampikkai
ceyuṭaṉirukkurār nīti mantiri Deshmukh. Kalki,* January 23, 1955.

mainstream press and would be known beyond their immediate places of origin. Their ranks included lawyers, retired administrators, and senior journalists who began their careers in the nationalist press. One such contributor, who went on to make his mark on *Swarajya* and later the Swatantra Party, was the Tamil Catholic Mariadas Ruthnaswamy. Trained in law, he went on to occupy a key role in the early non-Brahmin movement, contesting Brahmin hegemony of the professions. He also pursued a career in academia, serving as professor of history and later vice chancellor of a regional university.[140] An advocate of "conservative progress," Ruthnaswamy occupied himself with questions of political and constitutional theory and displayed a particular interest in issues of administration.[141] Legal education had sensitized graduates like him to issues of administration and influenced their language and understanding of politics.

The political affiliations of these contributors during the nationalist movement had been diverse. Some had been of the left. Others remained fiercely committed to the Raj. Still others were Gandhian Congress men like Rajagopalachari.[142] These figures all hailed from South India. What united them was a nostalgia for Victorian literature and culture and a persistently legal bent to their political commentary. These men received their education in an Indian university system in which English emerged as a distinct university subject related to preparation for the Indian Civil Service examinations.[143] It was also a form of education in British mores and culture.[144]

Such pursuits became secondary to their careers in the professions. These men became practitioner-scholars employed as government administrators or professionals fighting the Raj in the age of nationalism.[145] One section of them

140. On Ruthnaswamy's political career, see Baker, *The Politics of South India*, 27, 64.

141. Baker, *The Politics of South India*, 82–83. His demonstrated interest in administration comes out in Ruthnaswamy, *Principles and Practices of Public Administration* (Allahabad: Central Book Depot, 1962).

142. V. N. Naik, *Indian Liberalism: A Study* (Bombay: Padma, 1945).

143. Ram Nath and Rajendra Kumar Sharma, *History of Education in India* (New Delhi: Atlantic Publishers, 2000), 116–25. J. B. Harrison, "English as a University Subject in India and England: Calcutta, Allahabad, Benares, London, Cambridge and Oxford," in *The Transmission of Knowledge in South Asia: Essays on Education, Religion, History and Politics*, ed. Nigel Crook (Delhi: Oxford University Press, 1996), 155–90.

144. Gauri Viswanathan, *Masks of Conquest: Literary Study and British Rule in India* (New York: Columbia University Press, 2015).

145. On the implications of university education and government employment for Indian political consciousness, see Anil Seal, *The Emergence of Indian Nationalism: Competition and Collaboration in the Later Nineteenth Century* (Cambridge: Cambridge University Press, 1971), 1–24, 194–244.

had joined the Indian Civil Service after the passage of the Government of India Act of 1919, which steadily increased the recruitment of Indians into its ranks and posted them to work across the country.[146] Exposure to diverse settings broadened the scope of their interests beyond local concerns. Less tangibly, employment in this prestigious body tasked with administering the vast expanse of British India transformed them into men of affairs and social standing. The civil service "turned clerks into proconsuls, subalterns into strategists, traders into merchant princes—and daydreamers into philosopher-kings."[147]

For whom did these contributors write? *Swarajya* and *Kalki* formed a part of a growing print culture of the 1950s that catered to the reader's proclivity for acquisition and fed into gender-specific ideas about consumption.[148] The pages advertised a range of items for purchase: cooking oils, cars, toothpaste, paperback books, and bicycles. Household cleaning and consumer goods advertisements featured images of women and appealed to their traditional position as homemakers. These advertisements also showcased non-Western items now being mass-produced in factories, like cooking oil, *cāmpār* (lentil stew) paste, and *dhotis* (piece of unstitched cloth worn around the waist to cover the legs, see Figure 3.2). Advertising captures the presence of small-scale business enterprises, which are otherwise difficult to locate, and offers glimpses into consumption cultures.[149] The advertisement for dhotis highlights how business sought to appeal to potential customers to regard the importance of correct sizing of an Indian garment as seriously as they would a European one. The presence of both cheap items and more expensive goods on the pages of

146. Malti Sharma, *Indianization of the Civil Services in British India, 1858–1935* (New Delhi: Manak, 2001), 198–230.

147. Clive Dewey, *Anglo-Indian Attitudes: The Mind of the Indian Civil Service* (London: Hambledon, 1993), ix.

148. Aakriti Mandhwani "*Saritā* and the 1950s Hindi Middlebrow Reader," *Modern Asian Studies* 53, no. 6 (2019): 1797–815. Although she works on Hindi-speaking India, the observation applies to magazines like *Kalki* and *Ānanta Vikaṭan*.

149. Douglas Haynes, "Advertising and the History of South Asia: 1880–1950," *History Compass* 13, no. 8 (2015): 2361–74; Haynes, "Selling Masculinity: Advertisements for Sex Tonics and the Making of Modern Conjugality in Western India, 1900–45," *South Asia: Journal of South Asian Studies* 35, no. 4 (2012): 787–831. The history of consumption in South Asia remains understudied, especially in the postcolonial context. But see A. R. Venkatachalapathy, *In Those Days There Was No Coffee* (New Delhi: Yoda Press, 2006); Douglas Haynes, Abigail McGowan, and Haruka Yanagisawa, eds., *Towards a History of Consumption in South Asia* (New Delhi: Oxford University Press, 2010); and Haynes, *The Emergence of Brand-Name Capitalism in Late Colonial India: Advertising and the Making of Modern Conjugality* (London: Bloomsbury, 2022).

FIGURE 3.2. Dhoti Advertisement (*Swarajya*, January 4, 1964).

*Swarajya* blurs the distinction identified by scholarship on the colonial era, of mass journals advertising cheap goods and elite journals advertising expensive ones.[150] This was symptomatic of a change in attitudes toward consumption and the mass production of cheap goods. The magazines themselves were, in a sense, a form of elite consumption. Purchasing them offered the reader the opportunity to come off as knowledgeable and cultured in "good society."

Support for *Swarajya* and *Kalki* came from members of landowning and trading castes partaking in a broader small-enterprise-led transition away from agriculture in the region. Both magazines' proprietors were Brahmins, the dominant caste in decline. Their socially entrenched privilege and fluency in two languages allowed them to navigate multiple public spheres and conditioned their intellectual and political commitments. Advertisements and subscriptions for *Swarajya* came from members of the landowning Vellalar community

150. Haynes, *Small-Town Capitalism in Western India: Artisans, Merchants and the Making of the Informal Economy, 1870–1960* (Cambridge: Cambridge University Press, 2012), 362–63.

and mercantile Chettiars. All three communities turned to small forms of capitalism like agroindustry, textiles, and cements during this period. Brahmins and Vellalars liquidated their agricultural surpluses for investment. The Chettiars used their accumulated mercantile capital to finance enterprises across South and Southeast Asia and set up ventures of their own.[151]

*Swarajya* and *Kalki* expressed a new conservatism brewing during these years. They adopted a "rhetoric of reaction" on issues of political economy. Their pages featured contentions that new laws risked worsening the very problem they sought to mitigate and that such laws would not work out at all or would jeopardize institutions like the family.[152] This rhetoric was embedded in cultural, social, and political concerns. Resistance to land reform and the Hindu Succession Act also came from anxiety about disturbing the basic elements of the social structure and its associated culture and values. Seen in this light, it is not wholly surprising that *Kalki* also published serialized versions of the epics and novels about ancient India. Nor is it remarkable that *Swarajya* reported on classical music concerts, published essays about the histories of Indian cities, and reviewed translations from Sanskrit hymns. Maintaining the existing order of things went along with celebrating the spirit of the past.

*Kalki* embraced this dual disposition perhaps most forcefully in its August 2, 1959, issue. It appeared the day after Swatantra's inaugural convention, which deliberately coincided with the death anniversary of Bal Gangadhar Tilak. The cover (Figure 3.3) and editorial, "Tilakar Tiruṇāḷ" (Tilak Remembrance Day) identified Rajagopalachari as the inheritor of the mantle of the nationalist movement.[153] According to the editorial, Tilak had made the freedom movement—or movement for Swatantra—under the Congress something more than a body that passed paper resolutions. Every year, Tilak Remembrance Day commemorated the "Father of the Movement for Swatantra." Gandhi, the editorial continued, subsequently led the people awoken by Tilak on a sacred path. He pursued Swatantra through *ahimsa* and satyagraha and achieved a

151. Damodaran, *India's New Capitalists*, 24–25 (Chettiars), 55–65 (Tamil Brahmins), 137–74 (Gounders, a Vellalar community). As Damodaran argues, the Chettiars were in decline as capitalists from the 1950s, but their involvement in mercantile activity remained unabated.

152. This corresponds to what the social scientist Albert Hirschman called the "perversity," "futility," and "jeopardy" theses, respectively, in his classic study of conservatism. See Hirschman, *The Rhetoric of Reaction: Perversity, Futility, Jeopardy* (Cambridge, MA: Harvard University Press, 1991).

153. *Tilakar Tiruṇāḷ* (Tilak Remembrance Day), *Kalki*, August 2, 1959.

FIGURE 3.3. Rajagopalachari, Heir to Tilak,
Gandhi, and Patel (*Kalki*, August 2, 1959).

miracle the world had never seen before, showing that India was a *puṇyatēcam*
(holy land). Patel, Gandhi's *taḷapati* (commander), saved India from disintegration by incorporating the princely states into the Indian Union. Practical
and principled, he served as a counterweight to the idealistic Nehru. After
Patel's death, an *āmām pāṭṭu pāṭara kūṭam* (chorus of yes men) merrily went
about affirming Nehru's designs. Congress was morphing into a communist
party.

At this juncture, with *paṇpāṭu* (culture) and *nākarikam* (civilization) on the
line, Rajagopalachari decided to start the Swatantra Party, the editorial continued. This, it affirmed, was the crowning achievement of a life that had
already seen several accomplishments and contributions to the country.

Rajagopalachari trusted in the *aṭippaṭai tarma uṭai* (fundamental dharma) of the people, the tenets of which were economic activity and individual liberty. The final sentence of the editorial said that joining the Swatantra Party was also a form of paying homage and respect to Tilak, Gandhi, and Patel. Dharma connoted both the order of the cosmos and a notion of duty; it became a code word for this new conservatism.

## Engaging the Neoliberals on Inflation, Formulating Permit-and-License Raj

"Dear Sir, I request you kindly to send a set of sample tracts advertised in the *Freeman*: answers to the clichés of Socialism. I shall be grateful for the favor."[154] So wrote Rajagopalachari on April 10, 1961, to the circulation department of the Foundation for Economic Education, the same American libertarian think tank from where the Lotvalas sourced books and articles. The Swatantra Party's economic adviser, B. R. Shenoy, kept party leaders like Rajagopalachari abreast of the latest literature produced by neoliberal economists in the United States and Western Europe.[155] These writings appealed to Rajagopalachari as anticommunist discourse, jiving well with his pro-Anglo-American foreign policy writings.[156] Rajagopalachari also familiarized himself with a selection of economic issues he would write about after becoming the guiding light of the Swatantra Party by reading the work of neoliberals.

After the party's founding, Rajagopalachari linked the demand for opposition more closely to free economy. The encounter with Shenoy led him to use inflation as a metaphor for Congress misrule. While doing so, Rajagopalachari developed permit-and-license raj, his lasting contribution to Indian politico-economic discourse and the rallying slogan for the Swatantra Party. He used discourses of neoliberalism to legitimate the Swatantra Party's policy positions in *Swarajya* and talk back to the Congress in the language of economics.

154. Rajagopalachari to Foundation for Economic Education, April 10, 1961, Installment IV, CRP.

155. M. R. Masani to C. Rajagopalachari, July 22, 1959, Subject File 41, Papers Related to the Swatantra Party, Installment VI–XI, CRP.

156. He first left India in 1962 for the United States and the United Kingdom, where he lobbied for nuclear disarmament. See Guha, "The Wisest Man in India," 51. For a discussion of his foreign policy writings, see Srinivasan, *Gandhi's Conscience Keeper*, 163–89.

Like the neoliberals he cited, Rajagopalachari occasionally spoke of economic affairs disembedded from their social and cultural contexts in *Swarajya*. Such a rhetorical choice linked Swatantra's aims to a wider transnational context and shed *Swarajya* of some of its agrarian nostalgia. But it would be a mistake to classify Rajagopalachari as completely of the mind of the Western men he cited, or even of Shenoy. Alongside his *Swarajya* writings, he offered constructive suggestions to Congress leaders in Delhi about economic administration that demonstrate more comfort with statist economic policy than his popular writing would aver. Furthermore, his avoidance of certain major issues in political economy points to a rather selective uptake of neoliberal positions.

B. R. Shenoy, a Reserve Bank monetary economist, transitioned to economic affairs commentary in the mid-1950s after taking up directorship of the School of Social Sciences at the University of Gujarat.[157] Much of Shenoy's early scholarly work was preoccupied with the negative consequences of inflation.[158] Indeed, for a monetary economist, and especially one who had experienced India's inflation during World War II, price stability was a central concern.[159] Shenoy first became prominent in the public eye after publishing a widely circulated "Minute of Dissent to the Panel of Economists on the Second Five-Year Plan" (1955). "No plan can be greater than the available resources," he argued, rejecting deficit financing by foreign aid.[160] According to Shenoy, American food aid prevented India from developing her own agricultural output. Deficits necessarily led to inflation. Shenoy made every effort to exert a wider influence on public opinion. He contributed frequently to the popular press and lectured across India.[161]

157. Trained at the Benares Hindu University and the London School of Economics, he was the first Indian to publish in the venerable *Quarterly Journal of Economics* (1931). After a career as a monetary economist, Shenoy moved to Gujarat to take up a position as director of the School of Social Sciences in 1954. See Aditya Balasubramanian, "Alone at Home, Among Friends Abroad? B. R. Shenoy from Austrian School Economist to Cold War Public Intellectual," in *A Functioning Anarchy: Essays for Ramachandra Guha*, eds. Nandini Sundar and Srinath Raghavan (New Delhi: Penguin, 2021), 165–79.

158. Shenoy, *The Bombay Plan: A Review of Its Financial Provisions* (Bombay: Karnatak Publishing House, 1944).

159. For more on this, see Raghavan, *India's War*, 347, and "First Memorandum on Inflation," December 12, 1942, Finance Department, Finance-I Branch, File 11(66)-FI-46, NAI.

160. Shenoy, "A Note of Dissent," reprinted in *Economic Prophecies: B. R. Shenoy*, eds. R. K. Amin and Parth Shah (New Delhi: Centre for Civil Society, 2004), 19–20.

161. Nicole Sackley, "The Road from Serfdom: Economic Storytelling and Narratives of India in the Rise of Neoliberalism," *History and Technology* 31, no. 4 (2015): 397–419, 406.

After learning of Shenoy from his commentary on the second plan, the British-Hungarian economist Peter Bauer of the London School of Economics (LSE) invited Shenoy to address the Mont Pelerin Society (MPS) at Oxford in 1959.[162] This postwar international thought collective sought to bring markets into new domains of social and economic activity and contest the dominance of statist economic ideas, in particular newly fashionable Keynesian economic thought.[163] Shenoy's speech cited the West German *Soziale Marktwirtschaft* (social market economy), which allowed the market mechanism to operate freely but guaranteed social security to correct for the inequalities it produced, as a model for India. He contrasted it with the East German socialist economy. The West German model, he argued, had "enormous development poten- tialities." Shenoy attributed its *Wirstchaftswunder* (economic miracle) to the dismantling of economic controls.[164] In a thundering voice, he departed from his written text and phrased India's choice as one between free market econ- omy and communism.[165]

The speech greatly impressed the society's leader, F. A. von Hayek, whom Shenoy had first encountered as a student at LSE. He immediately offered Shenoy membership in the society.[166] Wilhelm Röpke, whose ideas had a seminal influence on the policies leading to the West German economic miracle, shared a similar appraisal.[167] He considered the speech to be one that

---

Although Shenoy never attained the latter's popularity or influence, there is a parallel in this career transition to that of Milton Friedman, analyzed in Burgin, *The Great Persuasion*, 152–85.

162. On Bauer, see chapter 1.

163. Burgin, *The Great Persuasion*.

164. C. L. Grossner, *The Making of the German Post-War Economy—Political Communication and Public Reception of the Social Market Economy after World War II* (London: I. B. Tauris, 2009), 47–60.

165. "Sound Recordings of the Mont Pelerin Society Meeting at Oxford in 1959," Tape 20, Side 1, Box 61, Papers of the Mont Pelerin Society, Hoover Institution Archives, Stanford Uni- versity, Stanford, CA. Compare these to "Free Market Economy for India," mimeo, Folder 13, Box 79, Friedrich A. von Hayek Papers.

166. Hayek to Shenoy, October 20, 1959, Folder 13, Box 79, Hayek Papers, Hoover Institution Archives.

167. Röpke (1899–1966), a German economist hailing from the Austrian tradition, was an heir to a line of thought known as ordoliberalism. According to ordoliberals, the state must create institutions, such as a legal regime, which allow market forces to thrive. However, unlike earlier ordoliberals, he and his interlocutors were interested in the scale of the world rather than the nation state. Röpke was also interested in requirements for market society, which he be- lieved required European Christian values and restrictions on the rights of people of color. See Slobodian, *Globalists*, 11, 74, 88–9, 150–57. On Röpke's role in advising the West German

"very ably" addressed "the fallacies in the common policies of underdeveloped countries."[168] Röpke would continue to follow Shenoy's work appreciatively.[169] He helped organize for Shenoy's work to reach a German-speaking audience, just as MPS members in the United States connected Shenoy with periodicals there.[170] Shenoy thus became a node in the network of Western thinkers and publicists engaged in what they believed to be an ideological crusade.[171] Here was a battle for hearts and minds, whether or not it was explicitly stated in such terms to the public. The MPS used Shenoy as a kind of India informer.[172] Shenoy in turn used the set of contacts that the MPS opened to sharpen his own ideas in the absence of like-minded economists in India. He also used it widen the audience for his research, and to syndicate or republish Western economic thinkers' works for the Indian literate public.[173] By 1970, he had spoken at multiple annual meetings and been elected one of the MPS' few global directors.[174] In this way, he used the MPS to advance his own standing.

Shenoy courted the interest of dissident politicians of various hues, never orthodox enough to make much impact in India's policymaking community. As a youth, Shenoy had personal connections to the Hindu majoritarian elements in the Indian Nationalist Congress.[175] Almost three decades later, K. M. Munshi invited him to speak at the Bharatiya Vidya Bhavan on the

government, see Alfred C. Mierzejewski, "Water in the Desert? The Influence of Wilhelm Röpke on Ludwig Erhard and the Social Market Economy," *Review of Austrian Economics* 19, no. 4 (2006), 275–87.

168. Wilhelm Röpke to Trygve J. B. Hoff, October 6, 1959, Folder 18, Wilhelm Röpke Papers, Institut für Wirtschaftspolitik, Cologne, Germany (hereafter WRP). For references from this archive, I am grateful to Quinn Slobodian.

169. Shenoy, *Indian Planning and Economic Development* (New York: Asia Publishing House, 1963); Shenoy to Röpke, October 27, 1963, Folder 129, WRP.

170. Shenoy, "Der richtige Weg zu Indiens Fortschritt" in *Entwicklungsländer: Wahn und Wirklichkeit*, ed. Albert Hunold (Zürich: Erlenbach, 1961), 139–56; Shenoy, "The Right Road to Indian Progress," *Fortune*, April 1960, 136–37, 244, 246, 251, 253–54.

171. Magnus Gregersen to Röpke, June 4, 1962, Folder 133, WRP.

172. Sackley, "The road from Serfdom," 400, 406. Thanks to Shenoy, Röpke even received correspondence from Sadasivam alerting him of *Swarajya* and its interest in issues of political economy. See Sadasivam to Röpke, October 15, 1963, Folder 89, WRP.

173. See the correspondences in Folder 11, Box 33, Milton Friedman Papers, Hoover Institution Archives; Shenoy to Hazlitt, October 13, 1961, "B.R. Shenoy, 1961–78" file, Henry Hazlitt Digital Archives-Beta; Shenoy to Hayek, December 22, 1965, Folder 1, Box 50, Friedrich Hayek Papers.

174. Arthur Shenfield to Henry Hazlitt, July 26, 1974, "Sh-Z" file, Hazlitt Digital Archives, hosted by Universidad Francisco Marroquin, https://hazlitt.ufm.edu/index.php.

175. Balasubramanian, "Alone at Home, Among Friends Abroad?," 166–67.

welfare state.[176] Shenoy described his ideal Hindu economy as "a minimum state." In it, "each individual should be left free to pursue his lawfully chosen vocation." Furthermore, according to the rule of dharma, the state could not typically "enter the sphere of economic activities, which is the sacred domain of the private sector."[177] Shenoy preferred "lawfully chosen vocations" instead of the hereditary division of labor. He believed a new "free economy" could be fashioned without losing its attachment to traditional practices and, above all, to dharma, "like truth." Like Rajagopalachari, Shenoy did not believe that the state should disrupt the basic social order. Even though he did not come out explicitly in favor of caste, he did not condone state involvement in economic and social activity to dissolve it either.

Shenoy provided the party's top brass with briefings and clippings of his latest articles after becoming Swatantra's informal economic advisor.[178] A lightly revised version of his 1959 MPS speech, which delineated "free" and "controlled" economy through the example of East and West Berlin, appeared in *Swarajya* the following year.[179] Rajagopalachari began a regular correspondence with him. The senior statesman adopted the economist's binary between free and controlled economy. Asking "Do you want free economy?", Rajagopalachari shifted his commentary toward economic affairs.[180]

Shenoy sent Rajagopalachari his articles in the national and foreign press. Rajagopalachari studied them as he developed a new Indian conservatism around economic issues and concerns of public administration. Rajagopalachari wrote back asking questions and seeking clarifications about jargon. Shenoy explained patiently. Once explained, Rajagopalachari would write in *Swarajya*, citing Shenoy appreciatively. To Shenoy, the fact that consumption of food-grains and cloth—both industries under price controls—had not increased measurably meant that "so far as the masses of people are concerned, planning has produced next to no improvement." Consequently, he argued that "the benefits of planning have accrued, principally, to the privileged classes." These consisted of "Congress Party men by the thousands, corrupt officials

176. "Semantic Trojan Horse of Nehru Planning," *IL*, October 1, 1957.

177. Shenoy, "My Idea of a Welfare State," reprinted in *IL*, December 1, 1957.

178. Munshi, who joined the party after giving up his initial reservations, was one of the beneficiaries. See B. R. Shenoy to K. M. Munshi, 16 February 1961, Microfilm Accession 2290, File 291, KMM, 172.

179. Shenoy, "East and West Berlin: A Study in Free vs. Controlled Economy," *Swarajya*, August 6, 1960.

180. Rajagopalachari, "Which Is Better and Safer?" *Swarajya*, December 23, 1961.

responsible for the issue of licenses and permits, contractors engaged in the public-sector projects, the beneficiaries of community-development projects, traders, businessmen and industrialists."[181] Because of the taxation rates, "black incomes" were being held in "currency, gold, diamonds, and inventories which are not entered in the books." They were also being plowed into real estate, as reflected in the new buildings in urban areas. He enclosed a pamphlet in his letter to Rajagopalachari called *Inflation in India: Causes, Effects, and Remedies*.

Rajagopalachari was impressed and asked for confirmation that he understood the argument correctly; because consumption of food and cloth was relatively static, the beneficiaries of increased per capita income and economic growth were "those who have been benefitted by the licensing policies of the Government" and "those people who are absorbed in the expanded bureaucracy and the wage-earning classes in the industrial sector."[182] Inflation provided the key link to explaining stagnant consumption. Shenoy presented the very existence of inflation as immorality, rather than noting its increasing but moderate level.

Rajagopalachari's front-page *Swarajya* article of September 24, 1960, observed that "inflation, import restrictions, and other controls have affected the moral standards of the nation." The article began by confessing that it merely represented Rajagopalachari's best attempt to understand Shenoy's pamphlet. Echoing Shenoy, he contended that these characteristics of Indian economic life "have led to the emergence of a new undesirable profession engaged in touting for obtaining licenses, permits and contracts in illicit trafficking in import licenses and in smuggling." This new class employed "practices to become rich quickly without spending energy," paying off officials as needed.[183] Rajagopalachari concluded by stating that inflation and "excessive State interference" were "the two evils of the Indian economy today." The following month, Rajagopalachari began to label "licenses and permits" as an oppressive technology of the state.[184]

181. Shenoy to Rajagopalachari, August 27, 1960, Microfilm Accession No. 10937, Installment II, CRP, NMML.

182. Rajagopalachari to Shenoy, August 30, 1960, Microfilm Accession No. 10937, Installment II, CRP, NMML.

183. Rajagopalachari, "Deficit Financing Must Stop and Controls Must Go," *Swarajya*, September 24, 1960. On the cloth industry slump and the food-grains inquiry committee's concern with food price increases, see Veranda Kumar, *Committees and Commissions in India, 1957–73* (New Delhi: Concept Publishing Company, 1975), 140–43, 308.

184. Rajagopalachari, "Congressmen and Communists," *Swarajya*, October 22, 1960.

The term "permit-and-license raj" evoked a sentiment of public malaise. It first appeared in an appeal for financial support of the party: "Swatantra is as vital as Swaraj. 'Permit-and-license raj' must go. The battle for Swatantra has begun. Help the Election Fund," Rajagopalachari said.[185] Three weeks later, permit-and-license raj appeared in *Swarajya* for the first time.[186] Like Rajagopalachari's prose, the term was crisp and precise. He would use permit-license-raj, permit-license-quota raj, license-permit raj, and permit-license-regime interchangeably.

At the time of its coinage, permit-and-license raj connoted more than the dirigisme of the pre-liberalization economy with which it is associated today. It evoked an oligarchic coalition between Congress politicians, big business, and corrupt bureaucrats and served as a kind of critique of vested interests in Indian democracy. Congress politicians conducted expensive election campaigns and bribed voters with money secured from big businesses. Once elected, they advised bureaucrats to prejudicially award permits and licenses to big businesses or allowed those bureaucrats to allocate permits to the highest bidders. Such a political environment constituted a new kind of raj, indeed jeopardizing the freedoms won in the national movement. It came from Rajagopalachari's engagement with Shenoy and a longstanding concern about administrative and electoral corruption dating back to the 1920s. Emboldened by his interactions with Shenoy and armed with neoliberal economists' writings, Rajagopalachari wrote on a wide range of economic affairs throughout the 1960s.[187]

Rajagopalachari used work by MPS economists to legitimize the platform and ideas of the Swatantra Party in *Swarajya*. Particularly concerned by rising inflation, Rajagopalachari suggested that readers consult a book by British Liberal Party politician and MPS member Graham Hutton called *Inflation and Society*.[188] Hutton's chatty and lucid book argued that inflation emerged from centralizing political activity, offering examples of inflation dating back to the

185. "Swatantra to Raise 1 Crore Election Fund," *The Hindustan Times Weekly*, March 5, 1961: "Election Fund," *ToI*, March 6, 1961.

186. "Sidelights," *Swarajya*, March 25, 1961.

187. This paragraph follows Vasanthi Srinivasan's excellent chapter, "Freeing the Economy from 'Slogan Socialism,'" in *Gandhi's Conscience Keeper*, 76–122.

188. Trained in law and economics at LSE, Hutton then taught at his alma mater and edited the *Economist* before joining politics and reinventing himself as a popular writer and champion of free markets. A frequent contributor to the media, he helped set up the London-based free-market think tank called the Institute of Economic Affairs in 1955. See "(David) Graham Hutton," *Who's Who 2018 & Who Was Who Online* (Oxford, Oxford University Press, 2018), https://libsta28.lib.cam.ac.uk:2090/10.1093/ww/9780199540884.013.U165629; "The Economist" in

Roman Republic. This led to overreach and fiscal irresponsibility. Because increased tax collection could be politically cumbersome, governments instead ran large deficits and created inflation.[189] The social instability caused by rising prices weakened democracy and led to authoritarianism. Rajagopalachari saw a parallel effort to his own in Hutton's polemical book.[190] A steady stream of writings from Anglo-American authors like these supplied Rajagopalachari with material for his polemic.

These writings also helped identify Swatantra as part of a global movement. Rajagopalachari wrote an exegetic *Swarajya* column contrasting free and controlled economy in 1966, drawing on the writing of MPS stalwart Milton Friedman.[191] Rajagopalachari had met Friedman, a University of Chicago economist and the twentieth century's most well-known neoliberal, during the latter's 1963 visit to India.[192] On another occasion, the senior statesman reviewed Shenoy's friend Röpke's *A Humane Society*.[193] The 1962 Swatantra Party manifesto cited the defeat of Britain's Socialists and discarding of state socialism by the West German Social Democrats as evidence of a "worldwide trend against centralized, bureaucratic State Capitalism and towards the restoration of the primacy of the laws of the free market."[194] One party publication even pointed to similarity between Swatantra and the New German Social Democrats by providing a side-by-side comparison of their manifestos.[195]

Private correspondences underscore greater nuance in Rajagopalachari's thinking. They suggest that Swatantra was intended as a corrective for the excesses of the state pushing the economy away from its agrarian roots rather than

Peter Barberis, John McHugh, and Mike Tyldesley, eds., *Encyclopaedia of British and Irish Political Organizations: Parties*, (London: Printer, 2000), 414.

189. Graham Hutton, *Inflation and Society* (London: Allen and Unwin, 1960).

190. Rajagopalachari, "The Grinding of the Individual to Nothingness," *Swarajya*, March 25, 1961.

191. Rajagopalachari, "Prof. Friedman Deals with an Enigma," *Swarajya*, April 2, 1966. Friedman was most famous for his work on monetary policy and exchange rates. He received the Nobel Prize in Economics in 1976. See Lanny Ebenstein, *Milton Friedman: A Biography* (Basingstoke: Palgrave MacMillan, 2007).

192. Rajagopalachari to Masani, February 26, 1963, File 4, Box 1—"1963 Correspondence with CR," SP, NMML.

193. Rajagopalachari, "The German Verdict," *Swarajya*, December 31, 1960.

194. *To Prosperity Through Freedom: The Swatantra Party's Statement of Policy Adopted at the National Convention in Patna on March 19 and 20, 1960* (Bombay: Swatantra Party, n.d.), 9.

195. An appendix in which both party manifestos appear side by side is available in C. Rajagopalachari, *Towards Doom? Swatantra Series-I* (Bombay: Swatantra Party, undated).

an appeal to open all economic activity to market competition. To take one example, Rajagopalachari recommended a scheme to Finance Minister T. T. Krishnamachari to recover unaccounted foreign exchange during a time of scarcity. The idea was to promise import licenses and no legal punishment if holders surrendered their illegally begotten money.[196] In other words, he did not endorse abolishing import licenses altogether and letting market forces determine the exchange rate. In a practical letter to Nehru's successor, Lal Bahadur Shastri, Rajagopalachari recommended using the country's five-year plan resources to "take up a nationwide Road making and housing plan and make fuller employment the goal instead of increased national output except in the field of food-grains."[197] From this almost Keynesian advice, one can infer that Rajagopalachari found it acceptable for the central government to assume a kind of responsibility to provide housing and employment. Although he did not elaborate much on it, the proposed scheme did not say anything about private sector involvement or decentralized implementation. Rajagopalachari could see a salutary role for the Center in taking control of new domains of economic activity with the objective of improving rural life.

Omissions in his writing further suggest that even in this stage of his life, when Rajagopalachari most seriously engaged professional neoliberal economists, he was never a cheerleader for their ideas. At this time, neoliberals were seriously invested in making the case for free exchange rates in a fixed exchange rate world.[198] Rajagopalachari was silent on this question. He also appears to have had nothing to say about free trade versus protectionism; any serious neoliberal would have had strong views on the merits of free trade.[199] Perhaps most importantly, he did not share the growing understanding across the ideological spectrum of economics as an analytic and increasingly quantitative science.[200]

———

Rajagopalachari further elaborated upon free economy from his regional perch in the Tamil land. He used it as the basis of the demand for the opposition party

196. Rajagopalachari to T. T. Krishnamachari, July 18, 1965, Installment IV, CRP.

197. Rajagopalachari to Shastri, March 11, 1965, Installment IV, CRP.

198. Stedman Jones, *Masters of the Universe: Hayek, Friedman, and the Birth of Neoliberal Politics* (Princeton: Princeton University Press, 2012), 180–214.

199. Slobodian, *Globalists*, 27–54.

200. Agnar Sandmo, *Economics Evolving* (Princeton: Princeton University Press, 2011).

he founded in 1959. For Rajagopalachari, a breakaway figure from the Congress, free economy represented the culmination of decades of observation of the relationship between economic and social change and its relation to ethics and religion. He conceptualized a heightened responsibility for individual ethical practice to ensure adequate economic well-being for society rather than an expanding machinery of the state, which was prone to corruption. Crucially, Rajagopalachari imagined free economy to be the platform of an opposition party in a two-party democracy. This idea was the first dimension of opposition politics.

Rajagopalachari's interlocutors in *Swarajya* formed a distinct constituency for free economy from the ideological entrepreneurs and lapsed revolutionaries of the previous chapter. They represented an intellectual world of anglicized bilingual professionals of the former Madras Presidency with a deep appreciation of the agrarian society. Landowner cultivators were moving to a small-enterprise-based model of economic activity in that society. A new consumer ethos and genre of reading accompanied this transition. *Kalki* explained economic issues and advanced complementary views to *Swarajya* in its editorials and news roundups, reaching a major mainstream Tamil audience.

Nehru was not the dictator of Rajagopalachari's polemic. At the same time, the global development of nuclear weapons and the memory of the atom bombs dropped on Hiroshima and Nagasaki lingered in Rajagopalachari's mind. In an essay titled "Future of Democracy in Asia," Rajagopalachari warned that without good administration—the "bone of orderly democracy"—citizens could easily fall into the trap of accepting military rule.[201] Intrinsically fragile, democracy required constant vigilance.

Rajagopalachari sought to defend an agrarian order undergoing organic change against the designs of an expanding state. This defense of this order tied together economic and social conservatism. Thus, Rajagopalachari could speak of the value of dharma and point with dismay to the disintegration of the joint family. Social well-being was not an activity the state could do much about without veering into totalitarianism. Instead, families and charities should take responsibility for these social welfare activities.[202]

Selectively appropriated and mediated through pamphlets and correspondences with Shenoy, neoliberal language was one of the ingredients in the mix

201. Aditya Balasubramanian, "Contesting the 'Permit-and-Licence *raj*': Economic Conservatism and the Idea of Democracy in 1950s India, " *Past and Present* 251, no. 1 (2021): 187–221, 213; Rajagopalachari, "Future of Democracy in Asia."

202. This parallels the phenomenon observed by Cooper in *Family Values*.

that Rajagopalachari used after founding the Swatantra Party.[203] He perhaps sought to guard against charges of obscurantism and articulate his frustrations with the socialist planned economy more forcefully by discussing policy more narrowly and speaking back to dominant discourses in their own idiom. Gradually, he stripped discussions of the family and duty away from his writings. Rajagopalachari theorized permit-and-license raj, a coinage that brought together contemporary concerns of inflation, bureaucratic excess, and corruption in politics in one pithy phrase. It would form the fulcrum of the Swatantra Party's negative critique of the Congress.

203. Scholars have shown how, in the 1970s, "importing" professional Western economic expertise internationalized local conflict between factions of a formerly united group in the Global South. In this case, language rather than expertise is part of the "internationalization." The internationalization is also different because it did not involve changes to India's relationship with international institutions or legal infrastructure. See Yves Dezalay and Bryan Garth, *The Internationalization of Palace Wars: Lawyers, Economists, and the Contest to Transform Latin American States* (Chicago: University of Chicago Press, 2002).

# 4

# Beyond Ghosts

## VISIONS AND SCALES OF FREE ECONOMIES

SPEAKING TO an interviewer on Independence Day, August 15, 1959, at New Delhi's Vigyan Bhavan (Science Building), the modernist Nehru laughed off the creation of the Swatantra Party. "It is a ghost-like party, ghosts of the last century, ghosts of past ages," he said. The prime minister conceded that "of course, ghosts can make a nuisance of themselves—perfectly true." Those who took Swatantra seriously in circles of public opinion represented financial interests and did not appreciate the way the world was moving, he suggested. On the one hand, the Congress had made "deliberate attempts at organized thinking" on the "problem of an underdeveloped country catching up, the developing [of] a self-generating economy fairly rapidly." On the other, Swatantra appeared to stand for "freedom from everything." The new party's members "have not quite got out of the nineteenth century yet," Nehru teased.[1] If ghosts of the past had come to haunt India's political present, then the frail, five-foot-four-inch octogenarian C. Rajagopalachari did not exactly excite much fear.

Nehru died before the Swatantra Party became the nuisance that it did in the 1967 elections.[2] Subsequent scholarly and popular opinion has done little to dispute his assessment. Focused on interest groups and coalition-building, the social scientists of the 1960s largely agreed with the prime minister. The narrative persists that the party of zamindars, maharajas, and big business "died of embarrassment" after it was "abandoned without regret" by certain business groups.[3]

---

1. "Extracts from the Transcript of the Prime Minister's Press Conference Held at Vigyan Bhavan on August 7, 1959," File One, Box 6, SP, NMML.

2. See chapter 6.

3. Kaviraj, *The Enchantment of Democracy and India*, 130.

This prevalent, enduring characterization suffers from two shortcomings. First, it disregards big business' more complicated strategies of political influence and heterogeneous response to the creation of Swatantra. Neither of the two major conglomerates wanted to destroy their relationship to the Congress, honed carefully over decades. Even though India's largest industrial house, Tata Sons, helped finance organizations like the Forum of Free Enterprise, it also tried to use economic crisis as an opportunity to reorient Congress policy toward the interests of private business.[4] The Tata chairman no doubt contributed generously to the Swatantra Party, but he continued to provide larger sums to the Congress.[5]

India's second largest conglomerate, run by G. D. Birla, eschewed involvement in the Swatantra Party altogether. Nonetheless, the Birlas sponsored the *Eastern Economist* magazine, which skewered Congress economic policy every week.[6] When in 1955 Nehru asked Birla to be his envoy to the private sector, the latter simply asked, "What are the orders?"[7] Although Birla privately acknowledged to Rajagopalachari that "controls and interference by the Government and bureaucratic administration is [sic] the greatest stumbling block just at present in the advancement of economies" and "the Planning Commission is the commission of planned hurdles," he continued to believe that the Congress was the undeserving victim of good intentions.[8]

Further, the interest group approach takes a hollow and static view of how dominant castes and elite communities navigate the transition to democracy and state-led industrialization. Such an approach risks simplifying a more complex reality. By broadening it to take both interests and ideas seriously, the question of how communities attempted to protect their position atop a social order in a more complex fashion can be more adequately addressed. These communities drew on vocabularies coined and relationships forged during the nationalist movement. In the process, they embraced some new ideas and practices while rejecting others.

4. J.R.D. Tata, "Subjects for Discussion with the PM, 3 August 1958," typed notes, FP-NO-130, J.R.D. Tata Papers, Tata Central Archives, Pune. Chapter 2 and the latter part of this chapter provide more information about the forum.

5. Howard Erdman, *The Swatantra Party and Indian Conservatism* (Cambridge: Cambridge University Press, 1967), 173–74.

6. Medha Kudaisya, *The Life and Times of G. D. Birla* (New Delhi: Oxford University Press, 2003).

7. G. D. Birla to Jawaharlal Nehru, July 29, 1955, Birla Papers, NMML.

8. G. D. Birla to C. Rajagopalachari, May 31, 1963, Installment IV, CRP, NMML.

Alongside Rajagopalachari's negative idea of economic freedom from the permit-and-license raj of Congress rule, positive visions formulated by those who joined Swatantra's senior leadership informed the party's politics. This constituency included ex-administrators who had been engaged in projects of modernization in the former princely states, not merely feudal landlords and maharajas. More importantly, Swatantra's leaders from communities like the Kammas of Andhra Pradesh, the Patidars of Gujarat, and the Parsis of Bombay advanced specific ideas of change drawn from what was happening in their communities and regions. These figures distributed their ideas across genres of texts—the manifesto, the memoir, the children's book—and responded to various political constraints. To take these ideas seriously is not to provide an apologia for these figures, but rather to better understand their practices and aspirations.[9]

Like Rajagopalachari, the Kamma leader N. G. Ranga, the Patidar Bhailal-bhai Patel, and the Parsi Masani all shared some relationship to the web of interconnected periodicals and associations that provided the threshing ground for free economy. Each hailed from landowning or mercantile communities in southern and western India engaged in or moving toward industrial enterprise. Caste identity and interest played a profound role in shaping their politics and their visions of political economy.[10]

The regions of the Bombay and Madras presidencies from which Ranga, Patel, and Masani hailed had been predominantly ryotwari areas with revenue collection straight from the cultivator. The ideal of peasant proprietorship was a powerful one, however inaccurately it characterized a more heterogeneous reality. Regional history and identity became even more important in the context of the creation of linguistic states in the 1950s, which created new resource conflicts and political arithmetic. And finally, in the context of the Cold War, the global environment mattered. Each of these figures was an anticommunist who considered political economy to be a question about the future existence of the world. They came together to formulate the first secular ideology of an independent Indian conservative party.[11] The Swatantra Party's principles

9. Consider, for example the sympathetic approach taken in Ranajit Guha, *A Rule of Property for Bengal: An Essay on the Idea of Permanent Settlement* (Paris: Mouton, 1963).

10. This ideological dimension is an underappreciated aspect of how a traditional form of identity shaped and reasserted itself in the face of universal franchise and the Center's program for economic and social transformation. See Susan and Lloyd Rudolph, *The Modernity of Tradition: Political Development in India* (Chicago: University of Chicago Press, 1967).

11. "Swatantra Party's Stress on Incentives: 21-Clause Statement of Principles Adopted," *ToI*, August 3, 1959.

served as a kind of common minimum commitment around which such figures could rally.

The economy figures not merely in the understanding and creation of national identity. It is also important at the level of the scalar unit of the region and the locality and the social formation of the community and the caste.[12] Conceiving of economies across multiple scalar units, such as locality, region, nation, and even the world, the Kammas, Patels, and Parsis developed alternative visions and practices of political economy. These stood at odds with Government of India–directed centralized economic planning and implied its *state coordination* of national economic activity. They instead advocated *state facilitation* of private economic activity at different geographic scales than the nation.

If politics is a struggle for ideas—and certainly not always progressive ideas—then how did these leaders come to "see" and think about the economy? From what biases did they suffer? How, and to which constituencies, did they express themselves?[13]

## Ghosts? Princely India and Regional Modernity

Nehru's characterization of the Swatantra Party's membership and its associated program has some merit, although it is not the full picture.[14] In North India, the party drew numbers from the vote banks of ex-princes and ex-zamindars of a cluster of communities known as *rajputs* (sons of kings). This designation of lordly status associated with the Kshatriya varna in the fourfold hierarchy of the Hindu social order placed them just below Brahmins. Rajputs performed privileged military service and held titles to land and revenue in the British

12. In analyzing multiple geographic scales of economic thought, this chapter seeks to move beyond Tooze, "Imagining National Economies: National and International Economic Statistics, 1900–50," in *Imagining Nations*, ed. Geoffrey Cubitt (Manchester: Manchester University Press, 1998), 212–28; and Goswami, *Producing India*. On multiple scales, see A. G. Hopkins, "Interactions between the Universal and the Local" and Mark Metzler, "The Cosmopolitanism of National Economics: Friedrich List in a Japanese Mirror," in *Global History: Interactions Between the Universal and the Local*, ed. Hopkins (Basingstoke: Macmillan, 2006), 1–19, 98–130.

13. Hobsbawm, "Where Are the British Historians Going?" *Marxist Quarterly* 2, no. 1 (1955): 14–26; Quinn Slobodian, "How to See the World Economy: Statistics, Maps, and Schumpeter's Camera in the First Age of Globalization," *Journal of Global History* 10, no. 2 (July 2015): 307–32; Slobodian, *Globalists*.

14. This paragraph draws substantially from Howard Erdman's discussion in *The Swatantra Party and Indian Conservatism*, 120–40.

colonial period. They had a strong sense of identity and adopted specific symbolic and sartorial practices to form the archetype of lordly clans.[15] Rajputs in the Swatantra Party tended to be family members of ex-rulers. The ex-rulers themselves and their direct descendants typically preferred to stay aloof from politics, or they saw little point in parting company with the Congress.[16]

In certain former princely regions like Baroda, Mysore, and Travancore, more economically progressive leadership drove reforms. Swatantra attracted some support in all these states, putting up candidates for election and winning seats in the state legislative assembly.[17] Enlightened rajas and zealous *diwans* (prime ministers) promoted industrial activity in each of these three states from the late nineteenth century. Each had or developed a performance-based rather than hereditary bureaucracy. Baroda, later incorporated into Bombay State (1951) and then Gujarat State (1960), benefited from the comparative absence of large landowners. This allowed it to avoid major resistance to the ruler's programs. The further introduction of ryotwari settlement and a modern bureaucracy in the early twentieth century curtailed the power of feudal lords. State-sponsored industrialization consciously "mimicking" Europe gave way to large capital investment from outside thanks to accommodating policies. Both textiles and chemicals industries developed.[18] This hastened a shift away from agriculture by the 1940s.[19] Travancore, which would become a part of Madras, prioritized agroindustry, specializing in coir, rubber, and tea. Here, it was less state ownership than state facilitation, like tax incentives and public infrastructure, which provided fillip to the process of resource extraction and industrial growth.[20]

Mysore presents perhaps the most dramatic example of princely development in thought and practice. There, initial openness to private investment,

15. I have omitted a more detailed discussion that delves into the changes and spread of Rajput identity between Mughal and British periods for the sake of simplicity. See Bayly, *Caste, Society and Politics*, 8, 32–4, 51, 190.

16. Chapter 5 discusses Maharani Gayatri Devi of Jaipur, an exception to this rule.

17. Chapter 6 reviews these results.

18. Manu Bhagavan, "Demystifying the 'Ideal Progressive': Resistance through Mimicked Modernity in Princely Baroda, 1900–1913," *Modern Asian Studies* 35, no. 2 (2001): 385–409.

19. David Hardiman, "Baroda," in *People, Princes, and Paramount Power: Society and Politics in the Indian Princely States*, ed. Robin Jeffrey (New Delhi: Oxford University Press, 1978), 107–35.

20. I discuss these issues in the first section of "A Forgotten Famine of '43? Travancore's Muffled 'Cry of Distress,'" *Modern Asian Studies*, forthcoming.

which helped form coffee and gold mining industries, gave way to a major state-led plan of development. Development encompassed a range of activities. The Kingdom of Mysore pursued large irrigation and dam-building schemes, becoming home to India's first hydroelectricity plant. It also sponsored industrial concerns as diverse as soap factories and iron and steel works. In a subsequent stage of "mixed economy," private interests developed small industries based on agricultural products. Diwans played an especially powerful role in Mysore's industrial transformation. M. Visvesvaraya, an engineer and later diwan (1912–18), even coined the phrase "industrialize or perish."[21] An admirer of Japanese industrialization and supporter of the idea of development by forced marches, he later drew up the first economic plan for India.[22] Mysore's economic development complemented social reform and a new aesthetic culture, together bringing about a "princely modern" society.[23]

Ex-princely administrators and retired Indian Civil Service officers dominated the Mysore Swatantra Party. Members like M. A. Sreenivasan, the ex-diwan of Gwalior and J. M. Lobo Prabhu, an ex-Indian Civil Service officer who had served in Bombay and Madras, showed a keen interest in the "efficiency" of administration of the past when compared to its messiness under democratic conditions.[24] Their expertise in implementing economic policy differed from the professionalized forms gaining wider currency in the mid-twentieth century and focused more on policy planning. These members generally had an anti-politics approach to public administration, which led them to reject measures like caste-based reservation for government jobs.[25] They often showed antidemocratic sentiments and questioned the wisdom of universal franchise.[26] Although bureaucratic generalists would continue to play an

21. Bjorn Hettne, *The Political Economy of Indirect Rule: Mysore, 1881–1947* (London: Curzon, 1978), 223–334.

22. On Visvesvaraya, see Aditya Balasubramanian, "A More Indian Path to Prosperity? Hindu Nationalism and Development in the Mid-20th Century and Beyond," *Capitalism: A Journal of History and Economics* 3, no. 2 (2022): 333–78, 351–54.

23. Janaki Nair, *Mysore Modern: Rethinking the Region under Princely Rule* (Minneapolis: University of Minnesota Press, 2011).

24. On Lobo Prabhu, see the previous chapter.

25. The term "anti-politics," with respect to bureaucratic depoliticization of the problems of poverty and development, comes from James Ferguson's influential *The Anti-Politics Machine: "Development," Depoliticization and Bureaucratic Power in Lesotho* (Minneapolis: University of Minnesota Press, 1994).

26. Erdman, *The Swatantra Party and Indian Conservatism*, 139.

important role in the economic administration of independent India, the idea generators by this time were the planners.

Without a bourgeoisie typical of industrial capitalism, economic development had taken a form compatible with monarchy in select former princely states. Powerful bureaucrats associated with these projects therefore helped these states transition from feudalism. However, they did not have much interest in a new political order. They found camaraderie among the more decidedly feudal ex-royals of the Swatantra Party, sharing a kind of political nostalgia.[27]

## Agrarian Economic Internationalism from the Ryot: The Kammas and N. G. Ranga

Certain dominant agrarian castes from the former ryotwari areas were more open to embracing economic and political change than the nostalgic administrators. Sections of the Kammas and Reddys of the Northern Circars (see Map 4.1)—Telugu-speaking landowner-cultivator castes of the former Madras Presidency—threw their support behind the Swatantra Party. Both owed their original prosperity to success in agriculture, but they later took advantage of other opportunities.

N. G. Ranga, a Kamma leader and Swatantra's president, had some ties to those who articulated ideas about free economy in magazines like the *Indian Libertarian* and *Swarajya*. Yet, for the most part, he had long pursued a distinct yet complementary set of ideas and practices. Ranga believed that regional landed agrarian interests might be advanced through forms of collective action between agricultural nations in the international order. Ranga moved between multiple identities as an agrarian economist, a Gandhian, a peasant leader, and an Afro-Asian internationalist.[28] He was an expert publicist who wrote prolifically in English and Telugu. A detailed study of his writings and political

27. Erdman, *The Swatantra Party and Indian Conservatism*, 120–28.

28. On Ranga as publicist, see David Washbrook, "The Development of Caste Organization in South India," in *South India: Political Institutions and Political Change*, eds. Baker and Washbrook (New Delhi: Macmillan, 1975), 150–203, 175–80. Ranga's Telugu newspaper, *Ryotpatrika*, receives a brief mention in Washbrook, "Country Politics: Madras 1880 to 1930," *Modern Asian Studies* 7, no. 3 (1973): 475–531, 518. This section omits detailed discussion of Ranga's Telugu books for two reasons: several of them overlap substantially with their English equivalents, and the salient ideas discussed here receive fullest expression in English.

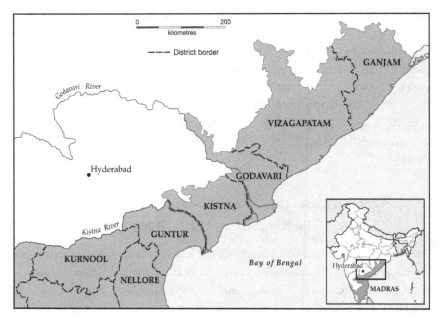

MAP 4.1. Northern Circars Region (Jenny Sheehan and CartoGIS, College of Asia and the Pacific, Australian National University, 2022).

activity illustrates how progressive anticolonial—and later, postcolonial—economic imaginaries of new world order, dubbed worldmaking in recent scholarship, can be compatible with national and regional systems and practices opposed to more radical change.[29] Reckoning with the imaginaries of worldmakers across multiple scales can help us better appreciate the political and economic trajectory of postcolonial societies, which are a history of both triumph and tragedy.[30]

29. Adom Getachew, *Worldmaking after Empire: The Rise and Fall of Self-Determination* (Princeton: Princeton University Press, 2019). I am suggesting that worldmaking can be compatible with more conservative ideas about national and local political economy and that attention to this can help us better understand the trajectory of societies after empire, especially because these worldmakers can go on to become powerful political actors at these scales.

30. For example, Black agrarianism as advocated by Booker T. Washington's Tuskegee Institute in the United States is conventionally understood as conservative. But Black communities in South Africa during the early twentieth century invoked the practices of the institute as a powerful form of antiracism (marked as they were by hierarchies of gender and class). At the transnational scale, then, the Tuskegee Institute and its legacy appear different from when

Ranga's idealized views of peasant proprietorship, small-town life, and economic transition were shaped by the prosperous history of his caste. Dam
construction in the mid-nineteenth century by Arthur Cotton on the Krishna
and Godavari rivers running through the Northern Circars led to large-scale
irrigation that transformed this area into a rice bowl.[31] Cash agriculture came
to predominate and reap the benefits of increasing integration into the world
economy. In these areas, freely flowing credit and mobile labor prevented debt
bondage and more extreme forms of landlordism. Rather than the *mirasdar*
estate or rural area, it was the mofussil town that formed the site of most economic activity. This "merging of town and countryside" led to a development
of a common culture. From the late nineteenth century, the residents of the
Krishna and Godavari delta grew increasingly literate, built homes of brick and
tile, and developed a thriving journalism industry.[32] Kammas began to receive
English-language education and to shift out of agriculture and into agroindustry. After the Great Depression, they further diversified investment of their
agricultural surpluses, moving into construction, cinema, real estate, and
transport. While still attached to agriculture, this caste was transitioning to
new kinds of enterprise.[33]

From a family of minor landowners, Ranga grew up in an environment of
expanding education and print culture.[34] He encountered British liberal,

---

examined purely at the national scale. See Julia Tischler, "'The Only Industry That Can Make
Us Hold Our Own': Black Agrarianism in South Africa from a Transatlantic Perspective,
ca. 1910–1930," *The American Historical Review* 126, no. 4 (2021): 1396–1423. I am indebted to
Meghna Chaudhuri for this reference.

31. Sunil Amrith, *Unruly Waters: How Rains, Rivers, Coasts and Seas Have Shaped Asia's
History* (New York: Basic Books, 2018), 3, 17–21, 39–40; David Washbrook, *The Emergence of
Provincial Politics: The Madras Presidency, 1870–1920* (Cambridge: Cambridge University Press,
1976), 91.

32. Washbrook, *The Emergence of Provincial Politics*, 92–94.

33. Carol Boyack Upadhya, "From Kulak to Capitalist: The Emergence of a New Business
Community in Coastal Andhra Pradesh, India," (unpublished PhD diss., Yale University, 1988),
106–9.

34. Linguistic change became a part of social reform efforts and a literary Telugu developed
closer to the spoken language from the 1910s. See Lisa Mitchell, *Language, Emotions and Politics
in South India: The Making of a Mother Tongue* (Ranikhet: Permanent Black, 2009). Socialist
ideas, which first appeared around 1920 in the Telugu periodical press, permeated across various
print forms, including novels, short stories, and poems. The economic challenges of the 1930s
helped generate interest in the revolutionary rhetoric of change and progress. See D. Anjaneyulu,

Gandhian, and leftist ideas in a Telugu public sphere experiencing a literary renaissance. Reminiscing on the period in his memoirs, Ranga describes a powerful social awakening: "I was opening my eyes into realization of the existence of a real world outside our twenty, fifty, or hundred villages in our Firka, Taluk and a few sleepy and smoky and dusty towns!"[35] He would continue to establish himself as a key figure in the mofussil intellectual world around his ancestral village of Nidubrolu.

Ranga abandoned plans to join the civil service after he arrived at Oxford in 1920. He gravitated toward social work and instead joined the Workers Education Association. By this time Gandhi assumed control over the freedom movement. Ranga would later recall that the experience of the atmosphere of political freedom in England sharpened his resolve to fight for the freedom of India.[36] Gandhi's interest in rural India and the mass character of the noncooperation movement of 1921 won Ranga over. His Oxford thesis on the economics of handloom weaving reflected this new interest.[37]

During these years away from home between 1920 and 1926, Ranga encountered ideas and policies that went on to inform his analyses of the Indian village and ideas for economic reform. He came across state-sponsored labor exchanges in England, France, Sweden, and Norway that might be used in India to redress rural unemployment.[38] Ranga was particularly struck by the example of Scandinavian countries, where government-appointed assessors and surveyors had suggested the best approach to land consolidation. The subsequent measures implemented took place with the express permission of landowners, honoring their property rights.[39] Visits to Scandinavia offered Ranga

"Impact of Socialist Ideology on Telugu Literature between the Wars," in *Socialism in India*, ed. B. R. Nanda (Delhi: Vikas, 1972), 244–60.

35. Ranga, *Fight for Freedom* (New Delhi: S. Chand, 1968), 59.

36. Ranga, *Fight for Freedom*, 80–81.

37. This later appeared as Ranga, *The Economics of Handloom (Being a Study of the Social and Economic Conditions of Handloom Weavers of South India)* (Bombay: D. B. Taraporevala Sons and Co, 1930).

38. As a professor of economics in the 1920s, Ranga wrote two volumes on *Economic Organisation of Indian Villages* (Bombay: D. B. Taraporevala and Co., 1929)—pioneering works that showed the realities of village social and economic life and the relative deprivation of peasants in zamindari areas. Later, in 1939, Ranga prepared a *Guide to Village Economic Survey* as part of the Kisan (Farmer) Publication Series of the All-India Kisan Sabha.

39. Ranga, *Fight for Freedom*, 83–84. On Swedish land redistribution, see Staffan Helmfrid, "The Storskifte, Enskifte, and Laga Skifte in Sweden: General Features," *Geografiska Annaler* 43, no. 1–2 (1961): 114–29.

a different vision of agrarian society. He came across folk schools that sought to teach a rural philosophy of life and encountered vibrant peasant political parties in Denmark and Sweden.[40] Finally, his encounter with the International Labor Organization (ILO) showed Ranga that international organizations could promote global class interests. This made him think about the possibilities of a body to advance the interests of the global peasantry.

In England, Ranga made friendships that broke racial barriers and shaped a lifelong commitment to the solidarity of Asian and African peoples.[41] This period extended the scale of his interests beyond the nation to the future of the world. Along with the Kenyan Jomo Kenyatta and the Trinidadian George Padmore, he joined the League of Colored Peoples.[42] A decade later, when Gandhi launched his Quit India Movement, Ranga sought to widen the demands of that movement and worked with his African friends to set up a Colonial and Colored Peoples Front agitating for all European empires to "Quit the Colonies!"[43] This moment spurred Ranga's creative thought about a new world order. His 1946 *Colonial and Coloured Peoples* argued that anticolonial leaders from nations with more successful freedom movements could help those of other nations in a "world organization."[44] Ranga's "skeleton

40. These recollections appear in Ranga, *Credo of World Peasantry* (Nidubrolu: Indian Peasant Institute, 1957), 443–7.

41. Ranga would keep in touch and meet with the pan-Africanist George Padmore well into the 1950s. See Ranga to Padmore, June 17, 1946; Ranga to Padmore, October 31, 1952, and Padmore to Ranga, June 8, 1955, reproduced in Ranga, *Agony and Solace: Correspondence, Statements, Speeches etc. 1936–74* (Nidubrolu: Kisan Publications, 1974), 60–61, 282–83, 316–17. Padmore's colleague Makonnen offers fond recollections of Ranga and Nehru and mentions their support of African leaders in preference to overseas Indians, who were allied with white settlers. See Makonnen, *Pan-Africanism from Within* (London: Oxford University Press, 1973), 190–91.

42. Ranga, *Fight for Freedom*, 92; Anne Spry Rush, "Imperial Identity in Colonial Minds: Harold Moody and the League of Colored Peoples, 1931–50," *Twentieth Century British History* 13, no. 4 (2002): 356–83; Takehiko Ochiai, "Harold Arundel Moody and the League of Colored Peoples," *Ryukoku Law Review* 52 (2019): 1–52.

43. The organization met in London twice, before and after the celebrated Fifth Pan-African Congress organized by Ras Makonnen and George Padmore. Neither the front nor the federation lasted long. See Marika Sherwood, "The All-Colonial Peoples Conferences in Britain, 1945," *Leeds African Studies Bulletin* 79 (2017/8): 113–24; On pan-Africanism as a vision of a new world order, see Adom Getachew, *Worldmaking after Empire: The Rise and Fall of Self-Determination* (Princeton: Princeton University Press, 2019), 69–70, 107–140.

44. Padmore would later recognize Ranga's ideas as anticipating the Trotskyist Non-European Unity Movement founded in Cape Town. See Padmore, *Pan-Africanism or Communism?* (London: Dennis Dobson, 1956), 358.

suggestions" for future world order included interest-free loans from rich to poor countries, special protections for colored minorities, an international social service "to train and help the colonial peoples," and a transnational agricultural development board. He suggested that traditional ways of living in villages should be respected and preserved.[45]

Following a brief career as professor of history and economics at Pachaiyappa's College in Madras, Ranga became a full-time politician in 1930.[46] He brought landowning cultivating castes like his native Kammas toward the cause of the anti-zamindari movement in his region by forming *sabhas* (associations); writing and spreading Telugu songs and stories; and rallying large crowds in protest (see Figure 4.1).[47] Ranga's Indian Peasant Institute provided education in economics, politics, and social service (see Table 4.1). At the national level, he cofounded the All-India Kisan Sabha. That group played a seminal role in bringing the peasantry behind the Indian Nationalist Congress. He was one of the architects of the project of Gandhian mass nationalism. Like Rajagopalachari, he participated in Gandhi's efforts to end untouchability by turning to creative writing. But Ranga expressed himself in the novel form rather than the short story. His *Harijan Nāyakuḍu* (Harijan Leader) (1933) tells the story of a Dalit social reformer who allies with Kammas of the ryots to fight violence and abuse, lobbies for Dalit access to schools, temples, and shared resources, organizes inter-caste marriages.[48]

45. Ranga, *Colonial and Colored Peoples: A Program for their Freedom and Progress* (Bombay: Hind Kitabs, 1946), 163–92.

46. Ranga was first elected to the Central Legislative Assembly in 1930 and again from 1934–46. Over the course of his life, he served on the Constituent Assembly (1946–51), the Rajya Sabha (1952–56 and 1977–79), and the Lok Sabha (1957–70, 1980–94). See "Ranga, Prof. Nayakulu N. G., 9th Lok Sabha, Members Bioprofile," http://loksabhaph.nic.in/writereaddata/biodata_1_12/1326.htm.

47. Although Ranga's own Northern Circars region was a ryotwari area, the Telugu-speaking areas that would become Andhra Pradesh in 1953 included tracts of zamindari land. See B. Reddy Prasad Reddy, "Anti-Zamindar Struggles in Andhra Rural Politics During the 1930s and 1940s," (unpublished PhD diss., University of Hyderabad, India, 1993); E. Koteswara Rao, "The Kisan Struggles in Andhra Pradesh—A Study of Kisan Struggles of Munagala and Challapalli Zamindaries," (unpublished PhD diss., Acharya Nagarjuna University, India, 2011).

48. Gail Omvedt, *Dalits and the Democratic Revolution: Dr. Ambedkar and the Dalit Movement in Colonial India* (New Delhi: Sage, 1994), 177. Gandhi used the term *harijan*, or "Children of God," to refer to those of ritually untouchable status. However, its paternalistic connotations have led to its replacement by Dalit, which is the preferred term used by these groups.

FIGURE 4.1. Ranga's All-India Kisan Sabha Conference at Bezwada, 1944 (Sunil Janah, *Photographing India* [New Delhi: Oxford University Press, 2013], 68–69).

Like Lotvala and his interlocutors, Ranga drifted politically rightward from his leftist origins. He came to express a strong anticommunism. Originally sympathetic to the socialism that penetrated India during the interwar period, Ranga's views changed after the communists joined the Congress as part of a united front in the 1930s. The Communist Party had to operate under cover and infiltrate other progressive groups in a clandestine fashion after being banned by the British. Figures like Ranga soured on them after they found their supporters becoming communists.[49] Over the next decade, a budding anticommunism put Ranga increasingly out of step with the Nehruvian Congress leadership. He urged caution against the more ambitious Congress proposals for land redistribution, worrying over their implications.[50]

At the Constituent Assembly, he spoke out against the creation of a strong Center on the grounds that "Mahatma Gandhi has pleaded over a period of thirty years for decentralization." Centralization "would only lead to Sovietization and totalitarianism not democracy." He defended the democratic potential of

49. Sarkar, *Modern India*, 257, 318, 333.
50. "Minute of Dissent by Shri O. P. Ramaswamy Reddiar and Prof. N. G. Ranga," in *Report of the Congress Agrarian Reforms Committee* (New Delhi: All India Congress Committee, 1949), 185–206.

TABLE 4.1. Syllabus for Weekend School

| January | February | March | April | May | June |
|---|---|---|---|---|---|
| 1. Education and its importance | 5. Comparative study of the Educational systems in dependent and independent countries | 5. Public Finance | 2. Annual income of Agricultural labour, labourer and public servants | 7. Imports and Exports | 5. Village Administration Now and Then |
| 8. Lives of great men and their services to the country | 12. Economics and its importance | 12. Public expenditure in the dependent and independent countries | 9. Planned Economics | 15. Indian Economics Now and Then | 12. Systems of Administration |
| 15. Village—Town Education | 19. Household Economics | 19. Taxes and their history | 16. Currency exchange and Banking | 22. A comparative study in economics of the dependent and independent countries | 19. Indian Administration, Village, Firka, Taluk, District, Province and Central |
| 22. What Sort of Education is Required | 26. Village Economics | 26. Economic factors, and the welfare of the masses | 23. The effects of exchange and currency on Agriculturists and merchants | 29. Economic Survey | 26. Local Administration in India and Other Countries |
| 29. The difference between old and present system of National Education | | | 30. Co-operation and insurance | | |

| July | August | September | October | November | December |
|---|---|---|---|---|---|
| 3. Police: Civil and Criminal Administrations | 1. Franchise | 5. Religions of Hindu, Buddhist, Muhammedan, Sikh, Jain, Parsi, and Christian | 3. The relation of Economics and Politics | 1. Communications of the World | 6. Nature Study |
| 10. Public Servants | 8. The difference between dependent and independent countries | 12. Harijan Movement | 10. Geography | 8. Agriculture, Minerals | 13. Food and Health |
| 17. Indian Act 1935–Congress | 15. Ways and means of getting independence | 19. Minority classes and tribesmen | 17. Indian Geography | 15. Home Industries and Factory Industries | 20. Man and his discipline |
| 25. Legislatures and Parties | 22. Nonviolent Imperialism and Socialism | 26. The relation of Religion to Politics | 25. World Geography | 22. How to conduct the Conferences and Meetings | 27. Examinations |
|  | 29. Constitutions of the World (a comparative study) |  |  | 29. Journalism |  |

*Source:* Ranga, *Adult Education Movement* (Rajahmundry: Andhradesa Adult Education Committee, 1938), 142–43.

the village *panchayat* as a unit of governance and objected to modernist critiques of caste-based inequality at the rural level.[51]

Never a cultural or linguistic nationalist, Ranga opposed "clubbing together regions of varying social, economic, and political developments . . . merely because their people spoke the same language."[52] He showed little interest in the movement for linguistic statehood of Andhra (Telugu-speaking regions of Madras Presidency) and the former princely state of Hyderabad as Andhra Pradesh. Events did not go his way. He cast his lot with the losing side in a factional battle for the control of Andhra politics.[53] In 1953, Andhra Pradesh became a separate state and later incorporated Hyderabad.[54] Ranga quit the Congress briefly to found the short-lived Krishikar Lok Party (Cultivating People's Party) before being brought back into the Congress fold in 1956 to form a joint front against the communists.[55]

Ranga developed a conviction that the dominant thrust of economic policy was antirural and dangerously close to subverting the right to property of all peasant proprietors. Although he applauded legislation that abolished the zamindari system, regional legislation to strengthen the occupancy rights of tenants and discussion of land ceilings in the second plan struck him as measures that went too far.[56] Ranga resigned from the Congress once again after the passage of the Nagpur resolution on Cooperative Farming.[57] His resignation letter declared, with characteristic exaggeration, that the resolution signaled "the commencement of demotion of peasantry into a new depressed class of the socialist age."[58]

51. Ranga, *Constituent Assembly Debates*, November 9, 1948.

52. Ranga, *Fight for Freedom*, 373.

53. Brian Stoddart, *Land, Water, Language and Politics in Andhra: Regional Evolution in India Since 1850* (London: Routledge, 2011) 180–85.

54. Guha, *India after Gandhi*, 186–89.

55. "See "Ranga, Prof. Nayakulu N. G"; A. M. Zaidi, *The Story of Congress Pilgrimage: Event to Event Record of Activities of the Indian National Congress from 1885 to 1985 Emanating from Official Reports of the General Secretaries* (New Delhi: Indian Institute of Applied Political Research, 1990), 200–2; Samantha Kathleen Watson, "The Limits of Self-Help: Policy and Political Economy in Rural Andhra Pradesh," (unpublished PhD diss., University of Manchester, 2012), 101.

56. C. Ramachandriah and A. Venkateswarlu, *Land Laws, Administration, and Displacement in Andhra Pradesh, India* (Hyderabad: Centre for Economic and Social Studies, 2014), 12–15.

57. See the previous chapter.

58. Austin, *Working a Democratic Constitution*, 43.

Ranga constructed an idealized peasant proprietor, which he deployed to defend rural propertied communities in ryotwari areas like the Reddys and the Kammas. He ignored distinctions of caste and class and unequal power dynamics between tenants and cultivators.[59] Three texts from the late 1950s represented the culmination of Ranga's views on the economy and the peasant proprietor's role: the historical credo, the rural economic survey, and the contemporary issue-based pamphlet. Each had antecedents in earlier output that included over sixty-five books in English and fifteen in Telugu.

Ranga's magnum opus, the five-hundred-odd page *Credo of World Peasantry* (1957), synthesized his interests in history and economics. The book heralded the awakening of the peasant movement that arose from "armors of co-operatives and parliamentary system of democracy and human rights."[60] It built on works like *The Colonial and Colored Peoples* and was congruous with Ranga's participation in groups like the International Federation for Agricultural Producers.[61] Consistent with Ranga's expression of discomfort with a strong Center and endorsement of village self-government at the Constituent Assembly, the *Credo of World Peasantry* advanced an ideal of decentralized democracy from the grassroots.[62] Although focused on reforming the capitalist world, Ranga considered the Soviet system to be equally anti-peasant because it alienated peasants from land ownership. The book wove regional class interests into a national and global framework.

The *Credo* was the most extensive of a vein of Ranga's writings that responded to communist allegations about peasants being insufficiently revolutionary. It was part history, part work of political economy, and part manifesto. Like Rajagopalachari's writings, it stylistically resembled oratory rather than written prose. Triumphal declarations and exaggerated assessments in the *Credo*'s pages reflected Ranga's background as a public speaker known for rallying peasants. At the same time, the *Credo* made claims to sophistication. Ranga peppered it with references to Marx's *Capital*, Dr. Sun Yat-sen's lectures, his own earlier

59. Washbrook, *The Emergence of Provincial Politics*, 70.

60. Ranga, *Credo of World Peasantry* (Nidubrolu: Indian Peasant Institute, 1957), 10.

61. Ranga, *World Role of National Revolution* (Nidubrolu: Kisan Publishers, 1945); Ranga, *The Colonial and Coloured Peoples: A Programme for their Freedom and Progress (New Delhi: Hind Kitabs, 1946)*; Ranga, *Revolutionary Peasants* (New Delhi: Amrit, 1949); Ranga, *Kisans and Communists* (Bombay: Pratibha, 1949); Ranga, "Message to the Tenth Anniversary of IFAP to be held on 19 May 1957 at Padua, USA," Serial Four, N. G. Ranga Papers, NAI.

62. Ranga, *Constituent Assembly Debates*, November 9, 1948; Austin, *The Indian Constitution*, 36.

books, and even surveys of the Food and Agricultural Organization (FAO) of the United Nations.

Shortcomings aside, the *Credo* comes off as neither simplistic nor lacking in conceptual clarity. In some ways, it reflects Ranga's own multiple identities as an economist, historian, peasant leader, and propagandist. The book's six appendices add to the multifaceted and slightly jumbled nature of the book. They include the "Credo of the Indian Peasant," excerpts from Ranga's speeches at the International Peasant Union, and a list of the objectives of the General Agreement on Trade and Tariffs.

Ranga painted the peasant as a sufferer of the unfortunate currents of world history. Wrenched from life in a "self-sufficient economy" of "Village Commonwealths" where agricultural surpluses could be drawn down in times of distress, the advent of feudalism forced peasants to produce more and more "under duress." Feudal interests extorted the farmer's agricultural surplus and left him/her vulnerable to the year's harvest. With the transition to capitalism and the internationalization of markets, an increasing number of middlemen came between producer and consumers. They provided "key services" and confused the peasant, leaving him/her at the margin of subsistence. The providers of key services could be private sector actors or bureaucrats who operated "the overall master mechanism of modern administration which regulates, permits, controls or commandeers almost every aspect of the complex social life of the present age." Most crucially for the peasant, key services had interfered with food production and distribution in India from the time of World War II. Ranga's was a version of Marx's argument about the alienation of industrial laborers, cleverly adapted for the case of the farmer.[63]

Peasants had actively adapted to changing political and economic currents of history but needed better representation in the postwar international economic system. They abandoned the joint family system, or tribal living with communal land ownership, in favor of peasant proprietorship by individual male adult family members. They participated in anticolonial nationalist projects, like the *kisans* who supported Gandhi in India. Arguing, without evidence, that that the supply inelasticity of agricultural produce was a structural feature of the world economy, Ranga demanded powerful intervention by nation states to ameliorate the consequences of low prices for agricultural output. He cited Franklin Roosevelt's New Deal "parity-price system" as a

63. Ranga, *Credo*, 11–43.

worthy model to emulate on a global scale.[64] The system guaranteed remunerative prices to agriculture to maintain farmer purchasing power.

Ranga offered two ideas to rival regional trading blocs formed by the superpowers and overcome unequal trading relationships between industrialized and agricultural nations. First, he suggested that Asian nations form their own regional trading bloc. He welcomed the proposals made at the recent Bangalore meeting of the United Nation's Economic Commission for Asia and the Far East, where delegates had presented proposals for "inter-shipping facilities" and "concessional freight-schedules." Second, he proposed that agrarian countries join hands in global forums to advocate for concessional terms of trade. Steps in this direction included the ideal of zero trade balances for all economies, as presented in the Havana Charter adopted by the UN Conference on Trade and Employment in 1947.[65] Ranga regarded both the regional trading bloc independent of the West and the zero balance of trade as parallels to the Gandhian idea of village self-sufficiency in the domain of international trade. He identified the FAO as "the governmental facet of the same awakening and world consciousness of peasants, the primary producers" and wanted to take the organization's activities much further.[66]

N. G. Ranga deployed a vivid metaphor to illustrate his vision of global agricultural price coordination. He suggested "a method quite analogous to Panama Locks or Volga-Don Canal Locks where the boats both on the higher and lower gradients are enabled to cross each other and go their own way without coming into clash." Practically, this meant that, first, individual countries should

64. On the Rooseveltian parity system, see Gary Libecamp, "The Great Depression and the Regulating State: Federal Government Regulation of Agriculture, 1884–1970," in *The Defining Moment: The Great Depression and the American Economy of the Twentieth Century*, eds. Michael Bordo, Claudia Goldin, and Eugene White (Chicago: University of Chicago Press, 1998), 181–224.

65. Ranga, *Credo*, 263–312. India had submitted a special report stressing the need for special accommodations to developing countries, acknowledging their lower level of industrialization at Havana. On the role of developing countries in setting the terms of the postwar international trading system, see Christy Thornton, *Revolution in Development: Mexico and the Governance of the Global Economy* (Berkeley: University of California Press, 2021), 121–45.

66. Unlike various other UN organizations, the United States and the United Kingdom did not originally support the FAO. Its origins trace to Australian demands for development sensitive to agrarian economies in 1946. See Martin Daunton, "Nutrition, Food, Agriculture and the World Economy," in *The Bretton Woods Agreement: Together with Scholarly Commentaries and Essential Historical Documents*, eds. Naomi Lamoreaux and Ian Shapiro (New Haven, CT: Yale University Press, 2019), 145–72.

set domestic agricultural prices to "develop the maximum amount of profit-able self-sufficiency" at a level fair to the peasantry. Subsequently, agrarian countries should negotiate bilateral agreements to coordinate quotas for commodities supplied to the world market and their prices.[67] The "gradients" referred to a range within which to keep internal and external price levels. Canals and dams had made Ranga's ancestral region of deltaic Andhra Pradesh prosperous. It was no coincidence that he kept these in his head when thinking about the governance of international trade. Though collaborative, Ranga's was not an internationalism that involved breaking down walls between coun-tries. Rather, his brand respected national sovereignty and worked within the international economic order without trying to overthrow it.

As a lifelong participant in organizations dedicated to Afro-Asian solidarity, Ranga also believed in advancing the cause of the world's peasants through informal transnational groups. He participated in the International Peasant Union, the latest in a line of informal transnational movements to represent those marginalized by the political and economic "center" by the "periphery." Started by exiled agrarian leaders from Eastern Europe, this anti-Soviet group was a foil to the Soviet Krestintern (Peasant International); it made very clear its bias toward the peasant proprietor rather than the landless agricultural laborer.[68]

Ranga adhered to a nationalist brand of internationalism. The cooperative units of his agrarian world order would "epitomize the essence of nineteenth-century liberalism, twentieth-century Gandhian Humanism and India's Pluralistic Social Traditions of peaceful growth." They would depend on "the mutual co-operation as between the various social and economic institutions from the Village Commonwealths and craft guilds up to their national super-structures." These cooperatives would serve themselves, not urban interests. Peasants would make production decisions. This organization aimed to bring out "individual enterprise and initiative" through "small-holdings" and "cottage-industrial homes." As distinct from the Soviet or Chinese "collectives," which were "gerrymandered" entities that accentuated class differences, the Indian cooperative ideal would bring peasants together.[69]

Ranga turned back to the genre in which he had originally made his name a year later, producing a village economic survey called *The Peasant and*

67. Ranga, *Credo*, 263–64.
68. Ralph L. Goldman, *The Future Catches Up: Transnational Parties and Democracy* (San Jose: Writers' Club Press, 2002), 58.
69. Ranga, *Credo*, 443–52.

*Cooperative Farming.*[70] His survey sought to show that small peasant holdings were productive and did not require nationalization and reorganization.[71] It responded to discussions about the appropriateness of cooperative farming for India. Ranga spoke in the language of the planned economic policymaker. He fought their economic indicators with data of his own to argue that peasant landholdings required no changes.[72]

Ranga's study examined the correlation between the size of landholding, the cost, and the output in owner-cultivated plots in an especially fertile area of Andhra Pradesh. It showed that producer surplus per acre increased as holdings got smaller. Income per farmer rose with the size of the farm, peaking at the medium-sized farmer, before declining again. Despite being draped in the garb of scientific presentation, the survey suffered from a lack of scientific rigor. Plots were not selected randomly, statistics collected did not account for differences in output based on the crop, and there was no way of verifying the data collected from the farmers.

Ranga's subsequent defense of the peasant proprietor abandoned any pretentions to scientific rigor. *Self-Employed Sector (Their Constructive Role in Planned Economy)* was a pamphlet that hoped to blunt the enthusiasm for agricultural land ceilings and link the peasant's plight at the hands of the Government of India to those of other constituencies.[73] Ranga contended that under the Hindu law of *mitakshara*, large holdings would be subdivided among male heirs over time, so as to obviate the need for land ceilings.[74] The gendered implications of this are worth noting in the context of personal law reform— he cited the tradition of exclusively male property inheritance rather than the more recent provisions of the Hindu Succession Act.[75] Next, the pamphlet proposed a reclassification of the economy into public sector, "private capitalist sector," "Self-employed Peoples' Sector," and a cooperative sector complementary to the self-employed sector. The peasant farmer in this people's sector was thus akin to "artisans, shopkeepers and retail traders," who "do not need

70. Ranga, *The Peasant and Cooperative Farming* (Nidubrolu: Indian Peasants Institute, 1958).

71. See chapter 3.

72. Menon, *Planning Democracy.*

73. N. G. Ranga, *Self-Employed Sector (Their Constructive Role in Planned Economy)* (Nidubrolu: Indian Peasant Institute, 1959).

74. Ranga, *Self-Employed Sector,* 1–34. See the discussion of personal law reform in the previous chapter.

75. See chapter 3.

any special protection or encouragement."[76] In this way, he theorized the peasant's commonality of interest with other groups who feared the increasing hand of the state.

Ranga's ideas and political career relied on the assumption of the undifferentiated category of the peasant. His experiences with the Indian communists reaffirmed his commitment to a unified peasant class. Like Rajagopalachari, he believed that communists focused on class struggle within the peasantry and hampered more unified collective action. Ranga looked to the Danish model of agrarian cooperatives for inspiration because they did "not seek to split up peasants into rich, middle, and poor sections and set up one against the other, to subvert their unity, and destroy them as a class."[77] He did not consider whether the appropriateness of the Danish model for India might be compromised by the conditions of the caste system. Instead, Ranga believed private property was the foundation of peasant self-employment. Contra Marx, Ranga constructed a revolutionary past and a freedom-loving identity for his idealized peasant. Perhaps unwittingly, this peasant proprietor model of a small property-based economy harkened back to the principles behind ryotwari settlement.[78]

Most of the constituents who elected Ranga to parliament did not speak English and would not deeply scrutinize writings like the *Credo* or the village economic survey. This material instead shows how, through his belief in a shared interest in property and his enmity to controls, a seemingly left-leaning agriculturist—one who helped shape early Congress planning and cultivated its peasant base—transitioned toward a party that claimed support for small business. Although Ranga represented interest groups, he re-evaluated and justified his precise positions once again as conditions changed. The *Credo*, the survey, and the pamphlet conveyed what alternative economic policy might look like.

76. Earlier pamphlets included *Guide to Rural Economic Surveys* (Madras: All-India Kisan Publications, 1939) and *Four Crore Artisans Hail the Gandhian Plan* (Bombay: Hind Kitabs, 1945).

77. Ranga, *Credo of World Peasantry*, 448.

78. Mohammed Mustafa, "The Shaping of Land Revenue Policy in Madras Presidency: Revenue Experiments—the Case of Chittoor District," *Indian Economic and Social History Review* 44, no. 2 (2007): 213–36. A synthetic overview of the ryotwari settlement—which comprised two-thirds of the landmass of Madras Presidency—and the other kinds of land tenure in this region appears in Dharma Kumar, *Land and Caste in South India: Agricultural Labor in the Madras Presidency during the Nineteenth Century* (Cambridge: Cambridge University Press, 1965), 6–34.

Conservative in terms of national politics and leftist in his interest in Third World peasant solidarity, Ranga was a mofussil intellectual elite with a global vision of an international coalition of peasants. His was a creative take on how to empower agriculturists to use the postwar liberal international order to their advantage and an example of how agriculturists navigated the transition to mass democracy in India. Even if economic policy had been brought beyond electoral politics to a sphere of economic and statistical "rationality" by the Congress, it remained embedded in political life.[79]

## Self-Sufficiency by Other Means? The Charotar Patidars and Bhaikaka Patel

Like Andhra's Kammas, the Patidars of the Charotar Tract in Gujarat are a landowning dominant caste who have successfully transitioned into agro-industry. From 1946, they commenced an experiment in cooperative economy that used the village as the basic unit of economic organization and focused on agricultural production. It was led by the private sector, although not without considerable state support. The economic cooperators of the Charotar Tract used their profits from agriculture to finance education and research initiatives through philanthropic trusts. This orientation is reflected in the emergence of two complementary flagship towns. In Anand, the Charotar Patidars developed a center for milk production. In the adjacent Vallabh Vidyanagar (Town of Knowledge), they established various educational institutions, the most substantial of which was a science and technology university. A strong sense of regional identity, caste-based cooperation and accumulation, and an openness to new ideas and foreign expertise have been at the heart of the Charotar Patidar's postcolonial fortunes.

Their home region of Gujarat—which would split off from Bombay to form its own state in 1960—has shaped the economic activity and identity of the Charotar Patidars. In medieval times, this terraqueous area formed a key Arabian Sea and Indian Ocean trading hub (see Map 4.2), attracting settlers from trading communities of the Middle East and other parts of Asia.[80] Both Brahmin

79. Partha Chatterjee, "Development Planning and the Indian State," in *The State, Development Planning and Liberalization in India*, 82–103.

80. Sheikh, *Forging a Region*. On the "mercantile ethos," see Suchitra Sheth and Achyut Yagnik, *The Shaping of Modern Gujarat: Pluralism, Hindutva and Beyond* (Delhi: Penguin India, 2005).

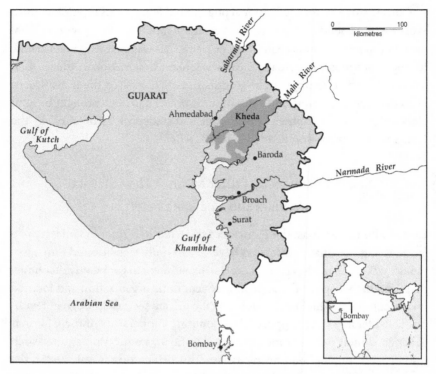

MAP 4.2. Gujarat and Kheda district during British Rule (Jenny Sheehan and CartoGIS, College of Asia and the Pacific, Australian National University, 2022).

and Bania (merchant) communities ran its educational institutions, making the distinction between intelligentsia and businesspeople more tenuous than in other regions. Commercial ethos was a component of Gujarati *asmitā*, or Gujarati-ness, the term coined by K. M. Munshi.[81] Asmitā also embraced the British description of mercantile and lettered Gujarati communities as "middle class." This went along with an understanding of development as commercially driven and private philanthropy as a strong element of self-identification. They tied upward mobility to educational attainment.[82]

81. See chapter 2.

82. Riho Isaka, "The Gujarati Literati and the Construction of a Regional Identity in the Late Nineteenth Century," (unpublished PhD diss., University of Cambridge, 1999). I am indebted

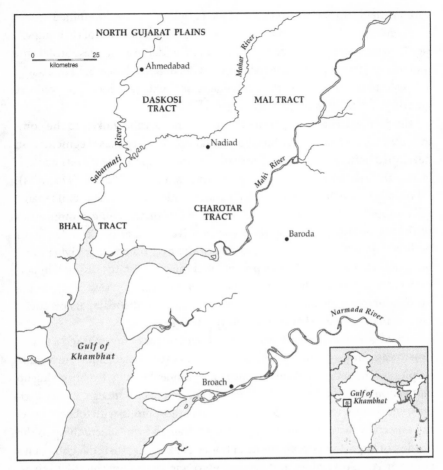

MAP 4.3. Agricultural Tracts (Jenny Sheehan and CartoGIS, College of Asia and the Pacific, Australian National University, 2022).

Schoolmasters and clerks carried ideas and concepts like asmitā from the city to mofussil areas of the fertile Charotar Tract. The region encompassing Nadiad, Borsad, and Anand subdivisions of the Kheda district of Bombay Presidency and the Petlad area of the former Baroda princely state (see Map 4.3).[83]

to Professor Ornit Shani for the reference. See also the discussion of the "mercantile ethos" in Sheth and Achyut Yagnik, *The Shaping of Modern Gujarat*, 1–6.

83. *Reports on Publications*, 1885, quoted in Isaka, "The Gujarati Literati and the Construction of a Regional Identity in the Late Nineteenth Century," 157.

Patidars made up about 12 percent of the population of the combined area.[84] The community's name comes from the Mughal-era practice of dividing village land into *patis* (strips), with each *patidar* (holder of a pati) responsible for procuring taxes proportionate to the area of the holding. Patis could be bought and sold to other Patidars in each village, or if village elders approved the granting of Patidar status to a non-Patidar.[85]

The political awakening of the Patidars is inextricably linked to the community's social history. Within the Patidar community, class segmentation developed between an elite minority of *Maṭadārs* responsible for revenue collection from their lineage groups, lesser Patidars, and the *Dharalas* (*Dharālās*). Of ritually untouchable status, the Dharalas tended to be agricultural tenants or laborers.[86] The matadars modeled themselves on the *bania* communities of the urban areas, adopting their competitive social ethic, "the desire for *sudharavuṃ*, self-improvement, and superiority over others," gift-giving practices, and eating habits.[87] They perpetuated their elite status through hypergamous marriages with lesser Patidars offering large dowries. To limit the number of marriageable females in their community, the matadars practiced female infanticide and banned widow remarriage.

From the mid-nineteenth century, cash settlement of revenue and a transition to cash crop agriculture helped the Patidars accumulate liquid, investible surpluses. The superior Patidars moved into moneylending, largely giving up cultivation. In several instances, Dharalas entered debt bondage. Lesser Patidars, who continued to cultivate, became more prosperous, with tobacco proving especially lucrative. Increasingly, they refrained from succumbing to the burden of large dowry obligations in hopes of marrying their daughters into superior Patidar families and formed marriage circles among themselves. Government credit schemes and debt reduction legislation after the 1899–1900 famine provided a means for the further rise of the lesser Patidars, as did migration across the country and to East Africa to pursue professional

84. *Census of 1921*, cited in Hardiman, "Baroda," 6.

85. In this way, they differentiated themselves from others in the *kanbi* cluster of cultivating communities in northern and western India. See David F. Pocock, *Kanbi and Patidar: A Study of the Patidar Community of Gujarat* (Oxford: Clarendon Press, 1972).

86. On the violence and extra-economic dynamics of the control exerted over the *dharalas*, see Vinayak Chaturvedi's highly innovative *Peasant Pasts: History and Memory in Western India* (Berkeley: University of California Press, 2007).

87. Bayly, *Caste, Society and Politics*, 221–23; Crispin Bates, "The Nature of Social Change in Rural Gujarat: The Kheda District 1818–1918," *Modern Asian Studies* 15, no. 4 (1981): 771–821, 795.

opportunities in trade and white-collar occupations. Dharalas began to organize in favor of a new political order.[88]

These currents of change formed the backdrop against which upwardly mobile lesser Patidars asserted their identity more explicitly.[89] They became outstanding exponents of Gandhian mass nationalism, protesting taxes and embracing the goal of "self-sufficiency" by boycotting Lancashire textiles and spinning khadi (Indian cloth). Further, the Patidars avoided excess, celebrated agrarian work, and valorized village life. They also coerced and committed violence against Dharalas, whom the British classified as a "criminal tribe" and restricted movement.[90] The Patidars' recognition as a caste from the 1931 census formally signaled a consolidation of community identity.[91]

The Gandhian Vallabhbhai, or Sardar (Leader) Patel, spearheaded the antitax *satyagraha* at Bardoli (1928). This brought him national fame and provided inspiration for other satyagrahas across the country.[92] Three years later, he became president of the Indian National Congress and would serve as Gandhi's deputy throughout the 1930s. Patel resisted measures by other leaders to move the Congress in a leftward direction. And while the likes of Rajagopalachari fell away from Congress during the Quit India Movement of 1942, preferring negotiation with the British, Patel remained loyal and participated closely in its execution.[93] He went on to serve as independent India's deputy prime minister and home minister (1947–50).

Sardar Patel had a hand in the experiments that commenced in both Anand and Vallabh Vidyanagar.[94] During the late colonial period, a Bombay-based British-owned dairy called Polson dominated the demand for Anand milk and set up a dairy infrastructure there. By 1946, Polson secured exclusive rights by

88. Chaturvedi, *Peasant Pasts*, 25–98.

89. Bates, "The Nature of Social Change in Gujarat"; Mario Rutten, *Farms and Factories: Social Profile of Large Farmers and Rural Industrialists in West India* (New Delhi: Oxford University Press, 1995), 92–105. On the credit co-operatives, which had limited success, see E. J. Catanach, *Rural Credit in Western India, 1875–1930* (Berkeley: University of California Press, 1970), 164.

90. Chaturvedi, *Peasant Pasts*, 101–62.

91. A. H. Somjee, "Social Mobility among the Patidars of Kaira," in *Contributions to Asian Studies*, ed. K. Ishwaran (Leiden, Netherlands: E. J. Brill, 1978), 105–13, 106.

92. Hardiman, "Baroda," 86–129; Sarkar, *Modern India*, 242.

93. See the discussion in Gandhi, *Patel: A Life* (Ahmedabad: Navajivan Trust, 1990), 66–230.

94. Ruth Heredia, *The Amul India Story* (New Delhi: Tata McGraw Hill, 1997), 8–16. On Sardar Patel, see chapter 1.

an order of the Bombay government. Subsequently, the company attempted to halve the purchase price and thus nearly eliminate the farmer's profits.[95] The concerned farmers approached Sardar Patel, who suggested they unite against Polson in two levels of cooperative: village-level milk production societies and a cooperatively owned dairy union. The individual village cooperatives would supply the milk, and the single cooperative union would process it and bring it to market.[96] This model enabled the Patidars to drive Polson and the middlemen out of business.

The Patidars who went to the Sardar that day encountered little trouble in forming village cooperative societies. To make their enterprise viable, however, they required outside expertise, ideas, and managerial talent. This brought a transnational dimension to their regional experiment. Their existing outdated machinery prevented the success of the cooperative enterprise. Furthermore, the dairy farmers did not have a sense of the latest production techniques. So they recruited a Michigan State University–trained engineer from the government-run Dairy Research Institute to manage operations.[97] The Patidars leveraged their network in the Congress through Sardar Patel to have their Kaira District Cooperative Milk Producers Union Limited (KDCMPUL) registered as a cooperative and become the chief supplier to the Bombay Milk Scheme.[98] Polson left Kheda. Within three years of KDCMPUL's founding, it had thirteen cooperative societies and 924 total members.[99]

Still, KDCMPUL lacked facilities to dry milk and continued to be captive to the fickle rhythms of consumer demand. Again, it turned to outside ideas and support. After studying the successful milk cooperatives in New Zealand,

95. Shankkar Aiyar, *Accidental India: A History of the Nation's Passage through Crisis and Change* (Delhi: Aleph, 2012), 157–60.

96. Abhijit Ghosh, "Embeddedness and the Dynamics of Strategy Processes: The Case of AMUL Cooperative, India," (unpublished PhD diss., McGill University, 2010).

97. The recruit, Verghese Kurien, would manage the operations while the Patidars' chosen leader managed increasing membership, handling government relations, and ironing out village issues. Kurien was born into the family of former finance minister John Matthai and hailed from the high-caste convert community known as the Syrian Christians in Kerala. After undergraduate studies in physics at Madras and a short stint at Tata Sons, Kurien pursued a higher degree in engineering in the United States. He first came to Kheda in 1949 and remained there for the rest of his career. See Verghese Kurien (as told to Gouri Salvi), *I Too Had a Dream* (New Delhi: Roli Books, 2005).

98. Ghosh, "Embeddedness and the Dynamics of Strategy Processes," 141.

99. Data from KDCMPUL, cited in Ghosh, "Embeddedness and the Dynamics of Strategy Processes," 136.

the Milk Union diversified production away from solely milk. It started to dry milk into powder, extending its shelf life. From UNICEF, it secured funding to purchase Danish machinery for a dairy-powder-producing factory. The company changed its name to the less clunky Anand Milk Union Limited (AMUL), which it uses to this day. By the end of the 1950s, the number of village cooperatives expanded to 138 societies with 33,068 members. Over the decade, AMUL increased its production by a factor of twenty-seven.[100] AMUL's fledgling success relied on the in-group ties of a dominant caste and favorable geography. With an openness to foreign investment, machinery, and ideas, the Patidars leveraged kinship ties and caste solidarity to become major players in agroindustry as "fraternal capitalists."[101]

The Charotar Patidars' experiment ran in parallel to top-down efforts directed by the Center toward community development from the 1950s.[102] In contrast to the Patidar experiment, the government scheme prioritized economic equity over increased output and sought to dissolve social distinctions rather than use them as a basis for localized development. However, landowning castes and village leaders benefited disproportionately from community development. Lower castes found themselves excluded from the fruits of the efforts, and dissenters were suppressed. The voluntary program failed to court much meaningful participation. Unlike in the Patidar case, agricultural yields did not improve. To break the cozy relationship between government officials working in the villages and local leaders, the government channeled resources

100. Ghosh, "Embeddedness and the Dynamics of Strategy Processes,"136.

101. This term comes from Sharad Chari's study of a parallel phenomenon in his excellent ethnography of the Tamil landowning cultivating community of Gounders. See Chari, *Fraternal Capital*. The Gounder turn to mass textile production began simultaneously but never took off until the 1980s. See Damodaran, *India's New Capitalists*, 152–53.

102. Model villages inspired by American and Gandhian decentralist thought had been conceived of in discussion with Nehru. They received financing and expertise from the U.S. government and the Ford Foundation as well as substantial allocations from the five-year plan budgets. A community projects administration sent on-the-ground workers to villages around India. They worked to bring about improvements to village economies by promoting small agriculture and the adoption of intermediate technology. They would also help run hygiene campaigns, distribute medicine, and rebuild public spaces. These programs aimed to bring about village solidarity, lift the weaker sections of the populace, and boost agricultural production. The program relied on *śramadān* (voluntary labor) rather than state investment, which was dispersed thinly across India. See Immerwahr, *Thinking Small: The United States and the Lure of Community Development* (Cambridge, MA: Harvard University Press, 2015), 55–82; Frankel, *India's Political Economy*, 102–9.

through democratically elected village panchayats (councils). The proposal for *panchayati* raj sought to reform the basic social structure of the village and empower its weaker sections.[103] This rival model of community development formed one source of tension between the Patidars and the Center.

While Anand headquartered the district's cooperative economy, Vallabh Vidyanagar became a training center and a site for the generation and exchange of ideas. It, too, had a Sardar Patel connection, as the town was established to effect his vision of a rural agricultural university. However, credit for its creation and success rests with Bhailalbhai, or Bhaikaka Patel (see Figure 4.2). Bhailalbhai spent most of his career working as a civil engineer for the government of the Bombay Presidency. He distinguished himself as executive engineer on the Sukkur Barrage in the northern area of Sindh (part of today's Pakistan). It was the largest single irrigation network of its kind in the world.[104] Bhailalbhai subsequently became the executive engineer for roads in Sindh before Sardar Patel called him to become the municipal engineer of Ahmedabad.[105] During the short span of time he served in this post (1940–42), Bhailalbhai constructed large roads, ensured access to water and electricity, and zoned the city into areas for industry, commerce, and education.[106] He left to initiate the Vallabh Vidyanagar project, which he called "a dream" in his memoirs.[107]

*Bhāīkākānām Saṃsmaraṇo* (Memoirs of Bhaikaka) filled over five hundred pages of Gujarati text.[108] It was dictated over the last two years of his life (1968–70) to a young assistant. Hyperbole, repetition, digressions, and the characterization of political disagreements as part of a Manichean struggle between good and evil attest to its oral quality. So too does the likely absence of any content editing. The memoirs are at one level an "ego document" of a

103. Immerwahr, 82–87; Frankel, *India's Political Economy*, 154.

104. He published a book about this experience as *Sukkura Bērējamāṃ Mārā Āṭha Varśa* (My Eight Years at Sukkur Barrage) in 1940. Ramesh Trivedi, *Educational Trajectory of Charotar Vidya Mandal: A Saga of Seven Decades*, trans. R.C. Desai and Salabha Natraj (Vallabh Vidyanagar: Charotar Vidya Mandal, 2015), 25. On the Sukkur Barrage's construction, see Daniel Haines, *Building the Empire, Building the Nation: Development, Legitimacy and Hydro-Politics in Sind, 1919–69* (Oxford: Oxford University Press, 2017), 1–52.

105. Bhailalbhai Patel, *Bhāīkākānām Saṃsmaraṇo*, 2nd edition (Ahmedabad: Sastum Sahitya Mudranalaya Trust, 1970), 105–254 (hereafter *BS*).

106. Dahyabhai Patel, "Foreword," in *Shri Bhailalbhai Patel 70th Anniversary Souvenir* (Vallabh Vidyanagar: Charotar Vidya Mandal, 1958), 7–13, 10–11.

107. Himanshu Upadhyaya, "Large Dams as 'Temples of Modern India?'" in *Intractable Conflicts in Contemporary India*, ed. Savyasaachi (Milton Keynes: Taylor and Francis, 2019), 86–103. Both chapters 17 and 18 of *BS* have *svapnā*, the Gujarati word for "dream," in their titles.

108. Upadhyaya, "Large Dams."

FIGURE 4.2. Statue of Bhaikaka Patel, Vallabh Vidyanagar (Aditya Balasubramanian).

proud Patidar's life as a civil engineer, creator of a rural industrial and educational township, and leader of the opposition in the Gujarat state legislative assembly.[109] At another, they provide an extraordinary vernacular perspective of the history and politics of local and regional economic development.

109. I borrow the term from Raza, *Revolutionary Pasts*, 20.

Bhaikaka's life is linked inextricably to that of his fellow Patidars. In turn, Patidar history is part of the history of Gujarat.

Bhailalbhai made his Vallabh Vidyanagar dream a reality by applying the principle of what he called *prabuddh swartha* (*prabud'dha svārta*, enlightened self-interest) to take the region's tradition of educational philanthropy to the next level.[110] Decades earlier, charitable trusts had provided the financial resources for a rural public library movement and the expansion of village schooling in the region, especially through the efforts of the Charotar Education Society (CES, est. 1916).[111] On the model of the CES, Bhailalbhai created a trust called the Charotar Vidya Mandal (CVM) to coordinate the project.[112] Instead of the government, the CVM secured land grants from five hundred Patidars to the area christened Vallabh Vidyanagar in return for half of their land back after the development of the area. Appealing to community interest as self-interest, the CVM further secured charitable donations from Charotar Patidars across the country and in the diaspora.[113]

Bhaikaka created an industrial cooperative that also operated by prabuddha swartha to build the physical edifices and infrastructure of the town. This Charotar Gramoddhar Sahkari Mandal (Charotar Village Cooperative Society) paid shareholders a 3 percent dividend and used half of the profits to help fund the CVM.[114] Units of the Sahkari Mandal included a metal factory, a machine shop, a hume pipe and tile factory, a carpentry shop, and a sawmill. Craftsmen trained at one of the units left to start their own business on occasion.[115] To an extent, the Sahkari Mandal delivered "self-sufficiency" by obviating the need to rely on building materials from elsewhere.

110. M. M. Patel, "*Prabud'dha svārtha*," in *Shri Bhailalbhai Patel 70th Birthday Souvenir* (Vallabh Vidyanagar: Charotar Vidya Mandal, 1958), 129; Patel, *BS*, 255.

111. Hardiman, "Baroda," 69–74; R. C. Desai and Salabha Natraj, *Educational Trajectory of Charotar Vidya Mandal: A Saga of Seven Decades*, trans. Ramesh Trivedi (Vallabh Vidyanagar: Charotar Vidya Mandal, 2015), 16.

112. Heredia, *The Amul India Story*, 112–16.

113. Patel, *BS*, 307–8. Through Sardar Patel's connections, the CVM got money from the Birla Group for an engineering college that became the Birla Vishwakarma Mahavidyalaya in 1948. However, the donation created subsequent fears that the Bombay government would renege on its promise to fund another such institution in Ahmedabad. Bhaikaka vowed never again to approach big business for funds.

114. Patel, *BS*, 307–8.

115. H. M. Patel, *The First Flush of Freedom: Recollections and Reflections* (New Delhi: Rupa and Co., 2005), 248.

Reading between the lines, it appears the prabuddha swartha of only some stakeholders factored into the creation of Vallabh Vidyanagar: shareholders, donors, and philanthropists. Nonelite non-Patidars received shorter shrift. The Sahkari Mandal paid artisans and laborers by the day. It compensated them partially in kind by educating their children. These workers most likely hailed from lower-caste origins. Bhaikaka noted with pride that they never joined the regional union when labor activists came to Vallabh Vidyanagar.[116]

Vallabh Vidyanagar's Sardar Patel University (SPU) opened its doors in 1955, combining science and technology education with instruction in community values and practices. It became a place of diverse theoretical and applied research.[117] By the late 1960s, its Agro-Economic Research Institute employed thirty field investigators and conducted empirically rigorous field studies to answer practical economic questions.[118] Beginning with the study of crop prices, the institute subsequently diversified its activities to look at issues of village and industrial political economy. It produced a series of village- and district-level case studies of economic conditions. These used survey methods to assess possibilities for industrial development by private investment and provided data about the conditions for private-sector-led industrial development of agroindustry.[119] Not far away, the Institute of Agriculture at Anand founded by Sardar Patel and K. M. Munshi, became affiliated with SPU. It researched crop varieties, planting, and harvesting.[120] Complementing this research, a cooperative training center trained "middle-level workers in the corporate sector."[121]

116. Patel, BS, 291, 301.

117. The University of Wisconsin is one of many "Land Grant" universities in the United States subsidized by a grant of land from the United States for the sake of promoting agricultural and technical education. See Colleges of Agriculture at the Land Grant Universities (Washington, DC: National Academies Press, 1995).

118. Ishwarbhai J. Patel to Ralph Borsodi, November 8, 1967, Folder 1, Box 2, Collection MC 34—Ralph Borsodi Papers, University of New Hampshire Archieves, Durham, NH, USA (hereafter Borsodi Papers).

119. Published titles included R. K. Amin, Economics for Engineers (Vallabh Vidyanagar: Charotar Book Stall, 1963); Amin, Mogri: Socio-economic Study of a Charotar village (Vallabh Vidyanagar: Charotar Book Stall, 1965); Amin, Valasan; Socio-economic Study of a Charotar village (Vallabh Vidyanagar: Charotar Book Stall, 1965); Amin, A Survey of the Industrial Potential of Kaira District (Vallabh Vidyanagar: Charotar Book Stall, 1966); Amin, Radio Rural Forums in Gujarat: an Observational Study (Vallabh Vidyanagar: Charotar Book Stall, 1966).

120. Jayeshkumar Vaghela, "Krushi Go Vidya Bhavan, Anand, 1939–2003: Its Contribution to Agricultural Extension," (unpublished PhD diss., Saurashtra University, 2017).

121. Patel to Borsodi, Folder 1, Box 2, Borsodi Papers.

Neoliberal ideas helped form the theoretical underpinnings of economic knowledge production at SPU. The head of the Agro-Economic Institute, R. K. Amin, studied under B. R. Shenoy and spent a brief period in Chicago working under Milton Friedman.[122] When Shenoy coordinated Friedman's travels in Gujarat during 1962, he took the American economist and his wife, Rose, to Anand and Vallabh Vidyanagar. Shenoy had Friedman deliver a lecture there. Rose would describe it as part of "Professor Shenoy's efforts to educate his people" and recalled the excursion to Gujarat as "a high spot in India."[123] Amin also sat on the Forum of Free Enterprise's essay committee, judging worthy contributions by high school and college students. He went on to run in parliamentary elections, joining the Lok Sabha on a Swatantra ticket in 1967.[124]

SPU's curriculum also incorporated the ideas of a man who embraced its rural mission and had been an inspiration for the development of free economy earlier in the decade. Ralph Borsodi, the American cooperative individualist and interlocutor of Ranchoddas Lotvala, served as a consultant to Sardar Patel University between 1959 and 1962.[125] Borsodi had become an admirer of Gandhi and believed a worldwide rural renaissance was a third way of development. He wrote a largely unintelligible book published by SPU called *The Education of the Whole Man*, which students read alongside their coursework.[126] This somewhat cryptic 452-page tome sought to provide an antidote to what Borsodi believed to be a narrow-mindedness caused by excessively specialized education that accompanied large factory production and urban living.

*The Education of the Whole Man* claimed to bring together ideas from different disciplines and various parts of the world. The first part of the book

122. Folder 10, Box 33, Friedman Papers.

123. Milton and Rose D. Friedman, *Two Lucky People: Memoirs* (Chicago: University of Chicago Press, 1998), 307.

124. "Members of Fourth Lok Sabha," Open Government Platform India, http://data.gov .in/catalog/members-fourth-lok-sabha-4th-march-1967-27th-december-1970.

125. "Pioneering in Education," *ToI*, November 24, 1963. Borsodi most likely first met Bhailalbhai on his three-month lecture tour in India during 1958. His School of Living had become financially unviable. He started a second model community called Melbourne Village and installed himself as chancellor of its university. However, Melbourne Village's inhabitants came mainly for the concessionary prices of land rather than for the social experiment. The university never got off the ground. See "The Social Whirl," *ToI*, September 28, 1958; Richard Crepeau, *Melbourne Village: The First Twenty-Five Years, 1946–71* (Gainesville: University of Central Florida, 1988).

126. Babubhai J. Patel, "Preface" to Borsodi, *The Education of the Whole Man* (Vallabh Vidyanagar: Sardar Vallabhbhai Vidyapeeth, 1963).

classified education into physical, intellectual, emotional, perceptual, "intro-spectional," axiological, and volitional types. This classification exhausted every conceivable aspect of life, according to Borsodi. The second part prescribed an integrated program of education for the stages of a person's life. Each chapter covered a separate stage from birth to death. In this way, the intellectual center adjacent to Anand adopted an individualist educational philosophy from an American who believed in cultural education and economic organization in small units. Borsodi's program of education uniquely complemented the cooperative economy.[127]

The allegedly self-reliant efforts at Vallabh Vidyanagar based on self-interest in fact required government assistance to achieve their intended results. Bhaikaka's critique focused more on the urban bias of government bureaucracy. Originally, he used his connection to Sardar Patel to secure approvals for land acquisition and building. However, red tape became more impenetrable after the latter's 1950 death. There was also a problem of urban areas receiving a disproportionate share of basic resources.[128] In a memorable section of *Bhāīkākānām Saṃsmaraṇo*, Bhaikaka discusses how villages received poorer quality food rations—red sorghum rather than wheat rice—thus necessitating purchases of food for students from the black market at three times the city price. He recalled with frustration the tension between trying to impart character to students at the university and violating laws to procure foodstuffs.[129]

Natural resource management-related conflict further set urban inhabitants against rural inhabitants and pitted Gujarati-speaking areas against Marathi-speaking areas of Bombay State. According to Bhaikaka, the Bombay government lost interest in two irrigation projects on the Mahi River after Sardar Patel's death. One project proposed to construct a canal in Kheda district on the right bank of the river and the other a dam on the left bank of the river. The

127. Borsodi himself went on to set up the International Foundation for Independence, which used grants from private foundations to provide loans for town and rural living projects in developing countries and piloted some forms of microlending in Mexico. Hoping to extend the scheme to India, he kept in touch with the Sardar Patel University after his return to the United States. See Ralph Borsodi to Ishwarbhai J. Patel, December 5, 1967, Folder 7, Box 1, Borsodi Papers; Stephanie Mills, *On Gandhi's Path: Bob Swann's Work for Peace and Community Economics* (Gabriola, Canada: New Society Publishers, 2010), 93–104.

128. "Need to Remove Disparity: Urban-Rural Areas," *ToI*, April 6, 1958.

129. Patel, *BS*, 323–27.

government's decision to take half of the change in the value of the land between the beginning and end of construction struck Bhaikaka as more extractive than in schemes pursued in the non-Gujarati areas. Bhaikaka wrote out a
plan for the canal in English, suggesting a scheme for financing. He argued that
without this canal, the network of tubewells in drought-prone Gujarat would
dry up.[130] Patel printed five thousand copies of it and ensured its wide circulation among influential politicians.[131] Canal construction began on the right
bank, although the dam project continued to meet resistance.[132] A much larger
dam project, over the Narmada River, never got off the ground during his
lifetime because of conflict about the depth of the dam.[133]

Land reform provided another flash point for controversy. Bhaikaka interpreted it to be part of a concerted attack by urban interests on rural India. The
Gujarat Tenancy and Agricultural Lands Act of 1948 provided security of tenure to cultivators, preventing them from being ejected arbitrarily by owners.
It also capped rents paid by the cultivators and alluded to future turnover of
land held over a certain ceiling limit.[134] Bhaikaka objected to these measures,
suggesting that the small size of most plots—five acres or less—forced owners
to augment their earnings by other means. For ages, like *andhā* (blind) and
*laṅgaḍā* (lame) men, landowner and farmer cooperated. In Bhaikaka's opinion, ideas of land to the tiller being entertained by the Congress-run Bombay
government from the mid-1950s destroyed this spirit of solidarity and fragmented rural society.[135]

130. Patel, *BS*, 360–62.

131. Bhailalbhai Patel, *Mahi Canal: Proposed Irrigation Project* (Vallabh Vidyanagar: Gramodhar Mudranalaya, 1953). Excessive extraction via tubewells began in the early twentieth century
after the widespread introduction of mechanized pumps. See the excellent discussion in Hardiman, "Well Irrigation in Gujarat: Systems of Use, Hierarchies of Control," *Economic and Political
Weekly* 33, no. 25 (1998): 1533–44.

132. "First Stage of Mahi Project Inaugurated," *ToI*, November 4, 1958; Dahyabhai Patel,
"Mahi Project: Letter to the Editor," *ToI*, August 25, 1959; *Project Performance Audit Report—
India: Kadana Irrigation Project* (World Bank: Operations Evaluation Department, 1981), 20–21.

133. Representatives of Bombay and Madhya Pradesh wanted a lower dam to reduce damage
done by the dam's reservoir; those of drought-prone Rajasthan and Gujarat wanted to construct
a dam as deep as possible to harness hydroelectricity and water for irrigation. See John R. Wood,
*The Politics of Water Resource Development in India: The Narmada Dams Controversy* (New Delhi:
Sage, 2007). Chapter 6 discusses this issue in further detail.

134. Nikita Sud, "From Land to the Tiller to Land Liberalization: The Political Economy of
Gujarat's Shifting Land Policy," *Modern Asian Studies* 41, no. 3 (2007): 603–37, 608–9.

135. Patel, *BS*, 340.

Bhailalbhai Patel relinquished control of daily affairs at Vallabh Vidyanagar and dedicated himself full time to politics after the passage of the Nagpur resolution in 1959. The next year, Gujarat won independent statehood. He orchestrated an alliance with the Kshatriya Sabha. The Kshatriya communities typically resented the upwardly mobile Patidars, who made up a fifth of the population of the newly constituted state and formed a powerful vote bank.[136] Undeterred, Bhailalbhai persuaded them that Congress' proposed land reforms posed a threat to their shared interests. With the support of these groups, the Swatantra Party would become chief opposition party in Gujarat and Bhailalbhai the leader of the opposition.[137] In this capacity, he traveled to every district and subdistrict of the state. He kept an eye out for sites where ports could be built and searched for industrial opportunities. In *Bhāīkākānām Saṃsmaraṇo*, Bhaikaka recalls how he measured the depth of the water in coastal areas and secured information on subterranean mineral resources like limestone, clay, copper, asbestos, and mica.[138] He never quite gave up the zeal of the project engineer. For him, political economy was about tangible local projects.

At the heart of the Vallabh Vidyanagar plan was ruralism, Bhaikaka reflected. It was also unmistakably modern. He believed that rural areas would not advance unless industries could operate there and provide nonagricultural employment. These areas required modern public goods like water works, drainage and education. Patel dedicated the latter part of his life to introducing small-scale machinery into villages so that industry could flourish.[139] Ironically, this small-scale vision was compatible with the large dam projects of Nehruvian India.[140] And, like in Nehruvian developmentalism, Bhaikaka's ruralism demonstrated little regard for the *adivasis* (term of self-identification used by native communities) it would displace. At the most, they figured as hindrances to realizing major aims.[141]

The Charotar Patidars "fraternally" directed their own turn to industry, benefiting from economic privilege, in-group solidarity, and community networks. They fashioned a cooperative economy and made use of outside

136. Bayly, *Caste, Society, and Politics*, 329–35.

137. Rajni Kothari and Rushikesh Maru, "Federating for Political Interests: The Kshatriyas of Gujarat," in *Caste in Indian Politics*, ed. Kothari (Bombay: Orient Longmans, 1970), 66–95, 79–86.

138. Patel, *BS*, 432.

139. Patel, *BS*, 540; 503.

140. Amrith, *Unruly Waters*, 175–228, 179.

141. Patel, *BS*, 362–63; Wood, *The Politics of Water Resource Development in India*, 108.

experts and technology to finesse their model as needed. Although they would require government assistance, the Patidars would not accept direction by the government. They retained control over processes of change and resisted more egalitarian reforms that could undermine their hegemony. In their political economy, the scalar units of the locality and the region predominated. There was little sense of nation. The broader global economy featured as a source of remittance capital and economic expertise.

## Free Enterprise and Free Trade, Great and Small: The Parsis and Minoo Masani

In addition to mofussil-dwelling traditionally agrarian castes in transition like the Kammas and Patidars, the Swatantra Party also attracted support from urban-dwelling, traditionally mercantile communities like the Zoroastrians, or Parsis. As of 1941, the approximately sixty thousand Parsis of Greater Bombay were half of the community's nationwide total and 4 percent of that city's population.[142] Fleeing religious persecution in Persia, this community began to settle in western India in the late seventh century CE (see Map 4.4) and learned Gujarati. They cultivated trading networks across the Indian Ocean during the early modern era and became major players in the opium trade with China.[143]

A section of the Parsi community moved into industrial activity in sectors like textiles and steel during the British colonial era, where political and moral concerns prevented the imperial masters from entering.[144] The canonical example was Tata Sons, which went on to become India's largest conglomerate.[145]

142. Leela Visaria, "Demographic Transition among Parsis: 1881–1971; I-Size of Parsi Population," *Economic and Political Weekly* 9, no. 42 (1974): 1735–41, 1737.

143. Tirthankar Roy, *A Business History of India: Enterprise and the Emergence of Capitalism from 1700* (Cambridge: Cambridge University Press, 2018), 40–68; Ghulam Nadri, *Eighteenth Century Gujarat: The Dynamics of its Political Economy, 1750–1800* (Leiden, Netherlands: Brill, 2009), 51–84; Jesse Palsetia, "The Parsis of India and the Opium Trade of China," *Contemporary Drug Problems* 35, no. 4 (2008): 647–78.

144. Mircea Raianu, "Trade, Finance and Industry in the Development of Indian Capitalism: The Case of Tata," *Business History Review* 92 (2020): 569–92; Ashok V. Desai, "The Origins of Parsi Enterprise," *The Indian Economic and Social History Review* 5, no. 4 (1968): 307–17; Amartya Sen, "The Commodity Pattern of British Enterprise in Early Indian Industrialization, 1854–1914," in *Second International Conference of Economic History, Aix-en-Provence, 1962*, vol. 2 (Paris and The Hague: Mouton, 1965), 781–808.

145. Mircea Raianu, *Tata: The Global Corporation that Built Indian Capitalism* (Cambridge, MA: Harvard University Press, 2021).

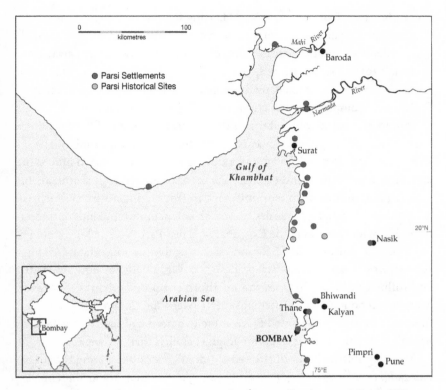

MAP 4.4. Parsi Settlement in Western India (Jenny Sheehan and CartoGIS, College of Asia and the Pacific, Australian National University, 2022).

This period also saw the Parsis adopt English education, customs, and practices so faithfully as to beat the colonizers at their own game.[146] They became adept at "Anglo-legalism" and were disproportionately represented in the city of Bombay's legal community.[147]

The Parsis showed an ambiguous attitude toward colonial rule, under which they had prospered. A vocal section of the community began to lead demands for moderate political reform and later *swaraj*, helping to found the

146. Seal, *The Emergence of Indian Nationalism*, 82–86, 110. Their habits of dress, dining, and domesticity are described in Simin Patel, "Cultural Intermediaries in a Colonial City: The Parsis of Bombay, c. 1860–1921," (unpublished PhD diss., University of Oxford, 2015).

147. Mitra Sharafi, *Law and Identity in Colonial South Asia: Parsi Legal Culture, 1772–1947* (Cambridge: Cambridge University Press, 2013), 4.

Indian National Congress in 1885.[148] During the interwar period, firms like
Tata came to support the anticolonial movement as their interests converged.[149]
After independence, the reorientation of economic development away from
trade and toward state-directed, heavy-industry-based capital accumulation
adversely affected not merely big business.[150] A much larger constituency of
Parsis could complain of restrictions on small enterprises and trade.[151]

Minoo Masani, a cofounder and the general secretary of the Swatantra
Party, came from a prominent Parsi family living in South Bombay. His involvement both in municipal politics and big business connected him to the
concerns of prominent and ordinary Parsis. Masani's writings illuminate his
staunch anticommunism, commitment to free trade and free enterprise
across multiple geographic scales, and involvement in various kinds of associations. He made a career in the Congress Socialist Party years after training in
law at the London School of Economics. During this time, he established himself as the right-hand man of Jayaprakash Narayan, a Berkeley-educated leftist
and follower of Gandhi from the northern region of Bihar.[152] However,
Masani quit politics in 1939 after tensions between the Congress socialists and
the communists of the United Front came to a head and the latter gained an
upper hand. This element of his biography parallels that of Ranga.

Masani published four illustrated children's textbooks during the 1940s:
*Our India* (1940), *Your Food* (1944), *Picture of a Plan* (1945), and *Our Growing*

148. Jesse S. Palsetia, *The Parsis of India: Preservation of Identity in Bombay City* (Leiden,
Netherlands: Brill, 2001), 277–319.

149. Manali Chakrabarti, "Why Did Indian Big Business Pursue a Policy of Economic Nationalism in the Interwar Years? A New Window to an Old Debate," *Modern Asian Studies* 43,
no. 4 (2009): 979–1038.

150. Jafari Farah, "Nutrition and Ecological Conditions among Parsis of Iran and India,"
(unpublished PhD diss., Karnatak University, 1995), 101–90, 106.

151. On the surveillance and criminalization of Parsis in the liquor trade, and of commodities
traders more generally, see De, *A People's Constitution*, 63–68; 86–99.

152. Narayan would go on to become the young hero of the Quit India Movement and a key
member of the Congress during the 1940s. However, he drifted away from organized politics
and instead became active in social work through the 1960s. Much of this involved bringing
together American anticommunist efforts and a movement for voluntary land donations and
decentralized economic activity, the Sarvodaya Movement. By the mid-1970s, he led the "total
revolution" against Congress. See Lydia Walker, "Jayaprakash Narayan and the Politics of Rec-
onciliation for the Postcolonial State and Its Imperial Fragments," *The Indian Economic and
Social History Review* 56, no. 2 (2019): 147–69, 150–53; Rakesh Ankit, "Jayaprakash Narayan,
Indian National Congress, and Party Politics, 1934–54," *Studies in Indian Politics* 3, no. 2 (2015):
149–63; Ramachandra Guha, *Makers of Modern India* (New Delhi: Penguin, 2010), 404–7.

*Human Family* (1950).[153] They show how private actors attempted to create idealized portraits of the nation in young hearts and minds even before the postcolonial state introduced textbook imagery.[154] During this time, the leadership of Oxford University Press in India moved steadily toward textbook production by Indian authors under the assumption that political change would bring new educational policies and syllabi.[155] Three of these four books appeared under Oxford's imprint. All were illustrated in a distinctive pedagogical style by a cartoonist from a leading advertising agency.[156] Each of these novel experiments in the communication of economic ideas went into multiple reprints and was translated into several different Indian languages. Other kinds of popular economic literature later replicated this style.[157]

*Our India* sold over half a million copies within seven years of its release.[158] Manmohan Singh, who went on to become finance minister and prime minister of India, credits *Our India* for sowing the seeds of his aspiration to become an economist.[159] "A craze. The book was a craze," former Swatantra politician

153. Minoo Masani, *Our India* (London: Oxford University Press, 1940); Masani, *Your Food: A Study of the Problem of Food and Nutrition* (Bombay: Tata Studies in Current Affairs, 1944); Masani, *Picture of a Plan* (Bombay: Oxford University Press, 1945); Masani, *Our Growing Human Family* (Bombay: Oxford University Press, 1950).

154. Partha Chatterjee, *Lineages of a Political Society* (Ranikhet: Permanent Black, 2011), 158–64; Roy, *Beyond Belief*, especially the images on 68, 113.

155. Rimi B. Chatterjee, *Empires of Mind: A History in India under the Raj* (Oxford: Oxford University Press, 2006); Rimi B. Chatterjee and Padmini Ray Murray, "India," in *History of Oxford University Press: Volume III—1866–1970*, ed. William Roger Louis (Oxford: Oxford University Press, 2013), 649–72.

156. Markus Daechsel, *The Politics of Self-Expression: The Urdu Middle-Class Milieu in Mid-Twentieth Century India and Pakistan* (New York: Routledge, 2005), 177.

157. A few of the many titles later imitating this style include *How We Live* (Bombay: Socialist Party, [n.d. 1948?]); *The Second Five-Year Plan* (New Delhi: Ministry of Information and Broadcasting, [n.d. 1956?]); and Babu Ram Misra, *The Plan and You* (Bombay: Orient Longmans, 1959). By the 1950s, textbooks accounted for over 60 percent of Oxford University Press' India sales. In subsequent decades, the publication of textbooks by presses grew to the hundreds of thousands per year. Chatterjee and Murray, "India," 668.

158. Jayal, *Citizenship and its Discontents*, 171. Three years later, the 2.12-rupee book had generated a gross profit (before subtracting overhead expenses and stock value) of 242,682 rupees. See Chatterjee, *Empires of Mind*, 446. Price data comes from the review "Hindustan Hamara," *ToI*, November 9, 1940.

159. Manmohan Singh interview by Charlie Rose, September 21, 2004, text reproduced in "Interview of Prime Minister Dr. Manmohan Singh on Charlie Rose Show," Government of India, Ministry of External Affairs, http://www.mea.gov.in/interviews.htm?dtl/4565/Intervie w+of+Prime+Minister+Dr+Manmohan+Singh+on+Charlie+Rose+Show.

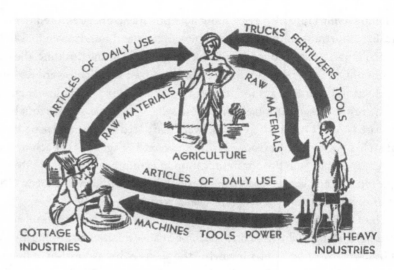

FIGURE 4.3. Circular Flow (Masani, *Our India*, 165. Reproduced with the permission of Oxford University Press India © Oxford University Press 1940).

Dr. H. V. Hande recalled.[160] An illustrated economic geography of the country, the book gave an idea of India's natural resource endowments, manpower potential, and standard of living. It also explained basic economic concepts (see Figure 4.3). *Our India's* visual style drew heavily from *Modern Man in the Making*, a book portraying human civilizational progress by Austrian social scientist and philosopher Otto Neurath.[161] Adopting Neurath's International System of Typographic Picture Education (ISOTYPE), the book sought to convey to children India's position vis-à-vis the world more tangibly and to impart an obligation to raise its level up to world standards (see Figure 4.4).[162] *Our India* encouraged readers to take up the challenge of nation-building. It was indicative of a widening of the conception of citizenship from a rights-based to a duty-based understanding.[163] The book appeared at around the same time that Rajagopalachari and Santhanam published *Ūrukku Nallatu*, the popular

160. Interview with Dr. H. V. Hande, Chennai, October 23, 2019.

161. Neurath, *Modern Man in the Making* (New York: Knopf, 1939).

162. Jordi Cat, "Supplement to Otto Neurath—Political Economy: Theory, Practice, and Philosophical Consequences," Stanford Encyclopedia of Philosophy, https://plato.stanford.edu/entries/neurath/political-economy.html and "Visual Education," https://plato.stanford.edu/entries/neurath/visual-education.html.

163. Jayal, *Citizenship and its Discontents*, 172.

**1910-1914**

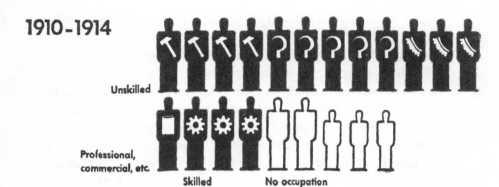

Unskilled

Professional,
commercial, etc.

Skilled          No occupation

**1920-1924**

Unskilled

Professional,
commercial, etc.

Skilled      No occupation

## Each symbol represents 250,000 immigrants

ISOTYPE

FIGURE 4.4. ISOTYPE in Neurath and Masani Versions (Neurath,
*Modern Man in the Making,* 95. Reproduced with the permission
of Penguin Random House © Knopf 1939; Masani, *Our India,* 36.
Reproduced with the permission of Oxford University Press India
© Oxford University Press 1940).

education reader that laid out a set of practices citizens could adopt for the advancement of the polity.[164]

In the aftermath of *Our India*'s success, Masani approached the Parsi firm Tata Sons for employment. Family friend A. D. Shroff, a fellow Parsi and a Tata director helped him get a job.[165] Masani brought out a "Studies in Current Affairs" series while working for the company's public relations arm.[166] To publicize the Bombay Plan, Tata's chairman, J.R.D. Tata, commissioned a work comparable to *Our India*, "rather in the style of that book and with the sort of illustrations it contains."[167] The plan was an industrialist attempt to sketch the contours of postwar development planning in India.[168]

Like the document it sought to explain, *Picture of a Plan* suggested vague "industrial control" by the state rather than nationalization. Masani departed from its text by invoking Gandhi's critique of modern industrial life and questioned the necessity of heavy industrialization. He suggested that the advent of modern technology allowed countries like India the opportunity of development via small towns and corporations using borrowed technology from abroad. This would "counter the tendency of highly mechanized large-scale industry to create unemployment."[169] Large-scale, enterprise-driven economic development in Nazi Germany and Soviet Russia had given way to "managerial revolution," wrote Masani, deploying an idea of the American former Trotskyist and wartime American intelligence agent James Burnham. "In Russia, things have been controlled much too much from the center and this has meant an unnecessarily large army of bureaucrats," he cautioned. Masani took pains to stress the importance of safeguarding liberty in any planned setup, quoting the American Declaration of Independence and Abraham Lincoln.[170] Serving at the time as a religious minority representative on the

164. See the previous chapter.

165. On Shroff, an eminent industrialist and one of India's representatives to the Bretton Woods Conference, see Sucheta Dalal, *A. D. Shroff: Titan of Free Enterprise* (New Delhi: Viking, 2000).

166. Other titles in the series included T.R.S. Kynnersley's *Roads for India* (1946) and F. E. James' *Battle for Health* (1946).

167. J.R.D. Tata to Purushotamdas Thakurdas, February 3, 1944, File 291, Part One, Thakurdas Papers, NMML.

168. On the Plan, see Chibber, *Locked in Place*; and Lockwood, *The Indian Bourgeoisie*.

169. Masani, *Picture of a Plan*, 22, 62; James Burnham, *The Managerial Revolution: What Is Happening in the World* (New York: The John Day Company, 1941).

170. Masani, *Picture of a Plan*, 38, 63.

Constituent Assembly's subcommittee on fundamental rights, he sought to strengthen protection of individual freedom.[171]

Masani endorsed American economic policy and Wilsonian liberal internationalism in *Our Growing Human Family: From Tribe to World Federation*.[172] The book traced mankind's progressive evolution from isolated individuals in prehistoric times to participants in world federation (see Figure 4.5). By this time, various anticolonial nationalists from the developing world had been disillusioned with the unequal integration of formerly colonized nations and racial hierarchy embedded implied by the Wilsonian project of a post–World War I international order.[173] They hatched alternative configurations of the transnational federation envisioning more equity among members, greater respect for diversity, and special procedures for mitigating inequality.[174]

Masani continued to credit Wilson with the "biggest and most hopeful of these efforts to reach forward to world Union." Masani's federation, to be moderated by the newly created United Nations, was utopian: "Though the nation-state will go, the nation will remain, just as the city remains though the city-state has disappeared. But nations will no longer speak through guns and battleships and bombers. They will express themselves in songs and ballads and dances."[175] The American open system of interstate trade provided a shining example for the world to follow; in contrast to European nation states hampered by tariff walls, the United States achieved more than the sum of its parts (see Figure 4.6).[176] Masani's narrative of mankind's progress drew from British writer H. G. Wells' Darwinian understanding of human history and visions of a universal world state of English speakers with Britain and the United States as its nucleus.[177]

Masani's attitude to gender and political economy relative to his contemporaries is hard to read. More than anything, this is a blind spot in his analyses.

171. "Minoo Masani," *The Times*, June 26, 1998.

172. This refers to the ideas of U.S. President Woodrow Wilson (1856–1924), who theorized the self-determination of nations and lay the intellectual groundwork for the League of Nations. See Erez Manela, *The Wilsonian Moment: Self-Determination and the International Origins of Anticolonial Nationalism* (Oxford: Oxford University Press, 2007).

173. Getachew, *Worldmaking after Empire*, 37–70; Manela, *The Wilsonian Moment*, 5.

174. Frederick Cooper, "Federation, Confederation, Territorial State: Debating a Post-Imperial Future in French West Africa, 1945–1960," in *Forms of Pluralism and Democratic Constitutionalism*, eds. Andrew Arato and Jean Cohen, (New York: Columbia University Press, 2018), 33–51; Getachew, *Worldmaking after Empire*, 107–41.

175. Masani, *Our Growing Human Family*, 93, 102.

176. Masani, *Our Growing Human Family*, 99–104.

177. Duncan Bell, *Dreamworlds of Race: Empire and the Utopian Destiny of Anglo-America* (Princeton: Princeton University Press, 2020), 152–202.

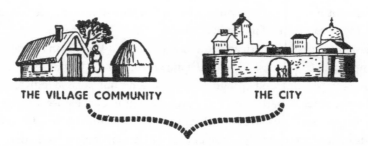

THE VILLAGE COMMUNITY          THE CITY

SURRENDERED THEIR AUTONOMY TO THE **NATION-STATE**

THESE NATION-STATES SOMETIMES EXPANDED INTO **EMPIRES**

THE TIME HAS NOW COME FOR THESE TO SURRENDER
THEIR SOVEREIGNTY TO A **WORLD FEDERATION**

FIGURE 4.5. From Village to World Federation (Masani, *Our Growing Human Family*, 101. Reproduced with the permission of Oxford University Press India © Oxford University Press 1950).

Across the four books, images of men dominate. Women do not fit meaningfully into the imaginaries of the future. *Our Growing Human Family* is the only book in which Masani discusses the role of women in society. In chapter 4, "A Wife, A Son, and a Slave," Masani suggests that the patriarchal family in which property inheritance took place through the male line coincided with

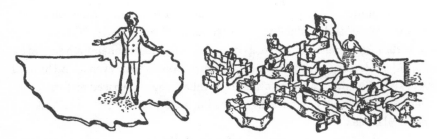

FIGURE 4.6. Free Trading America vs. Protectionist Europe (Masani, *Our Growing Human Family*, 102. Reproduced with the permission of Oxford University Press India © Oxford University Press 1950).

the introduction of settled agriculture. From then on, women became assets of men. Masani praises the matriarchal family of the southern regions of Travancore, Malabar, and Cochin, calling the nineteenth-century reforms to end this system "stupid." But he refrains from any normative assessment about patriarchy. More than anything, it seems to reflect an economic logic.[178]

Masani became a Cold War free enterpriser from the 1950s, operating as a dedicated polemicist in local and international groups. His Democratic Research Service (DRS) in Bombay published leaked documents with interpretive introductions from the Communist Party of India's (CPI) third (1953–54) and fourth congresses (1956). Masani himself wrote a history of the CPI.[179] By engaging in activities to discredit the communists, Masani satisfied a personal vendetta against them. This he had carried from the time they had infiltrated the Congress Socialist Party in the 1930s. In both the texts, Masani presented factually accurate evidence in a manner that sought to discredit the CPI.

Some scholars have alleged that Masani would seem the perfect CIA collaborator and local agent for the Americans.[180] However, we know that diplomats did not sound him out. Former U.S. ambassador to India Chester

178. Masani, *Our Growing Human Family*, 25–34.

179. A selection of the outfit's publications includes *Communist Conspiracy at Madurai: An Analysis of the Private Proceedings of the Third Congress of the CPI with Full Text of Documents* (Bombay: Democratic Research Service, 1954); *Communist Double Talk at Palghat: A Probe into the Private Proceedings of the Fourth Congress of the Indian Communist Party at Palghat Held in April 1956 with the Texts of Some Secret Documents* (Bombay: Democratic Research Service, 1956); *Indian Communist Party Documents, 1930–56* (Bombay: Democratic Research Service, 1957); *Kerala under Communism* (Bombay: Democratic Research Service, 1959).

180. On this characterization, see Benjamin Zachariah, *Nehru* (London: Routledge, 2004), 205.

Bowles complained in private correspondence of Masani's "blind bitterness against Nehru" and "instability." These tendencies could lead to "inaccurate or distorted" statements.[181] The risks of an unreliable local collaborator could be considerable in an environment of fake news. Bowles once even found himself accused of financing a procommunist Bombay magazine based on forged evidence.[182] It is unlikely that Americans financed or masterminded Masani's political career.

Masani did, however, involve himself with the International Congress for Cultural Freedom (ICCF) (see chapter 2), a group of artists and intellectuals championing freedom of expression that held a meeting in India in 1951. James Burnham, theorist of the managerial revolution, was one of the men in charge of diverting CIA funds to the Congress and had attended the meeting.[183] Members published periodicals and convened at conferences featuring prominent anticommunist academics, trade union leaders, and even socialists.[184] In 1952, Masani launched a monthly bulletin of the Indian branch of the ICCF called *Freedom First*, committed to the defense of "cultural freedom" in the face of totalitarian threats.[185] He believed the CCF could form the foundation of a sort of "worldwide anti-totalitarian 'fellowship.'"[186]

Cultural cold warriors could deviate from paths desired by their patrons.[187] Whether or not he knew of CIA funding, Masani used the CCF's resources opportunistically as part of political resistance to Nehru rather than for furthering American foreign policy objectives.[188] To the chagrin of the global CCF leadership, Masani's magazine, *Freedom First*, overtly mixed politics with

181. Bowles to Kennedy, November 18, 1952, Folder 267, Box 95, Papers of Chester Bowles, Manuscripts Collection, Yale University, USA. On Bowles' time in India, see Howard B. Schaffer, *Chester Bowles: New Dealer in the Cold War* (Cambridge, MA: Harvard University Press, 1993), 56–80.

182. Prakash, *Mumbai Fables*, 166.

183. Eric Pullin, "'Noise and Flutter': India, Propaganda, and Global Conflict, 1942–1963," (unpublished PhD diss., University of Wisconsin-Madison, 2009).

184. Saunders, *The Cultural Cold War: The CIA and the World of Arts and Letters* (New York: The New Press, 2000).

185. "The Open Society," *Freedom First*, June 1952, 1–2.

186. Roland Burke, "'Real Problems to Discuss': The Congress for Cultural Freedom's Asian and African Expeditions, 1951–1959," *Journal of World History* 27, no. 1 (2016): 53–85, 72.

187. In the Latin American context, see Patrick Iber, *Neither Peace Nor Freedom: The Cultural Cold War in Latin America* (Cambridge, MA: Harvard University Press, 2015), 18.

188. Pullin, "'Noise and Flutter'"; Pullin, "'Money Does Not Make Any Difference to the Opinions That We Hold': India, the CIA, and the Congress for Cultural Freedom, 1951–58,"

issues of cultural freedom. In late 1954, they forced Masani to start a separate literary magazine called *Quest* that omitted discussion of politics.[189] By this time, the CCF regarded Nehru as "the 'leading liberal alternative to Chinese Communism in India'" and had "sidelined Masani."[190]

Masani turned more actively to the related cause of free markets and free enterprise during the second plan period. He joined the Liberal International, which brought parliamentarians from across the world together and identified common objectives at annual meetings. The organization's manifesto listed as ideals the "free choice of occupation," "the right to private ownership of property and the right to embark on individual enterprise," and "consumer's free choice and the opportunity to reap the full benefit of the productivity of the soil and the industry of man."[191] Around the time Masani was elected as a patron of the Liberal International, the body held an annual meeting under the banner of "Free Economy in a Free Society." Key initiatives included the promotion of a European Common Market and free trade.[192]

Masani also played a significant role in Bombay-based Forum of Free Enterprise (1956–), founded by A. D. Shroff. The forum held weekly discussions by members and visiting speakers. Within four years of its inception, the forum had over a thousand members. It had sent a hundred booklets and leaflets to colleges and schools free of charge, sponsored five essay competitions, published 222 articles in the press, and produced twenty-nine newspaper supplements.[193] Financing came from the Tatas, members, and the founders. The forum printed writings from economists like Hayek and Friedman and hosted what became very famous annual speeches on the Union

*Intelligence and National Security* 26, no. 2–3 (2011): 377–98; Masani, *Against the Tide* (Ghaziabad, Vikas Publishing House, 1981), 54.

189. Pullin, "'Money Does Not Make Any Difference to the Opinions That We Hold.'"

190. Andrew Defty, *Britain, America and Anti-Communist Propaganda 1945–53: The Information Research Department* (London: Routledge, 2004), 206. See also Peter Coleman, *The Liberal Conspiracy: The Congress for Cultural Freedom and the Struggle for the Mind of Post-War Europe* (London: Macmillan, 1989), 152.

191. The Liberal International's ideology and expansion is discussed in their book. See Julie Smith, *A Sense of Liberty: The History of the Liberal International, 1947–1997* (London: Liberal International, 1997), v. Masani recalls his election to the Liberal International in memoirs of his life in independent India, *Against the Tide*, 88.

192. *The Liberal International (World Liberal Union)*, n.d., 12, Printed Material #137, Installment VI–XI, CRP, NMML.

193. "Brief Review of Activities," enclosed in A. D. Shroff to M. A. Master, October 19, 1960, Subject File 10, M. A. Master Papers, NMML.

Budget by the lawyer Nani Palkhivala.[194] These generally decried the high
levels of corporate and income taxation in the country and the presence of
multiple indirect taxes.[195] Shroff himself took an interest in the problem of inflation, writing multiple pamphlets attributing price rises to deficits of the Second
Five-Year Plan.[196]

Crucially, the forum's manifesto redefined free enterprise as entrepreneurship, the engine of social dynamism: "The man who first discovered fire was a
Free Enterpriser as also the man who invented the locomotive. . . . The shopkeeper and the merchant, the farmer and the artisan, the worker and the
manager . . . all these are Free Enterprisers."[197] Even if conceived of and participated in by Bombay Parsis, the language of "free enterprise" that Masani
embraced held broader appeal. The forum opened branches in Ahmedabad,
Bangalore, Calcutta, Delhi, and Madras, each of which had more than fifty
members by 1960.[198] Some of the regional branches translated the pamphlets
into local languages.[199] Studying voluntary associations in the city of Nagpur
in the 1960s, Robert Wirsing concluded that these could break forms of solidarity based on community and create new ones.[200] Free enterprise rhetoric
brought together sympathetic communities from various geographic loca-
tions in this case. Here was a more specialized, latter-day Libertarian Social
Institute.

The Forum of Free Enterprise was not a straightforward vehicle for the promotion of special interests. For one thing, big business' relationship to the forum was
far from smooth.[201] Shroff was dismayed that the Tata chairman, J.R.D. Tata,
caved to pressure from the Congress to restrain his criticism of Indian economic policy.[202] Nor did Masani merely represent big business interests in his

194. On Palkhivala, see chapter 6.
195. Kochanek, *Business and Politics*, 206.
196. A. D. Shroff, *An Inflationary Budget* (Bombay: Forum of Free Enterprise, 1959), and
Shroff, *Inflation Threatens Indian Economy* (Bombay: Forum of Free Enterprise, 1960).
197. "Manifesto of the Forum of Free Enterprise," *Forum of Free Enterprise*, http://www
.forumindia.org/booklet.htm.
198. "Brief Review of Activities"; Kochanek, *Business and Politics*, 207.
199. To take one example, Murarji Vaidya, *Towards a Self-Reliant Economy: Lessons of the Past*
(Bombay: Forum of Free Enterprise, 1966), was translated into Tamil as *Etirkāl Poruḷātārāmum
Kaṭanta Kāl Tavaṟukaḷum* (The Economy of the Future and Mistakes of the Past).
200. Robert Wirsing, *Socialist Society and Free Enterprise Politics* (Bombay: Vikas, 1977).
201. See chapter 1.
202. Dalal, *A. D. Shroff: Titan of Finance and Free Enterprise* (Delhi: Viking, 2000), 61.

forum activity. Therefore, the assessment of him as the "caricature of the cap-italist stooge" he once despised in his youth is incomplete.[203] His children's books presented a vision of the economy in which small industries using bor-rowed technology played a substantial role. His native South Bombay was filled with Parsi professionals, small-time capitalists, and merchants who made up the membership of the forum. Finally, the primary lobbying body of big business, the Federation of Indian Chambers of Commerce and Industry, and the leading company behind it, the Birla Group, was not involved in the forum and believed it to be unrepresentative of business interests.[204]

Masani ran successfully for parliament in the Lok Sabha elections of 1957. Despite never being a man of the masses, support from Jayaprakash Narayan helped him win election from a constituency in the latter's home state of Bihar. Masani's parliamentary speeches warned of the "tendency to over-idealize and glorify heavy industrialization." He attacked deficit-financing-induced infla-tion and taxation, saying, "We cannot invest resources that we do not possess." Masani alleged that India was turning away from the democratic way of life. He cautioned that the five-year plans and the "proliferation of the bureau-cracy" associated with the newly inaugurated state-led developmental projects were putting in place "a kind of bureaucratic State Capitalism as against Private Capitalism."[205] This language had much in common with the pamphlets now appearing from the Forum of Free Enterprise. Two years later at a forum event, Masani met Rajagopalachari and commenced discussions that led to founding of the Swatantra Party.[206]

Masani's free economy and society somewhat uncritically took inspiration from the United States. However, he believed that small traders, farmers, and entrepreneurs could move into small industry more readily thanks to technol-ogy transfers. The economy could therefore industrialize in a different fashion from European nations. This did not require a greatly active state, which Masani thought to be coercive when it ran deficits and produced inflation. Representative government would be democratic and republican, and political

203. Zachariah, *Developing India*, 257.

204. Kochanek, *Business and Politics*, 104–6.

205. "Speech on the Finance Bill in the Lok Sabha on August 26, 1957, and Speech in the Lok Sabha on May 28, 1957, during the General Discussion on the Budget," reprinted in Minoo Masani, *A Plea for Realism: Some Speeches Delivered in Parliament between May and August 1957* (Bombay: Popular Book Depot, 1957), 35–43, 1–10.

206. Speeches from the May 29, 1959, Bangalore meeting were reproduced as *For Freedom, Farm and Family* (Bombay: Forum of Free Enterprise, 1959).

opposition would be vibrant thanks to dutiful citizens. Internationally, free trade and federation would give way to a world government.

Masani considered communism and, later, even socialism, to be threats to this vision. He regarded the greatest experiment combining these ideologies, the Soviet Union, as a disaster. Conditioned by his anglicized Parsi ways and by leveraging community, city, and Cold War networks, Masani pushed for free enterprise and a communist-free India. Gradually, this mission led him into the electoral politics of opposition. Even if he made himself among the most visible, he was not a key figure either in the Tatas' efforts to influence the government or in the United States' Cold War activities in the region. It is better to see him, from his early years as an Oxford University Press author to his time as a pamphleteer engaged in the Forum of Free Enterprise, as mired in the print world of Bombay and seeking wider audiences.

Even though the highly westernized Masani considered himself a liberal, his anticommunism was constitutive of Indian economic conservatism. In the West, conservatism responded to socialism by incorporating the idea of limited power and rejecting the organic community in favor of the idea of an individual "exercising independence and force of character shored up by private property."[207] Its architects appropriated tenets of classical liberalism and constructed an appeal as an antitotalitarian cause.[208] Those holding conservative attitudes defined themselves as liberal in certain cases.[209] In India, the profound role of imperial liberal ideology in constructing political and educational institutions and informing governance had also contributed to the emergence of nationalist discourse in liberal idioms.[210] But Masani's position

207. Freeden, *Ideologies and Political Theory*, 355.

208. The standard definition of classical liberalism draws from John Stuart Mill's formulation as an individualist philosophy that assigns paramount importance to liberty and rationality and is underpinned by the understanding that these two concepts are interlocked with a notion of progress. See Freeden, *Ideologies and Political Theory*, 147–67. On the appropriation of its tenets by conservatives in the twentieth century, see Roger Scruton, *Conservatism: An Invitation to the Great Tradition* (New York: All Points, 2018), 103–26.

209. A single definition of liberalism became even more difficult because it was being reinvented simultaneously in countries such as the United States and Britain, which had a communitarian ethos and a concern for public responsibility toward improving human material needs and capacities. Freeden, *Ideologies and Political Theory*, 196. See also Katrina Forrester, *In the Shadow of Justice: Postwar Liberalism and the Remaking of Political Philosophy* (Princeton: Princeton University Press, 2019).

210. Mantena, *Alibis of Empire*; Bayly, *Recovering Liberties*.

was relationally conservative in a postcolonial environment where most other political groups self-identified as socialist.

———

N. G. Ranga, Bhaikaka Patel, and Minoo Masani produced positive visions of decentralized economies more firmly embedded in the world system than the Nehruvian equivalent, working across multiple scalar units. Their ideas underscore that Swatantra was invested not merely in critiquing the current trajectory of Indian economic policy and the dominant imaginaries of planning, but that it was also associated with alternatives. The various genres of literature they produced in that context illuminates that their economic ideas were far from ghostly visions of the past.

Although they threw up quite different visions and lived very different lives, some basic similarities unite Ranga, Patel, and Masani. Each had been shaped by their privileged hereditary communities of Kammas, Patidars, or Parsis. These communities had been willing to embrace foreign ideas, expertise, or machinery. Each had specific grievances concerning controls, bureaucratic red tape, food and agriculture, or land policy. Reflecting the interests of these communities, each of these three Swatantra leaders had an understanding that the state should pursue policies in favor of or to assist business and agriculture. They shared an openness to the liberal international economic order and United Nations organizations. They also all manifested a kind of anticommunism. That could be expressed explicitly, as in Masani's pamphlets, or in the doomsday warnings of the consequences of land ceilings in Bhaikaka's memoirs. As in the case of Rajagopalachari, education formed a key part of their politics. And they all kept relatively silent on issues of gender, not particularly concerned to incorporate women as more equal participants in political economy. As figures like Ranga, Patel, and Masani came together at the national level and made the case for decentralization, they also helped give an economic flavor to the debate about the relative powers of center and region in a federal system.

Of course, these slightly nebulous positive visions of free economy contradicted each other in minor ways. To take just one example, Ranga's views on price supports and canal locks to manage world trade and those of Masani's do not line up. However, these ideas got rationalized, consolidated, and translated again for the purposes of elections. The Swatantra Party's twenty-one principles brought out the lowest common denominator in the thought of these men. "Individual initiative," freedom of trade, and "increasing food production . . . through the self-employed peasant proprietor" appeared among its commitments. So did "incentives for higher production and expansion inherent in competitive enterprise."

Overall, the statement recommended "balanced development of capital goods, industries, organized consumer goods industries and rural industries that afford supplementary employment in small scale processing of the products of agriculture."[211] This required "decentralized distribution of industry" and reduced expenditure on "controls and official management with all its wastefulness and inefficiency." In agrarian areas, it required "a more effective program than is being followed at present in respect of irrigation and the supply of material, implements, credit and marketing facilities." Communicating this platform when the party hit the streets and its leaders sought to win votes would form the next part of opposition politics.

211. "Swatantra Party's Stress on Incentives."

# PART III

# Party Politics

# 5

# Communicating and Mobilizing

## FREE ECONOMY AS OPPOSITION

AROUND A THOUSAND delegates descended on the Central Studios in southern Bombay for Swatantra's inaugural convention between August 1 and 2, 1959. A short video from the first day shows the impeccably suited Parsi businessman and politician, Sir Homi Mody; the Sikh peasant leader Uddam Singh Nagoke of Punjab with two of his associates; and some party members from Andhra Pradesh entering the studios.[1] The camera cuts to a banner displaying the following words, attributed to Gandhi: "I look upon an increase in the power of the State with the greatest fear because, although while apparently doing good by minimizing exploitation, it does the greatest harm to mankind by destroying individuality which lies at the heart of all progress."

The first day of the convention is the birth anniversary of Bal Gangadhar Tilak, whose image adorns the dais along with those of Mahatma Gandhi and Sardar Patel.[2] Flanked by N. G. Ranga, a smiling, bespectacled C. Rajagopalachari emerges from a large black automobile. Walking stick in hand, he makes his way slowly toward the dais. The old man needs help climbing the stairs. There, he joins other party leaders representing various states. The camera pans to the audience, a sea of white. Most of them are wearing white kurtas. A few don Gandhi caps made of *khadi*. Minoo Masani calls the meeting to order. After an opening devotional song from the musician M. S. Subbulakshmi—the wife

---

1. "India: First Convention of Swatantra Party," Video Footage, Reuters Archive (Online), August 1, 1959, https://reuters.screenocean.com/record/1100640.

2. This paragraph follows "Swatantra Party Is Inaugurated: Pledge to Resist Inroads on Individual Freedom," *ToI*, August 2, 1959.

of *Kalki* editor T. Sadasivam and the only woman on the dais—the meeting begins at 10:30 a.m.

The audience listens to English speeches from Rajagopalachari, Ranga, and Masani. Rajagopalachari calls Swatantra not merely a party but a "movement for freedom as important and as serious as the movement for independence against the British rule." He continues, calling Swatantra a movement against "this misconceived progress of the Congress towards what will finally end in the suppression of individual liberty and the development of the State into a true Leviathan."[3] All three men allude to the threat to the agrarian social and economic order, calling it "family economy," "agricultural economy," or "rural life." These speeches are calculated to rile up the audience.

After this opening salvo, the top brass adjourns to a closed-door seminar in the nearby Bharatiya Vidya Bhavan.[4] They continue these discussions at the Bhavan the next morning before returning to Central Studios for a final session. A range of speakers from across the country addresses the audience, among them K. M. Munshi and V. P. Menon. At the conclusion of the convention, the party adopts a statement of principles that leaders finalized during the closed sessions. The document asserts the party's commitment to minimum government, economic growth, and social harmony. It welcomes those of all castes and creeds. Crucially, it embraces "a balanced development of capital goods industries, organized consumer goods industries, and rural industries that afford supplementary employment in the small-scale processing of the products of agriculture."[5] The last principle says that on topics not addressed by the previous principles, members are welcome to entertain their own positions.

At the convention, Rajagopalachari, Ranga, Masani, and their colleagues laid claim to the legacy of Tilak, Gandhi, and Patel. They presented themselves as caretakers of political freedom in the postcolonial age. As they saw it, Congress' socialism, which was slipping down the road to communism, endangered this freedom. Socialism sacrificed spirituality and the family, two pillars of Indian life, at the altar of material progress. Decrying cooperative farming, the "double fragmentation" produced by the Hindu Succession Act, and land

---

3. *Swatantra Party: Preparatory Convention* (Bombay: Popular Book Depot, 1959), 14–18. I am grateful to Mou Banerjee for helping me secure a copy of this pamphlet.

4. "'C. R.' Criticizes Congress Drift to Communism," *ToI*, August 3, 1959.

5. "Swatantra Party's Stress on Incentives: 21-Clause Statement of Principles Adopted," *ToI*, August 3, 1959.

reforms, they pledged to return the country to the constitution of 1950. Swatantra's leaders promised to uphold the fundamental right to property, freedom of trade, and commerce.

The logic of electoral politics required the Swatantra Party to attempt to push beyond the English-language associations and journals in which "free economy" had germinated, and even past the "small section of culturally equipped citizens" who inhabited India's "demographically limited" civil society.[6] Instead, it forced a reckoning with the unorganized domain in which most of India's recently enfranchised masses lived. To reach into this wider demographic, the party made efforts to overcome a "neighborly uncommunication" between English- and Indian-language publics.[7] This involved moving onto the streets and taking up localized issues. Although Swatantra might exploit established relationships of patronage to conduct such activity, it aimed at mobilizing people around economic ideas rather than attachments to caste and other forms of identity.

Efforts to spread political and economic ideas through various media and mobilization activity constituted the second dimension of opposition politics. Swatantra's leaders rewrote free economy as party doctrine, claiming to represent "middle-class" citizens "of the cities and the towns" who "must join hands with the peasants in the villages in defense of their rights and property."[8] Deploying a range of media, from gramophone recordings to cartoons, they sought to communicate in localized idioms. This project, at once polemical and pedagogical, aimed to widen the vocabulary of Indian politics. It illuminates how politicians and publicists engage with and communicate economic ideas. Engaging citizens in forms of protest and political participation that traced antecedents in anticolonial politics, the party yoked these to the economic concerns of the present. Seeking to create a politics of class, it reproduced the gendered conceptions of economic life prevalent at the time and aimed to make invisible the divisions of caste and religion that dominated the polity.

This process laid bare the limitations of both the imagination and take-up of the free economy project. Swatantra's various evocations of the middle class never quite mapped on to a substantial political constituency. Instead, they corresponded to various elite identities far removed from the middle of any

6. Partha Chatterjee, *The Politics of the Governed: Reflections on Popular Sovereignty in Most of the World* (New York: Columbia University Press, 2004).

7. Kaviraj, *The Imaginary Institution of India*, 9–38.

8. Masani, *Swatantra Party: Preparatory Convention*, 10.

kind of distribution of income or resources. Another related problem concerned the party's inability to escape the English-language origins of free economy. English had of course aided the spread of free economy across an elite stratum of people and indeed facilitated the coming together of party politicians from all over India. It was preferred to Hindi. However, the inability to translate free economy adequately into Indian languages—because of an inadequate number of bilingual intermediators and the more elite context of English usage—constrained Swatantra's attempts to attract support in a wider popular base.

Nevertheless, the party's efforts provoked responses. Ordinary people became conscious of Swatantra as part of their democratic practices and in certain cases came to see it as an economic ombudsperson or vehicle for voicing grievances. They wrote letters expressing their thoughts, filed petitions, donated money, and protested. These practices suggest consequences of the rise and fall of the Swatantra Party that go beyond the ballot box. They are part of a wider, material history of Indian democracy as a "dynamic and ongoing set of contestations" and "something one does."[9]

The open records of the Swatantra Party and its top brass allow a fine-grained picture of the design and execution of publicity and mobilization campaigns pursued in opposition to the Congress.[10] However, evaluating Swatantra's originality relative to its contemporary opposition parties in India is hard. Limitations in existing scholarly literature and access restrictions to the records of other parties that have survived to this day preclude such an assessment. All in all, such an exercise offers a valuable step in understanding the historical origins of how conservative parties in various geographic contexts use democracy to campaign for and attain power.[11] Their appeals have not

9. Lisa Mitchell, *Hailing the State: Indian Democracy between Elections* (Durham, NC: Duke University Press, 2023), 21. I am grateful to Professor Mitchell for permission to cite from her forthcoming book. See also Rohit De and Robert Travers, eds., "Petitioning and Political Cultures in South Asia," *Modern Asian Studies* 53, no. 1 (2019): 1–20.

10. This chapter breaks from the mold of social scientific research past and present by bringing together the study of the political and social power of economic ideas and of practices. These have tended to be studied separately. See the discussion in the introduction and chapter 4 of how the influential interest group approach to studies of Indian democracy prominent in the 1960s did not take ideology seriously.

11. Dunn, *Breaking Democracy's Spell* (New Haven, CT: Yale University Press, 2014); Pierre Rosanvallon, "Democratic Universalism as a Historical Problem," *Constellations: An International Journal of Critical and Democratic Theory* 16, no. 4 (2009): 539–49.

always been antidemocratic. Rather than a means to popular emancipation, democracy to them was a form of government that would stabilize society, with target constituencies as its anchors.

How did Swatantra weave together and consolidate the ideas of its leaders and put forth a platform for political opposition? In what ways did Swatantra attempt to mobilize economic discontent and create opposition consciousness in a largely unlettered society? What were the party's shortcomings and blind spots? And, to the extent that they did, how did ordinary citizens express themselves on the questions of economic and political life?

## "Ordered Progress" for the "Middle-Class Citizen"

Unlike its statement of principles, Swatantra's statement of policy took some time after the inaugural convention to be adopted formally. It sewed together the various conceptions of free economy of President N. G. Ranga, General Secretary Minoo Masani, Vice President K. M. Munshi, Mariadas Ruthnaswamy, and C. Rajagopalachari. Five experts, some of whom were not party members, prepared extended notes on specific issues.[12] Both the participants in the drafting of the statement of policy and those who contributed notes hailed from states in southern or western India.[13] Even as Swatantra's viability as a party owed to vote banks in North India, free economy as an ideology came from southern and western India. Crucially, the notes included one on economic policy by B. R. Shenoy, labeling inflation as a "crime against man."[14] Inflation became a key point of appeal against the Congress.

Masani drafted the original statement of policy. In preparing the final draft, he conferred with Munshi and incorporated suggestions from Rajagopalachari, Ruthnaswamy, and Ranga. Their respective contributions reflect the dispositions of these men. Thus, the original version prepared by Masani prioritized freedom of enterprise. Rajagopalachari and Ruthnaswamy's edits sought to add commitments to reconstructing villages and investing in

12. Munshi to Masani, January 26, 1960, Microfilm Accession 2291, File 295, KMM, 127.

13. The states were Mysore, Madras, Andhra Pradesh, Gujarat, or Maharashtra. Those who prepared minutes were Sir B. Rama Rau, B. R. Shenoy, Goutu Latchanna, H. M. Patel, and J. M. Lobo Prabhu; "Swatantra Party: Draft Minutes of Central Organizing Committee, 5 February 1960," Microfilm Accession 2291, File 295, KMM, 188–195, 195.

14. B. R. Shenoy, "Basic Economic Policy," [n.d. 1959], Subject File 41, Installment VI–XI, CRP, 735–47.

infrastructure connecting the village and the city. Both also wanted something in the statement of policy that committed to introducing rural public services. N. G. Ranga suggested peasant parity with the urban dweller and toning down the pro-free-enterprise language. His edits made the draft's disavowal of "laissez-faire" more prominent, and he removed cumbersome statistics unlikely to have much rhetorical force. As a peasant politician who had successfully won elections through popular appeal, Ranga had a better sense of what would work with the electorate than others. Munshi introduced a commitment to securing a minimum standard of food, clothing, and housing for all.[15] Reflecting Masani's position as the general secretary, the published version prioritized free enterprise.

The statement of policy argued that India did not have a free economy. It focused on four issues: inflation, taxation, corruption related to the size of the state, and the fundamental rights guaranteed in the constitution. The party projected an image of a select group marginalized by Congress economic policy: "The grinding effect of these combined pressures of stagnant income, rise in prices and excessive taxation has been particularly heavy on the middle classes which depend predominantly on fixed incomes. The middle classes, the backbone of society, are being victimized in the process."[16] The Swatantra leadership, and Masani especially, constructed a middle-class citizen for themselves to represent. The gendered language of the document suggested this was a male figure. He was the "peasant-proprietor, the artisan, the shopkeeper and the professional man" entitled to fundamental rights "which include the three human freedoms, namely the freedom to choose one's occupation; secondly, to pursue it without restraint within the limits of the Rule of Law; and lastly to dispose of one's income between spending and saving."[17] These freedoms did not actually exist as fundamental rights in the constitution.[18] Rather, the document appropriated the language of constitutional rights for the purposes of free economy to create the rights-bearing middle-class citizen. This citizen deserved commitment from the country's leaders to an honest rupee, free of inflation and its attending uncertainties.

Multiple rounds of drafting and attention to word choice indicate how seriously these leaders regarded the articulation of the party agenda. It was

15. "Draft Manifesto," Microfilm Accession 2293, File 14, KMM, 298–314.
16. *To Prosperity through Freedom* (Patna: Swatantra Party, 1960), 9.
17. *To Prosperity through Freedom*, 11.
18. On these, and Swatantra's activities related to them, see chapter 6.

another case of what Howard Erdman perceived as a "legalistic, constitutional-
ist strain" that reflected the training of three of these men in law.[19] The use of
the language of fundamental rights to describe the citizen's entitlements
was not accidental. It signaled the credentials of Masani, Mody, Munshi, Ranga, and
Rajagopalachari as delegates to the Constituent Assembly. Both Masani and
Munshi had been members of the fundamental rights subcommittee.[20] Rajagopalachari's copy of the statement pledged to restore the country to the 1950
constitution. Ranga conceived of the peasant's right to property as paramount,
viewing policies of land ceilings as a threat to this right. The idealized middle-
class citizen deserved his rights. The Swatantra top brass counted founding
fathers of the country among its ranks. These men invoked their distinguished status and role in the construction of the law of the republic to
strengthen their appeal.

To tackle what Ranga referred to as "the criticism against the party that
it consists of the better classes who are anxious to maintain the status quo
at all costs," the statement needed to embrace possibilities for change. The
leadership recast parts of its statement of policy to communicate an agenda
that seemed constructive and open to progress. Consider, for example, how
Ranga made a "positive land policy" out of his opposition to land ceilings
and cooperative farming that was still consistent with the statement of policy.
He rewrote the objectives in the statement to "a) increase food production,
b) preserve the harmony of rural life and c) achieve a sufficient measure of social
and economic equity" in the following way: "firstly, market compensation to
the landholders, secondly, completely voluntary nature of the transfers, and
thirdly, the building up of agriculture from below." Without committing to
what that building-up might entail, he described Congress agricultural policy
as an inadequate set of measures "merely giving better facilities for cultivation
such as credit, manures implements and the like." Drawing upon his knowledge
of small landholders liquidating their holdings in favor of other investment
opportunities, he suggested a policy of "gradual surrender."[21]

19. Erdman, *The Swatantra Party and Indian Conservatism*, 102.

20. On Munshi's role, see chapter 2. See A. K. Lal, *Secularism: Concept and Practice* (Delhi:
Concept, 1998), 145; Kalyani Ramnath, "'We the People': Seamless Webs and Social Revolution
in India's Constituent Assembly Debates," in *The Indian Constituent Assembly: Deliberations on
Democracy*, ed. Udit Bhatia (Oxford: Routledge, 2017), 181–95, 183; Austin, *The Indian Constitution*, 48.

21. N. G. Ranga, Untitled Note, n.d, Subject File 41, Installment VI–XI, CRP, 549–51.

Ranga criticized the inadequacy of Congress efforts to improve agricultural output and signaled his preference for a policy compatible with property rights and redistribution through this rewording. However, he never committed to any concrete steps toward progressive ends. Rhetorically remaking free economy for the purposes of mass electoral politics involved multiple sleights of hand like this. It meant attacking radical policies and presenting resistance to these policies as an embrace of change free of the heavy hand of the state. This class rhetoric deliberately avoided issues of caste and religious tension.

A large body of pamphlet literature conveyed various aspects of the statement of policy and sought to anchor the Swatantra Party's ideology more concretely. Pamphlets such as *Swatantra Speaks to the Poor* and *This Poor Man Prefers Swatantra* suggested that focus on "peasant proprietorship" and "people's enterprise" would "encourage a 'free economy' so that the doors can be thrown open to the poor." Through such literature, the party made claims to represent both Ranga's peasants and Masani's enterprisers, arguing that economic prosperity would trickle down for everyone's benefit. Two dedicated pamphlet series sought to advance these objectives: *Swatantra Public Education Series* and *For This We Stand*. The first, which had a print run of fifty thousand, attempted to widen voter knowledge about economic issues.[22] The second series comprised about twelve pamphlets that elaborated underemphasized aspects of the statement of policy.[23]

This illustrated literature illuminated economic concepts and depicted a "middle-class" citizen suffering life in the permit-and-license raj. Masani and his Forum of Free Enterprise colleagues based at the party's central office in Bombay drew upon their experience writing economic textbooks and pamphlets to create these materials. For the political tasks at hand, they increased the element of polemic in the party paraphernalia.

The pamphlet *Who's to Hold That Price Line?* highlights how the party literature sought to be simultaneously "factual and authoritative" and "plebeian and spicy," as Munshi once described their dual aims in an internal memorandum.[24] The fifteen-page pamphlet encapsulated the thrust of Swatantra's critique of Indian economic policy. It starts with a description of prices and inflation:

22. Titles included: *Socialism: An Ism Has Become a Wasm, Statism Rejected: Ceylon Shows the Way*, and *Inflation: Your Hidden Enemy*.

23. Titles included: *Fundamental Rights: Our Protection against Tyranny, The People Are Sovereign, Preparedness for Defense*, and *Why Swatantra Supports Tashkent Agreement*.

24. Munshi, "Publicity," October 24, 1959, File 2, Box 16, SP.

FIGURE 5.1. Factual (*Who's to Hold That Price Line?* [Bombay: Swatantra Party, n.d.]).

"Prices are expressed in terms of money, which in our country is the rupee. When there is an all-around increase in prices, economists call it inflation." Next, it defines money (see Figure 5.1). The pamphlet goes on to show money on a scale against goods and services and describes inflation as when excess printing of money disturbs that balance. Having provided these foundations, it explains in steps how direct and indirect taxes, state revenues, foreign aid, and deficit financing pay for the five-year plans. It shows how the heavy industry focus of the plans has generated income to spend but inadequate goods to purchase because of the neglect of agriculture and consumer goods industries.

So far, the pamphlet would appear indistinguishable from a textbook. The polemical turn comes later. In step one of Figure 5.2, heavy industry assumes human form as a fat government babu wearing a Gandhi cap huffing and puffing as he is allowed to run ahead of others who wonder "What's the idea in letting him go first?" In step two, the government worker is depicted as asleep on his desk as he sits on top of books called *Notes on Work* and *Efficiency*, presumably ignoring them. The accompanying text says, "As a rule, state enterprises are inefficient not only because there is complete divorce of responsibility from risk but also because of political interference." Thanks to their behavior, state enterprises lead to a "whirlpool of losses." Nevertheless, the size of government administration and its servants who "add little to the production of goods and

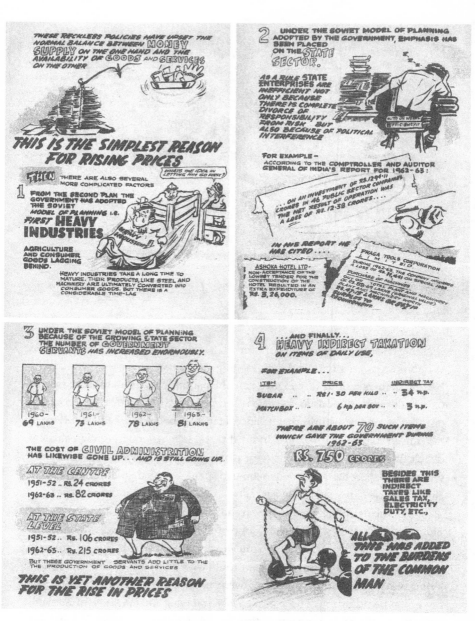

FIGURE 5.2. Spicy (*Who's to Hold That Price Line?*).

services" keeps growing. In step three, the government servants, illustrated as fat men, grow in size with time in a pictogram that conveys their increasing numbers. By the end, these government servants have become fat to the point of bursting. By contrast (step four), the skinny, distressed common man is weighed down by balls and chains, a metaphor for increasing indirect taxation. The pamphlet concludes by stating, "Unless economic laws are respected, prices will continue to soar." As in Rajagopalachari's *Swarajya* writings by this time, the pamphlet uses the imagery of the scales of justice and the language of "law" to portray the economy as simultaneously scientific and ethical.

*Who's to Hold That Price Line?* and pamphlets like it visually set up a binary between the state and the people. They show an increasingly distressed and impoverished skinny person against the emissary of the state growing fatter, richer, and lazier. Such materials portray someone from a "cherished community" under attack or at least under threat.[25] Another pamphlet, *18 Years of Socialism* (see Figure 5.3), presents a citizen being made false promises and placed under the burden of more and more taxes as a government servant grows taller and taller by standing on five-year plan documents. By 1967, the ordinary person can barely stand straight and kicks away the government servant and his plans, affirming his "new life."

Cynical cartoons in the periodical press inspired Swatantra's visual literature to give a face to the "middle-class citizen." The most influential of these was R. K. Laxman's *Common Man*. It appeared continuously from 1951 onward in India's most widely circulated newspaper, the *Times of India*. Swatantra seems to have copied this character (see the person depicted in Figure 5.3. and 5.4). The eponymous "common man" was the protagonist in an ill-fated, never-ending saga of democracy and development unfolding in the familiar settings of the village, the home, or the administrative office.[26] Elected officials and development specialists appear as incompetent and prone to corruption. Its author seems to suggest that the lofty ideals before the Indian nation state are quixotic at best. The common man was "a key register for the discourse of corruption . . . the ordinariness of these places and the daily routine make the discourse of corruption and its intimate tie with development

25. Charles Press, *The Political Cartoon* (Rutherford, NJ: Fairleigh Dickinson University Press, 1981), 50–79.

26. By 1960, the circulation of the *Times of India* had reached 158, 954. See *Press in India 1962—Part One*, 65.

FIGURE 5.3. Crushed by Taxation until He Rebels (*18 Years of Socialism* [Bombay: Swatantra Party, 1966]).

obvious."[27] Appearing week after week (see Figure 5.5), this figure became familiar to the reader.

*Common Man* spawned a genre of the "single-column pocket cartoon." It inspired cartoons by the artist Kevy Varma that appeared on the cover of *Eastern Economist* (from 1963) and *Thought* (from 1967), two magazines in the web that incubated the emergence of free economy.[28] It also inspired the character of *Kākājī* (Uncle) in Bombay cartoonist Bal Thackeray's Marathi cartoon weekly, *Mārmik* (Straight from the Heart).[29] Founded in 1960, the year Bombay State split into Gujarat and Maharashtra, *Mārmik* won acclaim for its biting satire and black humor. It took upon itself the task of representing the Marathi *maṇūsa* (man) and tapped into resentment about Muslims and immigrants to the city taking over. Wildly successful among literate Marathis, *Mārmik* served as a launching pad for Thackeray's politics of fear. In 1966, he started the Shiv Sena (Shiva's Army) party, which would rise to the forefront

27. I quote here from the excellent study by Ritu Khanduri, *Caricaturing Culture in India: Cartoons and History in the Modern World* (Cambridge: Cambridge University Press, 2014), 164–71, 164.

28. Khanduri, *Caricaturing Culture in India*, 191, 195. Information about the covers comes from the back issues of these magazines.

29. Khanduri, *Caricaturing Culture in India*, 164–66; Raj Thackeray, ed., *Bal Keshav Thackeray: A Photobiography* (Bombay: UBS Publishers, 2005), 60; Vaibhav Purandare, *Bal Thackeray and the Rise of the Shiv Sena* (New Delhi: Roli Books, 2012).

of Maharashtra politics.[30] Despite the differences between the projects for which these cartoons served, they all caricatured the incompetence of the developmental state and its politicians. This sowed the seeds of skepticism about the legitimacy of the Congress regime at large.

Masani and his colleagues had an ambiguous understanding of this target demographic. An early memorandum drawn up by the urbanite Masani described a group living in the cities but distinct from the "working class."[31] He later defined middle class as those with income of up to 25,000 rupees per year, in a country where output per capita was just about 2 percent of that amount.[32] Ranga, the former economist, spoke of a "salaried employee family budget," failing to elaborate further.[33] The party's strategy document for the 1962 elections redefined middle-class citizen based on some back-of-the-envelope calculations. The document spoke nebulously of those "who make up their own minds belonging to the educated and middle classes." It estimated this

30. Prakash, *Mumbai Fables,* 228–50.

31. Masani and Munshi, "Swatantra Party: Draft Manifesto," [n.d. 1961], Microfilm Accession 2291, File 296, KMM, 114–129, 119.

32. M. R. Masani, "Annexure: List of Demands—General Secretary's Letter 114," February 2, 1966, Microfilm Accession 2294, File 211, KMM, 130; *Economic Survey, 1974–5* (New Delhi: Government of India, 1974), 57.

33. "Tax Reduction Day (February 20, 1966): Points Made by Prof. N.G. Ranga, M.P. in His Speech Delivered at a Public Meeting Held at Vithalbhai Patel House, Rafi Marg, New Delhi," Microfilm Accession 10955, File 66, CRP, 183–85.

FIGURE 5.4. The Swatantra Party's "Common Man" (*The Rising Star* [Bombay: Swatantra Party, n.d. {1966?}]).

group to comprise a fifth of the purported 20 percent of voters whom the Swatantra leadership believed voted based on ideology, or 4 percent of the electorate. According to the document, this group required great effort to capture: "their vanity has to be satisfied." They required a personalized approach and "provision of transport" to the ballot boxes.[34] By the time of the 1967 manifesto, middle class meant the "self-employed man, whether he is a farmer, artisan, shopkeeper, or professional."[35]

Visually constructed by a group of men sitting in Bombay and reading its venerable *Times of India* newspaper, this middle-class citizen was presumably an English speaker living in urban areas, aware of the national news. There was no chiefly Indian language-speaking, rural small peasant proprietor or

34. J. M. Lobo Prabhu, "A Note on the Strategy for the General Election," Microfilm Accession 10963, File 90, CRP, 8–13.

35. "Draft Manifesto for the 1967 Elections," File Four, Box Four, SP.

# You Said It
### By LAXMAN

Why am I going abroad? Well, to study the conditions in our country, of course!

Utter lack of co-ordination, my friend—look at this road, neither the Telephones, nor the Water Works nor the P.W.D. has dug it up!

So, here we have our target, gentlemen—the zeroes are fixed, only we have to decide on a number now!

FIGURE 5.5. R. K. Laxman's *Common Man* in *Times of India* (*ToI*: July 12, 1958; October 29, 1959; March 15, 1960).

mofussil trader in this imaginary. The party used images and language most closely resembling their equivalents in the national newspaper media. As a demographic, however, the "common man" and "middle class" as presented in this visual literature defy straightforward description. The diversity of communities classifiable as middling in the income distribution divided by hierarchies of language, caste, and region render a solely material definition rife with problems. Historians of colonial India have defined this class as a partially westernized, English-speaking section of the populace employed in the professions and partaking of a consumption culture. Accounting for a very small and privileged fraction of Indian society, however, this group is hardly in the "middle."[36] The demographic expanded in the 1950s and 1960s. By 1971, a

36. Sanjay Joshi, ed., *The Middle Class in Colonial India* (New Delhi: Oxford University Press, 2010), xvii–xxix.

million people worked in the professions and university enrollment had increased sevenfold.[37]

The Swatantra Party defined its objectives in a statement of policy that prioritized free enterprise and envisioned an imaginary rights-bearing middle-class citizen as its core constituency. In defining this political imaginary, Masani, Munshi, Rajagopalachari, and Ranga staked their claims to legitimacy in their participation in the freedom struggle and enhanced the nobility of their objectives by using the language of constitutionalism. The middle-class citizen did not exist as a concrete entity. He—almost always referred to and presented as a man—had to be created by concentrated appeals to a small minority of the populace who might be swayed by ideology. A disproportionate amount of propaganda material targeted this group. Party leaders and workers reworked principles articulated in the statement of policy into an extensive pamphlet literature that sought to instruct as much as they did to persuade this citizen to become the middle-class citizen hemmed in by life in the permit-and-license raj.

Middle classness has never been a purely material designation. A staggering range of projects that unfolded across different countries from the late nineteenth to the twentieth centuries reveal how the contours of middle classness and the political activity and ideology of groups classified or self-identifying as such have been diverse. They have been products of material factors as much as concrete products of identity creation by ruling elites, or of self-identification.[38] The category seems to connote a buffer between other groups compatible with some notion of orderly modernization—a thinking class.[39] Swatantra's goal seems to have been to create from this group of people an anti-statist version of the salariat of postcolonial societies, "those with educational qualifications and aspirations for jobs in the state apparatus, the civil bureaucracy and the military," promising them "ordered progress" (see Figure 5.4).[40]

The substantial energy invested in conveying free economy as an electoral political ideology and constructing this middle-class citizen suggests that Swatantra accorded greater importance to its educational objectives than its

37. See chapter 1.

38. A. Ricardo López and Barbara Weinstein, "Introduction," in *The Making of the Middle Class: Toward a Transnational History*, eds. López and Weinstein (Durham, NC: Duke University Press, 2012), 1–24.

39. Barbara Weinstein, "Commentary on Part I: The Making of the Middle Class and Practices of Modernity," in *The Making of the Middle Class*, eds. López and Weinstein, 107–118.

40. Hamza Alavi, "Pakistan and Islam: Ethnicity and Ideology," in *State and Ideology in the Middle East and Pakistan*, eds. Fred Halliday and Hamza Alavi (New York: Monthly Review Press, 1987), 64–111. I am grateful to Srinath Raghavan for pointing me toward this concept.

electoral success. This order of priority both acknowledged the formidable challenge of defeating Congress and made use of the country's openness to voices of dissent to present an alternative. Rajagopalachari's letter drafted in advance of the 1967 polls presented this idea in characteristically moralizing terms: "Ours is a mission to spread political and economic education and we must firmly and devotedly stick to that work without caring for office or power. If office comes let us not shirk responsibility, but that is not our aim." He told his colleagues that they should be content "if others exercise authority, provided our principles are in substance accepted by them. What we aim at is to save the country from economic collapse and bankruptcy and to set it going on the honorable road of self-reliance."[41]

Articulating the Swatantra Party's role as fundamentally pedagogical was consistent with the Government of India's mission to offer a new electorate "political education." Through this, the government sought to familiarize Indians with the process of voting and the idea of democracy.[42] As privileged men with a background of public service, Swatantra's leaders saw it as their duty to educate, mirroring tactics to spread Congress ideology during the Indian nationalist movement.[43] However, in the initial stages they targeted a much more privileged stratum of Indians to advance the idea of the middle-class citizen and his importance to the success of Indian democracy.

## Courting a Wider Public

Minute-long gramophone recordings for the 1962 elections rendered into various regional languages lamented "insufficient goods, long queues . . . poverty . . . government is everything, and people are nothing." The solution to the crisis was to vote Swatantra, which would "free people from permit-license raj," raise output, food production, and prioritize agriculture.[44] Especially around election time, Swatantra attempted to promote wider consciousness

41. Rajagopalachari, letter draft, May 21, 1967, Installment VI–XI, CRP. On *niskama karma*, see chapter 3.

42. Kaviraj, *The Enchantment of Democracy and India*, 1–24; *Report on the First General Elections* (New Delhi: Election Commission, 1954), 212–13.

43. During the 1920s, students and teachers took on an especially important role in the Congress-led boycott of foreign cloth. See Pandey, *The Ascendancy of the Congress in Uttar Pradesh: Class, Community, and Nation in Northern India, 1920–1940* (London: Anthem Press, 2002), 70.

44. *Cīzoṁ meṁ kamī . . . lambī line . . . garībī . . . sarkār sab kuc hai, aur jantā kuc nahīṁ . . . Swatantra ko vote do, aur janatā ko permit-license rāj se āzād karo.* I consulted Hindi, Oriya, and Gujarati versions and translated from the Hindi. See 1962 General Election Propaganda

of its agenda and its underpinning ideas. The wider public it sought to court included speakers of Indian languages, literate workers, and professionals in small towns and rural areas.

Internal party memoranda mentioned the importance of appealing to the 45 percent of eligible voters whom the party leaders estimated did not vote.[45] Educating this "large class on whose votes Congress can be beaten" was of the utmost importance. From here, the party could recruit a broader base for a middle-class citizen. By a combination of "new ideas and methods" and sloganeering to "capitalize on discontent and disillusionment," the party leaders sought to capture the votes of this group.[46]

As Swatantra moved beyond the English-speaking core, it reworked the middle-class messaging in regional idioms. State branches of the Swatantra Party adopted bits and pieces of free economy in ways that corresponded better to the concerns of regional political economy and a widened conception of the middle class. Figures 5.6 and 5.7 reproduce some of the Hindi cartoons and slogans produced in the northern state of Madhya Pradesh for the 1967 elections. The cartoon *Yōjanā aur Pragatī kī Rāh Par!* (Figure 5.6, On the Path to Planning and Progress!) shows a fat *baḍe vyāpārī* (big trader) clothed in local garb with a Gandhi cap riding on the back of a donkey labeled "Congress." The frustrated animal fumes *samājvād* (socialism) from its nostrils as it tramples over workers, small traders, farmers, and *madhyam varg janatā* (middle-class people). For a new, strong government protecting *Dharm, Dhartī, Dhan, aur Dhandhā* (Dharma, Land, Wealth, and Occupation) and the end of permit-license-quota-raj, the solution was to vote Swatantra. The cartoon *Naye Zamīndār Sāhib* (Figure 5.7, The New Zamindar Sahib) depicts a similarly fat man wearing a Gandhi cap sitting on a throne called "Congress Party." The caption reads: "The old zamindar, rajas, and maharajas are gone. But in the era of Congress new zamindars have been born. To get rid of them, make the Swatantra Party strong."[47] Cartoons like

Recordings of Swatantra Party, Gramophone Company Record No. QC 1806, Sunny's Gramophone Museum and Records Archive, Plasannal, Kerala, India.

45. Lobo Prabhu, "A Note on the Strategy for the General Election." For the 1957 Lok Sabha elections, the correct number was a lower figure of 38 percent. "Turnout Lok Sabha Elections—1952–2004." *Election Commission of India*, accessed at http://eci.nic.in/eci_main1/votingprecentage_loksabha.aspx.

46. Lobo Prabhu, "A Note on the Strategy for the General Election."

47. *Purāne zamīndār aur rājeṁ maharājeṁ to samāpt ho gaye kintu Congressrūpī naye zamīndār ne ab janam liyā hai. Nayī zamīndārī khatam karne ke liye Swatantra Party ko tākatvar banāiye.* Microfilm Accession 2293, KMM, File 305, 311.

FIGURE 5.6. *Yōjanā aur Pragatī kī Rāh Par!* (On the Path to Planning and Progress!) (Abdul Kader Shaikh, image likeness of anonymous, low-quality image cartoon in Microfilm Accession 2293, KMM, File 305, 311).

these asserted that the Congress and its bureaucrats had replaced ex-zamindars and maharajas, who supported the Swatantra Party in the Hindi-speaking regions of North India.

The party aimed at a three-pronged publicity strategy that consisted of publishing a national party weekly, offering regular feeds to newspapers, and disseminating pamphlet literature.[48] It sought to tap into a growing reading public. In 1960s India, the reading public continued to grow. The number of registered periodicals grew from 6,435 in 1960 to 11,036 in 1970, with their combined circulation rising from 19.1 million to 29.3 million. Growth concentrated outside the country's four largest cities. By the end of the decade, the proportion of newspapers appearing from these four metropolitan cities had

48. Munshi, "Publicity."

FIGURE 5.7. *Naye Zamīndār Sāhib* (The New
Zamindar Sahib) (Abdul Kader Shaikh, image
likeness of anonymous, low-quality image
cartoon in Microfilm Accession 2293, KMM,
File 305, 310).

declined from 38 percent to 33 percent.[49] Instead, cities of over 100,000 people
accounted for an increased share of the growing number of periodicals.[50] New
weeklies, fortnightlies, and monthly journals tended to concentrate outside of
the metropolitan cities (see Table 5.1).[51] Through the print media, Swatantra
could attempt to reach into an enlarging mofussil audience.

49. Calculations based on data from *Press in India*, 1961–70.
50. *Press in India 1971—Part One*, 27.
51. *Press in India 1963—Part One*, 15.

TABLE 5.1. Newspapers Published, Classified by Centers of Publication

| Center of Publication | 1963 | 1964 | 1965 | 1966 | 1967 | 1968 | 1969 | 1970 | Annual Growth |
|---|---|---|---|---|---|---|---|---|---|
| Metropolitan Cities | 2,812 | 2,858 | 2,843 | 3,013 | 3,187 | 3,435 | 3,435 | 3,652 | 3.8% |
| State Capitals excluding Metropolitan Cities | 1,010 | 1,074 | 981 | 1,118 | 1,202 | 1,303 | 1,337 | 1,480 | 5.6% |
| Cities with Population one lakh and above | 2,173 | 2,360 | 2,311 | 2,499 | 2,707 | 2,901 | 2,978 | 3,138 | 5.4% |
| Towns with Population below one lakh | 1,798 | 1,869 | 1,771 | 2,010 | 2,219 | 2,380 | 2,531 | 2,766 | 6.3% |
| Total | 7,793 | 8,161 | 7,906 | 8,640 | 9,315 | 10,019 | 10,281 | 11,036 | 5.1% |

Source: Press in India, various. Prior to 1963, the statistics provided by the Government of India lumped state capitals and metropolitan cities together.

lakh = 100,000

Although the *Swatantra Newsletter* ended up appearing on a bimonthly rather than weekly basis, national dailies provided dedicated coverage of the party's activities.[52] Madras' *The Hindu*, which boasted a circulation of 120,966 in 1960, took particular interest in the activities of Rajagopalachari.[53] In its publicity efforts, Swatantra benefited from its leadership's connection to the press, which dated back to the nationalist movement. Correspondences about media strategy referred to these countrywide periodicals as "*nationalist* dailies and weeklies" (emphasis added).[54] Through the national media, the party enjoyed disproportionate media coverage relative to its size.

Denser publicity carrying party ideology came from periodicals published by party members or enthusiasts (see Table 5.2). They sought to awaken the reading public and reach the towns with Swatantra's message. Of one such effort, the party newsletter noted, "Through the medium of this paper, our Party is able to carry the message of Swatantra to the mofussil areas."[55] The sustainability of these publications varied. A half-dozen weeklies and newspapers appeared in the northern state of Uttar Pradesh, India's largest.[56] A Hindi version of *Swarajya*, called *Swarajya Sandesh* (*Swarajya Sandeś* or Swarajya Message), originally appeared in Delhi and Rajasthan.[57] *Sandesh* carried translated articles from *Swarajya*, Masani's *Freedom First*, and *Opinion*.[58] After about nine months of existence, in June 1965, copies circulated in all of the Hindi-speaking states.[59] Across them, the Uttar Pradesh state party disseminated the Hindi daily *Sainik* and Urdu fortnightly *Swatantra Raj*.[60] State-specific efforts included Bihar's *Swatantratā*, Maharashtra's *Swatantra Sandesh* (Swatantra

52. The weekly idea was scrapped on grounds of its alleged naiveté. Munshi to A. D. Shroff, October 24, 1959, see Microfilm Accession 2290, File 289, KMM, 392.

53. That year's figure for the most widely circulating daily, *The Indian Express*, was 206,709. *Press in India 1962—Part One*, 65. On Rajagopalachari's long connection to the editors of the *Hindu*, see Gandhi, *The Rajaji Story I*, 52, 289

54. N. Salivati to Sir Homi Mody, October 27, 1959, Microfilm Accession 2290, File 289, KMM, 357–60.

55. *Swatantra Newsletter*, November 1959 (hereafter SN).

56. *SN*, April–May 1960.

57. Her contributions are discussed in detail later in the chapter.

58. *Opinion* had been founded by A. D. Gorwala, an ICS mentor of H. M. Patel, Bhaikaka's successor at Vallabh Vidyanagar.

59. Gayatri Devi to K. M. Munshi, June 6, 1965, and Devi to Munshi, July 17, 1965, Microfilm Accession 2294, File 311, KMM, 37–38, 85.

60. S.K.D. Paliwal to K. M. Munshi, January 11, 1960, Microfilm Accession 2290, File 295, KMM, 106; *SN*, September 1960.

TABLE 5.2. Swatantra or Swatantra-Focused Periodicals

| Name | State | Language | Year Founded | Periodicity | Circulation | Official Party Newspaper (O) or Owned/Edited by Sympathizer (S) |
|---|---|---|---|---|---|---|
| *Berigai* | Madras | Tamil | 1952 | Fortnightly | 1,585 (1966) | S (S. S. Marisamy) |
| *Chanakyan* | Madras | Tamil | 1967 | Fortnightly | 1,000 (1967) | O |
| *Swarajya* | Madras | English | 1956 | Weekly | 15,502 (1967) | S (T. Sadasivam) |
| *Swarajya* | Uttar Pradesh | Hindi | 1956 | Weekly | 4,705 (1967) | S (Anand Sharma) |
| *Swarajya Sandesh* | Delhi | Hindi | 1964 | Weekly | NA | O |
| *Swatantra Path* | Uttar Pradesh | Hindi | 1964 | Weekly | NA | O |
| *Swatantra Patrika* | Andhra Pradesh | Telugu | 1965 | Monthly | NA | O |
| *Swatantra Patrika* | West Bengal | Bengali | 1960 | NA | NA | O |
| *Swatantra Raj* | Uttar Pradesh | Urdu | 1967 | Fortnightly | NA | O |
| *Swatantra Sandesh* | Gujarat | Gujarati | 1966 | Weekly | 2,118 (1967) | O |
| *Swatantra Sandesh* | Maharashtra | Marathi | 1965 | Weekly | 1,487 (1967) | O |
| *Swatantrata* | Bihar | Hindi | 1967 | NA | NA | O |

*Sources: Press in India*, various; papers of K. M. Munshi and C. Rajagopalachari. Circulation figures are reported inconsistently, so the most comparable set of figures has been assembled.

Message), and Orissa's *Swatantra Samachar*. There was even a *Swatantra Patrika* in West Bengal, where the party had a minimal presence.[61] It is unclear if any of these newspapers survived beyond the first few issues.

By contrast, party newspapers from southern and western India, where free economy originated, survived. One such newspaper, launched by an admirer of Rajagopalachari in 1965, was *Cānakyan*. It was named after the author of the *Arthaśāstra,* the ancient treatise on political economy. The newspaper ran an essay competition for youths on the "Role of Swatantra in Indian Politics."[62] Although it had no formal connection to the Libertarian Social Institute or the Forum of Free Enterprise, the contest resembled the earlier practices of these institutions. *Cānakyan* moved outside of its headquarters in Madras. One party worker reported to Rajagopalachari that from September 1966 he would distribute free copies in Virudhunagar, a business town some 300 miles away.[63] Gujarat's *Swatantra Sandesh* was another such publication that survived teething. It appeared weekly from 1966 on.[64] By 1967 *Swatantra Sandesh* enjoyed a circulation of 2,118 and *Cānakyan* of 1,000 (see Table 5.2).

Both *Swarajya* and *Kalki* provided information on Swatantra from Madras. *Kalki*'s managing editor Sadasivam took over *Swarajya* from July 1959.[65] He also became a Swatantra General Council member. Content occasionally overlapped between the periodicals, especially in *Kalki*'s new section called *Rājājiyin Karuttukaḷ* (Rajagopalachari's Opinions). *Swarajya* tended to reprint speeches delivered by party members and carry articles related to issues that interested its top brass. *Kalki*, with its mass readership, functioned more descriptively. The Tamil magazine reported and printed photos of party conferences and events. *Kalki* also carried appeals for donations signed by Rajagopalachari and allowed readers to mail them to the head office during election times.[66] Such

61. "Report of the Swatantra Party in the State of Bihar," March 21, 1960, Microfilm Accession 2292, File 299, KMM, Document Two (not paginated); *Swatantra Sandeś,* August 1, 1962, reproduced in Microfilm Accession 2294, File 309, KMM, 47–50; S. P. Agarwalla to K. M. Munshi, August 29, 1960, Microfilm Accession 2291, File 294, KMM, 80; *SN* April–May 1960.

62. J. Ramabhadran to C. Rajagopalachari, August 16, 1966, Microfilm Accession 10957, File 72, CRP, 102–3.

63. R.T.P. Subramaniam to C. Rajagopalachari, June 8, 1966, Microfilm Accession 10957, File 71, CRP, not paginated.

64. H. D. Sharma, "Swatantra Party in Gujarat—Rise, Growth and Decline (1960 to 1972)," (unpublished PhD diss., Gujarat University, 1976), 905.

65. T. Sadasivam to Homi Mody, June 30, 1959, File 1, Box 6, SP.

66. See, for example, *Kalki*, February 18, 1962, and February 25, 1962.

was the openly partisan nature of *Kalki* that Tamil-speaking readers interested in corresponding with Rajagopalachari and his associates addressed their letters to *Kalki Āciriyar* (Kalki Editor). A regional alliance in Madras also helped Swatantra and the issues it represented garner strong coverage in Tamil daily newspapers (see the next chapter).

All this suggests that Swatantra attempted to reach a much wider audience than indicated by the English pamphlet literature produced by the Bombay headquarters. The national press, dedicated party periodicals, and local print media published by party sympathizers carried free economy beyond its core. This is not to suggest that electoral success corresponded with the presence of this periodical literature. At this stage, elections continued to work in a clientelist fashion and the most substantial vote banks indeed came from the ex-Zamindari and princely areas (see chapter 4).[67] It means that where Swatantra managed to cross the English-Indian language divide to reach pockets of the growing reading public in India's interiors, it found interest in the free economy ideology. Not surprisingly, this tended to be in the very regions where free economy originated, in southern and western India.

To establish a coordinated pool of agents responsible for on-the-ground dissemination of party ideology, the Swatantra Party held study circles and training courses for its workers. Life members and workers numbered about fifty thousand by August 1969.[68] Training camps took place in states where the party had either a committed core of a few anglicized leaders who embraced the free economy discourse or where it enjoyed the support of local leaders who could command large crowds.[69] Coordinated jointly by the central office and state units, such events normally counted anywhere from twenty to a hundred participants. They combined efforts to "inculcate party workers with the philosophy of the party" with tactical advice on how to organize and operate in the field.[70]

67. See Weiner, *Party Politics in India* (Princeton: Princeton University Press, 1957); Rudolph and Rudolph, *The Modernity of Tradition*.

68. "Enrolment of Party Workers, Life Workers and Life Members as of 31 August 1969," File 1, Box 3, SP. The regional division of membership does not correspond cleanly to electoral footprint (** denotes unknown number, possibly zero): Andhra 9,713; Assam**; Bihar**; Bombay 1,300; Delhi 698; Gujarat 9,674; Haryana**; Himachal Pradesh 1,404; Kashmir 810; Kerala 3,017; Madhya Pradesh**; Maharashtra 513; Mysore 1,504; Orissa 6,395; Punjab 1,301; Rajasthan 7,386; Madras 5,678; Uttar Pradesh 2,610; West Bengal**.

69. These states were Andhra Pradesh, Bombay, Gujarat, Mysore, Orissa, and Uttar Pradesh.

70. SN, June 1961.

The breadth and intensity of these events could be quite substantial. Participants in a five-day training camp held in 1962 at Orissa discussed "Mass Psychology and Publicity, The Role of an Opposition in a Democracy, the Swatantra Party's Manifesto, Democratic Decentralization, and State Trading versus Free Trade."[71] Attendees of the more ambitious course of the central office in Bombay received lectures, watched documentary films, and got "practical training in party work." Over nine days, the course covered thirty-two topics.[72] A Gujarat study camp held two years later combined more abstract topics with case studies of local issues such as "repairing the primary school at Bhasan," "Transfer of a Nurse," and "irregular distribution of sugar by the supply department."[73]

These events provided opportunities to secure oaths of loyalty from party workers and inspire a proselytizing ethos. At one training event in Bangalore, a speaker urged workers to go into the field with the "zeal and enthusiasm of a missionary to try to convert men to come into the Swatantra fold by conviction rather than compulsion."[74] Training could be rigorous; in Orissa, where the party formed a coalition government in 1967, the daily program for the nine-day camp lasted from 5:30 a.m. to 9:30 p.m., with just three hours of break for lunch and rest.[75]

The most extraordinary of these efforts may have been the monthlong Volunteer Leaders' Training Camp of February 1966. The camp sought to create a core of committed volunteers who would subsequently recruit others. It brought together seventeen select volunteers in a village approximately twenty miles from Hyderabad, then the capital of Andhra Pradesh. They received "physical" training from a World War II veteran and "ideological" training from a Swatantra member of the regional legislative assembly. Delegates performed drills, flag-hoisting, road marches, and a guard of honor during the day. In the evenings, they worked to coin twenty-two slogans, two marching songs, and a flag song. They danced and played mimicry games. Finally, they marched the streets of the cities of Hyderabad and Secunderabad and sold party literature to shops to create "mass contact."[76]

71. *SN*, June 1962.
72. *SN*, August/September 1964.
73. *SN*, June 1964.
74. *SN*, October/November 1965.
75. *SN*, August/September 1967.
76. *SN*, March/April 1966.

Emphasizing the ties of its leaders to the freedom movement provided another way for Swatantra to broaden its appeal.[77] The party leadership recast the former objective of freedom from colonial rule as freedom from Congress' permit-and-license raj and emphasized the negative character of free economy. They invoked figures from the Congress before Gandhi and Nehru who focused primarily on asserting legal rights and lobbying for lower revenue collection from the colonial state. In one example, Rajagopalachari invited Khurshedben Naoroji to speak at the inaugural Swatantra state convention in the Tamil town of Coimbatore. She read out sections from her grandfather Dadabhai Naoroji's 1906 speech to the Congress. Dadabhai's "drain of wealth" theory provided an economic critique of empire. He had lobbied for an inclusive imperial citizenship for Indians within the framework of liberal capitalism that would enable them to be self-relying market agents.[78] Khurshedben quoted parts of the speech that compared individual freedom to one's breath. To conclude, she "exhorted the audience to regain the freedom which is now denied to the people."[79]

The details of the Coimbatore event point to particularities in Swatantra's ascent that characterized the party from its origins. Small commercial towns like Tamil-speaking Coimbatore constituted natural bases of support for the party because they were the home of small enterprises and salaried classes. Holding a state convention there would attract a crowd. Khurshedben's address reproduced the subordinate yet significant position of the female that characterized free economy and its associated politics ever since Kusum Lotvala started helping Ranchoddas with the Libertarian Social Institute.

Here again, the movement of free economy into the field through the Swatantra Party was a gendered process. Khurshedben had led an important political career of her own; earlier in life, she lobbied for women's participation in *satyagraha* as an opportunity for their "great awakening" and worked in often dangerous parts of the North West Frontier Province for Hindu Muslim unity. Despite her contributions to the nationalist cause, Khurshedben's claim

77. Munshi, "Publicity."

78. Vikram Visana, "Vernacular Liberalism, Capitalism, and Anti-Imperialism in the Political Thought of Dadabhai Naoroji," *The Historical Journal* 59, no. 3 (2016): 775–97. On Naoroji and his theory of the British drain of wealth from India, see Dinyar Patel, *Naoroji: Pioneer of Indian Nationalism* (Cambridge, MA: Harvard University Press, 2020).

79. *SN*, September 1960.

to legitimacy rested on her connection to her grandfather, and Mahatma Gandhi, for whom she had worked as a secretary in 1944–45.[80] She read out quotations of her grandfather instead of delivering her own remarks at Coimbatore.

Through these activities, Swatantra presented an alternative claim to represent the nation as its economic caretakers. Party leaders invoked a lineage of Congress leaders from the Bombay Presidency that included Naoroji, Gokhale, and Tilak. The same month of the Bombay event, Mariadas Ruthnaswamy addressed a crowd at the Tilak Smarak Mandir (Tilak Memorial Hall) in Bombay. He "urged the people of Maharashtra to be loyal to the ideals of individual liberty and enterprise fostered by their great leaders," including Tilak, the early nationalist leader.[81] Ruthnaswamy then visited the offices of Tilak's newspaper, where the late leader's grandson Jayavantrao Tilak greeted him.[82] Years later, Rajagopalachari unveiled a statue to commemorate the birth centenary of Gokhale. In his remarks, Rajagopalachari "pointed out that if Gokhale had been alive now, he would have died heartbroken after seeing the enormity of the tax burden imposed on the people." He specifically mentioned Gokhale's opposition to the salt tax levied by the British.[83] The irony of events like these was that they used the forum of mass address to invoke the leadership from a time when Congress' membership comprised mainly elite graduates and professional men.[84]

## Mobilizing Economic Discontent

Nevertheless, Swatantra did push beyond the elite confines of its originary environment and brought free economy into the politics of the streets. Activities exploited feelings of economic stagnation coming from the increasing

---

80. Working from far-flung and disparate archival fragments, Dinyar Patel painstakingly reconstructs what little information is available about Khurshedben. He suggests that the example of Khurshedben and Mridula Sarabhai changed Gandhi's views on the secondary role of women in the freedom movement, but it is not clear how Gandhi's comments in this regard changed his practices. See Dinyar Patel, "The Singing Satyagrahi: Khurshedben Naoroji and the Challenge of Indian Biography," in *A Functioning Anarchy*, 105–25.

81. See chapter 2.

82. *SN*, September 1960.

83. *SN*, May 1966.

84. Seal, *The Emergence of Indian Nationalism*. On Gokhale, see chapter 2.

prices and taxation of the 1960s. Swatantra engaged citizens in economic protest through organized campaigns against inflation and taxation. In addition,
the party mobilized people in opposition to specific government policies. It
presented itself as caretaker of citizens' economic welfare by amplifying grievances put forth by associations not formally connected to the party. These
efforts connected the practices of the elite associations from which the discourse of free economy had first emerged to the practices of economically
rooted mass-action from the nationalist movement. They presented opportunities to imprint free economy upon the minds of the masses.

A nationwide Anti-Inflation Day, held on September 18, 1960, sought to
create a link between the increasing levels of inflation and Congress misrule.[85]
Masani sent the pamphlets *Inflation—Your Hidden Enemy* and *The Fight
Against Inflation—Swatantra Party's Call* to each district leader across the
country.[86] Along with them, he sent a set of borrowed excerpts from a variety of
sources as talking points. These ranged from quotations from the Mont Pelerin
Society member Graham Hutton's anti-inflationary polemic, *Inflation and Society*, to official statistics about the budget and money supply from the Reserve
Bank of India. Masani offered the following as potential event slogans to chant:

1. Inflated currency, deflated economy
2. Inflation consumes the consumer and reduces the producer
3. Inflation hunts the hungry and swells the affluent
4. Down with Inflation

Statistics presented about the money supply showed a mere 5 percent increase
from the previous year. This material intended to convey fears of the possible
increase of inflation rather than the minor effects of this amount of inflation.
The approach made sense strategically because people could feel the pinch of
small cost increases.

Protesters wended their way through cities and towns across India during
Anti-Inflation Day. The most charged event took place in Poona, a small city
around ninety miles from Bombay. Participants burned an effigy of inflation and
signed a petition seeking President Rajendra Prasad's intervention to bring

85. Masani, "General Secretary's Letter No. 12, Anti-Inflation Day—September 18, 1960,"
August 12, 1960, Microfilm Accession 2292, File 297, KMM, 229–30.

86. The district is the government's unit of administration, institutions, and political organization just below the state.

down prices.[87] Poona's Anti-Inflation Day combined various forms of political engagement in service of a concept that had previously lived a tranquil life in the obscure pages of the *Indian Libertarian* and other such periodicals. In Madras city, a nearly two-mile procession terminated at Marina Beach, the most important local public space and a site for political gatherings. A "posse of motorcycle volunteers" led a group of cyclists and pedestrians through the city's streets as they carried Tamil placards with the slogans: "Don't be extravagant by spending others' money!"; "Encourage production!"; "No Controls!"; and "Don't ruin the country by printing notes!" Decorated vehicles bearing the portraits of Rajagopalachari and Gandhi accompanied them. [88]

Carrying his polemical rhetoric from *Swarajya* to the podium, Rajagopalachari regaled the Tamil audience for half an hour with similes and sarcasm. His speech invoked recent historical memory and made use of metaphors from the agrarian world of his early life. Recalling the evacuation of Madras during World War II and the conversion of assets to coins, he observed that in just under two decades, each rupee coin was worth just a quarter of its prior value. He used inflation to attack the overspending of the *ṭampāccāri thiṭṭaṅkaḷ* (vain or extravagant plans). Rajagopalachari likened the planners' hopes that the plans would work out in thirty years to planting tamarind seeds with hopes they would become trees, ignoring the threat of animals that could eat the seeds. He called the plans *puḷiaṅkoṭṭai thiṭṭaṅkaḷ* (tamarind seed plans), eliciting great laughter. Rajagopalachari used inflation to open an assault on the incompetence of the Congress-controlled state, indulging in just a little more excess than in his writings.[89]

"Education for the people on the realities of oppressive taxation and . . . warning to Government" provided the impetus behind the Anti-Tax Week of 1962 and Anti-Excessive Taxation Day of 1966.[90] These traced antecedents in Gandhian satyagraha, which had mobilized large groups of people in peaceful resistance. In line with that legacy, the guidelines Masani prepared for party workers began with a quotation from Mahatma Gandhi that taxes

87. *SN*, September 1960.

88. "Scrapping of Plan Urged: 'C. R.' on Curbing Price Line," *ToI*, September 19, 1960; "'Anti-Inflation' Day Celebrations," *IL*, 1 October 1960. On Marina Beach, see A. Srivathsan, "City and Public Life: History of Public Spaces in Chennai," in *Madras: The Architectural Heritage*, eds. K. Kalpana and F. Schiffer (Chennai: INTACH, 2003), 207–60, 213.

89. "Third Plan Schemes: C. R.'s Criticisms: 'Anti-Inflation Day' Observed," *The Hindu*, September 19, 1960.

90. "List of Demands," Microfilm Accession 10955, File 64, CRP, 186.

should benefit the whole society. But it was Ranga, gauging frustration with land taxes paid by his constituents, who conceived of this event.[91] The list of demands for Anti-Excessive Taxation Day in 1966 appealed across the urban-rural divide, calling for lower indirect taxes that hit urban professional classes and bringing down land and paddy taxes hitting agrarian landowners.[92] Reports from different states suggested similar activities to Anti-Inflation Day. By this time, Swatantra used its trained workers to address public gatherings. The party also began to co-opt professional associations in planning the events. In the Andhra Pradesh town of Rajampet, tailors, weavers, and members of backward class associations contributed to planning Anti-Excessive Taxation Day.[93]

Citizens familiar with the Swatantra ideology and committed to its economic agenda went deep into the South Indian mofussil for the purposes of Anti-Tax Day. Party organizers in the Tamil town of Kumbakonam recruited a Madras economic affairs journalist for the event and organized for him to travel 185 miles to address crowds.[94] Three hundred wall posters went up announcing the day's events in Madras' Salem district, where Rajagopalachari made his name as a lawyer and Congressman. Almost two hundred people participated in the Salem procession. They included "prominent advocates, about fifty businessmen, and many weavers" carrying placards and shouting slogans. They walked three miles as they wove around business localities and residential spaces. At the subsequent public meeting of approximately two thousand people, the party distributed five thousand pamphlets.[95]

Intended to anchor the party's efforts in concrete policy positions, targeted Swatantra events like these could also prompt confusion. Anxious party workers in the Tumkur district of Andhra Pradesh got confused by statements from the leadership that the party would dissolve if Congress reduced taxes by 50 percent. They worried that the party might be "satisfied only achieving the relief of taxation from the Congress" and abandon "its role to achieve some important principles [from the statement of principles], namely 2, 3, 10, 11, and

91. Ranga to Masani, January 28, 1966, reproduced in Microfilm Accession 10954, File 63, CRP, 6.

92. "Annexure: List of Demands," Microfilm Accession 2294, File 311, KMM, 130.

93. "Annexure A," SN, March–April 1966, 11–7.

94. Thurasai Rajagopal to C. Rajagopalachari, June 23, 1966, Microfilm Accession 10956, File 67, CRP, 251–53.

95. "Report of the Activities of the Salem Unit on the Anti-Excessive Taxation Day—20-2-1966," Microfilm Accession 10955, File 66, CRP, 158–158A.

21," which stressed freedom of the individual from state coercion of various forms and incentives for enterprise.[96]

Swatantra pursued goals consistent with its statement of policy in smaller, more public acts.[97] Government food policy tended to be the target of these signature campaigns, marches, and occasional hunger strikes. They concentrated around markets and shopping districts.[98] Some of these events were conducted by the party alone. Others were joint efforts with local action committees and interest groups.[99] Efforts could be substantial. Although the self-reported numbers cannot be taken at face value, some 2000 people allegedly gathered in 1965 to demonstrate against "the tightening up of various controls and the distribution of foodgrains." On another occasion, party workers in Bombay collected twenty thousand signatures demanding that the state government scrap food rationing.[100] Acquiring signatories for "monster petitions" could build solidarities and spread awareness of shared concerns about the intrusion of the state into new domains of resource control and regulation.[101] When the Bihar government increased the land levy in 1966, Swatantra collected five thousand signatures in one town and three thousand in another for an appeal demanding reconsideration.[102] In the metropolitan areas, Swatantra

96. R. Narasimhiah to C. Rajagopalachari, February 23, 1966, Microfilm Accession 10955, File 66, CRP, 212–15.

97. SN, January 1960; July 1960; September 1960.

98. SN, various; "Bulletin from the Bombay Party Secretary," Microfilm Accession 2295, File 315a, KMM, 129.

99. R. Krishnamurthi, secretary of Madras State Ryotwari Owners' Association, Kumbakonam, to K. M. Munshi, August 19, 1963, Microfilm Accession 2293, File 305, KMM, 211; S. Mustapha, secretary of All-Kerala Small Land Owners Association, Palghat, to K. M. Munshi, ibid (no date; not paginated).

100. SN, March 1969.

101. Recent scholarship demonstrates the relationship of the collective petition to vibrant political activity and engagement, challenging the traditional scholarly interpretation of supplication before authority. Rohit De notes the process of creating the "monster petition" as one that generated colonial anxieties in the nineteenth century and animated Mahatma Gandhi in "Cows and Constitutionalism," Modern Asian Studies 53, no. 1 (2019): 240–77. In a major contribution, Prashant Kidambi shows how collective petitioning integrated actors in protest of the intrusion of the state into new domains of urban life in Bombay after the outbreak of the plague in the late nineteenth century. Petitioning went along with activities like strikes and acts of violence. Kidambi argues that petitioning in the early twentieth century helped shape the contours of Bombay's urban civil society. See Kidambi, "The Petition as Event: Colonial Bombay, circa 1889–1914," Modern Asian Studies 53, no. 1 (2019): 203–39.

102. SN, January–February 1966.

experimented with service centers to target the middle-class, nonvoting citizen. Party workers in cities like Bombay and Delhi helped bring citizens' grievances to the attention of municipal officials and state governments. Occasional efforts like providing free lifts when bus drivers went on strike were part of an agenda to widen the party's scope to include socially responsible positive action.[103]

Swatantra still found popular mobilization profoundly challenging. The party's shortcomings in this regard entrenched the picture of an elite project. Some sections of the leadership felt uncomfortable with collective action. In one telling example, a resigning party member complained that the mainly retired civil servants who ran the Mysore unit "think that everything other than armchair politics is violence and communism." In the event, leaders had withdrawn the party from the opposition-wide support of the Bangalore water supply action committee's protest of water tax increases because of a threatened *hartāl* (voluntary cessation of all business activity). The resigning member questioned their understanding of civil disobedience.[104] As noted in the previous chapter, civil servants from princely states could be disdainful of democracy. A party well-wisher from a Tamil village wrote to Rajagopalachari that "the message of Swatantra has not yet permeated to the masses" for "want of enough organization and propaganda at village levels."[105] The president of the All-India Scheduled Castes League from the northern state of Madhya Pradesh raised similar concerns. After attending a party fundraiser at the luxurious Tata-owned Taj Mahal Hotel in Bombay, he complained to Rajagopalachari that "there is no place for poor, laborers, and especially scheduled castes/tribes in your party." He sensed a missed opportunity: "this is the time when we can finish the CONGRESS, but your party leaders hesitate to come close to the public."[106]

The deficit of charismatic leaders able to take the pulse of the masses went right to the top. General Secretary Masani could sound more like a business manager than a party leader. "A political party's success like that of a

103. *SN*, June 1960.

104. P. S. Sridhara Murthy to Rajagopalachari, April 15, 1966, Microfilm Accession 10965, File 97, CRP, 48.

105. S. Muthuswami Gounder to Rajagopalachari, July 20, 1966, Microfilm Accession 10957, File 71, CRP, 46–47.

106. Dhannalal M. Loudwal to Rajagopalachari, May 28, 1966, Microfilm Accession 10963, File 90, CRP, 35–36.

business concern depends on an observance of sound principles of organization and management," he observed in 1960.[107] He accorded more emphasis to discipline than mass contact and outreach to bring together the disparate groups composing the party. This style did little to capture popular imaginaries. Rajagopalachari critiqued the elite nature of Masani's Bombay public meetings: "You arrange chairs in front all-round the platform for private enterprise bosses and the crowd is kept in a large semi-circle far out with a feeling on their part that the meeting is not theirs, but they stand only as observers and by permission."[108]

Others shared this weakness. The late American political scientist Howard Erdman recalled a similar disconnect when shadowing Piloo Mody, the son of Homi Mody and another Swatantra leader with Tata connections. Out of sorts while campaigning in rural Gujarati, Piloo brought a mobile toilet with him. He addressed the crowd in English. A translator then conveyed the gist of his remarks to the Gujarati-speaking audience.[109] Rajagopalachari himself had weak oratorical talent. His message to voters for the 1967 elections, preserved in a gramophone recording, consists of the strained words of an unwell man, then eighty-eight years of age. Noticeably, Rajagopalachari suffers from labored breathing.[110]

The inability to tie the idealized middle class to real groups of people living in India further hobbled efforts at mobilizing this target demographic. Party leaders used the Hindi term *madhyam varg* and the Tamil term *naṭutturai vakuppu* to construct a narrative and offer solutions to middle-class distress. However, they came to no consensus on what the term meant. This failure points to the difficulties of bringing together a party composed of groups ranging from schoolteachers to ex-princely rulers around an ideology focused on economic concerns and a unified class identity.

How new were the "new ideas and methods" employed by Swatantra? It is hard to say.[111] Communication via the press and public meetings was certainly

107. Lala, *Beyond the Last Blue Mountain: The Life of J.R.D. Tata*, 344; SN, July 1960.

108. C. Rajagopalachari to M. R. Masani, November 17, 1962, Microfilm Accession 2294, File 19, KMM, 211.

109. Phone interview with Howard Erdman, April 3, 2015.

110. "Rajaji's Message," [n.d. 1967], Record QC 1805. Sunny's Gramophone Museum, Kottayam, Kerala.

111. On the paucity of research into democratic practice, see Sumit Sarkar, "Indian Democracy: The Historical Inheritance," in *The Success of India's Democracy*, ed. Atul Kohli (Cambridge: Cambridge University Press, 2001), 23–46.

nothing new.[112] The Congress undertook Mass Contacts Campaigns to attract
Muslim support during the 1930s.[113] Organized training camps and cadres
made up the backbone of support for the Hindu Nationalist Jan Sangh.[114] The
communists also ran petition campaigns against high prices and taxation.[115]
More innovatively, its affiliated Indian People's Theater Association had been
performing plays in towns and villages on political themes since the 1940s.[116]
Swatantra's appropriation of figures like Naoroji and Gokhale differentiated
the party from its competitors. Still, this was hardly a "new method." More
original was its emphasis on a set of economic concerns from the party's ideological position and the nationwide anti-inflation and anti-excess taxation
days. Swatantra used these activities to present itself as uniquely committed
to checking the excesses of the permit-and-license raj.

## Warding off "Carles-Marx" with "Swatantra Slogans"

A. C. Dutt found much to admire in the Swatantra pamphlet titled *Who's to
Hold That Price Line?* Even still, the lawyer from the northern city of Allahabad
in Uttar Pradesh suggested some improvements in a letter to the executive
secretary. Dutt corrected the pamphlet's definition of inflation from "an increase in the ratio between money and goods and services" to *just* an increase
in the ratio between money and goods. He did not say why. The original definition was not actually a mistake. Dutt also noted the incompleteness of the
pamphlet's list of causes of inflation. He supplied a few more: "insecurity
and lack of confidence of the people on [sic] the Government," "state owning"
that crowded out private ownership and greater output generation, and "government servants" who "usurp the resources of the country" and cause the

112. See, for example the discussion of the multiple tactics used in Pandey, *The Ascendancy of
the Congress in Uttar Pradesh*, 61–94. In the context of independent India, see Ramachandra Guha,
"Democracy's Biggest Gamble: India's First Free Elections in 1952," in *Decolonisation and the Politics
of Transition in South Asia*, ed. Bandyopadhyay (New Delhi: Orient Blackswan, 2016), 160–73.

113. Mushirul Hasan, "The Muslim Mass Contacts Campaign: Analysis of a Strategy of
Political Mobilization," in *India's Partition: Process, Strategy and Mobilization*, ed. Hasan (New
Delhi: Oxford University Press, 1993), 132–58.

114. Graham, *Hindu Nationalism and Indian Politics*, 15–20.

115. "Mammoth Petition to Lok Sabha: Check Prices & Cut Taxes, Govt. Told," *ToI*, September 14, 1963.

116. Sharmistha Saha, *Theatre and National Identity in Colonial India* (Singapore: Springer,
2018), 119–52.

"retardation of production." The final two extra causes had in fact appeared in the pamphlet. Next, Dutt pointed out that a high tax rate could provoke tax evasion, and that this too would raise prices, although he failed to provide a causal linkage between tax evasion and inflation. The letter concluded with a condemnation of planning, which Dutt considered as intimately connected to inflation: "Planning in our country is so faulty that it can be safely termed as a Planning Commission for the welfare of foreigners resulting in the sale of foreign goods and its ultimate exchange with Indian raw materials causing price increase."[117]

Dutt fell within Swatantra's target demographic, even if his letter was more extraordinary than representative of its reception. Still, it evokes the more widespread feelings that surface in the thousands of letters and petitions that passed the desks of Munshi, Rajagopalachari, and other senior party leaders. A university student wrote to Masani that "the state is expected to help the individual economic initiative rather than frustrate it, as far as the concept of free economy goes."[118] A Madras bookseller wrote to Ranga that the peasant leader's favorite term "'self-employment' can be made the basis of an important slogan . . . It represents a whole economic philosophy, including the decentralization of free thought" and be used to mobilize the small farmer and rural India.[119] Ramrai Mohanrai, chairman of the All-Bharat Middle Classes National Federation, congratulated Homi Mody for his Swatantra colleague's exposure of the "hollow and false" assertions by the Congress of the voluntary nature of cooperative farming.[120]

The content and quantity of material like this indicates a small, critical mass who saw Swatantra as a salient part of Indian political life. Ordinary people conveyed emotions about these experiences, showed nostalgia for earlier times, or indulged in fantasies about benevolent arbiters who could resolve their problems through their correspondences.[121] Opinions, expressions of discontent, and claims registered by the lettered public offer glimpses of the experience and imagination of the everyday state amid conditions of flux.[122]

---

117. Dutt to S. V. Raju, September 19, 1966, Microfilm Accession 10964, File 92, CRP, 172–73.

118. J. I Laliwala to Masani, January 12, 1970, File 3 Box 9, SP.

119. S. Y. Krishnamurty to N. G. Ranga, June 6, 1959, Ranga Papers.

120. Ram Rai Mohanrai to Homi Mody, October 21, 1959, File 1, Box 5, SP.

121. Julia Stephens, "A Bureaucracy of Rejection: Petitioning and the Impoverished Paternalism of the British-Indian Raj," *Modern Asian Studies* 53, no. 1 (2019): 177–202.

122. Gould, Sherman, and Ansari, "The Flux of the Matter."

Correspondents consisted of graduates and office-based professionals—lawyers, clerks, accountants, schoolteachers, or retirees—rich farmers, merchants, and shop owners. Rajagopalachari's Tamil- and English-language correspondents came chiefly from South India. Munshi received fewer such correspondences, somewhere in the hundreds. These came from the North, West, and the South. His interlocutors wrote in English and Hindi. Although they came from various levels of a wide range of people between the destitute and the wealthy, the correspondents did not normally hail from lower-caste backgrounds. To the extent that surnames denote caste, correspondents hailed almost exclusively from scholarly, agrarian landowning, or trading castes. Rajagopalachari's correspondents came chiefly from Brahmin, Chettiar, Gounder, and Marakkayar (Muslim merchant) communities.[123] Others hailed from Telugu-speaking Reddy and Naidu communities, also typically agrarian landowner cultivators and traders. Swatantra's message seems to have registered especially well with those whose economic interests it represented. Outside these communities, it enjoyed limited purchase.

Rural and urban Indians alike wrote in. These correspondents lobbied the political system by organizing in anticorruption leagues, income-tax sufferers associations, middle-class associations, and even ryotwari landowners' associations.[124] For them, democracy meant more than voting. These interlocutors fell into four broad types in terms of their connection to Swatantra: the Swatantra-aware; self-proclaimed party supporters requesting help; well-wishers and donors to the party describing local political developments; and declaimers or opinionated Indians like Dutt. Each of these types engaged with the party on a different level.

Those aware of Swatantra considered it an opposition party interested in socioeconomic concerns. Citizens sent copies of appeals and petitions in hopes of multiplying the probability that figures of influence could move these along. Failing that, they might hope that recipients publicize their claims

123. Some surnames are not associated with castes, and others have been adopted by individuals from upwardly mobile castes as part of a broader embrace of upper-caste ways of life known as *sanskritization*. See M. N. Srinivas, "A Note on Sanskritization and Westernization," *The Far Eastern Quarterly* 15, no. 4 (1956): 481–96.

124. See, for example, Microfilm Accession 2290, Files 290–94, KMM, and Microfilm Accession 10968, File 106, CRP. An article that mentions the Anti-Corruption Group's meeting is "*'Pēcātē! Ukkāru!!' Swatantra Kaṭci Piramukarukku Etirppu*" ("Don't Speak! Sit down!!" Opposition to Swatantra Leader) *DT*, September 28, 1964. The operating dynamics of these associations remain unexplored by scholarship, although their importance to the politics of civil society and the history of democratic practice in India may have been profound.

more widely. These attempts at amplification and escalation parallel the colonial-era practice of litigants filing multiple cases in different jurisdictions to maximize their chances of success.[125] In either the top left-hand corner of most of these documents or at the very end, the name of the Swatantra leader appeared alongside several others.

Sometimes these went from the district collector all the way up to the president of India. A lawyer following up with Madras' secretary of revenue about a stolen revenue form declaring an error in his favor on March 17, 1966, copied the prime minister, the chief minister, the district collector, and Rajagopalachari.[126] Two inhabitants of the Bedi village in Gujarat's Jamnagar district copied their request for a government inquiry into the corrupt food distribution practices by the licensees of the Marine Products Cooperative Society to a whole host of politicians. Their October 25, 1967, letter went out to the prime minister, the deputy prime minister, the minister of food, the local Swatantra parliamentarian and member of legislative assembly, Masani, "Shri Raj Gopalacharyajee, President, Swatantra Party, Madras," and the parliamentarians of nearby districts.[127] A copy of a letter to the president, from Ranga's native Guntur district, requested investigation into the black market of the liquor trade. It was addressed to "the all opposition parties [sic]," reaching Munshi.[128]

The petitions' signatories drew on the support of family, well-wishers, and local politicians to prepare them, as in colonial times.[129] Such support allowed those from the unlettered or semi-lettered public to partake of the process of claim-making. The son of an unlettered man in a Gujarat village protesting the seizure of his Philips transistor by customs officials scribbled over the typed appeal he had prepared with the observation that officials were doing this in "so many villages." Appealing to the incentives of his intended audience, he

125. Julia Stephens, "An Uncertain Inheritance: The Imperial Travels of Legal Migrants, from British India to Ottoman Iraq," *Law and History Review* 32, no. 4 (2014): 749–72, 751.

126. M. Peter to Revenue Secretary of Madras, March 17, 1966, Microfilm Accession 10956, File 67, CRP, 87–89.

127. Although Rajagopalachari had no such formal title, in the popular imagination, the proverbial Swatantra buck stopped with him. "Sub: Issue of license to *Dariyā'ī Utpādan Sahakāri Maṇḍalī* (Marine Products Co-operative Society) at village Bedi-Jamnagar District-Gujarat State," October 25, 1967, Microfilm Accession 10970, File 109, CRP, 419–21, 421.

128. Kolli Krishnamurthy to Munshi, n.d. Microfilm Accession 2291, File 295, KMM, 268–72, 272. On prohibition and control of the liquor trade during this time, which differed by state, see De, *A People's Constitution*, 32–76.

129. Rohit De and Robert Travers, "Petitioning and Political Cultures in South Asia: Introduction," *Modern Asian Studies* 53, no. 1 (2019): 1–20, 17.

concluded, "If you solve this question, it will be boon to Swatantra Party [sic]."[130] The Jai Hind (Victory to India) Estate Tenants and Shareholders' Association in Bombay asked Munshi to consider allegations against corruption in a government department. Its representatives offered to send further material as "our case will provide a good instance to the party to depose before the public the working of the Government Department."[131] Both letter writers appealed to the opposition party as a kind of ombudsperson.

Claimants could make tenacious attempts to escalate their cases. At times, they solicited politicians to intervene in processes involving the judiciary. In one case, a Tamil village widow abandoned building a tubewell on her land halfway because she never received the government loan that would allow her to construct the surrounding wall. Fellow villagers, who had grazing rights on the land, complained that farm animals and people could fall ill and die from the construction of the wall and sequestering of water resources for the tubewell, because the animals would not be able to move freely and there would be less common water to share. They filed petitions against her to the district collector and the superintendent of police. The widow then approached the collector of Tirunelveli district twice and wrote to the Kovilpatti revenue division officer, the Madras chief minister, three Tamil daily newspapers, and now Rajagopalachari. She asked that he publicize the issue so that people would not trust the government in the future and suffer a plight like hers.[132]

One woman writing to Rajagopalachari celebrated the "litigious nature of our people," thanks to which "many of the laws and other directives of the state Legislatures and that of Parliament have been struck down by our High Courts and the Supreme Court."[133] The case of the abandoned well fits right into the picture of rural life painted in the memoirs of Charuhasan, a lawyer in the mofussil town of Paramakudi in Madras State.[134] Disputes about land

130. Kadri Dusenbhai to Rajagopalachari, "Sub:—Seizure of My Philips Transistor, Chasis No. F. I. 11055," March 21, 1966, Microfilm Accession 10956, File 67, CRP, 215. His son H. K. Kadri prepared the letter in English and had his father sign in Gujarati.

131. J. A. Parikh to K. M Munshi, April 8, 1962, Microfilm Accession 2293, File 311, KMM, 46–47.

132. N. Sethurama Lakshmi Ammal to Rajagopalachari, December 27, 1966, Microfilm Accession 10964, File 94, CRP, 231–34.

133. S. Nagarajan to Rajagopalachari, August 19, 1966, Microfilm Accession 10957, File 72, CRP, 114. De, *A People's Constitution*.

134. Charuhasan, the brother of Tamil cinema legend and failed politician Kamal Hasan, would go on to quit his practice and become a well-known Tamil character actor. See Charuhasan, *Thinking on My Feet* (New Delhi: LiFi Publications, 2015), 40, 144.

jurisdiction and building rights came up every week. Cooperative credit societies, police officers, and even trial judges could be prone to corruption of various forms.[135]

Individuals and groups claiming to be supporters of the party wrote in for help and blamed Swatantra leaders for problems. Although their language no doubt exaggerates for demonstrative effect at times, these letters indicate the frustrations of economic life and tensions related to caste and class. It seems more likely that such tensions, rather than Masani's cartoons or the anti-inflation days, led people to express sympathy for Swatantra as an alternative to Congress. A man named V. L. Rajan wrote to Rajagopalachari on behalf of frustrated Madras pensioners who had been recently asked to vacate their homes by the local collector. The outgoing local elected officials from the Socialist Party and Madras Labor Union refused to turn over to the newly elected Congress leader proof of an agreement signed into law during Rajagopalachari's time as chief minister recognizing the pensioners' right to property secured after two decades of paying rent.

When the pensioners approached the concerned officials, they were sarcastically redirected to seek help from those for whom they had voted instead. Rajan noted that one of Swatantra's Madras legislative assembly members, H. V. Hande, was now helping them and speaking to the collectors. However, other parties' local bosses attempted to thwart these discussions.[136] Barely able to contain his anger, Rajan alleged that his adversaries paid off the new Congress legislative assembly member:

> When our will is with you, no government has the right to have this place vacated or sold. Under your leadership and on behalf of your party, I am challenging them ... Please send a telegram to [Prime Minister] Indira Gandhi, [President] Radhakrishnan, and [Defense Minister] Yashwantrao Chavan and get them to stop these shenanigans. We are poor people. We are at your feet, seeking protection.[137]

---

135. Interview with Charuhasan, Chennai, India, September 16, 2016.

136. For more on Hande, see the next chapter.

137. Eṅkaḷ uyil uṅkaḷ kaiyil irukkampōtu enta aracāṅkamum inta iṭattai kāli ceyyavō allatu virkavō, inta aracukku urimai illai eṉru uṅkaḷ talamaiyil uṅkaḷ kaṭciyiṉ cārpilum savāl viṭukiṟēn. Ākavē, nīṅkaḷ uṭaṉē Delhiyil Indira Gandhi am'maiyārukkum Jaṉātipati Rādhākrishnanukkum Rāṇuva Mantiri Chavanukkum uṭaṉē tanti koṭuttu, ivargaḷ kōṭṭattai aṭakka vēṇṭum. Iṅkuḷa ēḷaikaḷ ākiya nāṅkaḷ uṅkaḷ pātamtāṉ gati eṉru irukkiṟōm. V. L. Rajan to Rajagopalachari, March 31, 1966, Microfilm Accession 10956, File 67, CRP, 305.

Tensions between the laborers and retired professionals in the Pensioner Lines locality reached a fevered pitch. Rajan disparaged the underlings of the labor union and socialist leaders as *vēlai ilātatukaḷ* (jobless people). Elections had consequences. They could lead to power shifts that culminated in the undoing of a person's legal rights and, in this case, possible homelessness.

Another category of correspondents pledged support to the party without seeking action or favor from its leaders. Embedded in these letters at times were assessments of local party activity. Expressions of support could be quite touching. One supporter who had donated a total of 600 rupees over the last several months asked Sadasivam about the appropriateness of his contribution. He believed that the size of his donations reflected his ability to contribute but offered to send more if necessary.[138] A Brahmin supporter from a town near the Tamil temple city of Madurai described canvassing for Swatantra in marketplaces and near temples until exhausted by the heat. He wished he was stronger and pledged to distribute copies of *Cānakyan* from the following month.[139]

Party work could be difficult. The Madurai party supporter noted his resource constraints relative to Congress Party workers, forcing him to conduct meetings without microphones. This constraint limited his audience. His interlocutors, "restaurant cooks, rickshaw pullers, construction workers and even businessmen," cared more about caste than economic reform. "I figure they are sympathetic to our economic policy but have raised doubts about Rajagopalachari's hereditary education policy and caste-free, secular politics," he observed, pointing to the infamous scheme that ended Rajagopalachari's term as chief minister in 1954.[140] By contrast, the influential local Nadars, a historically lower-caste community now active in commerce, had supported the party quite heavily in this area.[141] Bringing free economy into the field rather than simply voicing discontent about the Congress required both overcoming the stigma of

138. S. Maruthavaanathesi to Sadasivam, November 20, 1961, Installment IV, SF 35, CRP, 85–86.

139. K. Ramanatha Iyer to Rajagopalachari, July 12, 1966, Microfilm Accession 10956, File 67, CRP, 308.

140. *Nagariluḷḷa camaiyal toḷilāḷarkaḷ, kaiyyu vaṇṭi toḷilāḷarlaḷ, kaṭṭita toḷilāḷarkaḷ mutalāna cāmāṉya makkaḷaiyum avargaḷ kūṭu irukkira iṭankaḷil kaṇṭu nām kaṭci koḷkaikaḷaiyum poruḷātāra uṇavu koḷkaikaḷaiyum pēriṭam eyiṟṟu koṇṭa pōtilum. Rājājiyin kalvi tiṭṭatukkum jāti pētamaṟṟa taṉmaiyilum, palar cantēkam teruvikka kēṭu varuṭṭam aṭaintēṉ.* RTP Subramaniam to Rajagopalachari, 8 June 1966, Microfilm Accession 10957, File 71, CRP, 33–37.

141. Robert Hardgrave, *The Nadars of Tamilnad: The Political Culture of a Community in Change* (Berkeley: University of California Press, 1969).

Rajagopalachari as a caste-prejudiced Brahmin and communicating in an intelligible idiom.

Perhaps the most unusual example of support came from the pen of one R. Bangaruswami, uncle and mentor of the historian of economic thought Srinivasa Ambirajan.[142] Bangaruswami braided together economic and political concerns and drew on the Tamil grammar of political communication to fashion an English-language attack on the Congress government's expanding bureaucracy. A Brahmin from the Kodaganallur village of Tirunelveli district, Bangaruswami sent Rajagopalachari "Swatantra Slogans" as a contribution to the party's attempts to court popular support. "Cryptic like sutras," these could "achieve a mantric character by mass repetition" in times of "stress and storm in public life." Bangaruswami presented a genealogy of nationalist slogans, from "Vande Mataram" (Mother India, I Bow to Thee), to "Quit India," which was responsible for "kindling fire and enthusiasm in a million hearts, in a million ways" to such an extent that "the [colonial] bureaucracy trembled to hear the words." Lamentably, the postcolonial government had lost the plot. Its "Grow More Food" scheme of the late 1940s had proved a "flat affair," Bangaruswami continued. The country continued to depend on foreign grain to feed itself.[143]

For Swatantra, Bangaruswami proposed the slogan "Drive Out the Congress." He offered a poem in excitement, which he hoped could be repeated across the country. The poem imported into English the Tamil form of aṭukkumoḻi. These were stacked sentences that built in intensity through repetition and alliteration. Political leaders used this technique in their public speeches.[144] The first stanza, with an aa-bb-cc rhyme scheme, went like this:

Drive out, drive out the Congress
That gives no redress
To the never-ending course of taxation,
Provoking a lot of trouble and ~~vexation~~ inflation

142. Ambirajan dedicated his first book to "my uncle R Bangaruswami." See Ambirajan, *A Grammar of Indian Planning* (Bombay: Popular Book Depot, 1959). On Ambirajan's own origins in Kodaganallur, see A. R. Venkatachalapathy, "Economist Extraordinaire," *The Hindu*, February 19, 2001, and V. R. Muraleedharan, "Scholar by Right," *The Hindu*, March 11, 2001.

143. The Grow More Food Scheme, initiated in 1943 after the Bengal famine, terminated in 1952 after it failed to meet its aims. Sherman, "From Grow More Food to Miss a Meal."

144. On aṭukkumoḻi, see Bernard Bate, *Tamil Oratory and the Dravidian Aesthetic: Democratic Practice in South India* (New York: Columbia University Press, 2009), 159–62.

And proclaiming its present devaluation
Is a sound scheme of revaluation![145]

The poem ended on a charged note: "We have had enough and need a change/ And Swatantra is within our range." Bangaruswami's native Tirunelveli district was famous for its bankers and writers. His letter brought together the form of the poet and the concerns of the banker.[146]

A final category of correspondents, opinionated Indians, ranged from supporters to naysayers of the Swatantra Party. They wrote long letters. These correspondences offered musings on the state of the nation and its economy. Some letters were filled with dense prose running over twenty pages long.[147] Others rhymed.[148] This was yet another instance of oral modes of public communication entering the written form.[149] Correspondents often complained of how the pursuit of money could dominate and corrupt a life. This called to mind the fifth principle of the Swatantra Party to "avoid the dominance of a purely materialist philosophy of life which thinks only in terms of the standard of life without any reference to its content or quality." To an extent, these problems emanated from the modernist vision of a planned industrialized country. At a regional level, they were a product of the acceleration of urban agglomeration in Madras State from World War II until the end of the 1960s.[150] This dynamic sharpened the distinction between the town and the city.

145. R. Bangaruswami to C Rajagopalachari, November 12, 1966, Microfilm Accession 10964, File 93, CRP, 109.

146. On Tirunelveli district's bankers, see volume 3 of the Government of India's 1930 *Madras Provincial Banking Enquiry Committee*, cited in Tirthankar Roy, *A Business History of India: Enterprise and the Emergence of Capitalism from 1700* (Cambridge: Cambridge University Press, 2018), 93. The most famous Tamil poet, Subramania Bharati and the author Pudumaipittan also hailed from this district. See A. N. Dev, *Indian Literature: An Introduction*, eds. Bajrang Tiwari and Sanam Khanna (New Delhi: Pearson, 2006), 125; and Lakshmi Holmstrom, ed. and trans., *Fiction's Pudumaipittan* (New Delhi: Katha, 2002).

147. P. S. Kalyanasundaram to C. Rajagopalachari, June 4, 1968, Subject File 46.2, Installment VI–XI, CRP, 152–69.

148. This practice was not limited to South India. Tharangini Sriraman, "A Petition-Like Application? Rhetoric and Rationing Documents in Wartime Delhi," *Indian Economic and Social History Review* 51, no. 3 (2014): 353–82.

149. See chapters 3 and 4.

150. R. Rukmani, "Urbanization and Socio-Economic Change in Tamil Nadu, 1901–91," *Economic and Political Weekly* 29, no. 51–52 (1994): 3263–72.

As Rajagopalachari's short stories conveyed forty years previously, move-ment to the city in search of economic fortune could be an unsettling and isolating experience. Dominated by the quest for income security, it could culminate in a loss of mores.[151] One A. Ramasamy Chettiar, who lived near the Muthupettai *panchayat* town in Thanjavur district and described himself as *parama ēḷai* (extremely poor), lamented the takeover of life by money. He worried about India borrowing money from the United States and the food shortages plaguing the nation. He had observed no improvement in the condi-tion and number of beggars, the hungry, and the unemployed.[152] India had been better off under the British, Chettiar surmised.

Anticommunism pervaded the lengthier letters. The language of socialism coming from the Center provoked anxieties among upper castes in a region that had seen a great deal of change. One temple priest from the large town of Udupi in Mysore wondered why the present government ignored the "writ-ings of Mr. Adam-Smith, Mr. Bukar [sic], Mr. Barnard Shaw [sic], and other great statesmen who held that the primary function of a government is protec-tion of person and property." Instead, he declared:

> The present Congress Government seems to have given up all the above hoary principles of good administration and have adopted the materialistic, immoral and anti-religious Comunist [sic] principles of Carles-marx [sic] and lenin-principles of terror, of expropriation, of regimentation, and of brain-washing and the architects of the so-called Socialistic pattern of society which is in fact Comunist [sic] Society . . . and they are going on merrily planning the insolvency of the Indian nation . . . They constitute the Directors of regimentation described by Mr Auldus [sic] Huxley in his future world.[153]

To be sure, the mofussil context for the interpretation of English-language texts produced juxtapositions unfamiliar to the westernized reader. Yet even after accounting for this, how the Fabian socialist Bernard Shaw became a guardian of property rights is unclear. Much clearer is the priest's anxieties

---

151. A. R. Venkatachalapathy, "Street Smart in Chennai: The City in Popular Imagination," in Venkatachalapathy, *In Those Days There Was No Coffee*, 59–72.

152. A. Ramasamy Chettiar to C. Rajagopalachari (in Tamil), February 1, 1968, Other Files—Number 9 (II), Installment IV, CRP, 252–55.

153. B. Ananthakrishna Achar to C. Rajagopalachari, April 16, 1959, Subject File 10, Install-ment VI–XI, CRP.

about left totalitarianism. Another correspondent, a village panchayat leader, worried that Swatantra's rise would weaken the Congress and pave the way for communist ascent.[154] On these grounds, he refused to support the party.

A broad section of the Indian populace knew about their right to vote as early as 1950, a full year before they cast their ballots.[155] From the subsequent decade, these correspondences indicate that the introduction of democratic government had started to produce a democratic social imaginary in the minds of some pockets of the enfranchised.[156] Practices such as multiple petitioning, escalation of claims, expressions of support for Swatantra, and declamations on the country's state of economic affairs offer evidence of this imaginary, influenced as they might be by prior practices or tinged with the occasional antidemocratic opinion. Responses to Swatantra's methods and communication tactics and awareness of party leaders as a conduit for making citizens' voices heard suggests a nascent opposition consciousness.

By no means was Swatantra the sole party responsible for creating opposition consciousness. Rather, people interpreted the opportunities and threats the party spoke of in sophisticated ways. They may have done the same in response to other parties. Indian citizens engaged Swatantra's leaders. They were not merely passive recipients of a pedagogical exercise. They come off as citizens with expectations about their entitlements in these invitations to dialogue of sorts.[157] Economic insecurity and observations about the abuse of public office provoked their discontent with the effects of the strategy selected for developing the country. That discontent generated great emotional distress as well as a sympathetic disposition toward Swatantra, culminating in a "politics of resentment."[158]

154. K. Kothandaraman, Chairman, Panchayat Union Council, Akkanaickenpalayam, Coimbatore District, to C. Rajagopalachari, November 27, 1961, Subject File 36, Installment IV, CRP.

155. Shani, *How India Became Democratic.*

156. Kaviraj, "The Empire of Democracy: Reading Indian Politics Through Tocqueville," in *Anxieties of Democracy: Tocquevillean Reflections on India and the United States,* eds. Partha Chatterjee and Ira Katznelson (New Delhi: Oxford University Press, 2012), 20–49.

157. On the pedagogical/dialogic dynamic, see Dipesh Chakrabarty, "The Legacies of Bandung: Decolonization and the Politics of Culture," in *Making a World After Empire: The Bandung Moment and its Political Afterlives,* ed. Christopher Lee (Athens: Ohio University Press, 2010), 45–68.

158. I borrow this term from Philip Nord's pioneering local history of shopkeepers in nineteenth-century Paris. Nord, *Paris Shopkeepers and the Politics of Resentment* (Princeton: Princeton University Press, 1986).

These letters and petitions also illuminate the different ways in which people conceived of economic life in their times. English-language correspondence more directly took up key economic policy issues. The Hindi and Tamil material normally concerned more localized individual or community grievances.[159] In part, this reflects that Swatantra's ideology originated in English-language discourse before its translation to Indian languages. Popular understandings of free economy took on different hues from party literature and propaganda. Nevertheless, they shared certain features: values of economic security and order, anxiety about the role of the state in economic life, perceptions of the corruption of the state, strong moral revulsion against debt, and a desire for fiscal rectitude. It is also possible that as part of the upward hermeneutic of ideas, these letters conditioned the way in which party leaders conceived of economic affairs and adjusted their views.[160] At the same time, their provenance from a limited demographic may have blinded Swatantra's leaders to the concrete achievements of this period of Indian history and even disconnected them from other issues.

## The Circumscribed Nature of Free Economy

The Swatantra Party spoke of an electoral politics "on which the attitudes taken by different candidates on various matters in the political and socio-economic spheres were the issues" that counted.[161] Its leadership hailed from relatively affluent or upwardly mobile communities and constructed an idealized political imaginary of the middle class that consciously avoided issues of caste and identity. On the one hand, this allowed Swatantra to become viable and to bury differences between a Hindu majoritarian like Munshi and a Parsi like Masani who embraced what he called a "nondenominational politics."[162] On the other hand, the strategy capped Swatantra's appeal.

Masani and Ranga drove Swatantra's popular outreach attempts. Neither had much interest in affirmative action to court the underrepresented. This

159. Discussion of a parallel issue about how the motivations and consciousness underlying workers' everyday politics differed from those of Union or Party leaders in colonial India appears in Rajnarayan Chandavarkar, *Imperial Power and Popular Politics*, 74–99.

160. Bayly, *Recovering Liberties*.

161. This was reprinted on the back of *Who's to Hold That Price Line?*

162. Masani, "What the Swatantra Party Stands For," n.d. File 5, Box 6, SP.

was consistent with their attitudes at the Constituent Assembly, where these men gravitated toward the idea that law should be blind to difference.[163] Neither Masani nor Ranga supported caste- or religion-based reservation of seats in legislatures. Both supported the reform of personal laws based on religion and endorsed the idea of a Uniform Civil Code. Masani himself actually went further than merely endorsing the idea. He even suggested adopting such a code within the next five to ten years.[164] By contrast, certain leaders from religious minority communities argued that such a code would impede the free practice of their religion.[165]

Consistent with this attitude, Swatantra neglected to reach out to marginalized sections of the electorate in ways that specifically recognized difference and disadvantage. Perhaps as a result, Swatantra's ranks at the state and national typically included just a few members from religious minorities or lower castes. They normally hailed from particularly elite backgrounds. A small coterie of well-to-do Parsis dominated the Bombay party organization.[166] Mysore parliamentarian Mohamed Imam and the Uttar Pradesh legislative assembly member Akhtar Ali were Muslims from ex-princely states. A former member of the Muslim League who served as an administrator in 1940s Mysore, Imam was a staunch anticommunist deeply invested in the cause of a

163. At the Constituent Assembly, Masani had tried unsuccessfully to introduce a clause in the Fundamental Rights section that "no impediments to marriages between citizens shall be based merely upon difference of religion." Minutes of the Sub-Committee on Fundamental Rights, March 28, 1947, Reproduced in B. Shiva Rao, ed., *The Framing of the India's Constitution: Select Documents*, vol. 2 (New Delhi: Indian Institute of Public Administration, 1967), 128, 163. I am grateful to Rohit De for the reference. The proposal attempted to overturn colonial law requiring interfaith couples to marry outside India or renounce their faiths. I first learned of this episode in Shruti V's illuminating blog post "Interfaith Marriage and the Constituent Assembly," *Article 14*, January 2, 2021, https://www.article-14.com/post/interfaith-marriage-the -constituent-assembly.

164. Shiva Rao, ed., *The Framing*, 128, 162. Masani believed that a system of proportional representation—instead of the first-past-the post system—would be better for everyone, minorities included. S. V. Raju, *Minoo Masani*, 54–55.

165. Sheshrao Chavan, *The Constitution of India: Role of Dr. K. M. Munshi* (Bombay: Bharatiya Vidya Bhavan, 2002); Leila Seth, "A Uniform Civil Code: Towards Gender Justice," *India International Centre Quarterly* 31: 4 (2005), 40–54; A. V. Thomas, *Christians in Secular India* (Rutherford, NJ: Fairleigh Dickinson University Press, 1974), 84.

166. See the membership rolls in File 1, Box 5, SP.

secular country with a two-party system.[167] He likely came from a landed background and played bridge in his spare time.[168]

More information exists about Akhtar Ali Khan, from Rampur. He became Swatantra's leader in the Uttar Pradesh legislative assembly in 1967. He enjoyed the support of an elite Muslim political organization called the Majlis-e-Mushawarat, created after a series of Hindu-Muslim riots in 1964. Majlis-e-Mushawarat aimed to support individual candidates sympathetic to the interests of Muslims and to better use the democratic process to become equal partners with Hindus in India's governance.[169] Akhtar's membership in Swatantra did not last long. The events leading to his dismissal indicate that Swatantra did not take minority concerns particularly seriously at the overall party level. He got suspended from the party for indiscipline after criticizing a pro-Israel statement made by Masani after the Arab Israeli War of 1967.[170]

Swatantra made some specific attempts to target women. On occasion, it appealed to them based on ideas of gender difference and complementarity to men.[171] Communication to women relied on appeals to their traditional economic roles as food procurers and providers. As an early *Swatantra Newsletter* noted, "They feel the present pinch of prices day by day as they have to run the households."[172] Swatantra sought to engage women in a manner consistent with an ideal of selflessness and service, complicit in the dominant understanding of the "male breadwinner as political citizen" that characterized these times.[173] To its credit, Swatantra refrained from the increasingly intrusive

167. Erdman, *The Swatantra Party and Indian Conservatism*, 133.

168. "Imam, Shri Mohamed." Fourth Lok Sabha, Member's Bioprofile, accessed at http://loksabhaph.nic.in/writereaddata/biodata_1_12/1196.htm.

169. During his time in the Assembly, Akhtar Ali Khan sought to restore the Urdu language as a second language in the state. Urdu had been the official language of the province in colonial times, but after Independence it slowly lost place to Hindi and Hindustani thanks to majoritarian efforts. Zaheer Masood Quraishi, "Emergence and Eclipse of Muslim Majlis-e-Mushawarat," *Economic and Political Weekly* 6, no. 25 (1971): 1229–34.

170. Quraishi, ibid; "U. P. Excise Minister," *ToI*, August 11, 1967.

171. Paola Bacchetta and Margaret Power have described this as an appeal to "essentialist-differentialist complementarity" that considers women as subordinates rather than separate but equal to men. Bacchetta and Power, eds., *Right Wing Women: From Conservatives to Extremists Around the World* (London: Routledge, 2002), 7.

172. *SN*, November 1959.

173. Anjali Bhardwaj Datta, Uditi Sen, and Mytheli Sreenivas, "Introduction: A Country of Her Making," *South Asia: Journal of South Asian Studies* 44, no. 2 (2021): 218–27, 220.

rhetoric of population control pursued by a Congress reckoning with economic stagnation during the 1960s.[174] However, the party leadership did not appear to be much concerned by the issue of lower female participation in elections than men either.[175] Not unlike the Congress, it ignored the labor and rights of the majority of women who worked in the agrarian economy and offered little imaginative thinking about new economic roles for them.[176]

Service and subordination to the household or family characterize Swatantra's attempts to court female voters. As mentioned, Khurshedben Naoroji served the memory of her family by reading out Dadabhai Naoroji's speech at a political rally. A flyer advertising Anti-Inflation Day in 1960 read, "Women are particularly requested to join the processions and attend the meeting."[177] This appeal did not extend to anti-tax fliers; rather it sought to engage women as procurers of food.[178] Seeking to promote female participation in activities conventionally associated with them, Swatantra's Bombay women's action committee ran free sewing classes in the slum area of Dharavi.[179] Known for his patriarchal sentiments, Rajagopalachari argued that jewelry gave "Indian womanhood financial security." He praised women for their prescience in accumulating gold while men who invested assets in banks saw inflation suck

174. Mytheli Sreenivas, *Reproductive Politics and the Making of Modern India* (Seattle: University of Washington Press, 2021), 92–154.

175. In the third (1962), fourth (1967), and fifth (1971) Lok Sabha elections, female participation was 16.7 percentage points, 11.2 percentage points, and 11.8 percentage points lower than men, respectively. See "Turnout Lok Sabha Elections—1952–2004."

176. Banerjee, "Whatever Happened to the Dreams of Modernity?" This neglect often led women toward precarious forms of activity in the informal economy. See Bharadwaj-Datta, "'Useful' and 'Earning' Citizens?" *Modern Asian Studies* 53, no. 6 (2019): 1924–55.

177. "The Swatantra Party Calls upon All Citizens to Observe 'Anti-Inflation Day,'" Microfilm Accession 2292, File 297, KMM, 267.

178. Women drove various anti-inflationary protests throughout the 1960s, almost a decade before their involvement in the Navnirman Andolan in the 1970s, as detailed in Radha Kumar, *The History of Doing: An Illustrated Account of Movements for Women's Rights and Feminism in India, 1800–1990* (New Delhi: Kali for Women, 1993), 102. In 1964, a women's organization staged at least three anti-inflationary protests in Delhi, the largest of which involved five hundred participants. *Peṇkaḷ Ārppāṭam! Delhi Caṭṭacapai Muṉṉāl!* ("Women's Demonstration! In Front of the Lok Sabha!!") *DT*, February 12, 1964; *Arici Vilai Uyarvu: 300 Peṇkaḷ Uṇṇāviratam! Piratamar Sāstri Vīṭu Muṉṉāl!!* ("Rice Price-Rise: 300 Womens' Fast! In Front of Prime Minister Shastri's House!!") *DT*, August 18, 1964; *Arici Vilai Uyarvukku Etirppu: 500 Peṇkaḷ Ārppāṭam! Delhi Caṭṭacapai Muṉṉāl!!* ("Anti-Rice Price Rise: Demonstration of 500 Women! In Front of the Lok Sabha!!") *DT*, September 8, 1964.

179. *SN*, February 1960.

away the real value of their rupees at his Anti-Inflation Day address on Marina Beach. When the country limited gold holding over a certain limit in a bid to deal with foreign exchange shortages in 1963, Rajagopalachari asserted that the Indian woman should speak out now as the finance minister was forcing her to get rid of gold, analogizing it to her right to question the husband if he sold her jewelry.[180]

Although not a single female name appeared in a fifty-eight-page list of people whom the Swatantra Party originally targeted for help in building their numbers in India's states, some elite women participated.[181] Gradually, in small numbers, women members entered the party's ranks. By 1969, the Swatantra General Council for 1967–69 included two women. Three participated in the state executive committees and councils. Still, none served on the Central Parliamentary Board.[182] Nine women ran for Lok Sabha seats under the Swatantra banner during the 1962 elections, and four won. Five years later, all three candidates won. In comparison, Congress put up thirty-three female candidates in 1962, of whom twenty-six were successful. Thirty-seven female Congress candidates ran in 1967, of whom nineteen were successful. As a proportion of the total candidates put up in each election, the Congress numbers were marginally higher. For both, women candidates numbered less than 10 percent of the total. The twelve women who ran on the Swatantra ticket were most likely prosperous: they either hailed from princely areas, had worked alongside their Gujarati political spouses, or came from the Tamil Gounder community.[183] At the state assembly level, an even smaller proportion of the party's electoral contestants were women.[184]

Lilavati Munshi was one of the few who sought election on the Swatantra ticket. A conservative woman nominated by the Congress to the Rajya Sabha in 1952–58, Lilavati made various contributions to the nationalist movement with her husband K. M. Munshi and served as vice president of the Bharatiya

180. *SN*, March 1963.

181. Subject File 38, Installment IV, CRP, 612–69.

182. "Appendix," *SN*, October 1967–January 1968.

183. *Statistical Report on General Elections, 1962 to The Third Lok Sabha*, vol. 2 (New Delhi: Government of India, 1962) and *Statistical Report on General Elections, 1967 to The Fourth Lok Sabha*, vol. 1 (New Delhi: Government of India, 1967).

184. Only twenty-one out of Swatantra's 2,552 contestants across assembly elections across states between 1962 and 1972 were female. Congress' record in each state was never worse and normally slightly better. Data compiled from *Statistical Reports*, Election Commission of India, various.

Vidya Bhavan. She played a key role in getting kissing and sex scenes banned from Indian films via the Cinematograph Act.[185] Lilavati's candidacy statement presented gender as a factor freeing her from vested interests during her 1962 parliamentary election campaign:

> Being a woman, I have one advantage. I neither want to do business nor get licenses. I do not need any special position nor status . . . When the Government works for the good of the people I should support it. If its work is not in the interest of the nation, I at least can raise my voice against it without being afraid of losing favor.[186]

Lilavati presented the woman as the conscience-keeper of society. The woman could be free of personal interests that kept businessmen silent in the face of bad governance. This was premised on the rejection of her potential role as an income-earning citizen.

While Lilavati Munshi lost her election, Maharani Gayatri Devi of Jaipur won hers, twice. She was elected to the Lok Sabha in 1962 and 1967. On the first occasion, she won the most one-sided contest in the history of democracy.[187] The victory mainly showed the hangover of princely rule. Describing a scene of peasants genuflecting and garlanding the maharani, *The Illustrated Weekly of India*'s profile offered the corrective: "This is not a scene from the distant past; you can see it happening today in some villages near Jaipur." When she asked for their vote, most of the men responded, "Of course we will. Are we not your subjects?" The women stayed silent, conventions prohibiting them from speaking in public.[188] Tragically, the maharani herself recalled feeling that the victory really belonged to her husband, the ex-maharaja.[189]

Gayatri Devi's legendary wealth and beauty led the English media in India and abroad to take great interest in her. They cared little for her ideas about governance.[190] *Current* ran an interview with the sensational title "Glamour Girl of Lok Sabha and Swatantra Party Talks to *Current*: Gayatri Devi MP."

185. Derek Bose, *Bollywood Uncensored: What You Don't See on the Screen and Why* (New Delhi: Rupa and Co., 2005), xvi.

186. Lilavati Munshi, "A Statement," Microfilm Accession 2294, File 307, KMM, 243–46.

187. Caroline Seebohm, "Fairy Tale with a Dark Ending," *New York Times*, March 13, 1977.

188. Ram Panjabi, "A Maharani's Election Campaign," *Illustrated Weekly of India*, February 25, 1962.

189. Gayatri Devi and Shanta Rama Rau, *A Princess Remembers: The Memoirs of the Maharani of Jaipur* (Philadelphia: Lippincott, 1976), 275.

190. See, for example, "Close-Up: Maharani on the Campaign Trail," *Life*, November 17, 1961.

FIGURE 5.8. Maharani on the Campaign Trail (*Illustrated Weekly of India*, February 19, 1967).

*The Illustrated Weekly of India* profile of the second campaign in 1967 featured eight pages of pictures of the maharani campaigning, with little accompanying text (see Figure 5.8).[191] Consistent with Swatantra's appeals to women, Gayatri Devi invoked the role of custodian of the home. Attacking municipal corruption that led to under-provision of cleaning facilities, she said in the same interview, "As I or you wouldn't like to keep our house dirty; similarly, the Municipality should be responsible enough to keep the city clean."[192]

Gayatri Devi worked as a committed manager and organizer for Swatantra during the time she did spend in India, although she traveled overseas often. She mediated disputes and opened a fair price shop for essential commodities like food in her constituency.[193] The princess rose to a prominent position on the party central executive committee, briefly served as the party's vice president. She even attempted to circulate a Hindi *Swarajya*.[194] However, she

191. "A Maharani's Battle for Votes," *The Illustrated Weekly of India*, February 19, 1967.

192. *Current*, October 5, 1963.

193. Gayatri Devi and Shanta Rama Rau, *A Princess Remembers*, 282–83, 290.

194. Gayatri Devi to Rajagopalachari, May 13, 1962, Subject File 30, Installment IV, CRP.

worried that her presence in the party fed the idea of the Swatantra Party as a party of reactionaries. She also perceived that the media's attention on her might be damaging to the party at large.[195]

Glimpses of less prominent women also appear in the history of the Swatantra Party. The *Swatantra Newsletter* reported that the majority of the fifteen thousand people at the Ramnad District Convention of November 1959 were women.[196] One Mrs. S. L. Pandey, head of the public relations committee of the party's central office in Bombay, planned the party's fourth anniversary celebrations. Her draft plan was extensive. Among other things, it listed balloons, leaflets, freely distributed pencils, rulers, exercise books, and "cloth bags to be distributed free mostly in labor area [sic]" as part of the event. Pandey proposed three possible topics for an essay contest: the spiraling of prices, free enterprise, and strikes against a totalitarian state.[197] The Bombay Swatantra Party women's committee involved itself in charity activities. It is questionable, however, whether such efforts translated into support from women.[198]

To the extent that marginalized minorities and women could participate in Swatantra, they participated selectively. Free economy remained a male, upper-caste or elite class economy. Mohammad Imam and Akhtar Ali hailed from immensely elite backgrounds. Politicians like Lilavati Munshi and Gayatri Devi owed their status in part to their powerful spouses. They appealed to women in their capacity as householders serving the family and the nation. The two Lotvala women had performed these roles of service as well: Bachuben through her involvement in municipal politics and Kusum through her stewardship of the Libertarian Social Institute. However, the pockets of Swatantra's female participation indicate that the woman could appear as an

195. Gayatri Devi to Rajagopalachari, February 16, 1961, ibid. Another ex-royal, Maharani of Gwalior Vijaya Raje Scindia, ran on the Swatantra ticket for the Lok Sabha and the Jana Sangh ticket for the state legislative assembly, winning both. She abandoned the Lok Sabha post and became a leader of the state opposition parties in a coalition called the Samyukta Vidhayak Dal. This ended her association with Swatantra. In the 1980s, she would go on to help found the BJP. See Vijayaraje Scindia with Manohar Malgonkar, *The Last Maharani of Gwalior: An Autobiography* (Albany: State University of New York, Press, 1987).

196. *SN*, January 1960.

197. S. L. Pandey to K. M. Munshi, July 6, 1963, Microfilm Accession 2293, File 305, KMM, not paginated.

198. *SN*, March 1963.

active economic agent in practice, even if not in thought. The Swatantra Party thus left out from its audience a significant proportion of the population eligible to vote.

———

Rajagopalachari wrote to Masani that it was on principles and promises rather than foundations of inherited mass support that Swatantra must stand or fall.[199] He was in no way deluded about Swatantra's chances of success at the ballot box. This lofty goal, as articulated in correspondence between two men never comfortable with the proverbial masses, shows their faith in democratic ideals and the nobility of political persuasion. Swatantra's leaders reanimated free economy and brought it to the center of this project, burying differences in the process. That keyword, coined by the Lotvalas, persisted in public discourse. The Swatantra leadership embraced and reanimated it as a slogan for political change.

Free economy went further than most political projects. To pursue a class-based politics around it, Swatantra created an idealized male middle-class citizen fighting for economic rights and then sought to mobilize the electorate to embrace that identity. The strategy was twofold. First, the party targeted a core constituency of English-speaking professionals in urban India with pamphlets that blended pedagogy and polemic. It supplemented these measures by targeting the press and mobilizing the masses around economic grievances to appeal to the broader public, especially those who did not vote. For this limited constituency, this politics offered a democratic, albeit not emancipatory, imaginary of "ordered progress" and offered an opposition politics.

Lack of funds, poor organization, and the inability to unite disparate party factions around a core ideology hobbled the Swatantra Party.[200] If the overwhelming influence of Masani and the Bombay English-speaking core leadership on the party's attempts to spread its message and its organization imposed some coherence, this also sowed the seeds of Swatantra's demise. Free economy could never quite escape its twin, English, with which it had been associated from its earliest days. The few mass leaders from the party's ranks played

199. Rajaji to Masani, February 27, 1964, File 3, Box Five, SP.

200. *Midterm Report* (Bombay: Swatantra Party, 1969); Bhanu Pratap Singh, "What Ails the Swatantra Party," n.d., Microfilm Accession 10955, File 65, CRP, 38; Undated meeting minutes [1968?], Subject File 43, Installment IV, CRP, 18–56.

only minor roles in defining attempts to disseminate party ideology among the masses. As one scholar of the Swatantra Party in Gujarat noted, "The type of literature that was distributed had been written from an All-India angle and had little relevance in the context of Gujarat. Most of the Party's literature . . . was written in the English language and the common man was deprived of it."[201]

How appropriate was free economy as a mass ideology? That a phrase like permit-and-license raj never had an Indian-language equivalent is revealing. How did the middle-class citizen of Swatantra's imagination correspond to what people looked like in India? To whom did such an identity appeal? Over 80 percent of the party's voters in the 1967 elections came from rural India. The urban salaried classes targeted did not provide much electoral support. In Madras State, where Rajagopalachari received voluminous correspondence, Swatantra's party workers were well settled in life and had stable jobs. They took no interest, by and large, in running for elected office.[202]

But by politicizing the language of economics and development and mobilizing people around economic issues, Swatantra offered a broadly secular nationalist alternative to the Congress. It united rather disparate groups around a common set of claims tracing origins in ideology. The party offered Indian democracy a new class-based politics for making economic claims and voicing grievances. Along with other opposition parties, it helped a group of Indians negotiate their enfranchisement by modifying their idioms and practices of mobilization. These would outlast Swatantra and many of its contemporaries. Inflation, taxation, and corruption would provide enduring impetuses for political mobilization of various kinds.

Swatantra offered a new political language and provided representation to new commercial groups and upwardly mobile professionals who were the products of a changing Nehruvian India. It was not a foregone conclusion that such disparate groups would loosely agree to Swatantra's platform, however fleetingly and tenuously forged. The ranks of these new classes would grow and continue with their politics of claim-making even after Swatantra died.

201. Sharma, 894.

202. S. S. Marisamy to Masani, [n.d. 1966], Microfilm Accession 10955, File 65, CRP, 164–68.

# 6

# Against the Tide

SWATANTRA IN OFFICE AND MEMORY

COMFORTABLY ENSCONCED in Sansad Bhavan, the circular Indo-Saracenic sandstone home of the Lok Sabha in Delhi, a jovial Minoo Masani prepared to give his maiden address as leader of the joint opposition parties. He scribbled "'Humpty Dumpty . . .' All the Queens horses" into his speaking notes for that day—March 21, 1967.[1] Forty-three members of his own party sat alongside him that day. This number exceeded the tally of any other opposition party (see Appendix). Swatantra had surpassed its own expectations.

Humpty, the Indian National Congress, had just lost seventy-seven seats in the 523-seat Lok Sabha in the general elections of 1967, decreasing its count from 361 to 283 (See Table A4 in the Appendix). Worse, the Congress lost its majority in the legislative assembly elections in seven out of sixteen Indian states.[2] Among the opposition parties, Swatantra capitalized best on the situation. Thanks to the merger of the ex-princely Ganatantra Parishad party into Swatantra, it even managed to form a coalition government in the eastern state of Orissa. Although the coalition did not last long, Swatantra managed to abolish land revenue taxation in the state. The party captured at least a tenth

---

1. To quote the nursery rhyme in full, "Humpty Dumpty sat on a wall. Humpty Dumpty had a great fall. All the King's horses and all the King's men couldn't put Humpty together again." Masani probably substituted "queen" for "king" because Indira Gandhi was the prime minister. See M. R. Masani, "Speech on the President's Address in the Lok Sabha on 21.3.1967," mainly typed notes, Serial No. 54, File Four, Masani Papers, NAI.

2. Kerala, Madras, Rajasthan, West Bengal, Orissa, Punjab, and Bihar. This does not account for the many subsequent defections and counter-defections that returned the Congress to power in states like Punjab and Bihar and removed it from power in Uttar Pradesh. See Frankel, *India's Political Economy*, 362–88.

of the assembly seats and became the official opposition party in Andhra Pradesh, Gujarat, and Rajasthan. The most surprising result of 1967 came from Madras, where an anti-incumbency wave washed away the Congress. Even the Congress Party's national president, K. Kamaraj, Rajagopalachari's old adversary, failed to win reelection.

Swatantra's success and Congress' misfortune did not last long. Analysis by political scientists suggested that most of Swatantra's electoral success owed to its ability to convert feudal relationships of power into legislature seats through votes from agricultural cultivators. This reality was at odds with the ideals and efforts of its founders and accounts for the dominant characterization of Swatantra as feudal.[3] More ominously for the party's survival, the Congress split in 1969 into the more conservative Congress (O) and the more radical wing headed by Nehru's daughter, Indira Gandhi, Congress (R). The Congress (O) slowly attracted away Swatantra's support. In the 1971 elections, the Congress (R) appealed directly to the electorate on a platform of "*Garībī Haṭāō!*" (Abolish Poverty!) and bypassed the state and local party magnates who had hitherto directed the electorate in a nearly patriarchal fashion.[4] It blew away the opposition, with the winning 352 seats in the Lok Sabha. In the end, Masani's own party, reduced to eight seats, would come to resemble the hapless Humpty. Shortly after the verdict, Swatantra disintegrated (see Table A5 and A6).

Nevertheless, Swatantra's significance exceeded its legislative returns.[5] Commentators noted that its rise brought a new ideological dimension to political debate and brought some of the divisions in the Congress into stark relief.[6] During the 1960s, it played a hand in some key developments in India's democratic history.[7] Swatantra sought to implant its idea of opposition

3. D. L. Sheth, "Profiles of Party Support in 1967," *Economic and Political Weekly* 6, no. 3/5 (1971): 275–88. For more information on these elections, see Tables 3 and 4 of the Appendix.

4. See Tables 5 and 6 of the Appendix. Kaviraj, *The Trajectories of the Indian State: Politics and Ideas* (Ranikhet: Permanent Black, 2011), 173–211, 179–80.

5. The electoral fortunes of Swatantra, and Indira Gandhi's rise to power have been discussed and analyzed by political scientists. See Rasam, *The Swatantra Party*, 111–177; Frankel, *India's Political Economy*, 388–434.

6. Kothari, "The Political Change of 1967."

7. Historical literature on Indian democracy has tended to focus on events of the preceding and subsequent decades. On the 1950s, see, for example, Ornit Shani, *How India Became Democratic*; De, *A People's Constitution*; Gyanesh Kudaisya, *A Republic in the Making: India in the 1950s* (New Delhi: Oxford University Press, 2017). Interest in the historical roots of contemporary authoritarianism in India no doubt has provided a powerful motivation for two recent scholarly

as a balancing force in a "one-footed democracy" and to advance free economy by using the institutions and processes of India's tripartite system of government.[8] What practices constituted this third dimension of opposition politics?

The memory of Swatantra and its leadership has made a recent return to the public mind decades after the party's early-1970s collapse. A range of figures have expressed hopes for the revival of Swatantra as a model for a new, rejuvenated opposition party since 2013. Where and from whom does this revivalism come? What has made this possible, and what are the possibilities for such a revival? And what from the history of free economy and opposition politics is worth keeping in mind today, both as caution and inspiration?

## Coalescing on Common Ground

Rajagopalachari's original idea on how to check one-party dominance was for a strong regional opposition party to offer competition to the Congress in each state. His logic ran that regional parties would exert pressure on the power of the Center and lobby for decentralized government.[9] After its founding as a national party, Swatantra pursued a modified version of this plan when it could. The party made use of regional credentials to insert itself into contests that sought to pit the opposition party of the region against the Congress at the Center through mergers, coalitions, and alliances of noncompetition.[10]

In two examples of successful alliances that handed defeat to the Congress, Swatantra shared with the dominant partner a commitment to strengthening the region vis-à-vis the Center and reversing the major thrust of current economic policy. First, in Uttar Pradesh, Swatantra briefly joined the Samyukta Vidayak Dal (United Parliamentary Group, or SVD) led by the Bharatiya Kranti Dal (Indian Revolutionary Floor, or BKD) to form a short-lived coalition government.[11] The BKD pursued a platform around farmers' interests

works on the Emergency of 1975–77. See Gyan Prakash, *Emergency Chronicles*; Jaffrelot and Anil, *India's First Dictatorship*.

8. Srinivasan, *Gandhi's Conscience Keeper*, 25–31.

9. See chapter 3.

10. *Cappāś, Jananāyaka Congress!* (Well Done, Democratic Congress!), *Kalki*, August 2, 1959; Rasam, *The Swatantra Party*, 24.

11. The Samyukta Vidayak Dal formed across the northern states, but Swatantra only partnered in Uttar Pradesh.

to redress economic policy's historically antirural bias.[12] It brought together smaller farmers from lower caste backgrounds. They had not benefited from the introduction of high-yield crops and fertilizers which had improved agricultural output and brought newfound prosperity to landowning castes during the 1960s.[13] Second, in Madras, Swatantra formed alliances with the Dravida Munnetra Kazhagam (DMK, or Progressive Dravidian Federation) in the 1962 assembly elections in Madras and entered into an overall DMK-led alliance in 1967.[14] Rajagopalachari himself played a crucial role in creating the Madras alliance.

The DMK's victory in the 1967 elections over the Congress created a viable two-party model in Madras, renamed Tamil Nadu (Land of the Tamils) by an act of the legislature two years later.[15] Since then, the Congress has never returned to power in that state. The DMK was defined by its commitment to anti-caste rationalism, social welfare, and Tamil identity. Swatantra did not share these objectives. Still, both parties asserted the interests of the region versus the Center and pointed out economic mismanagement by the Congress as exemplified by inflation. These were significant factors in the election.

Founded in 1949, the DMK represented the wing of the Dravidian movement that would end up embracing electoral politics. It had split off from the Dravidar Kazhagam (DK) of Periyar E. V. Ramaswami, the anti-caste rationalist leader who successfully galvanized popular sentiment against Rajagopalachari's government in 1937 and 1954.[16] The DMK developed a large following in the growing non-Brahmin student population after the Supreme Court struck down caste-based reservation of college seats.[17] Compared to the DK,

12. Paul Brass, *An Indian Political Life: Charan Singh and Congress Politics, 1967 to 1987* (New Delhi: Sage, 2014), 40–45.

13. Frankel, *India's Green Revolution: Economic Gains and Political Costs* (Princeton: Princeton University Press, 1971); Tim Bayliss-Smith and Sudhir Wanmali, eds., *Understanding Green Revolutions: Agrarian Change and Development Planning in South Asia* (Cambridge: Cambridge University Press, 1984).

14. In 1967, other partners included the Communist Party of India-Marxist, the Samyukta Socialist Party, and the Praja Socialist Party. See Barnett, *The Politics of Cultural Nationalism in South India*, 125, 136.

15. Barnett, *The Politics of Cultural Nationalism in South India*, 138. After the AIADMK split from the DMK in 1972, these two became the two major parties and the Congress occupied a distant third place.

16. See chapter 3.

17. In part to forestall such judicial action in the future, the text of the first amendment (1951) stipulated that nothing in the equal treatment provisions should prevent it from promoting

with which it shared the objective of annihilating caste, the DMK was not as explicitly anti-Brahmin. It also refrained from the DK's more incendiary activities like attacking religious idols to protest idolatry and burning copies of the constitution or the national flag in opposition to proposals for introducing Hindi as the country's official language. Leader C. N. Annadurai emphasized the ideals of *kaṭamai, kaṇṇiyam, kaṭṭuppāṭu* (duty, dignity, discipline).[18] Compared to Periyar, he did not disavow religion as vocally and adopted a more refined demeanor. Both DK and DMK made demands for a separate Dravidian nation until 1963. At that time, a constitutional amendment prohibiting secessionist activity led the DMK to drop the demand and instead embrace demands for greater autonomy for states.

The DMK's comparatively accommodating features compelled Rajagopalachari to send feelers in Annadurai's direction.[19] To be sure, cold calculation and opportunism factored into this move; Swatantra in no way shared the emancipatory and egalitarian program of the DMK. At the same time, a couple points of overlap made their alliance more than a marriage of convenience. Rajagopalachari commanded respect as a regional leader because of his steadfast refusal as chief minister to give in to Telugu speakers' demands for Madras city to become part of Andhra Pradesh in 1953.[20] His longstanding commitment to the development of Tamil literature and association with magazines like *Kalki* further bolstered these credentials.[21] From 1956, Rajagopalachari spoke out against making Hindi the country's official language.[22] He thus waded decisively into a greatly contentious debate. *Swarajya* and *Kalki* carried on a spirited anti-Hindi campaign in their pages. Swatantra passed resolutions opposing the imposition of Hindi as the national language.[23]

---

measures to redress social and economic inequality of "backward classes." See Austin, *Working a Democratic Constitution*, 94–100.

18. R. Kannan, *Anna: The Life and Times of C. N. Annadurai* (New Delhi: Penguin, 2010), 189. I am grateful to Pu Ko Saravanan for a discussion of Annadurai and this phrase.

19. Barnett, *The Politics of Cultural Nationalism in South India*, 124. The earliest indications of this were reported in the press in 1960. *Swatantra Kaṭci Ti Mu Ka Kūṭu!* (Swatantra Party-DMK Alliance!), *Dina Thanthi* (hereafter *DT*), October 13, 1960.

20. Guha, *India after Gandhi*, 187–89.

21. As Spratt notes, cultural and political wings of the Tamil movement came together in opposition to Hindi. Philip Spratt, *DMK in Power* (Bombay: Natchiket, 1970), 38.

22. Rajagopalachari, "'National' and 'Official,'" *Swarajya*, August 4, 1956; K. S. Ramanujam, *The Big Change* (Madras: Higginbothams, 1967), 37.

23. *Hindi Vēṇṭām! Āṅkilam Nīṭikka Vēṇṭum!!* (No to Hindi! English Must Last!!), *DT*, April 22, 1963.

The DMK's senior leaders had created trouble for Rajagopalachari's first ministry, participating actively in the anti-Hindi agitations under Periyar's lead during the late 1930s.[24] Now, some three decades later, they joined hands with their old adversary to set the issue up as a Tamil versus Hindi conflict. Politicizing this issue played to the DMK's strengths, as it counted gifted Tamil orators, writers, and actors among its ranks.[25] It became particularly important for the DMK after the party gave up the demand for a separate Dravidian nation. The party marked Republic Day, January 26, 1965, as a day of mourning and carried out the biggest protest in Madras history. Students burned Hindi books and marched to the secretariat demanding an amendment to the constitution protecting English. Across the state, the DMK flew black flags and burned effigies of the "demoness" of Hindi.[26] The Congress government responded with force and arrested 150 DMK leaders, including Annadurai himself.[27] This became the major issue in the elections.

This region-against-Center angle extended to issues of political economy. Both Swatantra and DMK believed in greater autonomy for states from the Center, with the DMK arguing for greater resource allocation to the South. Both parties mirrored each other's rhetoric of economic discontent. They levied charges of corruption against the ruling party, targeted the country's increasing foreign indebtedness as unwise policy, and bitterly opposed tax and price increases. A major DMK-led anti–price rise agitation in 1962 led to Annadurai's arrest. The issue became even bigger in the aftermath of back-to-back droughts in 1965 and 1966, prompting an increase in the scale of the protests.[28] Although Swatantra did not contribute much by way of numbers to these efforts, leaders' press writings and public statements consistently featured these themes. In one example, Rajagopalachari offered to dissolve the Swatantra Party if the Center removed all indirect taxes.[29]

Both parties leveraged their leaders' erudition to accentuate a contrast to the Madras Congress leadership. Nicknamed "Arignar" (Aṟiñar, Scholar), Annadurai wrote novels, plays, and film scripts. The DMK capitalized on the support of intellectuals and throughout the 1960s disseminated literature

24. See chapter 3.

25. Ramaswamy, *Passions of the Tongue*, 62–78.

26. Guha, *India after Gandhi*, 390–92.

27. Duncan Forrester, "The Madras Anti-Hindi Agitation, 1965: Political Protest and its Effects on Language Policy in India," *Pacific Affairs* 39, no. 1/2 (1966): 19–36, 24.

28. Ramanujam, *The Big Change*, 28, 30–36.

29. *Rājāji Nipantanai! Swatantra Kaṭciyē Kalaikka!!* (Rajaji's Condition! To Dissolve the Swatantra Party!!), *DT*, February 6, 1964.

bearing its ideology through the press. Reiterating his longstanding conviction that the poorly educated Kamaraj should not lead the Tamils, Rajagopalachari cast his lot with the Arignar and offered the scholarly Annadurai up as an alternative. Newspaper reports of DMK rallies reported workers yelling that the educated should rule, not the illiterate.[30]

Rajagopalachari's endorsement gave the DMK a kind of respectability in polite society, which had typically looked down upon the Dravidian party.[31] In fact, Annadurai asked Rajagopalachari to campaign for him in 1962.[32] The alliance also benefited the DMK because it had the effect of reducing multi-candidate contests to two-candidate and three-candidate contests. Additionally, Rajagopalachari helped attract the numerically small but socioeconomically powerful Brahmin community. He told members of his caste, "Brahmins! It is no sin to cast your vote for the Dravida Munnetra Kazhagam! Touching the sacred thread, I tell you that you must vote for the DMK."[33] The sacred thread, or *janeu*, connoted Brahmins' ritual status atop the caste order. By explicitly evoking it, Rajagopalachari suggested to Brahmins that they do their caste duty. Paradoxically, performing that duty meant casting a vote for the anti-caste DMK.

Pro-DMK sections of the Tamil press in turn painted Swatantra in a positive light. They provided coverage of the party and amplified common concerns. DMK leaders defended Swatantra against the charge of being a rich man's party, responding to such allegations by saying that Congress was the real rich man's party.[34] Swatantra and the other opposition parties also benefited from the mode and content of reporting by *Dina Thanthi* (Daily Wire), the most widely circulated Tamil daily, which enjoyed a circulation of 189,000 copies by 1962.[35] *Dina Thanthi* printed stories in a simple, spoken variety of Tamil, so that the literate could read them out to audiences in public spaces.[36] Its

30. Barnett, *The Politics of Cultural Nationalism in South India*, 137.

31. Kannan, *Anna*, 259.

32. *Annadurai Alaittār! Rājāji Varukirār!!* (Annadurai Called! Rajaji is Coming!!), *DT*, February 15, 1962.

33. Kannan, *Anna*, 302.

34. *Swatantra Kaṭci Paṇakkāra Kaṭciyā?* (Is the Swatantra Party a Rich Man's Party?), *DT*, August 9, 1965.

35. *Press in India, 1962—Part One*, 133–34. By comparison, the comparable second-most widely circulated daily *Dinamalar* was seventy thousand.

36. Francis Cody, "Daily Wires and Daily Blossoms: Cultivating Regimes of Circulation in Tamil India's Newspaper Revolution," *Journal of Linguistic Anthropology* 19, no. 2 (2009): 286–309, 291–93.

proprietor, Si Pa Adithanar, was an ardent Tamil nationalist and politician. Elected to the upper house of state parliament in 1964, he joined his Swatantra bench mate H. V. Hande in delivering speeches attacking the Congress government of the day.[37] Both were elected to the Madras legislative assembly in 1967, the year of the Swatantra-DMK alliance.

*Dina Thanthi's* editorial choices benefited opposition parties, even though the newspaper did not adopt an explicitly partisan approach to coverage. Catchy, sensational headlines were punctuated with multiple exclamation points. Stories on market price used onomatopoeic Tamil words like *kiṭukiṭu* (rapidly) for exaggerated effect.[38] A headline from June 6, 1966, for example, read, "Chili Price, Poison-Like Increase!"[39] The paper ran similar stories about tax increases. "Match Shortage! Cigarette Price Increase!! Consequences of New Taxes!!!" read a headline from April 25, 1962. "New Tax! New Tax on Kerosene and Cigarettes!!" read another from almost a year later.[40] Protests against rising taxes and inflation were important parts of the history of the 1960s. But *Dina Thanthi* went over and above merely covering them. Its pages presented taxation and inflation as wreaking havoc on the economy.

The 1960s marked the first chapter in a long history of opposition parties rallying around a vaguely defined "corruption" to produce waves of anti-incumbency in Indian electoral politics.[41] Inflation and the pinch of increased taxation have been and continue to be characterized as the symptoms of corruption and used to discredit regimes in power, more often than not the Congress.[42] This strategy allows opposition coalitions to downplay their own contradictions. It has even been a part of political contests famous for other issues such as language or ethnicity, like the 1967 DMK victory. Tarring the party in power at the Center as corrupt is also a way for regional parties to

37. Interview with H. V. Hande, Chennai, October 23, 2019.

38. For example, *Cāpāṭu Vilai Uyarvu! Chennai Hoṭelkaḷil!!* (Food Price Increase! In Madras Restaurants!!), *DT*, October 1, 1964; *Arici Vilai "Kiṭukiṭu" Uyarvu! Peyya Maḷai Kāraṇam!!* (Rapid Rice Price Increase! Rainfall the Reason!!), *DT*, November 17, 1960.

39. *Miḷakāi Vilai, Viśam Pōl Uyarvu!, DT*, June 6, 1966.

40. *Tīpeṭṭi Pañcam! Cigarette Vilai Uyarvu!! Putu Varikaḷin Etiroli!!!, DT*, April 25, 1962; *Putu Vari! Maṇṇeṇṇey, Cigareṭṭukku Putiya Vari!!, DT*, March 2, 1963.

41. Balasubramanian, "Anticorruption Development, and the Indian State"; Anil Nauriya, "Intolerance through the Years: 1934 to 1975 to 2015," *Mainstream* 52 (July 27, 2015), http://www.mainstreamweekly.net/article5764.html.

42. Pratap Bhanu Mehta points to the pervasiveness of inflation and corruption as key registers for political discontent in *The Burden of Democracy*, 158.

articulate their politics in a federal system. So, too, is asserting an antirural bias by a central government operating from a city. Through its allegiances, Swatantra helped contribute to this developing dynamic in a manner consistent with both its ideas of democracy and free economy.

## Performing Parliamentary Procedure

What happened once Swatantra got into office? Helmed by Masani, the party used parliamentary debate and procedure to increase the accountability of the ruling party and make the legislature more than a rubber-stamping institution. Amplifying this activity often required coming together with other parties having distinct agendas. In his memoirs, Masani acknowledged that the heterogeneity of opposition groups—ranging from the Jana Sangh to the communists—rendered much unity a futile attempt. Nevertheless, he welcomed the practice of opposition parties coming together when they could and recalled with contentment: "I have no reason to complain about the way in which the other parties, including the communists, behaved."[43] For arguably the most vocal Indian anticommunist of his age, this was quite an admission. Masani had great faith in parliament as a reasoning body for democracy. Responding to a press query on Independence Day in 1964, Masani said he considered free India's most outstanding achievement to date as "the maintenance of free discussion in Parliament, on the platform and in the Press." If it continued, he reckoned, "the possibility of removing all obstacles to correct thinking and action and to progress is still open and the basic goodness and intelligence of the people can be awakened."[44]

Swatantra made common cause with opposition parties in seeking to reverse key interventionist policies passed in the aftermath of the 1962 Sino-Indian War. These measures extended wartime powers under the Defense of India Rules to generate additional sources of finance for the government. The Gold Control Order, passed suddenly in January 1963, forced Indians to surrender all gold holdings except for personal ornaments. The order also prohibited the creation and trade of ornaments above 14-karat gold, threatening the

43. Masani, *Against the Tide*, 245; Masani, "United Opposition Front 'Difficult to Form': Masani Prefers Present System of Cooperation," *ToI*, June 8, 1963.

44. Masani, Response to Editor's Questionnaire in "The State of the Nation," *Illustrated Weekly of India*, January 26, 1964.

livelihoods of goldsmiths.[45] The Compulsory Deposit Scheme of 1963 obligated Indians to pay a certain proportion of their salaries into a government fund for a five-year period. They would receive their money and 4 percent interest after this time.[46] Congress lost three Lok Sabha by-elections to prominent critics of the Nehru government that year. One of them was Masani, elected from the Gujarat constituency of Rajkot.[47] The verdicts suggested that defeat by China and the introduction of repressive economic policies had unleashed popular discontent.[48]

Masani organized the first successful no-confidence motion in Indian parliamentary history by capitalizing on these issues.[49] Previous no-confidence measures never reached the threshold of fifty parliamentarians for formal recognition. Of course, the numbers secured would never be enough votes to topple the Congress. The motivation was partly pedagogical; "To move a vote of No-Confidence is a well-known Parliamentary means to educate the public as to why the opposition continues to oppose the party in power," Ranga wrote to Masani.[50]

Taking the floor, Masani the free enterpriser and anticommunist excoriated India's foreign policy of nonalignment. He also took aim at economic policy: "You cannot defeat the law of supply and demand. Prices, like water, will find their own level, and no amount of juggling will stop the laws of hydrodynamics or the laws of economics from having play."[51] The market fundamentalism of these lines indicated the hand of Shenoy, who vetted all of Masani's speeches on economic affairs.[52] Masani singled out how the regime was crushing the "backbone of the nation, the middle class" with rising taxes and prices,

---

45. "GOLD STOCKS NOT IN ORNAMENT FORM MUST BE STATED: Series of Steps to Curb Demand Announced," ToI, January 10, 1963. Two years later, to put the order on a more permanent footing, the government passed a Gold Control Act. See Sanjay Swarnkar, "The Gold Control Act of 1965, Its Socio-Economic Implications," Proceedings of the Indian History Congress 70 (2009–10), 1181–91.

46. "Deposits Scheme Only from July 1," ToI, May 27, 1963.

47. Frankel, India's Political Economy, 221.

48. J. C. Johari, Indian Polity (New Delhi: Lotus Press, 2004), 110. On the Sino-Indian war of 1962, see Raghavan, War and Peace in Modern India, 267–310.

49. M. K. Saini, "A Study of No-Confidence Motions in the Indian Parliament (1952–70)," The Indian Journal of Political Science 32, no. 3 (1971): 297–318.

50. Ranga to Masani, June 19, 1963, File 4, Box 1, SP.

51. Masani, Lok Sabha Debates, August 19, 1963, reproduced in File Four, Masani Papers, NAI.

52. Interview with S. V. Raju, Bombay, July 1, 2014.

demonstrating his flair for hyperbole.[53] Subsequent debate was an odd jumble of sometimes contradictory allegations. The left parties submitted their own no-confidence motion later, unwilling to join Swatantra. In the fallout from the event, left-leaning Defense Minister Krishna Menon resigned.

The true significance of such debates lay in the fact that dissent previously aired in a Congress working committee session had moved to parliament. Factions of the umbrella Congress had become their own parties. Opposition parties raised no-confidence motions eleven more times by the end of the decade. They forced the government to be accountable to the challenges of the period and engaged in unprecedented floor cooperation between themselves in the Lok Sabha.[54]

Complementing this activity, Swatantra performed the role of demanding accountability in other parliamentary forums. Allegations of corruption during regular debate reached a fever pitch and provoked measures like the first inquiry into ministerial corruption and dismissal of ministers on these grounds.[55] Masani became the first chairman of the Lok Sabha's public accounts committee from outside the Congress.[56] During his tenure (1967–69), the committee issued multiple criticisms of inefficiency and waste on the part of the sitting government. Among them were arrears in tax collection, overestimation of import requirements by the state trading corporation, unrealistic revenue estimation by the railways, and shortages of telephone cables in the country.[57]

The committee also launched a probe into the Indian Statistical Institute, then controlled by the cabinet secretariat and run by P. C. Mahalanobis, the statistician and architect of the Second Five-Year Plan. Its report suggested bringing the institute under control of the Ministry of Finance and abolishing Mahalanobis' post of secretary. Masani's spoken remarks accompanying the presentation of the report noted "the doubtful utility and excessive delays in compilation of statistics for the national sample survey and payment of large

53. Masani, *Lok Sabha Debates*, August 19, 1963.

54. Vikas Tripathi, "'Responsibility' and 'Accountability': Confidence and No Confidence Motions in the Indian Parliament," in *The Indian Parliament and Democratic Transformation*, Ajay Mehra, ed. (Abingdon: Routledge, 2018), 251–72.

55. Balasubramanian, "Anticorruption, Development, and the Indian State."

56. Masani, *Against the Tide*, 267–72.

57. "Progressive Rise in Tax Arrears: PAC Concern," *ToI*, August 8, 1967; "PAC Flays 'Unjustified' Ture Transaction," *ToI*, August 9, 1967; "PAC Flays Railways for 'Unrealistic Planning,'" *ToI* April 2, 1968; "Corporation in P&T Dept: PAC proposal," *ToI*, February 21, 1969.

amounts as grants to the institute without any evaluation of the work done and the cost at which it is done."[58] The report's scathing tone may have had more to do with Masani's animosity toward central planning than the severity of the findings. Nevertheless, the opposition leader raised a serious issue of favoritism and procedural irregularity in the allocation of public resources.

Regional efforts in the legislature paralleled Masani's national ones. Bhaikaka's memoirs offer an illuminating glimpse of how Swatantra operated as the official opposition in Gujarat. Bhaikaka Patel raised the state assembly's first no-confidence motion on the grounds that the government's incompetence at handling food shortages ought to disqualify the Congress from holding office.[59] To promote accountability, he moved a resolution asking ministers to declare their assets to the public.[60] He also used the discourse of corruption to perform the role of opposition party as a governance watchdog. Bhaikaka pressured the state government to investigate corruption in the cooperative societies and made allegations of ministers using office for personal gain.[61] And like Masani, Bhaikaka lobbied to give opposition more of a role in the committee work of elected assemblies. The Swatantra legislative assembly member who took up his seat after his retirement from politics became the first opposition member to chair the public accounts committee.[62]

Swatantra also pushed regional economic interests against the Center. Drawing on his skills and experience as a civil engineer, Bhaikaka took up the cause of the contentious interstate project to build large multipurpose dams on the Narmada River. The dispute arose because of a difference of opinion about the dam's goals. On the one hand, representatives of Bombay and the northern state of Madhya Pradesh wanted a lower dam to reduce damage done by the dam's reservoir. On the other hand, representatives of drought-prone Rajasthan and Gujarat wanted to construct a dam as deep as possible to harness hydroelectricity and water for irrigation.[63] Swatantra sponsored a 1966 Gujarat Legislative Assembly resolution to take up the project on a "war footing" because of the gravity of the state's food scarcity crisis. It passed unanimously. The next month, Bhaikaka represented the state in talks with the Madhya

---

58. "Vital Changes in Control of Statistics Institute Urged," *ToI*, April 3, 1969.

59. "Swatantra Leader Wants Gujarat Govt. to Quit," *ToI*, September 2, 1964.

60. "Gujarat Assembly Rejects Opposition Resolution," *ToI*, February 28, 1963.

61. *Patel, BS*, 438; "Parishad Leaders' Arrest Angers Gujarat MLAs," *ToI*, September 20, 1966.

62. Sharma, "Swatantra Party in Gujarat," 529.

63. Wood, *The Politics of Water Resource Development*.

Pradesh chief minister. He proposed that Gujarat would be able to raise money from citizen contributions to compensate Madhya Pradesh for submerged land.[64]

However, the many stakeholders across the three states thwarted further progress on resolving the issues, and the Center found it convenient to drag its feet on the matter. After the elections of 1967, Swatantra launched a campaign demanding the dam projects' completion within ten years. Bhaikaka organized a Khedut Sangh (farmer's union) and threatened major farmer protests if there were further delays.[65] While his efforts failed to meet their immediate objective, such activity helped make the Narmada issue one of enduring importance to regional politics.[66]

Swatantra took procedure seriously for its ability to create balance and accountability, perhaps more so than other parties. The party tried to vivify the parliamentary process through these efforts. Working from their position, Swatantra's legislators created pressures on the ruling party consistent with its platform of anticorruption and its members' legalism. The contrast between a figure like Masani and one like Bhaikaka, however, was that the latter managed to tie his parliamentary activity to popular mobilization. Masani, meanwhile, could appear to be screaming into a large void.

## Fundamentally Right (Wing)

Complementing its parliamentary activity, Swatantra mobilized citizens and appealed to the judiciary against perceived legislative overreach by the majority. Private property stood at the heart of the various articulations of free economy, whether or not explicitly stated. The party styled itself as the defender of the right to property and the right to constitutional remedies, two of the seven fundamental rights granted by the Indian Constitution.[67] The party sought to use the courts to balance out the legislature and the executive through petition campaigns and Supreme Court challenges. Swatantra inserted itself into the judicial history of postcolonial India.

64. Patel, BS, 446–60.

65. Sharma, "Swatantra Party in Gujarat," 695–96, 535–36; Patel, BS, 484–92.

66. The Sardar Sarovar Dam was ultimately only completed in 2019, after over three decades of protests by well-organized protesters on the grounds of ecological degradation and dispossession of *adivasi* communities. See Amrith, *Unruly Waters*, 292–95.

67. The others are the right to equality, the right to freedom, the right against exploitation, the right to constitutional remedies, and the right to freedom of religion. Part III, *Constitution of India*. The right to property would be removed by the forty-fourth amendment in 1978.

The right to property had been beset by contention from its origins. Debate at the Constituent Assembly centered on whether or not there was a right to compensation in the event of expropriation of property by the state, and whether the courts had a right to adjudicate the fairness of compensation in such cases.[68] Munshi and one section of the members of the assembly held the view that that the ultimate right to determine the parameters of adequate compensation in cases of expropriation by the government must rest with the judiciary. By contrast, a section of other delegates took a midway approach and pushed to exempt just zamindari land from judicial review. On the other end of the spectrum, Nehru believed that the courts ought to have no say in the matter.[69] The assembly eventually decided that the courts would have the right to determine the justness of the principle on which compensation was paid in all cases, but that the courts could not strike down expropriation legislation itself. Vallabhbhai Patel, the close colleague of Munshi and the most powerful man at the assembly, foreclosed the more radical options.[70]

The courts declared both company nationalization and land reform laws unconstitutional on the grounds of the timing and nature of compensation.[71] After Patel died in 1950, however, the balance of power in the legislature shifted toward Nehru. To advance the progressive aims of social and economic justice articulated in the constitution's nonjusticiable but ideologically charged directive principles of state policy, he succeeded in getting the first amendment (1951) and fourth amendment (1955) passed.[72] These facilitated zamindari abolition in various states, where the power to pass land reform legislation was vested. They also absolved the government from providing compensation in the event of a temporary transfer of ownership or property. However, neither touched the former ryotwari areas.

---

68. Austin, *The Indian Constitution*, 84–87.

69. V. Krishna Ananth, *The Indian Constitution and Social Revolution: Right to Property since Independence* (New Delhi: Sage, 2015), 55–79.

70. Austin, *The Indian Constitution*, 93.

71. For a detailed discussion, see Austin, *Working a Democratic Constitution*, 78–110.

72. The constitution says that "the State shall in particular, direct its policy towards securing . . . b) that the ownership and control of the material resources of the community are so distributed as best to subserve the common good c) that the operation of the economic system does not result in the concentration of wealth and means of production to the common detriment." Articles 39B and C, *Constitution of India*. On fundamental rights, see chapter 1.

The bill to bring a seventeenth amendment to the constitution was intro-duced in the Lok Sabha on May 5, 1963. Under its provisions, states could pass land ceiling legislation in non-zamindari areas without judicial challenges. Like the first and fourth amendments, it originated in response to recent court decisions. The Supreme Court decision had ruled against a land reform bill in the southern state of Kerala on the grounds that the category of land in ques-tion was not protected from judicial review of compensation by the first and fourth amendments and that the amount offered was inadequate. The amendment thus sought to remedy this ambiguity by broadening the kinds of land that could be seized without judicial review to special local tenures and ryotwari settlement. It further listed 124 state land reform acts not chal-lengeable in court.[73]

Ranga took the lead in Swatantra's efforts to mobilize against the seven-teenth amendment bill. In an emphatically worded letter to Masani, he asserted: "It is wrong to treat the *patta*-holders of land [under the ryotwari system, those holding documents that gave them landholding rights and assigned responsibility for paying revenue tax] as equivalent to the intermedi-ary rent-collecting Zamindars and Inamdars and to penalize crores of Pat-tadars of Gujarat, Punjab, Assam, Andhra, Madras and Mysore and Maharash-tra." Confronted with the logical extension of the principle underpinning zamindari abolition to ryotwari settlement, he bristled. To counter the pro-posed amendment, Ranga outlined immediate actions: "I am suggesting to peasants in all the Ryotwari areas to send post-cards to the Lok Sabha protest-ing against this bill."[74] Ranga ignored the diversity of land sizes and tenures in the former ryotwari areas and the landlordism prevalent in certain areas. He clung to an idealized notion of the ryotwari patta (title deed) holder as small peasant proprietor.

Ranga joined Dahyabai Patel, son of Vallabhbhai Patel and a Swatantra Party member of the Rajya Sabha (upper house of parliament), in offering two further grounds for opposition to the seventeenth amendment. Versions of these concerns had characterized free economy from its origins.[75] The first

73. Austin, *Working a Democratic Constitution*, 110–11.

74. Ranga to Masani, June 19, 1963.

75. These later appeared in A. P. Jain, ed., *Lawless Legislation: Why Swatantra Opposes the 17th Amendment?* (New Delhi: Swatantra Party, 1963). Jain, an ex-minister for food and agricul-ture, was himself not a Swatantra Party member, but he made common cause with the party on this matter. Siegel, *Hungry Nation*, 178–79.

argument concerned corruption in the executive branch. The public purpose of land expropriation, Ranga reckoned, "becomes the sweet will of the Local Minister, the revenue board and all the other offices." Compensation "will depend on the manner in which his pockets are lined and his palm is oiled." Affirming the sanctity and primacy of the judiciary, he protested, "it cannot be left to the sweet will and pleasure of the Executive as the amendment seeks to make it. It must be a question to be left to the decision of the Court."[76] Speaking in the upper house of parliament, Dahyabai offered an anticommunist argument. His logic ran that the amendment must be understood as part of a sequence. It came after two amendments to the constitutional right to property, visits to China to study collective farms, and the Nagpur resolution. Taken together, these developments suggested that India was steadily moving toward Chinese- or Soviet-style totalitarianism.[77] Of course, the fear of the consequences of the legislation for power relations between the landed and the landless slipped out. "Once the peasant proprietor is declared as an intermediary; the squatter automatically styling himself as the cultivator will be in a position to claim the land," a colleague noted.[78] They did not say why this was such a bad eventuality.

Swatantra took action to prevent these events from coming to pass. Ranga wrote to Nehru personally, asking him to suspend action on the bill. He reproduced the line from his 1959 book *Self Employed Sector* (see chapter 4) that if rural areas were to face land ceilings, then parallel ceilings on urban, industrial, professional, and commercial incomes should follow.[79] Swatantra submitted a strongly worded memorandum to the president alleging that the amendment encroached "on the Fundamental Right to property of no less than 60 million families in India who own and cultivate some land."[80] Citing a 1951 clarification by the law minister that the Lok Sabha would not pass a bill abrogating the right to judicial review, the memorandum appealed to the president to send the bill back to parliament. Further, in what appears weak and even desperate, the memorandum suggested that the assurances given not to dispossess "ryotwari tenants" actually meant "any land held under ryotwari

76. Ranga, "Monstrous Legislation," in *Lawless Legislation*, 11–30, 23–24

77. Dahyabhai Patel, "Road to Communism," in *Lawless Legislation*, 43–46.

78. Jain, "Introduction" in *Lawless Legislation*, 7.

79. Austin, *Working a Democratic Constitution*, 112.

80. "Memorandum to the President on the 17th Amendment Bill," [n.d. 1964], Microfilm Accession 2295, File 314a, KMM, (not paginated).

settlement." By extending the definition of "estate," the constitution would "stand disfigured by an article amounting to a deep riddle," it concluded.

Apart from these letters, Swatantra performed various actions signaling its objections. The party organized public gatherings on the issue across the country. On September 14, 1963, three members of legislative assembly from Madras hosted a daylong conference against the amendment in the Tamil temple town of Pazhani.[81] Six days later, Swatantra members of parliament walked out of the Lok Sabha, objecting to the bill's very existence.[82] The party subsequently flooded parliament with petitions from all over the country, collecting thousands of signatures.[83] The next year, it led five thousand delegates to a Kisan Sammelan (Farmers Convention) on a march to Sansad Bhavan in protest.[84] Andhra Pradesh party members trained in the law represented farmers in court, fighting against land ceilings legislation.[85]

Neither the arguments adduced against the bill nor these spirited mobilization efforts prevented its passage or the Supreme Court's upholding of the measure.[86] The significance of these activities lay in the fact that they represented Swatantra's first and perhaps only successful attempt at mobilizing mass support for an issue that almost exclusively affected rural landed interests. In other cases, like inflation or taxation, the issue cut across classes and the urban-rural divide. Similarly, the other issues spurred action across the political spectrum of opposition parties. By contrast, Swatantra accounted almost wholly for opposition party-led protest of the seventeenth amendment.

Some months before seventeenth amendment bill passed, the Congress working committee adopted a resolution on democracy and socialism promising "fundamental changes in the social structure."[87] But the figure meant to take India on that journey, Jawaharlal Nehru died that year. Foreign exchange

---

81. *Madurai Zillā Swatantra Kaṭci (Araciyal Kaṭṭa) 17-āvatu Tiruntu Kaṇṭaṉ Makānāṭu, Paḷani* (Madurai District Swatantra Party Convention to Condemn 17th Amendment at Pazhani), September 14, 1963, Microfilm Accession 2293, File 305, KMM, 2723.

82. "Swatantra Group Walks Out of Lok Sabha," *ToI*, September 20, 1963.

83. *SN*, November 1963.

84. "Protest Against 17th Amendment: Peasants' Rally," *ToI*, March 31, 1964.

85. *SN*, October–November 1965.

86. *Sajjan Singh v. State of Rajasthan*, 1965, AIR 845. Even though the Supreme Court subsequently ruled in the 1967 Golak Nath case that parliament could not curtail any of the fundamental rights, the verdict did not apply ex post facto to laws passed, saving the seventeenth amendment. Austin, *Working a Democratic Constitution*, 196–202.

87. Austin, *Working a Democratic Constitution*, 116.

crisis and realignment of political forces in the party organization arrested progress toward these lofty aims. As a condition for accepting financial assistance from Western donors, Nehru's successor, Lal Bahadur Shastri, pursued minor trade liberalization reforms and devalued the currency to boost exports.[88] However, Shastri died suddenly in 1966. The Congress Party "syndicate" of elderly male state party bosses installed Nehru's daughter Indira Gandhi as the prime minister. Led by Kamaraj, the syndicate calculated that she would be a pliable leader and allow the party organization to direct the government.

The results of the 1967 elections and 1968 by-elections embarrassed the Congress and set in motion events that brought to a head the tensions between party and government.[89] The syndicate inserted aging conservative leader Morarji Desai as finance minister and deputy prime minister as a check on Indira Gandhi, just in case. They seriously underestimated the new prime minister. Allying with the more radical elements of the Congress Forum for Socialist Action, she cast herself as a progressive leader. Divisions between an Indira faction and a party organization faction grew. The Indira faction painted its foes as a "reactionary" group, even though the syndicate comprised a more ideologically heterogeneous bunch. Tensions sharpened. By November 1969, the party split into the Indira-led Congress (R) and the party organization's Congress (O).

Swatantra surfaced in the judicial history of this period on either side of the Congress split, making important contributions to Supreme Court cases on bank nationalization and the abolition of the princes' privy purses. On July 19, 1969, upon receiving Indira Gandhi's instructions, the president of India signed an ordinance nationalizing the country's fourteen largest banks. The measure went further than the earlier policy of "social control" and sought to demonstrate Indira's commitment to progressive change.[90] That evening, Rustom Cavasji Cooper, a Parsi businessman and Swatantra Party treasurer, heard about the ordinance on the radio while hosting a dinner party at his Bombay home. The next day, he flew to New Delhi to prepare to file a writ

88. The best account appears in Engerman, *The Price of Aid*, 240–62. See also Kudaisya, "'Reforms by Stealth,'" and Mukherji, "India's Aborted Liberalization."

89. This paragraph sketches the discussion in Robert Hardgrave, "The Congress in India—Crisis and Split," *Asian Survey* 10, no. 3 (1970): 256–62; Austin, *Working a Democratic Constitution*, 173–95; and Frankel, *India's Political Economy*, 388–419.

90. Austin, *Working a Democratic Constitution*, 215.

petition to the Supreme Court against the ordinance.[91] Under article 32 of the Indian Constitution, citizens enjoy the fundamental right to move the Supreme Court by proceedings for the enforcement of fundamental rights. In Delhi, Cooper met Swatantra's lawyer, Nani Palkhivala. A fellow Parsi and eminent legal practitioner, Palkhivala worked on several famous Supreme Court cases related to fundamental rights. He also cowrote the definitive treatment of Indian income tax law.[92] Palkhivala's ideological sympathies rested with his client. Although not formally a Swatantra member, Palkhivala attended early meetings of the Bombay branch of the party and became president of the Forum of Free Enterprise in 1968.[93] His annual speeches under the forum's auspices, excoriating what he considered the national budget's excessive, complex tax provisions, became popular and received wide media coverage.[94]

Masani and his fellow Swatantra parliamentarian Narayan Dandeker joined Palkhivala and Cooper to plot.[95] That day, they contacted some fifty prospective allies who might lend their names to a petition. They found one taker, the Jana Sangh leader Balraj Madhok. Two petitions came of the meeting.[96] One, filed on behalf of Masani and Madhok, challenged the ordinance on grounds that the power to issue an ordinance exists only if parliament is not in session. The petition argued that the grounds for promulgating the ordinance never existed because parliament was to convene just two days after the president issued the ordinance. It further alleged that the ordinance was promulgated "with a view to sidetracking the full, normal, effective functioning of the Houses of Parliament." This, the petition suggested, infringed upon their fundamental rights to freedom of expression and freedom of occupation as members of parliament.[97] The idea that the ordinance obstructed their occupation by preventing debate in parliament was a stretch, even for these pettifoggers. The court refused to entertain Masani and Madhok's petition.

91. R. C. Cooper, "Why I Moved the Supreme Court," *Himmat*, February 20, 1970. I am grateful to Ian Kumekawa for helping me secure a copy of this article.

92. M. V. Kamath, *Nani A. Palkhivala: A Life* (New Delhi: Hay House, 2007).

93. Minutes of the August 12, 1959, Meeting of the Swatantra Party Organizing Committee for Greater Bombay, File One, Box 6, SP.

94. Kamath, *Nani A. Palkhivala*, 365–75.

95. Masani, *Against the Tide*, 300–302.

96. Cooper, "Why I Moved the Supreme Court."

97. Writ Petition Settled by N. A. Palkhivala in the Matter of M. R. Masani and Balraj Madhok vs. Union of India, July 21, 1969, File 2, Box Five, SP.

The court did, however, consider a slightly amended version of Cooper's petition after the ordinance passed as a law some weeks later.[98] According to the petition, the law violated the right to equality before the law (article 14) because it selectively nationalized just fourteen banks. It also violated the right to practice one's occupation freely (article 19) by preventing the banks from performing nonbanking business. It violated the right to just compensation (article 31) because the compensation to shareholders was inadequate.[99] The Supreme Court ruled in Cooper's favor, striking down the law for violating articles 14 and 31. The judgment stated that the law contravened article 14 by interfering with the activities of some banks and not others. It also noted that the law violated article 31 because its provision for compensation in the form of government securities redeemable in ten years did not constitute equal indemnification.

The judgment in *R. C. Cooper v. Union of India* (1970) established two key precedents. First, it evaluated the effects rather than the object of legislation. Second, the court established that the other legal violations—like the rights of the company—did not bar the court from considering violations of the rights of the individual.[100] A revised nationalization law adjusted to these provisions passed through parliament shortly thereafter, allowing the banks to continue their nonbank activities and offering the option of compensation to shareholders in cash.[101]

Later that year, the home minister introduced a bill to derecognize the titles of Indian princes and thereby remove their privy purses, or tax-free salaries paid by the government. Swatantra objected to the twenty-fourth amendment bill for a couple of reasons. On a personal level, it violated the agreement with the princes in exchange for their accession to the Indian Union, as negotiated by Sardar Patel with help from V. P. Menon under Rajagopalachari's tenure as governor general.[102] The recent death of Menon, an early member of Swatantra, magnified the personal stakes. From an interest perspective, the legislation threatened to adversely affect the ex-princes among the party members. P. K. Deo, an ex-prince and Swatantra member of parliament, spoke out

98. "Bank Act Is Challenged in the Supreme Court," *ToI*, August 29, 1969.

99. Austin, *Working a Democratic Constitution*, 216.

100. Rajeev Dhavan and N. S. Nahar, "The Compensation Conundrum: Socialism at the Bar of the Supreme Court," *Journal of the Indian Law Institute* 20, no. 3 (1978): 406–37; R. S. Gae, *The Bank Nationalisation Case and the Constitution* (Bombay: N.M. Tripathi, 1971), 190.

101. Austin, *Working a Democratic Constitution*, 219–20.

102. Basu, *V. P. Menon*.

immediately against bill on the floor of parliament. He argued that it undermined the constitution and infringed upon the right to property.[103] In solidarity with such figures, R. C. Cooper convened a fundamental rights front and
appointed a former chief justice of the Supreme Court as chairman. Although
in theory nonpartisan and open to everyone, the National Headquarters of the
Swatantra Party coordinated the front's activities.[104] In August 1970, the front
held a two-hundred-delegate convention in Bombay addressed by Ranga,
Palkhivala, and Cooper. At that event, the chairman suggested that the amendment "changes private property into state property." He defended the right to
property both as an incentive to work and the basis for freedom.[105]

After the twenty-fourth amendment bill failed to pass by one vote in the
Rajya Sabha, Indira Gandhi organized for it to be reintroduced as a presiden-
tial ordinance. In response, several princes filed writ petitions contesting the
ordinance. The Supreme Court recognized the petition of Madhav Rao Scindia, a Bharatiya Jana Sangh member of parliament legally represented by
Palkhivala. Once again, Palkhivala succeeded in his efforts. In *His Highness
Maharajadhiraja Madhav Rao Scindia v. Union of India* (1971), the court struck
down the measure, ruling that the president had no power to amend the constitution. Writing separately from the majority opinion, another judge noted
that the ordinance also infringed upon articles 19 and 31.[106]

The citizen and the opposition party are the unacknowledged participants
in the "great constitutional confrontation" of the late 1960s and early 1970s
between parliament and the courts.[107] The citizen filed the writ petition. The
opposition party used the courts to overcome numerical disadvantages in parliament, mobilizing the right to constitutional remedies. It registered its opinions in public and organized citizens.[108] Just as Swatantra defended cash

103. Austin, *Working a Democratic Constitution*, 225.

104. Draft Minutes of the Executive Committee, Swatantra Party, Bombay Region, July 15,
1970, File 1, Box 3, SP.

105. "Power to Amend Constitution May Lead to Despotism," *ToI*, August 31, 1970.

106. *H. H. Maharajadhiraja Madhav Rao vs. Union of India*, 1971 AIR 530.

107. Austin, *Working a Democratic Constitution*, 171.

108. On the courts' mediating function in this respect, see Namita Wahi, "The Right to
Property and Economic Development: How Property Saved Democracy in India (1950–1978),"
April 29, 2021, University of Wisconsin-Madison Center for South Asia Spring 2021 Lecture
Series, https://www.youtube.com/watch?v=nCsLA2b6CCw. The presentation comes from a
project building on Wahi, "The Right to Property and Economic Development in India," (un-
published SJD dissertation, Harvard Law School, 2014).

against inflation and income against taxation, it defended that more illiquid form of wealth—property—against the state.

At the base of this activity stood a particular idea of how democracy and constitutions should work, best summarized by Munshi in a public speech he gave in opposition to the seventeenth amendment bill.[109] "Democratic constitutions are intended to be a stabilizing factor, not subject to frequent changes," he said. Pointing to the American experience of just twenty-two amendments in 175 years, he lamented that India had passed seventeen in thirteen years. India's leadership "is unreconciled to the role of the judiciary as the arbiter and interpreter of the Constitution," he asserted. This had taken place, to some extent, because "with the death of Sardar Patel, the built-in two-party system in the Congress came to an end." The party sought to bring that stability in the face of change by moving debates out of the Congress working committee and into parliament.

## Remembering Swatantra, Reviving Swatantra?

Swatantra pursued an opposition politics to stabilize democracy by balancing out the Congress and advancing the cause of free economy. It came alive at a time when uncertainty about one-party dominance loomed, when new ideological agendas were being woven into the fabric of Indian democracy, and new solidarities looked to displace older ones. To reduce the Congress' massive electoral footprint, the Swatantra Party collaborated with regional parties. The party raised no-confidence motions and involved itself in parliamentary committees to create mechanisms of accountability. Such activity brought the dominant party before the public eye in unprecedented ways. Finally, Swatantra mobilized people in defense of property and lobbied the judiciary to check legislative power.

Economic ideas more consistent with the various articulations of free economy would gain greater purchase socially, ideologically, and in practice over subsequent decades. That trend has accelerated since the end of the Cold War and the 1991 liberalization of the Indian economy. And in subsequent

109. Munshi, "Implications of the proposed 17th Amendment," in *Lawless Legislation*, 68–70. A classic reading of how the ideas and activity in opposition can be understood as parts of a coherent whole is Quentin Skinner, "The Principles and Practice of Opposition: The Case of Bolingbroke versus Walpole," in *Historical Perspectives: Studies in English Thought and Society in Honor of J. H. Plumb*, Neil McKendrick, ed. (London: Europa, 1974), 93–128.

decades, opposition parties have displaced the Congress from power at the national and state level with increasing regularity.[110] Campaigns against corruption and inflation, like the DMK's in 1967, have featured prominently in these successful anti-incumbent efforts.[111]

Swatantra itself has not been a part of these developments. Infighting within the party's ranks resulted in various fissiparous tendencies. These intensified after poor results in the 1971 elections. The party was reduced to nothing after Rajagopalachari's death shortly thereafter.[112] More systemically, Indian electoral politics changed structure and registers in the 1970s. Leaders made impassioned appeals to eliminate poverty and provide welfare subsidies to sectional interests. Political entrepreneurs from lower-caste backgrounds representing identitarian recognition concerns rose to prominence.[113] Agrarian owner-cultivators who prospered during the Green Revolution pursued politics around increasing agrarian subsidies from the state. They did not meaningfully transition to new enterprise activity and therefore demand pro-business policy.[114] In such an environment, Swatantra's platform would not have had much take-up. No less crucially, the importance and strength of the solidarities forged and the reputations cultivated in the nationalist movement had been crucial to Swatantra's creation. The passage of time and the delinking of state and national elections in 1971 weakened these ties.

India adopted some pro-business policies beginning in the second half of 1970s and select market reforms in the decade after that.[115] Mounting of international pressures and the country's increasingly precarious balance of payments drove these policy changes, rather than any major internal political constituency. It was not so much ex-Swatantra members politically organized in new parties as it was technocrats who rose to prominence in policymaking

110. Ruparelia, *Divided We Govern: Coalition Politics in Modern India* (New York: Oxford University Press, 2016); Frankel, *India's Political Economy*.

111. Nauriya, "Intolerance through the Years."

112. The party's decline is covered systematically in Rasam, *The Swatantra Party*, 143–79.

113. On this phrasing, see Nancy Fraser and Axel Honneth, *Redistribution or Recognition? A Political-Philosophical Exchange* (London: Verso Books, 2003). On this emergent constituency, see Frankel, *India's Political Economy*, 626–91.

114. Rudolph and Rudolph identified this constituency as "bullock capitalists." *In Pursuit of Lakshmi*, 52–53.

115. Srinath Raghavan, "Decoding the Emergency," *Seminar* 677 (January 2016), https://www.india-seminar.com/2016/677/677_srinath_raghavan.htm; Dani Rodrik and Arvind Subramanian, "From 'Hindu Growth' to Productivity Surge: The Mystery of the Indian Growth Transition," NBER Working Paper 10376, (March 2004), https://papers.ssrn.com/sol3/papers.cfm?abstract_id=519165.

and had experience and training in international economic institutions who championed these reforms.[116] The state did not abandon its earlier economic paradigm so much as it changed its domains of intervention and nonintervention. For example, the government intensified its control over the banking sector and nationalized industries like coal while it experimented with dropping certain import duties.[117] It was only from the liberalization of the Indian economy in the 1990s that a comprehensive shift could be detected.[118] With that change, the Indian economy of the preceding four decades came to be labeled with Rajagopalachari's moniker: permit-and-license raj. The term's original connotation of an oligarchic coalition between the dominant party, big business, and elite bureaucracy was forgotten.

The new politics of the 1970s and beyond coincided with the emergence of new, chiefly upper-caste Hindu commercial interests. These players owed their rise to two factors: government policies restricting monopolies and industrial concentration by established business houses, and the undergoing of a broader economic transition into manufacturing and then tertiary sector growth.[119] As electoral politics gravitated toward poverty alleviation and identity concerns, these groups became disillusioned with secularism, the state, and democratic ideals. They gravitated to the majoritarian upper-caste politics of Hindu nationalism, the new electoral vehicle for which was the Bharatiya Janata Party (BJP).[120]

Economic liberalization and the ascent of Hindu nationalism have characterized Indian politics and economy since the 1990s. A wave of anti-incumbency took down the Congress-led United Progressive Alliance (UPA) coalition government in 2014. The verdict brought the BJP a majority in the Lok Sabha on the back of a campaign targeting the corruption of the ruling party.[121] It is in this context that Swatantra, long forgotten, has returned to public memory. Delhi's Nehru Memorial Museum and Library held a conference called "Swatantra: Principles, People, Politics" on February 3, 2018. That day, 27,000 documents from the defunct party office in Bombay arrived at the

---

116. Balasubramanian, "Is India in the History of Neoliberalism?," 57–58.

117. Das Gupta, *State and Capital in Independent India*, 142–76.

118. There is a vast literature on this topic. One useful account is Vijay Joshi and I.M.D. Little, *India's Economic Reforms, 1991–2001* (New Delhi: Oxford University Press, 2001).

119. Das Gupta, *State and Capital in Independent India*, 177–217; Rudolph and Rudolph, *In Pursuit of Lakshmi*, 28–29.

120. Blom Hansen, *The Saffron Wave*, 8.

121. Andrew Wyatt, "India in 2014: Decisive National Elections," *Asian Survey* 55, no. 1 (2015): 33–47; Irfan Ahmed and Pralay Kanungo, eds., *The Algebra of Warfare-Welfare: A Long View of India's 2014.*

library for safekeeping and access to researchers.[122] The principal organizer of the event, a Delhi-based think tank called the Center for Civil Society, has spearheaded the initiative to digitize *Freedom First, Indian Libertarian,* and the pamphlets of the Forum of Free Enterprise through a portal called IndianLiberals.[123] That center has also produced edited volumes on B. R. Shenoy, Milton Friedman, dissent on socialism, and *Ārtik Swatantra* (Economic Swatantra).[124] It is the most straightforwardly neoliberal organization in India, tracing its origins in grants from the ideologically similar Atlas Network.[125]

Complementing these neoliberals, sections of business and the pro-business media have declared their desire for the party's revival. An unsigned editorial of the *Mint* business daily dating to 2016 made the case that C. Rajagopalachari is the "icon" India needs today.[126] A businessman now involved in social entrepreneurship expressed similar sentiments some months later in the same paper.[127] More recently, an independent researcher with a Muslim name suggested that "India needs a resurrected Swatantra party" to represent agriculture and small industry in a way that transcends religion and caste. He noted the urgency of such a resurrection in the context of the dominant BJP's "totalitarian statist turn and adhering to ruthless crony capitalism."[128]

Of another persuasion are liberal public intellectuals like Amartya Sen and Ramachandra Guha. While the two have disagreed on the manner in which one may appropriate India's past, both are committed to religious pluralism and have unambiguously condemned the BJP on grounds of majoritarian

122. "Concept Note—Swatantra: Principles, People, Politics," *Centre for Civil Society,* http://ccs.in/sites/default/files/swatantra-concept-note.pdf; "#Redefining Swatantra," Twitter hashtag, at https://twitter.com/hashtag/RedefiningSwatantra.

123. "Indian Liberals: An Online Archive of Indian Liberal Writings," *Indianliberals.in,* http://indianliberals.in.

124. Parth Shah, ed., *Friedman on India* (New Delhi: Centre for Civil Society, 2000); Parth J. Shah, ed., *Profiles in Courage: Dissent on Indian Socialism* (New Delhi: Centre for Civil Society, 2001); Parth J. Shah and R. K. Amin, eds., *B. R. Shenoy: Theoretical Vision* (New Delhi: Centre for Civil Society, 2004); Shah and Amin, eds., *Economic Prophecies*; Parth J. Shah, *Ārtik Swatantra kā Saṅgharś* (New Delhi: Centre for Civil Society, 2005).

125. Balasubramanian, "Is India in the History of Neoliberalism?"; On the Atlas Network (previously Foundation), see Timothy Mitchell, "The Work of Economics: How a Discipline Makes Its World," *European Journal of Sociology* 46, no. 2 (2005): 297–320.

126. "C. Rajagopalachari: The Icon India Needs Today," *Mint,* December 9, 2016.

127. Narayan Ramachandran, "A Yawning Gap in India's Political Spectrum," *Mint,* August 21, 2017.

128. Faisal C. K., "Why Today's India Needs a Resurrected Swatantra Party," *The Wire,* January 17, 2021.

ideology and practice.[129] In a public address, Sen expressed his wish that the Swatantra Party would be revived and pointed appreciatively to the constitutionalism of Minoo Masani.[130] Guha has asked whether India has any conservative intellectuals to speak of and has pointed to C. Rajagopalachari as a worthy model for a rejuvenated Indian conservatism.[131] Though neither would join such a party or even vote for it, they believe that it could help protect democratic institutions.

Finally, those who have embraced Hindu nationalism have appropriated Swatantra's name and history. The renewed *Swarajya* magazine bears the logo "Read India Right."[132] Founded the year the BJP won its Lok Sabha majority, the magazine appears monthly in English. It also has a digital daily "avatar" called #*Swarajya* and launched a Hindi website in 2018. This "Swarajya 2.0" calls itself a "61-year-old independent media start-up." By their own admission, "the founders of the twenty-first-century *Swarajya* merely see themselves as custodians of Rajagopalachari's legacy."[133] The tenets of its editorial philosophy listed on the magazine website are democracy, free markets, individual freedom, individual enterprise, gender equality, and equality of opportunity. Also listed are "Secularism which does not pander" and "Separation of religion from politics." The #*Swarajya* website lists its commitment to a "reduced role of the state in general" but notes that the state might be more effective in "Defense, Internal security, Foreign policy, Justice system, Facilitating business, Investing in the national interest, Physical and social infrastructure."[134] *Swarajya* has unambiguously embraced the politics of religious majoritarianism.[135] One of its

129. On their differences about the appropriation of India's past in the present, see Ramachandra Guha, "Arguments with Sen: Arguments about India," *Economic and Political Weekly* 40, no. 41 (2005): 4420–25, and the response in Sen, "Our Past and Our Present," *Economic and Political Weekly* 41, no. 47 (2006): 4877–86. For their opposition to a Modi-led BJP from 2013 onward, see "Amartya Sen: As an Indian Citizen, I Don't Want Modi as My PM," *ToI*, July 22, 2013, and Guha, "The Man Who Would Rule India," *The Hindu*, February 8, 2013. Their commitment to pluralism is articulated in Sen, *Identity and Violence: The Illusion of Destiny* (New York: Norton, 2006) and Guha, *India after Gandhi*.

130. Amartya Sen, *A Wish a Day for a Week* (London: Penguin, 2014).

131. Ramachandra Guha, "In Absentia: Where Are India's Conservative Intellectuals?" *Caravan*, March 1, 2015, http://www.caravanmagazine.in/reportage/absentia-ramachandra-guha-indian-conservatives.

132. "Swatantra: Principles, People, Politics," http://indianliberals.in/swatantra/.

133. "About Us," #*Swarajya*, https://swarajyamag.com/about-us.

134. "Our Editorial Philosophy," #*Swarajya*, https://swarajyamag.com/editorial-philosophy.

135. See, for example, R. Jagannathan, "Saat Khoon Maaf: With Article 370 Gone, Modi and Shah Now Have the Nation Fully Behind Them," #*Swarajya*, August 5, 2019; R. Jagannathan,

contributors, former Swatantra legislative assembly member H. V. Hande, has since authored a biography of Rajagopalachari and joined the BJP.[136] Reflecting on the differences between the Swatantra and the BJP in conversation, he pointed out Rajagopalachari's "softness" on Muslims and that the BJP's cadre-basis in the Rashtriya Swayamsevak Sangh (RSS) has allowed it to be the mass party that Swatantra never was.[137]

Resurgent interest in the Swatantra Party is noteworthy and even welcome in the face of a new one-party dominance. Bearing in mind the range of actors that supported Swatantra in the 1960s, the diversity of voices interested in the Swatantra today might even be salutary for its prospects. An economic program to attract the support of business and the "new middle classes" who have asserted themselves since the liberalization reforms might hold appeal across identity groups and offer competition to the BJP.[138] At the same time, the omissions and elisions of this revival are concerning. Nothing in this discourse has yet parsed distinctions between center and region, conservatism and liberalism, or human and economic freedom. Generally missing from these debates are Indian-language interlocutors, Muslims, and those who trace origins from middle or lower castes. And in the weakened institutional context of parliament and the Indian judiciary, a renewed Swatantra would have to focus more on popular mobilization to achieve its goals. That was the Achilles heel of the original party.

Men who had embraced Gandhi's program of interreligious harmony like Rajagopalachari, Masani, and Ranga, set Swatantra's agenda. The party managed to avoid practicing an overt religious majoritarianism that characterized elements of the party's leadership by rallying almost exclusively around economic issues. Masani aspired for India to become a "modern, non-denominational Indian society."[139] There were limitations to the willingness

---

"Hinduphobic Alliance Muddies the Water in Battle Against CAA; India Must Not Let Hindus Down Again," #Swarajya, November 27, 2020. Jagannathan is the editorial director of #Swarajya.

136. Hande has written seven articles in Swarajya. "Hande," https://swarajyamag.com /author/548683/dr-h-v-hande; Hande, Mutaṟiñar Rājāji (Chennai: Sri Mahameru Trust, 1999). Initially, he moved on to a successful career in the AIADMK party, which split off from the DMK and emerged as its chief rival. During the 1970s, Hande became Tamil Nadu's health minister. But after the death of the AIADMK's founder in 1987, Hande joined the BJP.

137. Interview with Hande, Chennai, October 23, 2019.

138. Leela Fernandes, India's New Middle Class: Democratic Politics in an Era of Economic Reform (Minneapolis: University of Minnesota Press, 2006).

139. Masani, "A Call for Consolidation," SN, August/September 1970.

of such a Hindu majority party to accommodate minorities, but it did not exclude them as a matter of principle.[140]

An anecdote is illustrative. In 1970, Rajagopalachari condemned the RSS-affiliated *Organiser* newspaper (see chapter 2) for publishing historical stories about warlike Muslim kings and tyrants: "Not only do such stories serve no current purpose, but they do great harm." Instead, he encouraged the magazine to "adopt a more reasonable attitude when dealing with events and sections of people who are permanent elements of our society and who are ready to cooperate in all our national efforts though they are not willing to give up their religion."[141] The editor K. R. Malkani, a cofounder of the BJP's predecessor Bharatiya Jana Sangh, responded by asserting the veracity of the stories he published. He told Rajagopalachari that the elder statesman's objection was "on par" with the "secularists" who objected to *bhajans* (Hindu prayer songs) being played on the All India Radio. "Sir, we find that Muslims and Marxists are everywhere coming together," he wrote.[142]

Malkani might have been dismayed to learn of the views of one K. Syed Ahmed, president of the Ceylon Muslim Writers' Association and vice president of the All-Ceylon Tamil Writers' Federation. His letter to Rajagopalachari exposes the bigotry of the *Organiser* editor: "The false ideology of socialism has no place in our country . . . I pray to God to render you all health and strength to lead us to the righteous path," he wrote.[143] As the Swatantra idea is repurposed for the political present, its emissaries and enthusiasts may find solidarities in unlikely places and remain vigilant about disingenuous appropriations of both the party's and India's history.[144]

———

Free economy and the Swatantra Party came to life after India won freedom from the British Raj, once the consensus forged among anticolonial nationalists of diverse persuasions broke down. By the end of the 1950s, new economic

140. Ranga, *Fight for Freedom*, 255, 259.

141. "Dear Reader," *Swarajya*, June 27, 1970, 30.

142. K. R. Malkani to C. Rajagopalachari, June 19, 1970, File 118, Installment III, CRP.

143. M. K. Syed Ahmed to C. Rajagopalachari, March 25, 1967, File 104, Installment III, CRP.

144. G. Balachandran, "Religion and Nationalism in Modern India," in *Unravelling the Nation: Sectarian Conflict and India's Secular Identity*, Kaushik Basu and Sanjay Subrahmanyam, eds. (New Delhi: Penguin, 1996), 81–129.

interests had emerged and the Nehruvian model of planned developmentalism encountered roadblocks. As India's literate public expanded in size, ideological entrepreneurs representing various causes across India's urban spaces came together to critique Indian political economy and economic policy during the second plan period. They drew upon Cold War–era discourses of neoliberalism and tried to reconcile them with India's history and current conditions. Interacting in associations and writing in periodicals, they threshed out their own common-sense ideas to help make the economy the new domain for debate on the nation. Their free economy offered an ideological foundation for Indian conservative politics to develop in a distinctively mid-twentieth century form that blended an anticommunism, which invoked the fear of totalitarianism, with advocacy of unfettered commercial exchange and the defense of property.

Situated in distinct contexts of region, language, caste, and political economy, the keyword "free economy" took on multiple meanings as it circulated, moving across metropole and mofussil alike. Most clearly, it meant opposition to the "socialistic pattern of society," which Rajagopalachari dubbed permit-and-license raj. At the time, no other party explicitly disavowed the ruling party's socioeconomic objectives. Free economy could also mean N. G. Ranga's self-employed economy of peasants, Masani's country of free enterprisers. It could be, to those Indians who took it upon themselves to write to the Swatantra leadership, a rhetoric for the expression of economic resentment. Of course, free for some meant unfree for others; the unspoken dimensions of the free economy discourses point to a patriarchal household division of labor, patterns of lower-caste exploitation, and not much freedom for the woman.

Free economy's ambiguity allowed it to serve as a point of consensus agreed upon by diverse figures, whose social commitments ranged from cosmopolitan individualism to a parochial family orientation. The lowest common denominator of the varying visions of free economy were a decentralized economy with strong private property rights, which prioritized small industry and embraced agriculture. An antistatism, rather than an anarchism, pervaded these visions; the state would avoid its own commercial activity in such an economy and create a supportive environment for private economic activity when necessary. It would not occupy the commanding heights of the economy.

The partisans of free economy interacted with libertarians and neoliberals in the Western world, finding occasional overlap in their concerns. In fact, the content of their formulations shared more with those of American individualist anarchists than neoliberals. Indian protagonists engaged more with the polemical content of neoliberal utterances rather than theories of institutional design. They appropriated elements of these discourses for their political aims, as a layering over of their own economic ideas to respond to official Indian discourses on economy. This helped them wage a battle of ideas against the threat of communism.

Free economy became relevant for India's democracy as a platform for a project that this book has described as opposition politics, embodied by the Swatantra Party. This was at one level an idea of an economically conservative party to balance out India's "one-footed" democracy, imagined most coher-ently by Rajagopalachari but tracing antecedents in the *Indian Libertarian*. Rajagopalachari's stature and appeals to dharma and ordered progress played a crucial role in attracting interest for this project across a range of political actors. Next, opposition politics rejected the anti-politics of development. It involved disseminating free economy in Indian-language publics and attaching it to a concrete political project. As they entered the world of party politics and elections, Swatantra's leadership rewrote free economy for a middle-class rights-bearing citizen. To win popular support, the party tapped into a vein of discontent around issues such as inflation and taxation to establish itself as an alternative political player at the all-India level. It provided an economic edu-cation for voters from the lettered public and managed to mount what was at the time the largest organized political challenge to the Congress. As it did so, it drew on antecedent practices, most of them associated with the nationalist movement. These ranged from propaganda to mass protest. These efforts courted responses that showed how, in certain quarters, people understood opposition to the Congress as a forum for claim-making and expression. Finally, opposition politics meant using India's institutional political machinery to forge coalitions and fight for free economy from elected office. Swatantra mobilized sections of the populace and used India's political institutions to provide checks and balances to the party in power before the elections of 1971 swept it away.

Democracy is too often invoked to signify not merely a procedure of rule but also a set of values—freedom, rights, and progress among them.[145] This conflation can mislead us and compromise our understanding of how distinct

145. Dunn, *Democracy: A History.*

projects of democracy have emerged and unfolded.[146] In India, the introduction of democracy before industrialization or the advent of mass literacy could mean that elections merely turned feudal relationships converted into legislative seats. No better example exists than the Maharani Gayatri Devi's thumping victories under the Swatantra Party banner. At the same time, democracy could carry the promise of emancipation for the masses and mean unprecedented empowerment for historically disadvantaged groups like Dalits.[147] Across the world, the recent rise of ethnomajoritarian regimes has taken place in both democratic and nondemocratic fashion. India is a peculiar case of the postcolonial society in which this process has taken place electorally. Consistently peaceful transfers of power have taken place between regimes for seven decades. But the Indian example also points to the risks that endure even after procedural democracy becomes ingrained in the postcolony. Projects like Swatantra's can help us imagine alternative possibilities and solidarities to check the worst excesses of the present, even if they stand far apart from our utopias.

146. Kaviraj, "An Outline of a Revisionist Theory of Modernity," *European Journal of Sociology* 46, no. 3 (2005): 497–526. This is indeed one of the shortcomings of the otherwise excellent recent scholarship on neoliberalism.

147. Jaffrelot, *India's Silent Revolution: The Rise of the Lower Castes in North India* (New York: Columbia University Press, 2003); Shani, *How India Became Democratic*; Shani, "India's Democracy before the Democratic Discontent, 1940s–1970s," *History Compass* 20, no. 6 (2022), https://doi.org/10.1111/hic3.12742.

# Electoral Results

TABLE A1. Swatantra's 1962 Results in State Assemblies

| State | Total Seats | Seats Contested | Seats Won | Percentage of Votes Polled |
|---|---|---|---|---|
| Andhra Pradesh | 300 | 141 | 19 | 10.6 |
| Assam | 105 | — | — | — |
| Bihar | 318 | 259 | 50 | 17.5 |
| Gujarat | 154 | 106 | 26 | 24.2 |
| Madhya Pradesh | 288 | 43 | 2 | 1.2 |
| Tamil Nadu | 206 | 94 | 6 | 7.9 |
| Maharashtra | 264 | 9 | — | 0.4 |
| Mysore | 208 | 59 | 9 | 7.2 |
| Punjab | 154 | 42 | 3 | 3.9 |
| Rajasthan | 176 | 92 | 36 | 17.2 |
| Uttar Pradesh | 430 | 167 | 15 | 4.8 |
| West Bengal | 252 | 26 | 0 | 0.6 |

Source: Rasam, *The Swatantra Party*, 74.

TABLE A2. Results of Major National Parties in the 1962 Lok Sabha Elections

| Party | Percentage of Popular Vote | Seats Won |
|---|---|---|
| Indian National Congress | 44.7 | 361 |
| Communist Party of India | 9.9 | 29 |
| Swatantra Party | 11.1 | 20 |
| Bharatiya Jana Sangh | 7.9 | 18 |
| Praja Socialist Party | 6.4 | 14 |
| Republican Party | 6.8 | 12 |

Source: *Key Highlights on General Elections, 1962 to the Third Lok Sabha*, (New Delhi: Election Commission of India, 1962), 56.

TABLE A3. Swatantra's 1967 Results in State Assemblies

| State | Total Seats | Seats Contested | Seats Won | Percentage of Votes Polled |
|---|---|---|---|---|
| Andhra Pradesh | 287 | 89 | 29 | 9.9 |
| Assam | 126 | 12 | 2 | 1.4 |
| Bihar | 318 | 127 | 3 | 2.4 |
| Gujarat | 168 | 148 | 66 | 38.2 |
| Haryana | 296 | 12 | 3 | 3.2 |
| Madhya Pradesh | 234 | 21 | 7 | 2.6 |
| Tamil Nadu | 270 | 27 | 20 | 5.3 |
| Mysore | 216 | 47 | 16 | 7 |
| Orissa | 104 | 101 | 49 | 22.5 |
| Rajasthan | 184 | 107 | 49 | 22.2 |
| Uttar Pradesh | 425 | 211 | 13 | 4.9 |
| West Bengal | 280 | 21 | 1 | 0.8 |

*Source*: Rasam, *The Swatantra Party*, 101.


TABLE A4. Results of Major National Parties in the 1967 Lok Sabha Elections

| Party | Percentage of Popular Vote | Seats Won |
|---|---|---|
| Indian National Congress | 40.8 | 283 |
| Swatantra Party | 8.7 | 44 |
| Bharatiya Jana Sangh | 9.3 | 35 |
| Communist Party of India | 5.1 | 23 |
| Samyukta Socialist Party | 4.9 | 23 |
| Communist Party of India (Marxist) | 5.1 | 19 |
| Praja Socialist Party | 3.1 | 13 |

*Source*: *Key Highlights on General Elections, 1967 to the Fourth Lok Sabha* (New Delhi: Election Commission of India), 75.

TABLE A5. Swatantra's 1971 Results in State Assemblies

| State | Total Seats | Seats Contested | Seats Won | Percentage of Votes Polled |
|---|---|---|---|---|
| Andhra Pradesh | 287 | 20 | 2 | 2 |
| Assam | 114 | 1 | 1 | 0.6 |
| Bihar | 318 | 49 | 2 | 0.7 |
| Delhi | 150 | 6 | 0 | 0.5 |
| Gujarat | 168 | 47 | 0 | 1.8 |
| Mysore/Karnataka | 216 | 28 | 0 | 0.6 |
| Orissa | 140 | 115 | 36 | 17.4 |
| Punjab | 104 | 4 | 0 | 0.03 |
| Rajasthan | 184 | 119 | 11 | 12.3 |
| Tamil Nadu | 234 | 19 | 6 | 3 |

*Sources: Rasam, The Swatantra Party, 153; Statistical Report on General Election, 1971 to State Legislative Assemblies and Statistical Report on General Election, 1972 to State Legislative Assemblies, various.*

TABLE A6. Results of Major National Parties in the 1971 Lok Sabha Elections

| Party | Percentage of Popular Votes | Seats Won |
|---|---|---|
| Indian National Congress (R) | 43.7 | 350 |
| Indian National Congress (O) | 10.5 | 16 |
| Jana Sangh | 7.4 | 22 |
| Swatantra | 3.1 | 8 |
| Samyukta Socialist Party | 2.4 | 3 |
| Praja Socialist Party | 1.1 | 2 |
| Communist Party of India | 4.7 | 23 |
| Communist Party of India (Marxist) | 5.1 | 25 |
| Dravida Munnetra Kazhagam | 3.9 | 23 |
| Others | 11.1 | 32 |
| Independents | 7.1 | 11 |

*Source: Key Highlights on General Elections, 1971 to the Fifth Lok Sabha, 76.*

# NOTE ON SOURCES

PAINTING A COHERENT picture of the past requires suturing together the fragments it leaves us, which can entail procuring them from far-flung places and reading across languages. In this book, I make use of sources in English, Gujarati, Hindi, and Tamil. Hiteshi Bhatt translated the Gujarati material; all other translations are my own. Core material comes from the private papers of C. Rajagopalachari and K. M. Munshi, two of the largest archival collections available in India. These rich repositories include statements of party ideology and activity, thousands of petitions and letters from constituents, and exchanges between leaders and officials of the Nehruvian state. In addition, I consulted the recently collected and open papers of the Swatantra Party. I have read these sources alongside fragments from the formal archives of the Indian state and collections strewn across Germany, the United Kingdom, and the United States. These mainly concerned individual and institutional interlocutors of my protagonists. Owing to the paucity of the secondary literature on the topics considered, I have also cited excellent unpublished doctoral dissertations found either on ProQuest or Shodhganga, the open-access online repository for Indian doctoral theses.

I read across multiple kinds of published sources. Libraries in India and the United States and online portals furnished me with collections of periodicals like *Indian Libertarian, Indian Rationalist, MysIndia, Swarajya,* and *Thought.* Digitized newspaper repositories of the *Times of India,* available on the ProQuest historical newspapers database, and *Dina Thanthi,* available at their head office in Chennai, provided information about national and regional events. Published materials produced by the Government of India—including statistics on the Indian press, industrial licenses, and election returns—furnished me with statistics on India's postcolonial economic and social history. The voices of the historical actors explored in these pages came out most clearly from the various genres of texts they wrote and the fora where they spoke. These include everything from moralistic short stories to children's books, voice recordings to films. I found them in various libraries all over the world and scattered across multiple websites.

I also interviewed four people whose reflections offered a living archive of memory. S. V. Raju, former executive secretary of the party, met with me in Bombay in July 2014 and answered many queries about party organization and Minoo Masani. Howard Erdman, professor emeritus at Dartmouth College and author of *The Swatantra Party and Indian Conservatism*, graciously shared memories of his experiences in India and reflections on the party over a phone conversation in March 2015. Both have since passed away. I sincerely regret that I am unable to share this work with them. S. Charuhasan, the mofussil lawyer and later character actor in Tamil cinema, shared memories of his early career with me in October 2019 at his Chennai home. That same month, Dr. H. V. Hande, former Swatantra Party legislative assembly member and All-India secretary, met with me twice at his Chennai hospital to discuss the party's presence in Madras/Tamil Nadu and his experiences as a legislator.

# SELECTED BIBLIOGRAPHY
# AND ABBREVIATIONS


## Physical Archival Collections

### Asian and African Studies Collections (AASC), the British Library (BL), London, UK

European Manuscripts
India, Pakistan and Burma Association Papers (MSS EUR 158)
 File 356: Swatantra Party
India Office Records
 Legislative, Political, and Judicial Files
 File 12/167: Ranchoddas Bhavan (Lotwalla) and son Narotam


### Houghton Library, Harvard University, USA

Ishill Additional Papers (MS AM 1614)
Series II. Letters to Joseph Ishill
 Folder 23: R. Bhavan


### Hoover Institution Archives, Stanford University, USA

Milton Friedman Papers
 Box 33, Folder 11: B. R. Shenoy
Friedrich A. von Hayek Papers
 Box 79, Folder 13: B. R. Shenoy
Mont Pelerin Society Papers
 Box 61 (Sound Recordings): Mont Pelerin Society Meeting at Oxford, 1959


### Institut für Wirtschaftspolitik, Cologne, Germany

Wilhelm Röpke Papers (WRP)
 Folders 89, 129, 133

## Manuscripts Collection, Yale University, USA

Chester Bowles Papers (MS 628)
Part III, Series I: U.S. and International Correspondence
  Box 95, Folder 67: Donald Kennedy

## National Archives of India, New Delhi, India (NAI)

Government of India
  Ministry of Finance
  Ministry of States
Private Collections
  M. R. Masani Papers
  K. M. Munshi Papers (KMM), on microfilm
  Sardar Patel Papers
  N. G. Ranga Papers

## Nehru Memorial Museum and Library, New Delhi, India (NMML)

C. Rajagopalachari Papers (CRP)
  Installments II, III, IV, V, VI–XI
  Microfilm Collections
G. D. Birla Papers
  Correspondences
Indulal Yagnik Papers
  Correspondences
John Matthai Papers
  Microfilm Collections
M. A. Master Papers
  File 10: Forum of Free Enterprise
Purushotamdas Thakurdas Papers
  File 291: Bombay Plan
Swatantra Party Papers (SP), Uncatalogued
  Boxes 1, 3, 5, 6, 9, 16

## Special and Area Studies Collection, George A. Smathers Library, the University of Florida, USA

Joseph Ishill Papers
  Box 1C, Folder 17: R. B. Lotvala

## Sunny's Gramophone Museum and Records Archive, Plassanal, Kerala, India

Swatantra Party Recordings

## Tamil Nadu State Archives, Chennai, India (TNSA)

Government of Madras Presidency
   Development Branch

## University of New Hampshire, Durham, NH, USA

Ralph Borsodi Papers (Collection MC 34)
   Correspondence
   Box 1, Folder 7: N–Pi
   Box 2, Folder 1: Pa–Pi

## Tata Central Archives, Pune, India

J.R.D. Tata Papers
   Speeches File

## Digital Archives

Henry Hazlitt Digital Archives-Beta, powered by Universidad Francisco Marroquin
   http://www.hazlitt.ufm.edu
Reuters Online Archive
   https://reuters.screenocean.com

## Newspapers and Periodicals

Bombay Chronicle (BC)
Cooperative Socialist
Caravan
Current
Dina Thanthi (DT)
Eastern Economist
Economic and Political Weekly
Freedom First
Free Economic Review (FER)
Hindu
Hindustan Times
Illustrated Weekly of India
Indian Libertarian (IL)
Indian Rationalist
Kalki

Libertarian
Libertarian Socialist
Life
Mint
MysIndia
New Reasoner
Reason
Statesman
Swarajya
#Swarajya
Swatantra Newsletter (SN)
Thought
Times of India (ToI)
Times (London)

## Official Government Publications

*Administrative Reforms Commission: Report on Machinery for Planning.* New Delhi: Government of India, 1968.

*Administrative Reforms Commission: Report on State Administration.* New Delhi: Government of India, 1969.

Chopra, P. N., ed. *The Gazetteer of India: Indian Union Vol. 3-Economic Structure and Activities.* New Delhi: Government of India, 1975.

Chopra, P. N., ed. *The Gazetteer of India: Indian Union Vol. 4-Administration and Public Welfare.* New Delhi: Government of India, 1978.

*Constituent Assembly Debates, 1946–50. New Delhi: Government of India.* https://eparlib.nic.in/handle/1234456789/4.

*Direct Taxes Enquiry Committee: Final Report.* New Delhi: Ministry of the Finance, 1971.

*Economic Survey, 1974–5.* New Delhi: Government of India, 1974.

*Hazari, R. K. Industrial Planning and Licensing Policy: Final Report.* New Delhi: Planning Commission, 1967.

*Industrial Policy Resolution, 30th April 1956.* New Delhi: Government of India Press, 1956.

*Key Highlights on General Elections, 1962 to the Third Lok Sabha.* New Delhi: Election Commission of India, 1962.

*Key Highlights on General Elections, 1967 to the Fourth Lok Sabha.* New Delhi: Election Commission of India, 1967.

*Key Highlights on General Elections, 1971 to the Fifth Lok Sabha.* New Delhi: Election Commission of India, 1971.

*Press in India.* New Delhi: Ministry of Information and Broadcasting, 1956–71.

*Report of Central Direct Taxes Administration.* New Delhi: Administrative Reforms Commission, 1969.

*Report on the Committee on Distribution of Income and Levels of Living: Part One—Distribution of Income and Wealth and Concentration of Economic Power.* New Delhi: Planning Commission, 1964.

*Report on the First General Elections.* New Delhi: Election Commission, 1954.

*Report of the Committee on Taxation of Agricultural Wealth and Income.* New Delhi: Ministry of Finance, 1972.

*Report of the Committee on the Prevention of Corruption.* New Delhi: Ministry of Home Affairs, 1964.

*Report of the Indian Delegation to China on Agrarian Cooperatives.* New Delhi: Planning Commission, 1957.

*Report of the Industrial Licencing Policy Inquiry Committee.* New Delhi: Government of India, 1969.

*Report of the Working Group on Industries.* New Delhi: Government of India Committee on Unemployment, 1972.

*Statistical Report on General Elections, 1962 to The Third Lok Sabha.* Vol. 1. New Delhi: Government of India, 1962.

*Statistical Report on General Elections, 1967 to The Fourth Lok Sabha.* Vol. 1. New Delhi: Government of India, 1967.

*The Second Five-Year Plan.* New Delhi: Ministry of Information and Broadcasting, n.d.

## Published Primary Sources

*18 Years of Socialism*. Bombay: Swatantra Party, 1966.

Amin, R. K. *Economics for Engineers*. Vallabh Vidyanagar: Charotar Book Stall, 1963.

Bauer, P. T. *United States Aid and Indian Economic Development*. Washington DC: American Enterprise Institute, 1959.

Borsodi, Ralph. *The Education of the Whole Man*. Vallabh Vidyanagar: Sardar Patel Vallabhbhai Vidyapeeth, 1963.

Chander, Krishan. *Ek Gadhe kī Ātmakatā*. New Delhi: Hind Pocket Books, n.d.

Charuhasan, S. *Thinking on My Feet*. New Delhi: LiFi Publications, 2015.

Chopra, P. N., ed. *The Collected Works of Sardar Vallabhbhai Patel*. New Delhi: Konark, 1998.

Devi, Gayatri, and Shanta Rama Rau. *A Princess Remembers: The Memoirs of the Maharani of Jaipuri*. Philadelphia: Lippincott, 1976.

Elenjimittam, Anthony. *Cosmic Ecumenism via Hindu-Buddhist Catholicism: An Autobiography of an Indian Dominican Monk*. Bombay: Aquinas Publications, 1983.

———. *Philosophy and Action of the R.S.S. for the Hind Swaraj*. Bombay: Laxmi Publications, 1951.

*For Freedom, Farm and Family*. Bombay: Forum of Free Enterprise, 1959.

Gajendragadkar, K. B. *Legal Rights of Hindu Women: Discussion of Some Necessary and Urgent Reforms*. Bombay: Indian Institute of Sociology, 1942.

———. *Prize Essay on Why the Present Hindu Law of Survivorship Applicable to Joint Family Property Should Be Abolished*. Bombay: Indian Institute of Sociology, 1939.

Goel, Sita Ram. *How I Became a Hindu*. New Delhi: Voice of India, 1982.

Jain, A. P., ed. *Lawless Legislation: Why Swatantra Opposes the 17th Amendment?* New Delhi: Swatantra Party, 1963.

Mahajan, Mehr Chand. *Background of the Kashmir Problem*. Bombay: Libertarian Social Institute, 1959.

Malkani, K. R. *Principles for a New Political Party*. New Delhi: Vijay Pustak Bhandar, 1951.

*Manifesto of the Forum of Free Enterprise*.

Masani, Minoo. *Against the Tide*. Ghaziabad: Vikas Publishing House, 1981.

———. *A Plea for Realism: Some Speeches Delivered in Parliament between May and August 1957*. Bombay: Popular Book Depot, 1957.

———. *Bliss It Was in That Dawn*. London: Arnold Heinemann, 1977.

———. *Our Growing Human Family*. Bombay: Oxford University Press, 1950.

———. *Our India*. London: Oxford University Press, 1940.

———. *Picture of a Plan*. Bombay: Oxford University Press, 1945.

———. *Why This Starvation? Some Facts about Food*. Bombay: New Book Company, 1943.

———. *Your Food: A Study of the Problem of Food and Nutrition*. Bombay: Tata Studies in Current Affairs, 1944.

Mehta, Ashoka. *Economic Consequences of Sardar Patel*. Bombay: Socialist Party, 1949.

*Midterm Report*. Bombay: Swatantra Party, 1969.

Neurath, Otto. *Modern Man in the Making*. New York: Knopf, 1939.

Patel, Bhailalbhai. *Bhāīkākānām Saṃsmaraṇo*. 2nd ed. Ahmedabad: Sastum Sahitya Mudranalaya Trust, 1996. (BS).

———. *Mahi Canal: Proposed Irrigation Project*. Vallabh Vidyanagar: Gramodhar Mudranalaya, 1953.

Patel, H. M. *The First Flush of Freedom: Recollections and Reflections.* New Delhi: Rupa and Co., 2005.

Rajagopalachari, C. *Ātma Cintaṇai.* Madras: Lodhra Press, 1935.

———. *Chats Behind Bars.* Madras: S. Ganesan, 1931.

———. *Cokraṭār.* Madras: The Sadhu Press, 1922.

———. *Rājāji Kataikaḷ.* 10th ed. Chennai: Vanthi Pathippakam, 2010.

———. *Rājāji Kaṭṭuraikaḷ.* 2nd ed. Madras: Pudumai Pathippakam, 1944.

———. *Satyameva Jayate: A Collection of Articles Contributed to Swarajya and Other Journals from 1956 to 1961.* 2nd ed. Madras: Catalyst Trust, 2005.

———. *Stories for the Innocent.* Bombay: Bharatiya Vidya Bhavan, 1964.

———. *The Second Book of the Kural: A Selection from the Old Tamil Code for Princes, Statesmen, and Men of Affairs.* Madras: Rochouse and Sons, 1937.

———. *Towards Doom? Swatantra Series-I.* Bombay: Swatantra Party, undated.

———. *Vedanta: The Basic Culture of India.* New Delhi: Hindustan Times, 1946.

Rajagopalachari, C. and K. Santhanam. *Ūrukku Nallatu.* Madras: Rochouse and Sons, 1939.

Ramanathan, S. *Two Years of Congress Rule.* Madras: Madras Legislature Congress Party, 1939.

Ranga, N. G. *Agony and Solace: Correspondence, Statements, Speeches, etc. 1936–74.* Nidubrolu: Kisan Publishers, 1974.

———. *A Guide to Village Economic Survey.* Madras: All-India Kisan Publishers, 1939.

———. *Adult Education Movement.* Rajahmundry: Andhradesa Adult Education Committee, 1938.

———. *Credo of World Peasantry.* Nidubrolu: Indian Peasant Institute, 1957.

———. *Economic Organisation of Indian Villages.* 2 vols. Bombay: D. B. Taraporevala Sons and Co., 1929.

———. *Fight for Freedom.* New Delhi: S. Chand, 1968.

———. *Four Crore Artisans Hail the Gandhian Plan.* Bombay: Hind Kitabs, 1945.

———. *Guide to Rural Economic Surveys.* Madras: All-India Kisan Publications, 1939.

———. *Kisans and Communists.* Bombay: Pratibha, 1949.

———. *Revolutionary Peasants.* New Delhi: Amrit, 1949.

———. *Self-Employed Sector (Their Constructive Role in Planned Economy).* Nidubrolu: Indian Peasant Institute, 1959.

———. *The Colonial and Coloured Peoples: A Programme for their Freedom and Progress.* New Delhi: Hind Kitabs, 1946.

———. *The Peasant and Cooperative Farming.* Nidubrolu: Indian Peasants Institute, 1958.

———. *The Economics of Handloom (Being a Study of the Social and Economic Conditions of Handloom Weavers of South India).* Bombay: D. B. Taraporevala Sons and Co., 1930.

———. *World Role of National Revolution.* Nidubrolu: Kisan Publishers, 1945.

Ranganathan, Airavatham. *English or Linguistic Chaos.* Bombay: Libertarian Social Institute, 1959.

Rangarajan, Mahesh, Deepa Bhatnagar, and N. Balakrishnan. eds. *Selected Works of C. Rajagopalachari.* 3 vols. New Delhi: Nehru Memorial Library and Orient Blackswan, 2013/2014.

*Report of the Congress Agrarian Reforms Committee.* New Delhi: All India Congress Committee, 1949.

Ruthnaswamy, Mariadas. *Principles and Practices of Public Administration.* Allahabad: Central Book Depot, 1962.

Sanyal, B. S. *Culture: An Introduction*. Bombay: Asia Publishing House, 1962.

———. *Ethics and Meta-Ethics*. Delhi: Vikas, 1970.

———. *Introduction to Logic*. Ajmer: Sachin Publications, 1979.

Scindia, Vijayaraje, and Manohar Malgonkar. *The Last Maharani of Gwalior: An Autobiography*. Albany: State University of New York, Press, 1987.

Shenoy, B. R. *The Bombay Plan: A Review of Its Financial Provisions*. Bombay: Karnatak Publishing House, 1944.

Shukla, Srilal. *Rāg Darbārī*. 2nd paperback ed. New Delhi: Rajkamal Prakashan, 2021.

Shroff, A. D. *An Inflationary Budget*. Bombay: Forum of Free Enterprise, 1959.

———. *Inflation Threatens Indian Economy*. Bombay: Forum of Free Enterprise, 1960.

Spratt, Philip. *Diamat as Philosophy of Nature*. Bombay: Libertarian Social Institute, 1958.

———. *Blowing Up India: Reminiscences and Reflections of a Former Comintern Emissary*. Calcutta: Prachi Prakashan, 1955.

*Swatantra Party: Preparatory Convention*. Bombay: Popular Book Depot, 1959.

*Three Modern Indian Plays*. New Delhi: Oxford University Press, 1989.

*Tomorrow Is Ours*. New Delhi, Films Division, 1955.

*To Prosperity through Freedom: The Swatantra Party's Statement of Policy Adopted at the National Convention in Patna on March 19 and 20, 1960*. Bombay: Swatantra Party, n.d.

*Towards a Self-Reliant Economy: Lessons of the Past*. Bombay: Forum of Free Enterprise, n.d.

Vaidya, Murarji. *Towards a Self-Reliant Economy: Lessons of the Past*. Bombay: Forum of Free Enterprise, 1966.

*Who's to Hold That Price Line?* Bombay: Swatantra Party, n.d.

*Working for the Plan*. Bombay: Films Division, 1956.

# INDEX

*Figures, maps, notes, and tables are indicated by f, m, n, and t following the page number.*

Arya Samaj (Society of the Aryan Race), 56, 73
Atlas Network, 292
Austrian school of political economy, 87

Babri Masjid Mosque, 73n93
Bacchetta, Paola, 260n171
Bachman, Jessica, 93n182
Bandung Afro-Asian Conference (1955), 93n179
Bangaruswami, R., 254–55, 254n142
Bardhan, Pranab, 10n28
Bauer, Peter, 49, 49n139, 148
Bentham, Jeremy, 86
Bhagini Samaj, 65
Bharati, Subramania, 255n146
Bharatiya Jana Sangh Party, 7–8, 74, 90
Bharatiya Janata Party (BJP), 8, 291, 294
Bharatiya Kranti Dal (BKD), 270
Bharatiya Vidya Bhavan, 52, 96, 99, 105, 115, 214
Bhavan's Journal (magazine), 99
Birla, G. D., 158
Birla, Ritu, 47n127
Birla Group, 188n113, 207
Birla Vishwakarma Mahavidyalaya, 188n113
BJP (Bharatiya Janata Party), 8, 291, 294
BKD (Bharatiya Kranti Dal), 270
Black agrarianism, 164n30
Blitz (magazine), 97, 97t
Bombay: communism in, 60–61; Hindu-Muslim conflict in, 61–62, 63; Indian National Congress and, 57; land tenure system in, 42; Lotvala in, 53–57; maps of, 54f, 55m; urbanization in, 44, 46; World War I and, 58–59
Bombay Milk Scheme, 184–85
Borsodi, Ralph, 69–70, 84, 190n125, 191n127; Education and Living, 70; The Education of the Whole Man, 190–91
bourgeoisie, 9–10, 9n27
Bowles, Chester, 203–4
Brahmins: agricultural surpluses liquidated for investment by, 144; in caste order, 3n5, 116n14; in Gujarat, 180; Kashmir and, 74

bureaucracy: growth of, 34–43, 37t; public sector plan outlay, 37–38, 38t
Burke, Edmund, 92, 124, 133
Burnham, James, 200, 204

Cānakyan (newspaper), 236
Center for Civil Society, 292
Central Intelligence Agency (CIA), 68, 95, 203–4
Central Statistical Organization, 28
Ceylon Muslim Writers' Association, 295
Chander, Krishan: Ek Gadhe kī Ātmakatā (The Autobiography of an Ass), 43–44
Chari, Sharad, 185n101
charitable endowments and trusts, 124–25, 124n55, 188
Charotar Education Society, 188
Charotar Gramoddhar Sahkari Mandal, 188, 189
Charotar Tract, 179, 181, 181m, 185
Charotar Vidya Mandal (CVM), 188
Charuhasan, 251, 251n134
Chatterjee, Partha, 10n28
Chettiar, A. Ramasamy, 256
Chettiars, 144, 144n151
Chibber, Vivek, 9n27
Chinoy, Mumtaz, 65
Chodorov, Frank, 78n116
CIA. See Central Intelligence Agency
civic duty, 123
class conflict, 10, 43–50, 48t
classical liberalism, 5n13, 208n208
Colonial and Colored Peoples Front, 167
Committee on the Prevention of Corruption, 47
communism: in Bombay, 60–61; Lotvala and, 67. See also anticommunism; specific political parties
Communist Party of Great Britain, 101
Communist Party of India: ban on, 95, 169; Dange expelled from, 62–63; on democracy as step to dictatorship, 7–8; electoral success of, 82n130, 115; Indian National Congress and, 25n17; libertarianism and,

## A NOTE ON THE TYPE

This book has been composed in Arno, an Old-style serif typeface in the classic Venetian tradition, designed by Robert Slimbach at Adobe.